THE ALL-VOLUNTEER FORCE AFTER A DECADE

Retrospect and Prospect

Pergamon Titles of Related Interest

Art, Davis & Huntington REORGANIZING AMERICA'S DEFENSE: LEADERSHIP IN WAR AND PEACE

Goodpaster & Elliott TOWARD A CONSENSUS ON MILITARY SERVICE

Hunt & Blair LEADERSHIP ON THE FUTURE BATTLEFIELD

Record REVISING U.S. MILITARY STRATEGY

RUSI/BRASSEY'S DEFENCE YEARBOOK 1983

RUSI/BRASSEY'S DEFENCE YEARBOOK 1984

Sarkesian BEYOND THE BATTLEFIELD

Sheraden & Eberly NATIONAL SERVICE

Taylor et al. DEFENSE MANPOWER PLANNING

Related Journals*

DEFENSE ANALYSIS

*Free specimen copies available upon request.

THE ALL-VOLUNTEER FORCE AFTER A DECADE

Retrospect and Prospect

Edited by

William Bowman, Roger Little and G. Thomas Sicilia

PERGAMON-BRASSEY'S
International Defense Publishers

Washington   New York   Oxford   London   Toronto   Sydney   Frankfurt

Pergamon Press Offices:

U.S.A.   Pergamon-Brassey's International Defense Publishers
                         1340 Old Chain Bridge Road, McLean, Virginia, 22101, U.S.A.

                         Pergamon Press Inc., Maxwell House, Fairview Park,
                         Elmsford, New York 10523, U.S.A.

U.K.   Pergamon Press Ltd., Headington Hill Hall,
                         Oxford OX3 0BW, England

CANADA   Pergamon Press Canada Ltd., Suite 104, 150 Consumers Road,
                         Willowdale, Ontario M2J 1P9, Canada

AUSTRALIA   Pergamon Press (Aust.) Pty. Ltd., P.O. Box 544,
                         Potts Point, NSW 2011, Australia

FEDERAL REPUBLIC   Pergamon Press GmbH, Hammerweg 6,
OF GERMANY   D-6242 Kronberg, Federal Republic of Germany

BRAZIL   Pergamon Editora Ltda., Rua Eça de Queiros, 346,
                         CEP 04011, São Paulo, Brazil

JAPAN   Pergamon Press Ltd., 8th Floor, Matsuoka Central Building,
                         1-7-1 Nishishinjuku, Shinjuku, Tokyo 160, Japan

PEOPLE'S REPUBLIC   Pergamon Press, Qianmen Hotel, Beijing,
OF CHINA   People's Republic of China

Library of Congress Cataloging in Publication Data
Main entry under title:

The All volunteer force after a decade.

    1. Military service, Voluntary--United States--
History--20th century--Congresses. 2. United States--
Armed Forces--Recruiting, enlistment, etc.--Congresses.
I. Bowman, William. II. Little, Roger, 1939-
III. Sicilia, G. Thomas.
UB323.A64 1985   355.2′2362′0973   85-3489
ISBN 0-08-032405-3
ISBN 0-08-032409-6 (pbk.)

Printed in the United States of America

Contents

Preface

This book is the outgrowth of a conference held at the U. S. Naval Academy November 2-4, 1983 to commemorate ten years of experience with an armed force composed solely of volunteers. The impetus for the conference was a series of discussions between members of the Economics Department at the Navel Academy and the Office of the Secretary of Defense, Manpower, Reserve Affairs, and Logistics (OSD/MRA&L). Funding of the conference was made possible through OSD/MRA&L, while coordination for the conference was provided by Dr. G. Thomas Sicilia of OSD/MRA&L (director of accession policy), and Dr. Roger D. Little and Dr. William R. Bowman of the Naval Academy (professor and chairman, and associate professor of economics respectively). Special gratitude is extended to Dr. Lawrence J. Korb, assistant secretary-OSD/MRA&L, the major sponsor of the conference, whose overall interest, guidance, and financial support made the conference a reality.

From the beginning we desired that the conference be academic in nature, allowing ample opportunity for interaction, debate, and opposing views as well as formal presentations. To assist us in selecting authors of formal presentations, a Speaker's Committee was assembled. The committee was composed of Martin Binkin, The Brookings Institution; Professor Richard S. Elster, Naval Postgraduate School; John D. Johnston, Syllogistics, Inc.; James Lacy, Center for Naval Analyses; and H. Wallace Siniako, The Smithsonian Institution. We owe particular thanks to these military manpower experts for their positive response, good counsel, and guidance on topics and recommendations for speakers and discussants. To assure that interaction, debate, and opposing views were offered, we allowed sufficient time for the discussants to react to the formal presentations and to the views of the other discussants. Their comments are included at the end of each part of the book. Perhaps as important, we reserved time for questions and encouraged participation from the audience. Their questions and comments were taped and edited. They are also included at the end of each part of the book together with the identity of the commentator where possible. Unfortunately, because of audio problems, a full transcript of remarks in the last part was not possible.

One of the highlights of an effort of this nature is the involvement of top-level policymakers and creative thinkers in the field. We were most fortunate to have Secretary of Defense Caspar W. Weinberger, Assistant Secretary of Defense Lawrence J. Korb, Martin Anderson, Senior Fellow at the Hoover Institution, and Charles C. Moskos, Jr., professor of sociology at Northwestern University, address the conference. Secretary Weinberger's address was included as part of the Naval Academy's Forrestal Lecture Series in order to expose the entire Brigade of Midshipmen to the All-Volunteer Force issue.

Planning for the conference necessitated close cooperation between OSD/MRA&L and the Naval Academy. Many individuals lent invaluable service to bring the conference and this volume to fruition. First, we would like to recognize the support of Assistant Secretary Korb and the superintendents of the Naval Academy who served during the planning and execution phases of the conference—Vice Adm. Edward C. Waller, USN and Rear Adm. Charles R. Larson, USN. We would also like to recognize the services of members of the Naval Academy's economics department, especially Maj. Robert L. Wolf, USMC, and members of the OSD/MRA&L staff, particularly LTC Doug Patterson and Jeannie McHugh. We also wish to thank members of the public works department of the Academy for their help and the staff of the Officer's and Faculty Club for providing excellent banquet meals. Our appreciation is extended, additionally, to Joyce Subinski and Kathy Kaplan, who performed the secretarial functions for the conference, and to Darlene Batten and Rosanne Rowe, who assisted in the preparation of the manuscript. Lastly, we wish to thank Kevin Maxwell and Dr. Franklin D. Margiotta of Pergamon Press for their encouragement and direction in putting together this volume and Angela Piliouras for her careful editorial work.

Introduction

The All-Volunteer Force (AVF) has enjoyed numerous successes and overcome numerous problems since its inception in 1973. Not surprisingly, there has been a continuing debate over the merits of the volunteer versus conscripted force throughout the AVF's ten-year history. This debate has subsided recently in light of the high-quality recruit the military services have been able to attract since 1981. The debate is far from over, however, due to a number of issues including the reduction in the size of the military-aged youth population, changing force structure demands, increasingly complex and sophisticated weapons systems, a fluctuating economy, and the high cost of maintaining a quality volunteer force. Debate and discussion in the decade ahead promise to be as lively as in the first decade. This conference attempted to review the record of the first ten years under the volunteer force policy and to forecast the next ten years. Specifically, the conference addressed the all-volunteer decision, experience to date, future manpower supply and requirements, and alternative policies for manning the forces in the years ahead.

The 275 conference attendees were a bipartisan mixture of the key military and civilian figures involved in the setting of military manpower policy in the Nixon, Ford, Carter, and Reagan administrations. They included past members of the Gates Commission, the Defense Manpower Commission, the recent Military Manpower Task Force, presidential advisors, and various defense and service assistant secretaries and their deputies who were responsible for manpower policy over the past ten years. Attending as well were past and present directors of the selective service system and past and present uniformed military manpower experts including recruiting commanders, deputy chiefs of staff for personnel, and members of the Office of the Joint Chiefs of Staff. Other participants included key congressional staffers, leading scientific researchers in the field, and representatives from the General Accounting Office, the Congressional Budget Office, the Office of Management and Budget, the press, the service academies, and service advertising agencies.

The conference was divided into four sessions. The first session reviewed the Gates Commission report projections and traced the history of the AVF from its inception through 1983. The focus was on the key issues affecting both the first-term and career enlisted forces, women, and minorities, plus the economic and compensation considerations that helped to shape the enlisted force.

The second session centered on the impact of technology, weapons systems, and military force size on the need for high-quality and experienced personnel in the next decade. Specifically, the discussion centered on the impact and interplay of the new, more sophisticated weapons and support systems, emerging technologies, and changing manning requirements as they affect the needed quality and experienced mix of people.

The third session focused on the active and reserve manpower supply for the next decade. Specifically addressed were trends and forecasts for such key variables and parameters as the budget, economy, pay compensation trends, and congressional and public attitudes.

The final session was designed to link the earlier conference presentations and focused on alternative personnel procurement strategies and policies for meeting future requirements. Using the lessons learned over the first ten years (session 1), real world constraints (session 2), and supply (session 3), the volunteer, conscription, and national service options were considered.

In addition to the views presented in the formal sessions, four speakers presented their views of the military manpower debate (Part I): Secretary of Defense Caspar W. Weinberger; Dr. Lawrence J. Korb, assistant secretary of defense for Manpower, Reserve Affairs and Logistics; Dr. Martin Anderson, advisor to Presidents Nixon and Reagan; and Dr. Charles C. Moskos Jr., leading sociologist on military manpower matters from Northwestern University.

The consensus reached by the conference was that the armed forces, manned solely with volunteers, was in good shape at the end of FY 1983. The volunteer concept remains sound and no serious consideration of a return to conscription should occur for several years. However, a few people noted that, while temporarily silenced, the all-volunteer/draft debate is not over. The debate would return should we experience increased difficulty in recruiting and retention.

There was also general agreement that, since the volunteer force will be a fact of life for the foreseeable future, the nation must make the commitment to assure that it continues to work well. Secretary Weinberger best summarized this precept by announcing that the AVF experiment was over and that from now on the Department of Defense will no longer refer to our military as the All-Volunteer Force. They are simply our armed forces.

Finally, there was consensus that, whether we have a volunteer or a draft system, the Department of Defense faces real manpower challenges later this century due to the rising cost and sophistication of our new weapons systems. This challenge will be exacerbated by the smaller youth pool from which to draw recruits and the possibility of a larger military force. It was generally agreed that while recruiting will demand a great deal of attention in the coming years, the real manpower challenge in the next ten years is likely to be in the training and retention areas.

Part I
POLICY ISSUES

1 The All-Volunteer Force in the 1980s: DoD Perspective

CASPAR W. WEINBERGER

There might seem, on the face of it, to be a certain irony in my coming to the United States Naval Academy to reflect on America's ten-year-old all-volunteer armed forces. For almost a century and a half, the Naval Academy has attracted young men—and today, young women as well—who freely chose the difficult, dangerous, and honorable career of serving in their nation's armed forces. You have always been volunteers.

But it is precisely the caliber of the young men and women here today that makes the Naval Academy such an appropriate site for this conference on the future of our All-Volunteer Force. Your talent, and dedication, and spirit remind us that from the beginning of our history the United States has relied for its defense on the quality of a free people. We have relied on this quality not just in our officer corps but in every rank, not just in those who have freely volunteered, but also in those who have been called by their nation.

I was serving in the cabinet as secretary of health, education, and welfare in 1973, and I remember very well the debate over the All-Volunteer Force. Above all I remember hearing some of our men and women in uniform express their skepticism about whether we could maintain the necessary quality in an All-Volunteer Force.

It was an honest concern. And it grew deeper in the late 1970s, when our military leaders saw dramatic declines not just in the quality of our new recruits, but also in the morale of our career personnel. The peacetime All-Volunteer Force, many concluded, was an unsuccessful experiment, and it was time to draw it to a close.

Today, just ten years after the United States inducted its last draftee, these doubts have largely been stilled. Not only are all the services more than meeting their recruiting goals, but the quality of new entrants has never been higher.

In terms both of the proportion of high school graduates and the proportion of enlistees scoring above average on the standard military entrance tests, our enlistees in 1982 and 1983 rated

1

better than new entrants at any time during the draft. They also rate significantly better than the youth population as a whole.

Of course these statistics are just general indicators of quality—the real test comes in training and performance. And what I am hearing from military leaders in every service is that our men and women in uniform have never been better qualified, better prepared, or more dedicated.

Just last month Admiral Watkins, chief of naval operations, told the crew of the *USS New Jersey*, stationed off Beirut, "It is really incredible for all of us who went through the terrible '70s to see the Navy turn around the way it has over the past three years. Today our people have great pride, spirit, and enthusiasm, the like of which I have not seen in my 34 years of commissioned service."

Recently, through both tragedy and triumph, we have seen even more of this quality. President Reagan told us of the young marine, too badly wounded to talk, who used every ounce of his strength to write a short message which he handed to the marine Commandant, General P. X. Kelly. His message contained just two words: "Semper Fi."

The army Chief of Staff, Gen. John A. Wickham Jr., recently returned from visiting troops who were wounded in Grenada, and he told me about a severely wounded soldier who was wearing a combat infantry badge and purple heart on his hospital pajamas. When news photographers started to take his picture, he asked them to "wait a minute," and reached into his pocket to pull out a small American flag that had been stitched onto his combat fatigues. He stuck the flag above his decorations and said, "OK, now you can take your pictures, because this is what I am proudest of."

This is our All-Volunteer Force. These are the men and women who have freely accepted the danger, hardship, and discipline of military life, the family separations and long hours without overtime pay, the mud, the jungle, the desert, the heat, and the bone-chilling cold. America has never been protected by a finer military.

So what have we learned in a decade? First, we have learned that the All-Volunteer Force can be not just a success, but a huge success. This is good news for the young people of America, both for those who seek opportunities in the armed forces and for those who seek a different future. And it is good news for a nation that puts the highest value on individual choice and freedom.

But we have learned something even more important—or at least we should have. We have learned that the United States cannot evade its commitment to quality without endangering its defenses. And that means we cannot evade our commitment to give our men and women in uniform the rewards, the opportunities, and the tools they need to do their job and do it well.

This will seem a harsh judgment, but I believe that at least part of the criticism levelled against our All-Volunteer Force was really just a smoke screen. Behind the smoke screen was a basic unwillingness to pay the price of giving our armed forces decent compensation for their contribution to their nation's security. Then there was a fear that we could not attract enough educationally qualified people unless we had a draft—that fear has been completely dispelled by the facts.

By the time this administration took office in 1981, the United States was paying a steep price for neglecting our men and women in uniform. Inflation eroded pay and benefits. Inadequate defense budgets forced training cutbacks and delays in replacing obsolete equipment. Morale in our armed forces plummeted, and we began to lose many of our most experienced and talented people.

Today these problems may seem far behind us. I have already mentioned that our new enlistees are the best-educated in the history of America's military. Our retention statistics are equally encouraging. So far this year, over 68% of all eligible personnel have reenlisted, compared to only 55% in 1980. In the navy and marines, reenlistments are up to unprecedented levels, and 91% of the new recruits are high school graduates. That is especially good news for the midshipmen who will soon be out in the fleet training and leading these sailors and marines.

These improvements, of course, partly reflect the better pay, benefits, and training opportunities which were enacted when President Reagan took office. But I believe they also reflect our nation's renewed respect for the sacrifice and dedication of our men and women in uniform. You who have chosen a service academy and a military career already, I believe, have sensed and responded to this change: the 1,356 entering members of the class of 1987 were chosen from among 13,568 applicants.

It is a great pleasure to cite these improvements in our armed forces. But let me also offer a warning. We cannot afford to travel down the same road again. If we were once again to shortchange our men and women in uniform, the results, if anything, would be worse than they were in the late 1970s. Young people contemplating a military career—making the same calculations which you as midshipmen so recently considered—would see not just reduced incentives but a pattern of inconsistency and repeated neglect. They would look elsewhere. One important element of our commitment to quality, then, must be a commitment to decent rewards; a second must be a commitment to opportunity.

It angers me when I hear the off-hand comment that an All-Volunteer Force is somehow a mercenary force—and that this is proved by the high minority representation in the ranks. Those who cite the fact that blacks make up 13% of the overall youth population, and a bit more than 20% of our total military strength, should also take the time to discover that black enlistees are more likely to be high school graduates than their white counterparts, and also that they are more likely to reenlist. They should also take the time to look into the outstanding war record of black and Hispanic Americans.

But there is an even more important point here. Our armed forces attract a higher proportion of minority recruits because our armed forces offer opportunities for training, leadership, and advancement—better opportunities, it appears, than many of these young men and women have found in the rest of our society.

I am reminded of "Chappie" James, the seventeenth child of a poor black family in Florida, who started working odd jobs at the age of twelve to earn plane rides and flying lessons. The day the air force pinned on his fourth star, he told those gathered to celebrate that his promotion was important "by the effect it will have on some kid on a hot sidewalk in some ghetto." I suspect that hundreds of such youths have been inspired by the example of General James, and of Lt. Col. Charles Bolden, Naval Academy class of '68, the Marine Corps' first black astronaut, and of other outstanding leaders like them. We should be proud to think that these young people look to the U. S. military for a chance both to serve their country and to change their futures, just as we are proud to see more than 600 midshipmen from minority backgrounds here at Annapolis today.

In my view, however, the most rewarding development we have seen in our armed forces over the past decade has been the tremendous expansion of opportunities for women. Ten years ago an audience of midshipmen would have been an audience of young men. Today there are 320 women preparing for careers as naval officers here in Annapolis, and thousands more young women are entering the officer corps of all our services. By opening up more military careers to women, we are fulfilling our commitment to quality and providing our armed forces with a tremendous new source of talent and leadership.

Likewise, over the past decade we have seen a more than fourfold increase in the proportion of women in our enlisted ranks. Again, this seems to me to be a tremendous vote of confidence in America's armed forces by young women who are seeking new opportunities to shape their own futures.

Women, thanks to their own efforts, have made tremendous strides in the civilian job market over the past decade. Still, I think we would all acknowledge that it remains difficult for women to break into many traditionally male careers. Service in the armed forces offers young women a chance to learn how to operate heavy equipment, or repair jet engines, or apply the newest computer techniques. Service in the armed forces also gives young women a chance to build supervisory skills and gain confidence in their leadership ability.

On July 19, I issued a statement reaffirming that "no artificial barriers to career opportunities for women will be constructed or tolerated." In this light, I was very pleased that the army decided just last month to reopen thirteen of twenty-three career fields which had been closed to enlisted female soldiers. At this time only forty-nine, out of a total of 351 skill categories, are closed to women. Those that are closed, are closed only because of the probability of direct combat involvement.

Our commitment to quality, then, means a commitment both to decent rewards and to full opportunity. But a commitment to quality also means giving our talented and highly-trained forces the weapons and equipment which make full use of their ability.

In the past few years there has been an increasingly lively debate over how we should equip our forces, and, more specifically, over how heavily we should rely on advanced technology. I welcome this debate, which I believe reflects the increased interest in our defense posture. All the same, I have been concerned to see some groups and individuals who are hunting for an excuse to reduce our defense budget's seize on the notion that we could make do with a larger number of less expensive, less sophisticated weapons.

Many who make this case have little understanding of just how technologically advanced Soviet weapons have become, often with the aid of technology bought or stolen from us. If our weapons cannot counter this threat, then they are useless. But I am also concerned that some critics who would blithely revamp our modernization program have not stopped to think about what implications their proposals might have for the future of our All-Volunteer Force.

Technology, it turns out, is a great force multiplier. Consider the example of the *Ticonderoga*-class cruiser, one of the most sophisticated new ships in our navy: indeed, a ship that some have argued is too sophisticated. These cruisers carry a crew of about 360. By contrast, the now-retired *Albany*-class cruisers, which had far less capability, required a crew almost three times that size.

We need to remember that personnel-related costs make up almost half our defense budget. The Soviets, by comparison, spend only about 15% of their defense budget on personnel. But they are also willing to conscript huge numbers of their citizens and to provide these conscript forces with low pay and few amenities.

We should also keep in mind that however eager some members of Congress may be to buy less expensive weapons and equipment, they have shown little willingness to increase the size of our forces. Already they have reduced our requested end strength by almost 43,000 men and women.

Finally, there is something even more important left out of these calculations and that is the value of human life. Technology is not only a force multiplier; it also saves lives. When we spend the money to use steel in the superstructure of *Arleigh Burke*-class destroyers, when we equip the M-1 tank with ballistic doors that close quickly to protect the crew if the ammunition stores are hit, we are reflecting our commitment to do all we can to protect the lives of the men and women who are risking their own for our freedom.

I want to end by delivering two messages: one to you, the midshipmen of the U. S. Naval Academy, the other both to you and to your fellow citizens. To the midshipmen I would say, quite simply, that our All-Volunteer Force offers you a new challenge. The men and women you will lead when you leave here as naval officers are men and women who have freely chosen to serve. They will be asking more of the armed forces, which means they will be asking more of you. Ultimately the success of our All-Volunteer Force depends not just on the quality of their rewards, opportunities, and tools, but also on the quality of the leadership they receive. I am confident that you will be more than equal to this challenge; indeed, I believe that this challenge is part of what is bringing more and more of our brightest young people back into military service.

To the participants in this conference, and to all the American people, I would say that the experiment is over. We know now that an All-Volunteer Force can succeed, and we know what it takes to make it succeed. We need have only the will, the perserverance and the commitment to quality.

Therefore, from today it will not be the policy of the Department of Defense to speak about our military as the all-volunteer armed forces. From today, that can go without saying. Our men and women in uniform, including the midshipmen here today, are simply the armed forces, and the finest armed forces this country has ever known.

2 Military Manpower Training Achievements and Challenges for the 1980s

LAWRENCE J. KORB

For the past decade, our nation has been protected by an all-volunteer armed force. At present, its continued future looks bright, but this has not always been so.

Early in this decade, this administration faced a crisis situation in the manpower area. The armed forces were undermanned, we could not attract sufficient numbers of recruits to fill the ranks, recruit quality in terms of test scores and educational levels had reached all-time lows, morale had plummeted, and our career personnel were leaving in great numbers. The cumulative effect of a number of years of inadequate pay and compensation, and a national lack of pride for our men and women in uniform had taken their toll.

Upon taking office, this administration moved quickly to correct the problem. Today there is overwhelming evidence that these efforts have paid off. Dignity has been restored to military service, and I am pleased to report to you that from a manpower view, our military forces are in excellent health.

In the near future we plan to announce officially the status of military manpower for the conclusion of FY1983. However, I would like to share with you some preliminary results focusing primarily on the enlisted force.

First, let us take a look at the active forces. All four services again met their authorized strength targets, as they have since 1981. More noteworthy, this success was accomplished while increasing the size of the active forces by nearly 75,000 people or almost 4% over the past three years.

Similarly, in FY1983 all services met their recruiting objectives, swearing in 305,000 new recruits, 25,000 returning veterans who had prior service, and commissioning 34,000 new officers.

Quality, too, is up. The entrance test scores and the educational levels of new recruits not only exceeded those of the civilian youth population, but also were significantly better than were experienced during conscription. I am happy to report that this is also true for the army which traditionally has had the most difficult time attracting high-quality recruits.

Let me be more specific: about 74% of the eighteen through twenty-three-year-old youth population possess high school diplomas. In FY1983 the number of new recruits possessing a high school diploma was 91%. By way of comparison, in 1980, department-wide, only 68% of new recruits held diplomas. The army number in 1980 was a dismal 54% high school graduates. We began to turn this around in 1981 when under this administration, the DoD figure rose to 81%, a DoD all-time high. That same year the army reached 80%—also a record high. This year, the department achieved a record-setting 91% high school diploma graduate rate. The army achieved 88%—the highest in its history. By way of comparison, during the Vietnam-era draft, the army's average was 77%. Lest the other services feel neglected, they, too, had banner years: navy, 91%; marine corps, 92%; and air force 98%.

With regard to scores on the Defense Department entrance aptitude test, we again have a great success story to announce. In 1983, 91% of DoD accessions scored in the average or above categories on the Armed Forces Qualification Test, that is, categories I through III; this compares to 69% in 1980. In this measure of quality, FY1983 was better than any year of the draft, but this story gets better. DoD-wide, 41% scored in the above average category (categories I and II). This is the highest ever attained. The army's 37% was also an all-time high. The comparable figure for the youth population is also 37%. These are excellent results because people in this range have the ability to gain entrance to colleges and universities rather than enlist; for purposes of comparison, the 1980 number for the army was only 15%.

Our results also show that we stopped excessive losses from the career force and reenlistments increased significantly. In fact, in FY1983, DoD continued its record-breaking success of 1982. As a consequence, the career force is growing in size, experience, and quality at a rate much faster than the increases in our overall manpower strength. To illustrate, there are about 50,000 more NCOs (E-5 to E-9) in FY1983 than there were in FY1980 and over 100,000 more people with greater than four years' service.

The selected reserve end strength reached a low point in 1979. Our preliminary results show that there are now over 198,000 more selected reservists than at the end of FY1979—a 25% increase. This puts the selected reserve at the highest mark in the AVF. It is also the second highest strength we have ever had in the selected reserve, just 1,300 short of the 1959 record high, a figure we will surpass this fiscal year. Further, like the active force, quality in the reserves has also increased dramatically.

In sum, the revitalization of our All-Volunteer Force has been a success. But what of the decade ahead? We all know the number of youths is declining, while at the same time we will be expanding the size of our forces to provide manpower for the increasing number of weapons entering into the inventory. We will also have to deal with a situation in which economic growth will increase private sector competition for the same manpower resources needed by the military.

In my opinion, returning to conscription is not a viable alternative. We neither will—for we just do not have the political consensus to do it—nor should we do it. The good old days of the draft were not really that good, and bringing back conscription would result in a whole new set of problems which, in my opinion, would be much worse than those faced by an all-volunteer military in peacetime. In addition, not only would the draft fail to save money, as a number of people argue, but I believe it would be more expensive because a conscript force would have much higher turnover and less experience. Moreover, military forces consisting entirely of volunteers gives the nation greater flexibility in foreign policy. Public acceptance for military involvement in complex situations is much lower when the services are composed of draftees.

We can continue to make the all-volunteer system work, that is, we can continue to recruit and retain sufficient numbers of quality people, as long as the American people support the military, the pay system is fair and competitive and, to use President Reagan's phrase, it remains an honor to wear the uniform of the country. Do not lament the fact that personnel costs consume a very large portion of the defense budget and do not be seduced into thinking that it would be better to do other things with that money: it is money well spent. In the final analysis, it is people, not hardware, that will bring us military victory. Further, do not lament the fact that the force composition is changing, and that we have more women in uniform today than under the draft. Women should be in the force; they are an integral part of the force; they are doing well, and they are here to stay. Women are not simply an afterthought or temporary source of personnel we used just to get us through tough recruiting times. The number of women in the force is growing and will continue to grow, as will the opportunities in both traditional and nontraditional fields. Be assured that under this administration women in the military will be able to fulfill their potential or, to borrow an army phrase, they will continue to be "all that they can be."

I would like now to switch from the present to discuss some of the ways we are preparing to meet the challenges of the future. First, we are greatly expanding our efforts to learn as much as we can about the recruiting market and what makes its various segments tick. We have expanded our market surveys to include research for both active and reserve forces, for both new recruits as well as returning veterans. We are conducting research on the propensity of these groups toward military service and how and why their attitudes change. We are looking, via a national test, at the effects of both national service-specific and joint-service advertising as well as the effects of local advertising.

We are also evaluating various enlistment incentives liked the Army College Fund and enlistment bonuses. Finally, we are looking ahead to potential alternative markets such as college-bound youth, older enlistees, and prior-service personnel, to name but a few groups.

One especially exciting project we are pursuing with the services is a recuiting early warning system. We need to have some advance warning if and when a recruiting downturn might occur and we need to gain some idea of the severity of that downturn. With that knowledge, we can be proactive rather than run the risk of repeating our dismal record of being reactive—which has been costly, inefficient, and detrimental to our readiness.

Another area of potentially high payoff is a joint-service program designed to develop job performance measures and then link these measures to military enlistment standards. This linkage would provide the services with a means to match recruits more precisely with the jobs for which they are best suited, thus leading to improved on-the-job performance. The availability of job performance measures would also provide an opportunity to improve our evaluation of technical training courses and assist in choosing the best individuals for reenlistment into the career force.

Another exciting area is computer adaptive testing or CAT. Unlike the paper and pencil entrance examination we now give, CAT permits a much more precise determination of aptitude and ability. Under CAT, test questions will be specifically tailored to the ability of the individual (i.e., if a question is answered correctly, a more difficult question follows, and so on, until the correct aptitude level is met).

We also are working with occupational data to link military and civilian occupational data for recruiting, retention, and mobilization efforts. This data base will enable us to: (1) provide youth with better information about military occupations and training opportunities; (2) develop linkages with labor and education manpower supply sources so that we can locate the types of recruits we need; (3) provide school counselors with resources needed to counsel young people about military occupational and training opportunities; and (4) study military-civilian comparability issues such as pay and, for mobilization purposes, occupational specialty.

Finally, we are pursuing initiatives to improve the way we collect, use, and analyze training information and data. We hope to cluster activities in the training area and in the data and analysis area into collocated services and DoD centers of excellence. This effort has a large potential. It will allow the training community to train future recruits to operate and maintain the new system being implemented.

In conclusion, the AVF has proven it can work well. We remain committed to the view that an all-volunteer military is the prime peacetime option for both now and the foreseeable future. But we must not be complacent; we must prepare now to meet the challenges of the rest of this century.

On its tenth birthday, the AVF gets high grades. With proper planning and support, I am sure that this will also be true ten years from now.

3 The All-Volunteer Force Decision, History, and Prospects

MARTIN ANDERSON

The first responsibility of any decent government is to protect the life, liberty, and property of its citizens, not only from their fellow citizens, but also from the potential aggression of other countries. It would be nice to live in a world where you did not have to worry about getting your head bashed in by your neighbor, but we don't. And as long as envy, greed, and the lust for power lurk in the hearts of men, we won't.

We live in an increasingly dangerous world. As that danger increases, so does the importance of our national defenses. And at the core of those defenses lies our armed forces. Raising and maintaining an armed force that has the combat capability to cope with the threats facing our nation is, and must continue to be, at the top of the list on the national policy agenda of the United States.

The subject of this conference, the All-Volunteer Force, is a vital one. For not only does it involve the preservation of the United States as a free nation in a largely totalitarian and hostile world, but the way we go about raising the military manpower necessary to accomplish that goal has far-reaching social, economic, and political implications for our society.

As I looked over the list of participants, I noticed many old friends and it brought back memories of many discussions and debates on this issue that have taken place during the past fifteen years or so. And as I thought about them one thing struck me. Some of us may have disagreed on what the best way was to raise and maintain an armed force, but we didn't disagree on the necessity of raising one. There may be some people in this country who, out of ignorance or cowardice or malice, are opposed to a strong military force and who flinch from the possibility of confronting malevolent, violent people. However, as I look around the room, I think it is fair to say that while we may disagree about how we should do it, there is a totally shared conviction that it is mandatory that this nation have an armed force whose combat capabilities are superior to those of any hostile power that threatens us.

The military manpower policy issue we are addressing in this conference is not whether we should have an armed force, nor how large that force should be, but rather the issue is one of how we should go about raising that force. Should we continue to rely on an all-volunteer force, as we have now done for the last decade? Or should we return to a draft similar to the one we had for over twenty-five years following World War II? Or should we radically change our military manpower policy and adopt a program of mandatory universal national service?

As we attempt to answer these questions I think there are two basic criteria that must be kept in mind as we wade through the complex questions that are involved in judging any method of raising an armed force. The first and foremost criterion is the effect on this nation's military capability. The second criterion is the social, economic, and political effects on our society. In this regard, the policy issue of military manpower is unique, for no other issue involves both foreign and domestic policy considerations to such a degree.

Most of us are familiar with the intense, sometimes bitter, debate that preceded the end of the draft in the United States. The opposition to ending the draft was powerful and widespread. It was opposed by most senior military men, by many congressmen and senators, by much of the National Security Council staff, by the editorial board of the *New York Times*, and by a substantial part of the public.

There were serious warnings and predictions that our national security would be weakened; that we would have an armed force composed either entirely of blacks, or primarily of the poor, the ignorant, and the misfits of our society; that it would be enormously expensive; and that it would not work. The bottom line was the clear implication that a volunteer force would not be inclined to fight and, to the extent that it did, it wouldn't fight very well.

Since the end of the draft, over ten years ago, the warnings have continued. With a few exceptions here and there, there has been a continual flow of reports in the media from academicians, military personnel, reporters, columnists, and elected officials questioning and attacking the all-volunteer force concept. In the late 1970s, after more than five years of experience with an all-volunteer force, even the chairman of the Senate Armed Services Manpower and Personnel Subcommittee pronounced that "the all-volunteer force may be a luxury that the United States can no longer afford," and seriously proposed a "minimally" coercive national service program as an alternative.

Yet the All-Volunteer Force rolled on. And the reasons were fairly simple. When the changeover to the All-Volunteer Force began in 1973, the Defense Department and the individual services, especially the army, were faced with what was probably the most difficult, largest personnel management problem that any organization has dealt with in this country. And they handled it brilliantly.

Let's look at the essence of what they accomplished. In terms of sheer size the number of men and women on active duty consistently has met the goals set by our overall military strategy during the last ten years. And the quality of these men and women laid to rest the unconscionable slurs on their mental, physical, and moral capacities. We can argue about a hundred details, but the main, overriding thrust of what happened is sharp and clear. In size and strength the All-Volunteer Force is proving itself to be superior to a partially drafted one.

I think it was all summed up rather well last August by Gen. John A. Wickham Jr., the chief of staff of the army, who said he was so pleased with the quality of today's army that "we don't need the draft now."[1] And then General Wickham went further, saying: "They are the best in my 33 years of service. They'll fight, and they are as patriotic as you or I. They follow orders, and they die."[2]

A few months later some of those men that the general was talking about proved—in Lebanon and in Grenada—that what he said was true.

So far our armed forces have done an extraordinary job in solving the management problems associated with moving from a drafted force to an all-volunteer force. If you look at all the major policy changes our government has initiated during the last fifteen or twenty years, the move to an all-volunteer force easily stands out as one of the most successful.

But the fact that we have been successful in implementing a major policy change in how we go about raising our armed forces does not mean that we have solved all of our armed manpower problems. It is also important to note that many of the problems that remain are independent of what method we use to raise manpower. For example, one of the most serious problems remaining concerns our reserve forces. At times it has been argued that an all-volunteer force lacks flexibility in time of crisis. The National Advisory Commission on Selective Service, which was chaired by Burke Marshall, concluded in 1967 that if the draft were ever abolished, "the sudden need for greater numbers of men would find the nation without the machinery to meet it."

The flexibility of an armed force to quickly mobilize its manpower and resources to meet a sudden, serious threat to national security is critical in today's world. We need a substantial amount of combat-capable manpower that can function almost immediately. And we also need a way to strengthen that active force base quickly and decisively.

A draft in such a situation is virtually useless, and excessive reliance on it could place us in great danger. Even with the names and addresses of young men neatly listed on computer printouts, it would take at least three to four months to contact them, to induct them, and to hastily train them, if the training facilities were in fact ready. The end result would be hundreds of thousands of teenage soldiers, some serving reluctantly, almost all with no experience and little training, flooding into the ranks of the armed forces, many months too late.

As the Defense Manpower Commission appointed by President Ford noted in its report in 1976:

> The changing nature of war and its technology will not allow for any lengthy period of time for national mobilization for a major conflict. Thus, the national security relies on the ability to mobilize our reserve forces from a peacetime, "citizen soldiers" status to a combat-ready status in a relatively short time.

What is vital to our national security is a large, well-trained reserve force; one that is really ready. We need a force that can be called into service in a matter of days, not months, in case of an emergency.

Unfortunately, our reserve forces today have significant shortfalls in numbers, in training, and in equipment. The reserves have been too low on our priority list for too long, including both the period of time when we had the draft and now, when we do not. I doubt if there is much disagreement about the urgency of building a reserve force that is both strong and ready. But, of course, the question is how.

First let me suggest that there is something that we should *not* have done. After the Soviets invaded Afghanistan, our shocked national leaders obviously felt it was necessary to do something to indicate to the Soviets that we took their aggression seriously. President Carter could have called for the restoration of the draft. He could have called up the reserves, but instead he began draft registration.

President Carter was right in his belated recognition of the potential military threat that the Soviet Union poses to world peace and to our security. But taking down the names and addresses of the young men of America under the threat of jail or a large fine was a weak and possibly dangerous response. What the Soviets would understand is a clear, effective move to strengthen the combat capability of our armed forces. Registration does not do this. Instead it can easily lull us into a truly dangerous state of complacency.

The fact that we have millions of young men registered for the draft has caused too many of us to sigh contentedly, feeling more secure because we know that in the event of an emergency we will be able to summon this huge manpower pool to our defense. It wouldn't be so bad if the only things wrong with this scenario were that large segments of the list contain out-of-date addresses, or that we would not be able to accept draftees within the first week of an emergency mobilization because our training facilities would not be ready, or that we would not produce any combat-ready troops for three or four months after that.

The real problem is that by having draft registration and a potential draft as a ready crutch we are fooling ourselves into believing that we can safely continue to ignore the importance of building a credible way to increase our military manpower swiftly in a time of crisis.

Too many people still believe that our military manpower problems can be solved by returning to a draft. And they view the existence of registration as a proxy for the existence of the draft. And consequently they have turned their efforts and talents to solving other problems.

Unfortunately the existence of draft registration, and a belief that a military draft can be right around the corner, can be used as a reason by some and as an excuse by others not to take the hard steps that will strengthen our reserve forces to the point where they can effectively back up our active forces.

It is doubtful if the Soviets are upset by draft registration anywhere near to the degree that we are calmed by it and the prospect of the draft. They seem to be fully capable of distinguishing between computer lists of young, untrained, potential draftees and a significantly strengthened reserve force. They seem to be able to tell when we are just stamping our feet or when we are shouldering our arms.

Well, what should be done? Let me make some suggestions.

First, we should think seriously about repealing draft registration. Besides taking up an inordinate amount of time and political capital, it really doesn't seem to work very well. In September 1982 the General Accounting Office reported that address information for between 20% and 40% of the registrants of those to be called first in the event of an emergency could be outdated. They estimated that at the end of eight years, 75% of those addresses might be outdated. But more importantly, as long as we have draft registration, too many of us will see it as a talisman that will somehow produce magical results.

Second, we should adopt a policy that makes it clear that from now on the reserve forces of the United States are serious business, not a pleasant place to have an occasional paid weekend. Anyone staying in or signing up for the reserves or the National Guard should have the clear understanding that in the event of a military threat to this country, they will be the first called to supplement our active forces, regardless of whether they are married, have children, or know a congressman.

Third, we must arm the reserves and National Guard with modern weaponry and other equipment that is fully comparable to what our active forces have.

Fourth, we should take steps to encourage more people to join the reserves and, for those already serving, to reenlist. These steps should include improved recruiting efforts, competitive levels of pay, reenlistment bonuses, and improved management of our current reserve forces.

Fifth, we should seriously consider an effective program of lateral entry into the armed forces so that more mature men and women, from their late twenties through their forties and perhaps in some cases up through their sixties, could enlist for a period of time, both in the active forces and in the reserves. This could provide the armed forces with a vast new potential pool of talented people.

Finally, our national leaders should continue to make every effort to explain clearly and comprehensively why it is so necessary for us to build up and to maintain such powerful defensive forces. They should explain it again and again.

The history of this country's response to a call to arms shows that Americans have always turned out in overwhelming numbers when they felt their country was threatened and they believed that our cause was a just one. There is no evidence to suggest that this would not also be the case today.

But if the only way we can convince our young men and women to participate in the defense of this country is to threaten them with jail or a stiff fine, then the leadership of this country has failed. It has failed to persuade our people of the seriousness of the situation and the validity of the course of action proposed to deal with it.

We have spent too much time in the past making lists and dreaming about legions of troops who will arrive too late. Let us devote our time in the future to arming and training a combat-ready active and reserve force that is clearly stronger than any other on this earth. And let us raise and train this armed force in a manner consistent with the principles of freedom on which the country was founded.

NOTES

1. *Washington Post*, 9 August 1983.
2. Ibid.

4 The Marketplace All-Volunteer Force: A Critique

CHARLES C. MOSKOS, JR.

We can all take pleasure that recruitment and retention is going so well in today's All-Volunteer Force. Although the viability of the AVF in times of economic prosperity continues to remain in doubt, we hope the military manpower establishment has learned one important lesson from the recent upturn in recruitment. We have been rich and we have been poor in the manpower of the AVF, and rich is better than poor. The word from the units in the field is unmistakable: that the type of recruits entering the armed forces *does* make a difference.

My concern, however, is not with enlisted quality or manpower quantity. My concern is with the very fundamentals of the marketplace approach to military manpower, an approach that warps our understanding of the armed forces. Even if current standards of military manpower could be maintained into the foreseeable future (a probability I view as slight), there are profound reasons for concern with the direction the AVF has taken. A marketplace philosophy clearly underpinned the rationale of the 1970 *Report of the President's Commission on an All-Volunteer Force*, better known as the Gates Commission report—the very same report being honored at this conference on the AVF.

The Gates Commission was strongly influenced by laissez-faire economic thought and argued that primary reliance to recruit an armed force should be on monetary inducements guided by marketplace standards. This dovetailed with the system analysts who had become ascendant in the Department of Defense under both Democratic and Republican administrations. Whether under the rubric of econometrics or system analyses, such a redefinition of military service is based on a set of core assumptions. First, there is no analytical distinction between military systems and other systems in terms of cost-effective analysis, even between civilian enterprises and military services. Second, notions of goal commitment, morale, and unit cohesion are difficult to measure, therefore they are inappropriate objects of analysis. Finally, the ideas of citizenship obligation or social representativeness are incidental concerns in manning a military force. Such a mindset has contributed to moving the American military toward an occupational format.

The policy corollaries for military manpower of the marketplace mentality are as follows: (1) recruit pay must be substantially higher than during the draft; (2) more compensation should be up front in the salary i.e., "visible," rather than in kind or deferred, thereby allowing for a more efficient operation of the marketplace; (3) military compensation should as much as possible be linked to skill differences of individual service members, again allowing for a more efficient marketplace; and (4) the career force should become a larger proportion of the enlisted force, the presumption being that this will reduce personnel turnover.

These trends replace the concept of the citizen soldier with that of economic man. It is highly symbolic that as of January 1983, members of the armed forces are counted as part of the labor force for the first time in American history. Other indicators of the trend toward the occupational format include (1) the rise in attrition (i.e., failure to complete an enlistment)—a movement in all but name toward a system of indeterminate enlistments; (2) the increasing proportion of military members living off-post—a separation of work and residence locales; (3) the growing number of enlisted members holding second jobs outside the military—an undermining of the service member's role commitment to the military; and (4) an increasing reliance on contract labor to perform tasks previously carried out by military members.

There is also an excessive bias in econometric analysis to view only qualified data as reliable, an exclusive preference for numbers over adjectives. Yet when the qualitative or "anecdotal" reports came into conflict with the rosy picture of recruits given by the quantitative data of the 1970s, time proved it was the "soft" rather than the "hard" data that were the more accurate. A solid anecdote is to be trusted more than a slippery statistic.

Sober economists, of course, regard their models as conceptual devices for explaining certain tendencies, not as blueprints for completely describing or predicting actual events. There is a general consensus among first-rank economists that the need is to reason on the basis of actual observations as opposed to abstract assumptions about human behavior. Or as phrased in the March 1983 issue of the *American Economic Review*, "There are two things you are better off not watching in the making: sausages and econometric estimates." There should be a rule that when quantified data run contrary to common sense, professional judgments, or field observations, first question the quantified data rather than the common sense.

A sheerly econometric logic would lead one to conclude: (1) anyone who joins or stays in the service when he or she could earn a better salary outside the military is stupid (or at least unaware of alternatives); (2) we should pay patriotic service members less (because they would stay in the military at lower recompense) than those motivated only by economic concerns; and (3) the most cost-effective enlistment practice would be to recruit from Third-World nations.

Even on its own terms, there are problems with the kind of approach used by AVF econometricians. With regard to recruiting, for example, there are certainly different elasticities between the combat arms and the technical services. Different elasticities also characterize subgroups within the youth population.

The most serious failing of the econometric approach to military manpower, however, is the inability to anticipate, or sometimes even comprehend, second and third order outcomes of a marketplace AVF. Every marketplace proposal should be accompanied by an institutional impact statement before it is seriously considered. Let me mention some of these secondary and tertiary consequences.

A marketplace model means that military members should be paid no more or no less than is necessary to meet recruitment and retention goals. This, in turn, means an inevitable movement to replace the "pay by rank" system with one based on "pay by skill" (a euphemism for pay by shortage). The outcome would be a constant churning of the compensation system to adjust to ever changing shortages and overages. A pay-by-shortage system coupled with a salary system also means emphasizing individual over group incentives.

The "front-loading" of compensation toward the junior enlisted ranks compresses enlisted pay grades. A first sergeant in the draft era made five times the income of a PFC compared to only twice that income today. In fact, an E-3 in 1983 earns the equivalent of about $15,000 if he or she lives off post, as an increasing number are doing. The number of marrieds at the junior enlisted levels is about twice that of the draft era. Even barracks are redesigned to insure greater individual privacy, thus converting the NCO into a shift boss rather than one who has broad leadership responsibilities.

Completely unanticipated by the Gates Commission was the rise in the number of female service members. One inevitable outcome was joint-service marriages. Today, about one-quarter of all enlisted women have military husbands. The long-term consequences of joint-service marriages are barely acknowledged, much less appraised for their impact on military effectiveness.

One of the current issues in the manpower agenda is the costs of military retirement. Rarely mentioned is that the considerable costs of the retirement system are aggravated by shifting to a salary system and by increasing the career proportion of the military force. Thus, the marketplace approach raises the pressure to do away with the present military retirement system. It is certainly not for me as a sociologist to remind my economist friends that there is no free lunch.

Cost-effectiveness principles also mean elimination of programs that promote cohesion but cannot be quantified as contributing to learning skill. Thus, there are constant pressures to do away with unit dining facilities, decentralized personnel systems, parades, and morale and recreation programs.

Contrary to expectations, the personnel turnover rate over the course of the AVF has not been much different from that of the peacetime draft era, despite the fact that the average length of initial enlistment is now much longer than during the draft era. What has changed is the kind of turnover. During the draft era, almost all separations were due to expiration of term of service (ETS). Under the AVF, personnel losses due to attrition and desertion have matched, or even exceeded, ETS separations. We are observing, in effect, the phenomenon of military members being "fired" or "quitting," much in the manner of civilian enterprises. That there is a differential consequence on unit cohesiveness between soldiers who leave the service after successfully completing their tours and those who are prematurely separated (even if both groups serve the same length) escapes the grasp of manpower analaysts. It is dismaying to hear leading policymakers say attrition is not a problem if end strength figures are met.

A lesser secondary consequence of the AVF is the creation of hundreds, if not thousands, of well-paid jobs for manpower analysts, defense consultants, advertisers, and the like. Without my being too cynical, they have a vested interest in the marketplace AVF, and it is hard to imagine them holding their printouts or accounts and slipping quietly away.

The most far-reaching consequence of the marketplace AVF is that it ultimately reduces recruiting an armed forces to a form of consumerism, even hedonism, which is hardly a basis for the kind of commitment required in a military organization. It is noteworthy that the 1982 *Military Manpower Task Force: A Report to the President on the Status and Prospects of the All-Volunteer Force* chaired by Secretary of Defense Caspar W. Weinberger, curtly dismissed the notion that any form of national service could have anything to do with military recruitment. God forbid, that manning our armed forces be contaminated by the idea of citizen obligation.

Men and women act from self-interest to be sure, but they have different opinions of what that interest is or what really serves their interest. The largest cash sum in the world cannot buy most people's willingness to go into combat. In the long run, by attaching a market value to military service, econometricians and the military manpower establishment have cheapened rather than enhanced the value many soldiers and many Americans believed military service had.

Part II

PRELUDE AND PERFORMANCE TO DATE

Introduction

ROGER T. KELLEY

On the day a formal cease-fire ended our involvement in the Vietnam War, the United States ceased using conscription to man its armed forces. Preparation for that day had begun in 1969 when President Nixon appointed a commission chaired by then Secretary of Defense Thomas S. Gates to study the feasibility of an all-volunteer force. The president's conviction that the draft should and could be ended rested on three foundations, one demographic, one social and economic, and one political. The demographic truth was self-evident: the "baby-boom" generation would mature during the 1970s providing a large cohort of young people available to man a volunteer force. Second, while the lottery draft was "fair" in that everyone had an equal chance of serving, draft exemptions and the economic burden on those selected made it "unfair" after the fact. Third, the end of an unpopular war made it timely to attempt a clean break with the draft as soon as possible. So, setting aside the deeper philosophical question of a citizen's responsibility to his country, the Gates Commission provided immediate and sufficient justification for ending conscription.

The panel was generally upbeat in its ten-year assessment of the realities of the decision to establish a volunteer force. While the commission's approach and findings have been criticized and challenged, it is generally conceded that their expectations and projections have stood the test of time.

In reviewing a decade of experience with first-term enlisted volunteers, Gary R. Nelson finds that force-level targets have been adequately met and that the recruit quality has improved. Higher than expected attrition in the early years has declined recently as the services have enlisted more high school graduates. Yet, Nelson warns that better recruiting strategies and a better understanding of pay and unemployment effects are necessary in order to maintain acceptable quality as the eligible youth population shrinks by 20% over the next ten years. Finally Nelson notes that a major problem during the first decade of the volunteer force was the lag between the time that a recruiting/retention problem was first observed and the time the programming budget and congressional system took action to resolve it. In this regard, Nelson endorses the need for an early warning system that would allow the quick identification of upcoming problems and expedite the process to resolve them.

Addressing the complementary "careerists" part of the enlisted force, C. Robert Roll, Jr. and John T. Warner find the Gates Commission remarkably mute on this subject. Indirectly and implicitly, the commission expected a volunteer force to be career oriented and hence older and more productive. In fact this has occurred, and Roll and Warner argue that additional productivity gains would result from even larger proportions of careerists in high-skill areas. The military compensation system is the key tool in affecting proper policies in this area.

In the final chapter addressing the Gates Commission's projections, Martin Binkin and Mark J. Eitelberg examine the growing role of minorities and women in the enlisted force. The authors find the commission failed to perceive the trend toward higher numbers of minorities in the military. Minorities now comprise about one third of the enlisted force compared to the projection of under one fifth. Buoyed by the Equal Rights Amendment, the proportion of women has increased from 2% to 9%. Whether such trends should be viewed as constituting opportunities for social mobility and equal opportunity or whether they imply lower readiness because of evidence that proportionately fewer minorities and women possess the aptitude to absorb growing training requirements is a substantive concern for the next decade.

The chapters in Part II reflect a consensus that the Gates Commission was correct in its assessment that an all-volunteer force concept would work in a peacetime atmosphere. There is debate and controversy over whether it is the appropriate way to man our armed forces and whether this approach can be maintained. But, there is also a growing understanding of how the All-Volunteer Force can be made to work in order to meet less than wartime manpower demands. Assuming no major conflicts, our growing understanding of how to recruit and manage a volunteer force adds significantly to the likelihood that this experiment can be sustained through the next decade.

5 The Supply and Quality of First-Term Enlistees Under the All-Volunteer Force

GARY R. NELSON*

INTRODUCTION

The fundamental concept of the All-Volunteer Force is the exclusive reliance on volunteers to meet the demand for first-term enlisted personnel. The reliance only on volunteers (not on conscripts) has resulted in major changes in the recruitment and management of military personnel and in the lives of America's youth. This chapter reviews and evaluates the experience of the military services in meeting their demands with first-term enlistees during the ten years since the end of the draft. The review generates a number of lessons on the policies and management of the AVF which will be important in the years ahead.

America came to the AVF after prolonged experience with using a draft to supplement available volunteers for military service. The draft had been a fixture in the life and concerns of American youth for over three decades, from the mobilization in 1940 that preceded U.S. involvement in World War II to the end of the Vietnam War in 1973. While the size of draft calls varied during that period, American youth were inducted into the armed forces every year except 1947 and 1948. More than 14.9 million were drafted from 1940 through 1973. Millions more sought enlistment in the military services as a result of the draft. Additional millions were

*The author is grateful to James E. Arnold for his assistance in data collection and review of the Gates Commission volumes. Helpful comments were received from William K. Brehm and Dr. Matthew Black. This chapter draws heavily on a number of works dealing with the AVF, including the president's *Military Manpower Task Force* report, *America's Volunteers, Profile of American Youth*, and past contributions by Dr. Richard W. Hunter and myself to the Hoover Institution and the University of Rochester jointly sponsored conference, "Registration and the Draft." I am also indebted to my colleague, Dr. Lawrence Goldberg, for help in shaping some of the key ideas herein on enlistment supply analysis. The errors, however, are all my responsibility.

channeled into occupations and activities, namely defense industries, colleges and graduate schools, because of exemption or deferment from the draft. Marriage and fatherhood were also in this category.

The AVF resulted from the confluence of several factors:

- The understandable unpopularity of a lengthy and inconclusive war.
- The rapid growth in the youth population as a result of the baby boom. Therefore, continuation of the draft during peacetime would take only a small percentage of eligible males.
- A growing difficulty in choosing those for military service during the Vietnam War. No longer were students, fathers, and those in certain occupations or callings to receive favored treatment. Although the draft lottery provides equity *ex ante*, that is—everyone has an equal chance of being called, it penalized those who were selected.

Of all these factors, I believe the most important was the growth in population. In the 1950s, because of the small depression-era youth cohorts and the large demands for military personnel during the cold war era, about 80% of eligible young men were needed to provide the officer and enlisted personnel required by the active and reserve forces. Table 5.1[1] shows that the percentage dropped to 60% prior to the Vietnam War and to only one-quarter in the first four years of the AVF.[2]

Prior to the Vietnam War, the selective service system had made major changes in its selection criteria to cope with the rapid growth of military-aged youths. Deferment categories were broadened to include fathers first and then husbands. Even with new categories of deferment, the draft could not begin to absorb all new entrants. Under the "oldest first" draft policies, the age of inductees had risen steadily in the early 1960s. Without the Vietnam War and the great increase in the demand for military manpower, the pressures for the AVF may have occurred much sooner.

We can never establish whether the AVF was primarily a product of the population boom or a product of the joint effects of the Vietnam War and the population. My personal view would favor the former explanation. It seems inevitable that with a favorable ratio of accessions to population we would at some time have attempted an experiment with the AVF.

Table 5.1. Supply and Demand for Young Men (In Thousands)

Years	18-Year-Old Males	Estimated Military Elig.	Average Male Accessions*	Percent of Eligibles
1954-1957	1,089	804	643	80.0
1958-1961	1,217	907	555	61.2
1962-1965	1,464	1,126	659	58.5
1966-1969	1,782	1,445	1,017	70.4
1970-1973	1,932	1,598	672	42.1
1974-1977	2,104	1,747	459	26.3
1978-1981	2,156	1,783	425	23.8

Source: America's Volunteers: A Report on the All-Volunteer Armed Forces, Office of the Assistant Secretary of Defense (Manpower, Reserve Affairs and Logistics) (Washington, DC: Government Printing Office, 1978) p. 190, and adapted from Richard V.L. Cooper, *Military Manpower and the All-Volunteer Force* (Santa Monica, CA: Rand Corporation, 1977) R1450-ARPA.

*Male accessions include officer and enlisted accessions in both the active military and the reserve components.

The Gates Commission

The President's Commission on an All-Volunteer Armed Force was formed in 1969, at the direction of President Nixon, "to develop a comprehensive plan for eliminating conscription and moving toward an all-volunteer armed force."[3]

The Gates Commission conducted approximately two dozen research projects in a variety of areas. The most germane for this chapter and for the recommendations of the commission were on the demand for enlistees, including both quality and quantity, and the supply of personnel to military service. The latter projects gave us the first significant cluster of econometric studies of military labor supply, studies covering first-term enlistees, reenlistees, and officer accessions. The Gates Commission used these results to develop proposals for manning an AVF at force sizes ranging from two to three million.

The Gates Commission report and studies provide a basis to judge the commission against the experience of the AVF in its first ten years in several different areas:

- The demand for nonprior-service (NPS) enlistees and the turnover rate of the AVF.
- The quality of recruits measured by educational attainment and test scores.
- The supply of enlistees and their sensitivity to military pay, civilian economic conditions, recruiting programs, and other variables.

Objective

This chapter tries to fulfill several purposes. In particular, it seeks to:

- Review the results of ten years with the AVF
- Identify the major AVF issues during this period
- Provide a comparison of the results with the predictions of the Gates Commission
- Summarize the major lessons learned concerning the management of the AVF

The Introduction is followed by a review of the AVF experience of the past ten years, a concise treatment of current knowledge of the major factors affecting enlistment supply, including pay, unemployment, recruiting programs, population, and a discussion of the management and policy lessons learned in the past ten years.

THE AVF EXPERIENCE: 1974-1983

The United States has completed ten years in maintaining a military force of over 2 million persons without resorting to the draft. While this has been a peacetime era of remarkably constant military force sizes, there were significant fluctuations in some of the major factors affecting the AVF:

- Two deep recessions, bottoming in 1975 and 1982-1983, marked the AVF period. They surround a period of moderately good economic conditions.
- Congress and the executive branch have, at times, restricted funding for AVF-related programs: first-term military pay, recruiters, advertising.
- The G.I. Bill, a generous program of educational benefits, was replaced with a far less valuable program in January 1977.
- From 1976 to 1980 the entry test used to qualify recruits for military service was badly misnormed at the lower ranges. Consequently, recruiting results were actually far worse during this period than were measured at the time.

There were other factors affecting the AVF during this time period, including a growing degree of sophistication in the management of recruiting and other activities connected to the AVF. Following is a review of the experience of the past ten years.

Force Size and NPS Enlistments

The transition to the AVF occurred simultaneously with the decline in active strength at the end of the Vietnam War. The active force inventories were 2.65 million in 1964, 3.5 million in 1968, and they declined to a figure of approximately 2.1 million during the AVF era (Table 5.2).

Table 5.2. Active Duty Military End Strengths[1], FY1964 to 1983 (In Thousands)

	1964	1968	1970	1972	1974	1975	1976	1977	1978	1979	1980	1981	1982	1983[2]
Army	973	1570	1322	811	783	784	779	782	771	758	777	781	780	780
Navy	668	765	692	588	546	535	525	530	530	522	527	540	553	558
Marine Corps	190	207	260	198	189	196	192	192	191	185	189	191	192	194
Air Force	857	905	791	726	644	613	585	571	570	559	558	570	583	592
Total DoD[3]	2687	3547	3066	2322	2161	2127	2081	2074	2061	2024	2050	2082	2109	2123

Source: Data on 1964-1970 are from *America's Volunteers: A Report on the All-Volunteer Armed Forces*, p. 191.
  Data on 1972-1981 are from OASD(MRA&L) (MP&FM) Accession Policy.
  Data on 1982-1983 are from OASD(PA).

[1] Includes only reimbursable active duty military personnel (excludes active duty military personnel paid from civil functions, reserve, and National Guard appropriations).
[2] This is the first fiscal year for which reserve personnel on full-time active duty for training and administration of reserves (TARs) are not counted again active duty end strength appropriations.
[3] Numbers may not add due to rounding.

Thus, the AVF has remained at the lower end of the range of force sizes (two million to three million) considered by the Gates Commission. Except for a shortfall of about 25,000 at the end of FY1979 and smaller amounts in other years, the military has achieved its planned strength during the AVF era.

Although military force sizes have remained relatively constant, the number of NPS enlistments has generally declined throughout the period (See Figure 5.1 and Table 5.3). The numbers reflect a gradual stabilization of the military force following the end of the draft.

Figure 5.1. Nonprior Service Active Duty Enlisted Accessions by Service, FY1974-1983

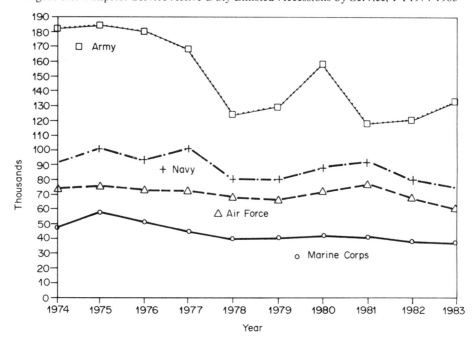

Table 5.3. Nonprior Service Active Duty Enlisted Accessions (000) Selected Fiscal Years

	1964	1968	1972	1974	1975	1976	1977	1978	1979	1980	1981	1982	1983
Army	267.7	533.1	187.2	182.2	184.7	180.2	168.4	124.0	129.3	158.2	117.9	120.4	132.7
Navy	90.0	117.5	86.9	91.7	101.1	93.5	101.6	80.3	79.6	88.0	92.0	79.8	75.0
Marine Corps	38.8	95.9	57.7	47.9	57.8	51.2	45.0	39.6	40.2	41.8	40.9	38.1	36.9
Air Force	89.3	90.5	86.0	73.8	75.6	72.9	72.5	68.0	66.6	71.8	76.9	67.5	60.5
Total DoD[1]	485.8	837.1	418.8	395.5	419.2	397.8	387.5	312.0	315.8	359.8	327.8	305.7	305.1
Total Inductions	151.0	340.0	27.0										
Accessions as a Percentage of DoD[2] End Strengths	20.8	27.4	19.4	21.0	22.8	21.9	21.7	17.5	17.8	20.5	18.5	17.0	16.5

Source: Data on 1964-1970 are from OASD(MRA&L) (MP&FM) Accession Policy.
    Data on 1983 are from OASD(PA).
    Data on inductions are from Richard V.L. Cooper, *Military Manpower and the All-Volunteer Force* (Santa Monica, CA: Rand
    Corporation, 1977) R1450-ARPA, p. 20.

[1] Numbers may not add due to rounding.

[2] $$\frac{(\text{NPS Enlisted Accessions})_t}{\frac{1}{2}[(\text{Enlisted End Strength})_{t-1} + (\text{Enlisted End Strength})_t]}$$

Turnover rates have declined from an average 21.9% in the first four years of the AVF (FY1974-1977) to an average of 18.5% in the last four years (Figure 5.2).[4] Even now, the rate of NPS enlisted accessions is greater than projected by the Gates Commission. NPS accessions have averaged 327,000 over the past four years, in comparison to the Gates Commission projection[5] of about 270,000 for a force of 2.1 million (Table 5.4). A major factor, however, was the high rate of losses of individuals during the first term of service.

Figure 5.2. DoD Turnover Rates,[a] FY1974-1983

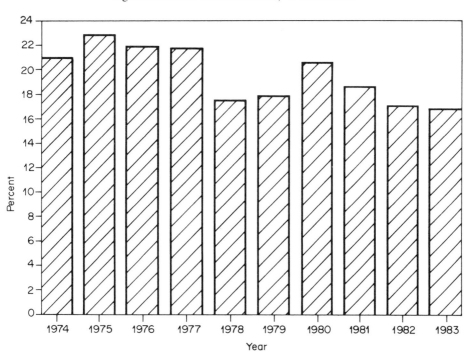

[a] Fiscal year turnover rates were computed by dividing yearly NPS enlisted accessions by enlisted active duty and strengths at each
  endpoint.

Table 5.4. Gates Commission Projection of NPS
Enlistments Required to Support Different Force Sizes
(In Thousands)

Force Size	NPS Enlistments
2,000	259
2,100[a]	271[a]
2,250	290
2,500	332
3,000	410

Source: The Report of the President's Commission on an All-Volunteer Armed
Forces (New York: Macmillan Co., 1970) p.42.

[a] Interpolated values.

First-Term Attrition

An unexpected development of the AVF was an increase in the number of first-term enlistees not completing their contracted term of service. In FY1971, during the draft era, 26% left prior to the end of the first thirty-six months of service. In FY1974 the comparable number was 37%. First-term attrition is costly in several ways:

- Losses may represent potentially productive trained man-years and hence a less capable force.
- Higher losses produce larger requirements for NPS enlistments and may require more recruiters or higher pay for recruits.
- Higher losses create additional costs for training and other turnover-related items.

Because of these costs the secretary of defense in the past has directed the services to achieve reduction in first-term attrition. Table 5.5 shows the growth for both high school degree graduates (HSDG) and non-high school degree graduates, in the first-term attrition rate since the cohort entering in FY1971. More recent declines probably reflect the management attention paid to the attrition problem.

Table 5.5. 1971-1978 Cohorts First Term Attrition,
Percentage Losses, 0-36 Months of Service for
Male NPS Accessions, Total DoD

	HSDG	Non-HSDG
1971	18.2	39.7
1972	21.0	41.6
1973	23.2	46.3
1974	26.0	50.9
1975	26.6	51.4
1976	26.2	50.2
1977	24.0	49.1
1978	23.6	45.3

Source: Data for 1971-1975 are from America's Volunteers: A Report on the All-
Volunteer Armed Forces Office of the Assistant Secretary of Defense (Manpower,
Reserve Affairs and Logistics) (Washington, DC: Government Printing Office, 1978)
p. 208. Data for 1975-1978 are from Officer and Enlisted Personnel Management
OASD (MRA&L).

The factors underlying the increase in first-term attrition have never been clear. It occurred in all services and for all quality groups. It cannot be explained by the mix between draftees and volunteers or by other quantitative changes. Perhaps a subtle but pervasive shift in philosophy occurred—a force that became a "volunteer-in" force also became "volunteer out." Without the presence of the draft, where conscripts and enlistees had an obligation to fulfill, commanders were less patient with below average enlistees. In one sense, higher first-term attrition may be a "benefit" of the AVF in that it confers greater management flexibility. Nevertheless, it is an expensive form of flexibility.

One striking factor about first-term attrition is its strong relationship to level of education. High school diploma graduates are one-half as likely to leave before the completion of the term of service as nongraduates (Table 5.5). About 50% of nongraduates are attrition losses. Those who are successful in *completing* high school are successful in *completing* a term of military service. This is an important factor in assessing the quality of enlistees.

The Quality Dimension

From its inception the principal concern of the AVF has been the quality, not the quantity of enlistees.

The term "quality" has come to mean the attributes the individual brings into military service rather than performance measures while on military service. The two most commonly referenced attributes are receipt of a high school diploma and entry-level test scores. The test used to measure the aptitude of new recruits is the Armed Services Vocational Aptitude Battery (ASVAB). The ASVAB is used by the military services to determine eligibility for enlistment and qualification for particular military jobs.[6] Four subtests of the ASVAB are combined to form the Armed Forces Qualification Test (AFQT), the primary determinant of enlistment eligibility.

Measures of quality or of performance after entrance in the military are one of three kinds. The first measure, training-school outcomes, is the traditional basis of military aptitude standards. Classroom measures, while useful, are not the same as performance on the job. Indeed, concern exists that the premium on paper-and-pencil performance in both aptitude tests and the classroom may unwarrantedly strengthen the correlates.

A second measure of performance is attrition during the first-term. No matter how job-proficient, a person is of no value if he has left military service. We have shown the strong relationship between high school diploma graduation (HSDG) and completion of the first term of service.

The third measure, performance on skill-based tests while serving with a military unit, requires more detailed discussion. A study recently completed by David Armor and others at Rand investigated performance of the Military Occupational Specialty infantry (MOS) on the Skill Qualification Test (SQT). The test, which includes "hands-on" performance in critical tasks, is probably more closely related than classroom performance to actual performance on the job. Armor et al. found a strong relationship between performance on the SQT and both the AFQT score and the combat arms aptitude component of the ASVAB. The relationship with high school graduation, while positive, was not nearly so strong.

Both AFQT scores and high school graduation appear to be useful indicators of success in later service.

High School Diploma Graduates. The high school diploma graduate (HSDG) category has a strong correlation with attrition rates. The importance of this measure, plus particular recruiting problems in the army, has led the Congress to impose a minimum 65% high school graduation percentage on male enlistees in the army.

The record of the AVF in HSDG percentages appears in Figure 5.3 and Figure 5.4 and in Table 5.6. Over the past ten years HSDGs as a percent of NPS accessions have averaged 74%, in comparison to 71% in the ten years preceding the AVF. Recent years have been far superior to the average. DoD-wide HSDG percentages were 85% for FY1981, 86% for FY1982, and 89% for the first half of FY1983. In comparison, in the 1980 youth population 72% of males and 77% of females were high school diploma graduates.[7]

Figure 5.3. Percent HSDG Nonprior-Service Enlisted Accessions by Service, FY1974-1983

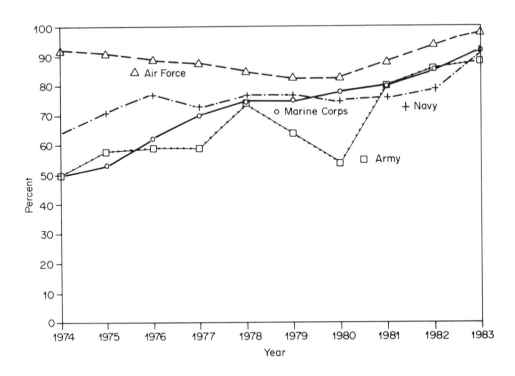

Figure 5.4. DoD HSDG Nonprior-Service Enlisted Accessions, FY1974-1983

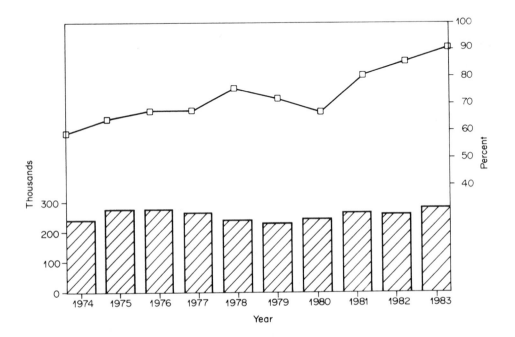

Table 5.6. Percent HSDG[1] Nonprior-Service Enlisted Accessions Selected FY1964-1983

	1964	1968	1972	1974	1975	1976	1977	1978	1979	1980	1981	1982	1983
Army (%)	70	71	61	50	58	59	59	74	64	54	80	86	88
Navy (%)	57	82	71	64	71	77	73	77	77	75	76	79	91
Marine Corps (%)	61	58	52	50	53	62	70	75	75	78	80	85	92
Air Force (%)	84	93	83	92	91	89	88	85	83	83	88	94	98
Total DoD (%)	69	74	67	61	66	69	69	77	73	68	81	86	91
Total HSDG DoD[2] (In Thousands)	335	620	280	240	275	275	265	240	230	245	265	260	280

Source: Data on 1964-1968 and 1982 are from *Military Manpower Task Force: A Report to the President on the Status and Prospects of the All-Volunteer Force* (Washington, DC: Government Printing Office November 1982) p. II-4.
Data on 1972-1981 are from *Profile of American Youth*, p. 20.
Data on 1983 are from OASD(PA).

[1] Does not include GED certificates.
[2] Numbers rounded to the nearest 5000.

Beneath the long-term DoD-wide averages lie some particular factors that deserve comment:

- Year-to-year fluctuations in HSDG percentages are significant and represent both supply and demand factors. A year such as 1978 reflected low demand (and a relatively high HSDG percentage). Recent experience unquestionably represents a surge in supply.
- The range in variation in HSDG percentages under the AVF is significantly greater than in the previous ten years. The maximum range under the draft was 68 to 78%; under the AVF the low was 61% (in FY1974) and the high 89% (in FY1983). The AVF is not nearly so self-regulating as the draft; consequently, it places a premium on the management of both supply and demand factors.
- The significant differences in HSDG percentages by service do not match differences in the requirements for NPS enlistees. In particular, the army has been over ten percentage points below the other services during most of the AVF era. The army has had about 40% of total DoD recruits in most recent years. As a result partially of this large demand, the army has had greater difficulty than the other services in meeting its recruiting targets.[8] Recently this gap between the army and the other services has closed sharply. Favorable recruiting conditions have made it easy for all of the services to achieve high percentages of HSDGs. Also, the army makes extensive use of enlistment bonuses and for the past two years has made use of the Veterans Educational Assistance Program (VEAP), a generous program of educational benefits.

The general trend in HSDG percentages has been strongly positive in the ten years of the AVF. The demand for NPS enlistees has declined because of a decline in personnel turnover as the AVF has matured (see Table 5.5). The economy is weaker now than it was at the beginning of the AVF. And finally, the AVF programs are better employed and better managed as we have become more expert in their use.

AFQT Scores. AFQT scores have been the most widely used, long-term barometer of NPS enlisted accessions. AFQT scores are divided into five categories as shown in Table 5.7. The table compares the 1980 U.S. male population age eighteen to twenty-three with NPS male enlisted accessions in FY1982 and in earlier peacetime and wartime eras. Mental category V enlistees are barred by law from enlistment and, partially in response to AVF testing and recruiting problems between 1976 and 1980, Congress has restricted each service to at most 20% in category IV.

The major problem with test scores during the AVF period occurred in FY1976, when a new test (the ASVAB) was introduced. The test was seriously misnormed for category IV enlistees.

Table 5.7. AFQT Scores Among the Male Youth Population
and Nonprior-Service Recruits, 1952-1982

Category Percentiles	I 93-100	II 65-92	III 31-64	IV 10-30	V 0-9
1980 Male Youth	5	35	29	23	8
Nonprior-Service Male Accessions					
AVF 1982	3	34	50	13	0
AVF 1980	3	24	42	32	0
AVF 1975	4	34	56	6	0
Vietnam War 1968	6	32	38	25	0
Cold War 1957	8	25	43	24	0
Korean War 1952	6	22	32	39	0

Source: Profile of American Youth Office of the Assistant Secretary of Defense (Manpower, Reserve Affairs and Logistics) (Washington, DC: Government Printing Office, 1982) pp. 15, 69.

Figures may not add due to rounding.
Male youth population age 18 to 23.

As a result, the services were taking in enlistees classified as category III who were really category IV (see Figure 5.5). This error continued for five years, through FY1980. During the period of misnorming, instead of around 5% in category IV for DoD, the percentage was greater than 25%. The category IV percentage for the army exceeded 45%.

Figure 5.6 and Table 5.8 show the percentage of NPS accessions in category IV for each service in selected years, 1974-1983. In the recent years 1981 through 1983, the percent scoring in category IV has declined sharply from the misnormed years. The percent in category IV for this period is comparable to the best years in the pre-Vietnam era.

Table 5.8. Percent AFQT Category I-III NPS Enlisted Accessions,
Renormed Scores, Selected FY1964-1983

	1964	1968	1972	1974	1975	1976	1977	1978	1979	1980	1981	1982	1983
Army	79	72	82	82	90	89	59	61	54	50	69	81	88
Navy	89	84	80	97	95	94	80	82	79	82	88	89	92
Marine Corps	91	78	80	92	96	96	76	73	72	73	87	91	94
Air Force	96	84	92	99	100	99	95	94	90	91	93	94	98
Total DoD	85	75	83	90	94	93	73	75	70	69	82	87	92
Total I-III DoD[1] (In Thousands)	415	630	350	355	395	370	285	235	220	250	270	265	280

Source: Data on 1964-1975 are from *America's Volunteers: A Report on the All-Volunteer Armed Forces*, p. 197.
         Data on 1976-1979 are from Accession Policy OASD(MRA&L).
         Data on 1980-1983 are from OASD(PA).

[1] Numbers rounded to the nearest 5000.

A major factor in using test scores as an entry standard is the strong interaction with race and ethnic groups. Table 5.9 depicts the AFQT distribution of the 1980 youth population by race and ethnic group. Both blacks and Hispanics score significantly below the remainder of the population. Black scores are particularly low, with a mean percentile score of only seventeen. Three-fourths of the black youth population score below category III. Median scores for black enlistments are nearly twice as high as scores for the overall black population (thirty-three to seventeen). Hispanic scores are somewhat higher than blacks', but 59% fall into categories III and IV.

Figure 5.5. Percentage Distribution on Nonprior-Service Accessions by Armed Forces
Qualification Test (AFQT) Category IV; Fiscal Years 1961-1981.
(Total DoD Left, Army Right)

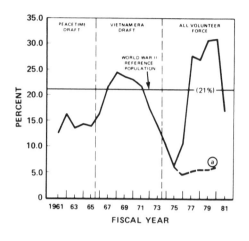
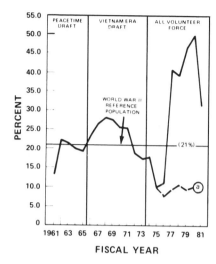

Source: *Profile of American Youth*, Office of the Assistant Secretary of Defense (Manpower, Reserve Affairs and Logistics) (Washington, DC: Government Printing Office, March 1982) pp. 17-18. Data on 1961-1970 accessions are from Office of Assistant Secretary of Defense (Manpower, Reserve Affairs, and Logistics). Data on 1971-1981 accessions provided by Defense Manpower Data Center.

[a] Broken lines show the percentage of accessions scoring within the respective AFQT category, as originally reported prior to the discovery of test miscalibration. Solid lines for this period (FY1976-1980) reflect the percentage of accessions based on test scores that were later renormed.

Figure 5.6. Percent AFQT Category I-III Enlisted Accessions, by Service, FY1974-1983

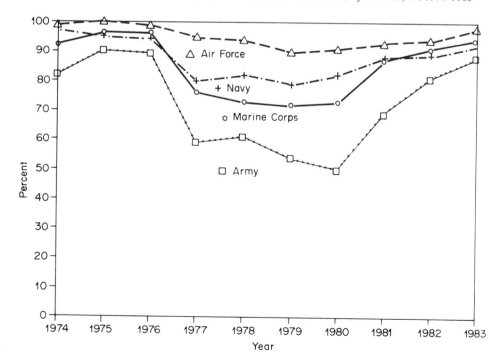

Table 5.9. Distribution of 1980 Youth Population
by AFQT Category and Racial/Ethnic Group[a]

AFQT Category	Percentile Range	Total Population (%)	White[b] (%)	Black[c] (%)	Hispanic (%)
I	93-100	4	5	_d	1
II	65-92	33	39	7	13
III	31-92	32	34	21	27
IV	10-30	24	19	46	39
V	1-9	7	3	26	20
Median Score of Population		51	59	17	23
Median Score of 1981 Enlistees				33	

Source: Profile of American Youth, pp. 7, 22, 24.

a Youth population age eighteen to twenty-three.
b Includes all racial and ethnic groups except blacks and Hispanics.
c Excludes Hispanics.
d Less than 0.5%.

Representation

A major concern about the All-Volunteer Force has been that it is somehow unrepresentative of the U.S. population. The claim has been made that the middle class has abandoned the military; that we have an army of the poor and disadvantaged; that minority groups serve out of proportion to their number in the population. Criticism continues that this means that the poor and the minorities would suffer disproportionate casualties in time of war. This view holds that military service is a "burden" that must be shared equally among all groups.

Interestingly, criticism of the representation of the AVF has not come from groups representing the poor and minorities. For these groups, any attempt to reduce the poor and minorities on active duty would be seen during peacetime as a job issue. This alternate view holds that no one bears a burden as long as all enlistments are voluntary in return for the personal and professional opportunities of military service. Blacks and other groups would view any attempt to impose quotas as an act of discrimination.

The subjects of concern here are black representation in the force, the socioeconomic status of members, geographic representation, and the use of women in the military. Because chapter 7 deals explicitly with women and minority representation, this subsection is extremely brief. Much of the material is based on the report of this administration's *Military Manpower Task Force: A Report to the President on the Status and Prospects of the All-Volunteer Force.*[9]

Table 5.10. Blacks as a Percent of Active Duty Strength, FY1982

	DoD	Army	Navy	Marine Corps	Air Force
Officers	6	8	3	4	5
Enlisted	22	33	12	21	17
TOTAL:	20	30	11	20	15

Source: Military Manpower Task Force: A Report to the President on the Status and Prospects of the All-Volunteer Force (Washington, DC: Government Printing Office, 1982) p. II-13.

Black Representation. Blacks have a greater representation in the enlisted forces than in the U.S. population as a whole. Twenty percent of the U.S. military is black, compared with 13% of the youth population and 12% of the general population. Blacks represent 22% of the enlisted force but only 6% of officers (Table 5.10).

Blacks have a higher propensity than whites to both enlist and reenlist. The analysis of the Gates Commission supports this conclusion for reenlistments but not for enlistments. The Gates Commission, in fact, argued that blacks would show a smaller increase than whites in voluntary enlistments as a result of a first-term pay increase. In fact, blacks have enlisted out of proportion to their percentage of the eligible population. This is particularly true of the army. Table 5.11 shows black enlisted accessions in the army as a percent of total army enlisted accessions.

Table 5.11. Black Enlisted Accessions in the Army
as a Percent of Total Army Enlisted Accessions

Fiscal Year	Black Males	Black Females	Total
Draft Years			
1964	12	19	13
1968	13	19	13
1972	15	18	15
AVF Years			
1974	28	20	27
1976	25	18	24
1980	28	40	30
1981	26	37	27
1982	23	30	25

Source: *Military Manpower Task Force: A Report to the President on the Status and Prospects of the All-Volunteer Force* (Washington, DC: Government Printing Office, November 1982) p. II-14.

Socioeconomic Status. The question of socioeconomic status is a most difficult one to address for military personnel. No data on social origin are collected by the military services. An analysis of civilian and military youth, age eighteen to twenty-one, as part of the National Longitudinal Surveys, was made in 1979. It compares military personnel with total civilian youth population and with civilian youth who are employed full-time. The comparison includes education and occupation of parents and the youth's own educational expectations (Table 5.12). Because of the ages included, the military population consists primarily of enlisted personnel. One would expect a higher percentage of officers to come from professional families where parents had education beyond high school.

The data show that military enlisted youth came from about the same socioeconomic background as employed civilian youth. And though the background is somewhat less favored than for the total population, military enlistees had the full range of backgrounds. In educational expectations, interestingly, military youth are more ambitious than both total youth and employed youth. Military service either attracts those with aspirations for higher education or encourages those it does attract to seek more education.

Table 5.12. Comparison of Selected Characteristics of Males in the Armed Forces and Civilians, Age 18-21, 1979 (Percent)

	Civilians		Military	
Characteristics	Total	Full-Time Employed*	All Services	Army Only
Education of Parents	100	100	100	100
Less than 12 Years	23	27	23	31
12 Years	42	49	45	43
13 Years or More	35	24	32	26
Occupation of Parents	100	100	100	100
Professional or Managerial	31	21	23	22
Sales/Clerical	12	12	11	8
Blue Collar	44	53	52	53
Service	9	9	12	15
Farming	4	5	2	2
Educational Expectations	100	100	100	100
Less than 12 Years	8	10	2	2
12 Years	35	48	27	31
13-15 Years	17	25	25	30
16 Years or More	40	17	46	37

Source: "National Longtitudinal Survey of Youth, Labor Force Behavior," Ohio State University. Cited in report of *Military Manpower Task Force*, p. II-12.

*"Full-time employed" excludes those who are unemployed, those still in high school, and those enrolled in college full-time.

Geographic Representation. An extensive analysis of the geographic distribution in the study *America's Volunteers: A Report on the All-Volunteer Armed Forces* showed that there were virtually no differences between NPS enlistees and the general population.

Women in the Military. The group most underrepresented in military service is female youth, although there has been significantly greater participation of women in the military in the past decade. From only 1.3% in FY1971, women in the enlisted force had grown to 9.0% by FY1982 (Table 5.13). Increased participation of women not only provides increased job opportunities for women but increases the supply of potential recruits. I have found no recommendations of the Gates Commission that urged greater participation of women in the military.

Table 5.13. Female Enlisted Personnel (Percent)

	FY1972	FY1982
Army	1.8	9.6
Navy	1.1	7.7
Marine Corps	2.1	4.5
Air Force	2.0	11.3
DoD	1.6	9.0

Source: *Military Manpower Task Force: A Report to the President on the Status and Prospects of the All-Volunteer Force* (Washington, DC: Government Printing Office, 1982) p. II-18.

Enlisted Standards

The transition ten years ago from the draft to the AVF has also provided for a subtle but profound shift in some important areas of personnel management. The services have much greater management control today over who enters and who remains in military service.

During the draft era, standards for induction as well as for enlistment revolved around questions of who must serve. Entry-level standards were simple and tended to be low in comparison to today's standards. Relatively low standards made it possible for more to serve and made it difficult for individuals to avoid military service by intentional poor performance or by dropping out of school. Not only did the standards apply to draftees and to the army, but the air force and the navy both took substantial percentages of category IV enlistees during the draft era. Today, occupational-based standards have made the services far more selective about who enters.

Because equity and draft avoidance are of less concern today, the services are able to use principles of supply and demand to narrow or tighten enlistment standards. Most recently, in a healthy recruiting market, it is no surprise that standards for both enlistment and retention have been increased. Standards include weight standards, occupations open to women, entry-level test scores, and various programs to limit reenlistment. In fact, because of the problems with the ASVAB from 1976 to 1980, a careful enforcement of retention standards is a wise policy.

As Stephen Herbits[10] and others have pointed out, the flexibility to raise standards in times of excess supply is an important benefit of the AVF. It is equally important to recognize that, if supply declines, it may be necessary to adjust standards to increase the supply of recruits.

THE DETERMINANTS OF ENLISTMENT SUPPLY

The conceptual framework for enlistment supply is one of individual choice. Individuals are said to choose among available employment opportunities and usually choose the one that offers the best combination of financial inducements and nonmonetary rewards. Military enlistments depend on economic, demographic, and policy variables such as:

- *Military pay and allowances* are the wage rates the military offers to potential enlistees and reenlistees.
- *Civilian wages* are those alternatives available outside the military to prospective recruits.
- *Civilian unemployment rates* reflect the availability of jobs in the civilian sector.
- *Educational benefits* have historically been available to those serving in the military. The Vietnam-era G.I. Bill expired in December 1976, and was replaced by a less costly (and less valuable) benefit.
- *Enlistment standards* determine who is eligible to enlist and what military occupations are available to them.
- *Recruiting programs*, particularly recruiters and advertising, are used to "sell" enlistment in the military, and evidence shows they play an important role in enlistment supply.
- *Eligible population* of males at the prime age of enlistment (seventeen to twenty-one years) has an obvious bearing on the number who choose to enlist in the military. The decline in the youth cohort throughout the 1980s and into the next decade figures prominently in the concerns about the future viability of the AVF.

Because of the unique nature of military service, it is understandable that nonmonetary aspects of service play a major role in individual decisions to enlist. The desire to serve, the benefits of military training, patriotism, and the appeal to the individual of belonging to a strong institution are undoubtedly important, as are public attitudes toward national defense. We have made less progress in measuring these factors and relating them to military enlistments than we have with the economic aspects of military and civilian employment. Nevertheless, these other factors do play a strong role in military enlistment.

The first problem in measuring trends in enlistment supply is to identify the "supply" of enlistees rather than the demand. The best metric of the supply of first-term enlistees is enlistment contracts for male high school graduates in the upper mental categories. These were clearly supply-limited during this period. Contracts signed are a better measure of supply than enlisted accessions because (1) the contract signing is closer to the time the individual makes a supply decision, and (2) the timing of accessions is affected by the openings in entry-level training.

The supply-limited group consists of male, nonprior-service enlisted contracts who are high school diploma graduates in AFQT categories I to IIIA (percentile scores 50-100). Females, non-high school graduates, and those in the lower half of the mental score distribution have been limited by demand factors during the period of the AVF.[11]

From FY1976T[12] to 1979 supply-limited enlistments declined dramatically, from 142,000 for DoD as a whole to 83,000, based on renormed AFQT scores. This decline of 42% was masked for basically two reasons: the problem in the norming of the AFQT went undetected until 1980, and the demand for new recruits was at times very low, particularly in FY1978. Following FY1979, economic trends and a number of corrective measures acted together to sharply reverse this trend. And, faced with a recognized problem, the recruiting commands may also have spurred the recruiting forces to new efforts. By FY1982, the number of enlistment contracts for male HSDGs in the upper half of the test score range exceeded the figure at the beginning of the period.

Figure 5.7. Male HSDG Enlistment Contracts, Category I-IIIA, by Service, FY1976T-1983

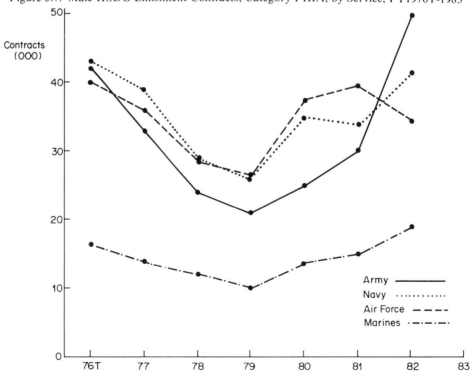

Figure 5.7 and Table 5.14 show the number of I-III HSDG male enlistment contracts by service for FY1976 to 1982. Enlistment supply is generally V-shaped over this period for each service, reaching its nadir in every case in FY1979.

Figure 5.7 shows the trends in the DoD enlistment supply for FY1976T to 1982 and trends in several key factors affecting military enlistment. The sharp dip and subsequent rebound of enlistment supply closely matches the trends in both civilian unemployment rates and the ratio of military to civilian pay. This strong apparent relationship is corroborated by a large number of detailed studies of military enlistments. The relationship is less apparent between enlistment supply and trends in youth population and military recruiting programs. The population trends, while very strong over the decade, show little change on a year-to-year basis. The numbers of recruiters with production goals experienced a sharp jump in FY1980 in response to a recognition of a serious recruiting problem, but otherwise remained constant. The evidence on the importance of recruiting programs comes not so much from an analysis of time-series data but from a detailed cross-section analysis of enlistment supply across a large number of recruiting districts.

Table 5.14. Enlistment Supply Measure, 1976 to 1982
I-IIIA Male HSDG Enlistment Contracts
Renormed Scores (In Thousands)

	1976[a]	1977	1978	1979	1980	1981	1982
Army	42.1	32.8	24.0	20.9	24.7	29.8	49.6
Navy	43.3	38.7	29.1	26.0	34.8	34.3	41.5
Marine Corps	16.4	13.8	11.6	9.9	13.4	14.9	18.7
Air Force	40.4	35.9	28.6	26.3	37.4	39.3	35.7
DoD	142.2	121.2	93.3	83.1	110.3	118.3	145.5

Source: Lawrence Goldberg, "Analysis of Enlistment Supply in FY1976T-1982." Unpublished paper, June 1983.

[a] Period October 1, 1975 to September 30, 1976

Research on Enlistment Supply

Researchers have contributed to our understanding of enlistment supply through literally dozens of empirical studies over the past fifteen years. Most of the studies have sought to determine the effect of economic variables such as military and civilian earnings and civilian unemployment rates and the contribution of recruiting programs to military enlistment supply. The earliest group of studies were prepared for the Gates Commission in 1969 and 1970. More recent efforts have been sponsored by the Office of the Secretary of Defense (OSD) and the military services or have emerged from the academic community.

Tables 5.15 through 5.18 summarize the major findings from over twenty different studies. The studies cover each of the four services. The tables show estimates of elasticities for four key variables:

- Relative pay
- Unemployment
- Recruiters
- Population

The tables indicate the period of the data and the cohort of enlistees examined. The studies generally can be put into one of four types of analyses: time-series analysis, cross-section analysis, combined cross-section and time-series analysis, and analysis of microdata. Each has its own characteristic strengths and weaknesses.

Table 5.15. Elasticities from Time-Series Studies

Service	Author	Period of Data	Cohort	Pay	Unemployment	Recruiters	Population
					Elasticities		
Army	Fechter (1970)	Quarterly 58:1-68:4	1-3	1.24-1.67*	0	—	1.0[a]
	Fechter (1978)	Quarterly 58:1-74:2	1-3	0.97*	0.23	—	1.0[a]
	Fernandez (1979)	Monthly 70:7-78:9	1-2	0.88	0.24	.07	1.0[a]
	Grissmer (1978)	Monthly 70:6-75:7	1-2 HSG	1.22*	0.42*	—	1.0[a]
			3 HSG	1.68*	0.37*	—	1.0[a]
	Dale & Gilroy (1983)	Monthly 75:10-82:3	1-3A HSG	0.6-1.5*	1.1-1.3*	0	1.0[a]
	Ash, Udis & McNown (1983)	Semiannual 67:2-79:2	All	0.88-1.09*	0.13	—	1.0[a]
Navy	Fernandez (1979)	Monthly 70:7-79:9	1-2	0.63*	0.65*	—	1.0[a]
	Goldberg (1979)	Quarterly 71:3-77:4	1-3A HSG	0.13	0.51*	1.27	5.0
	Greenston & Toikka (1978)	Quarterly 70:3-77:4	1-2 HSG	0.36	0.61*	—	0.28
			3 HSG	0.22	1.65*	—	0.02
	Grissmer (1978)	Monthly 70:6-75:7	1-2 HSG	0.94	0.50	—	1.0[a]
			3 HSG	1.55	0.35	—	1.0[a]
	Dale & Gilroy (1983)	Monthly 75:10-82:3	1-3A HSG	0.5-1.8*	1.0-1.3*	—	1.0[a]
	Ash, Udis & McNown (1983)	Semiannual 67:2-79:2	All	0.88-1.18*	N.R.	—	1.0[a]
Marine Corps	Cralley (1979)	Monthly 73:7-79.9	1-2 HSG	—[b]	0.79*	0.36[a]	.60[a]
			3A HSG	—[b]	0.79*	0.60[a]	.30[a]
	Fernandez (1979)	Monthly 70:7-79.9	1-2	0.06	1.37*	0.62	1.0[a]
	Grissmer (1978)	Monthly 70:6-75:7	1-2 HSG	0.74*	1.25*	—	1.0[a]
			3 HSG	0.57*	0.62*	—	1.0[a]
	Dale & Gilroy (1983)	Monthly 75:10-82:3	1-3A HSG	1.5-3.1*	1.0-1.3*	—	1.0[a]
	Ash, Udis & McNown (1983)	Semiannual 67:2-79:2	All	0.31-0.35	N.R.	—	1.0[a]
Air Force	Fernandez (1979)	Monthly 70:7-79.9	1-2	0.29	0.63	—	1.0[a]
	Grissmer (1978)	Monthly 70:6-75:7	1-2 HSG	0.84*	0.95	—	1.0[a]
			3 HSG	0.99*	-0.24	—	1.0[a]
	Saving (1980)	Quarterly 70:3-77:4	1-2 HSG	0.96	0	—	1.0[a]
			3 HSG	2.38	0	—	1.0[a]
	Dale & Gilroy (1983)	Monthly 75:10-82:3	1-3A HSG	0.9-1.6*	1.0-1.1*	—	1.0[a]
	Ash, Udis & McNown (1983)	Semiannual 67:2-79:2	All	.09	N.R.	—	1.0[a]
Total DoD	Cooper (1977)	Semiannual 71:2-76.1		0.95-1.23*	0.11-.27	—	1.0
	Grissmer (1978)	Monthly 70:6-75:7	1-2 HSG	0.89*	0.46	—	1.0[a]
			3 HSG	1.15	0.29	—	1.0[a]

Source: References based on Goldberg (1982) and Dale & Gilroy (1983). See bibliography.

* Statistically significant at 0.05 level.
[a] Assumed value.
[b] Took on assumed values to estimate other parameters.

Table 5.16. Elasticities from Cross-Section Studies

Service	Author	Sites	Period	Cohort	Pay	Elasticities		
						Unemployment	Recruiters	Population
Army	Gray (1970)		1964		1.5*	—	—	
	Goldberg (1975)	States	1973	HSG	1.12*	—	0.23[a]	0.34[a]
	Huck & Allen (1977)	States	1975	1-3A HSDG	1.16*	0.34*	0.34*	0.65*
	Moore et al. (1974)	States	1972	HSG	0.60*	0.23*	—	1.0 [a]
			1973	HSG	0.65*	—	0.28	0.72[a]
Navy	Borack & Siegel (1981)	Districts	1977	HSDG	0.43*	0.16*	0.97	N.R.
			1978	HSDG	0.29*	0.13	0.77	N.R.
			1979	HSDG	0.26	0.08	0.70	N.R.
	Goldberg (1975)	States	1973	HSG	—	0.16	0.41*	-0.14
	Huck & Allen (1977)	States	1975	1-3A HSDG	0.61*	0.03	0.56*	0.44*
	Moore et al. (1974)	States	1972	HSG	-0.86	0.15	0.75	0.25[a]
			1973	HSG	-0.19	0.23	0.64	0.36[a]
	Morey (1981)		1976-1978	HSG	0.17*	0.18	0.73*	0.25*
	Jehn & Shughart (1978)	Districts	1973	HSG	1.22*	0.30*	0.12/0.68[b]	N.R.
			1975	HSG	1.26*	0.02	-0.14/0.69[b]	N.R.
Marine Corps	Cralley (1979)	Offices	1978	1-2 HSG	0.89*	—	0.36*	0.60*
				1-3A HSG	0.56*	—	0.49*	0.44*
	Goldberg (1975)	States	1973	HSG	—	—	0.81	0.29
	Huck & Allen (1977)	States	1975	1-3A HSDG	-0.18	-0.06	0.37*	0.57*
	Moore et al. (1974)	States	1972	HSG	—	0.11	0.18	0.82[a]
			1973	HSG	-0.31	-0.08	0.26*	0.74[a]
Air Force	Goldberg (1975)	States	1973	HSG	0.63*	0.14	0.83*	0.08
	Huck & Allen (1977)	States	1975	1-3A HSG	-0.11	0.25*	0.73*	0.20*
	Hooper et al. (1980)	Offices	1977-1978	ALL	—	—	0.65	0.13
	Moore et al. (1974)	States	1972	HSG			0.84*	0.16[a]
			1973	HSG	0.23	0.17	0.69*	0.31[a]
DoD	Moore et al. (1974)	States	1972	HSG	0.12	0.20*	—	1.0 [a]
			1973	HSG	0.23	0.11	0.41*	0.59[a]

Source: References based on Goldberg (1982) and Dale & Gilroy (1983). See bibliography.

* Statistically significant at 0.05 level.
[a] Assumed value.
[b] Second value holds goals per recruiter constant.

- *Time-series analysis* has typically examined the variation in worldwide enlistments over time as a function of key explanatory variables. While time-series analysis appears to provide positive estimates of the effects of pay and unemployment variables, it has been less successful in measuring the contribution of recruiting program changes or of population growth. Time-series analysis is not a particularly rich source of variation in the factors affecting enlistments, although national unemployment and pay data are reasonably easy to collect. Moreover, time-series analysis must confront the strong seasonal patterns in enlistment behavior and must specify the leads and lags in the key variables. In all, the time-series studies have made a useful contribution to the literature on enlistment supply.

- *Cross-section analysis*, which examines variation in enlistments across recruiting districts or states, is a richer source of data. It permits the analyst to relate enlistments to cross-section variations in earnings and unemployment and to measure the return to more intensive use of recruiters. Cross-section analysis places a premium on careful data collection and measurement of variations in earnings and wages, unemployment, population, and recruiter programs. The statistical problems related to imperfect measurement ("errors in variables") can produce serious underestimates of the contributions of key variables to enlistment supply. It is not surprising that the most successful efforts have tended to invest very heavily in data collection.

The objective of supply analysis is frequently to project variations over time, and with cross-section analysis this is frequently difficult to do.

Table 5.17. Elasticities from Joint Cross-Section Time Series Studies

| Service | Author† | Sites | Period | Cohort | Pay | Elasticities | | |
						Unemployment	Recruiters	Population
Army	Goldberg (1982)	Navy Districts	Annual: 76-80	1-3A HSDG	2.22*	-0.06	0.72*	0.39*
	Goldberg (1983)	Navy Districts	Annual: 76-82	1-3A HSDG	1.86*	0.26*	0.93*	0.09
	Cotterman (1982)	States	Monthly— 74:10-81:3	1-3A HSDG	0.37	—	1.30*	—
Navy	Goldberg (1982)	Navy Districts	Annual: 76-80	1-3A HSDG	0.93*	0.29*	0.74*	0.42*
	Goldberg (1983)	Navy Districts	Annual: 76-82	1-3A HSDG	0.81*	0.27*	0.59*	0.47*
	Cotterman (1982)	States	Monthly— 74:10-81:3	1-3A HSDG	0.70*	—	0.98*	—
Marine Corps	Goldberg (1982)	Navy Districts	Annual: 76-80	1-3A HSDG	0.38*	0.26*	1.00*	0.27
	Goldberg (1983)	Navy Districts	Annual: 76-82	1-3A HSDG	0.55*	0.36*	0.94*	0.12
	Cotterman (1982)	States	Monthly— 74:10-81:3	1-3A HSDG	1.33*	—	1.52*	—
Air Force	Goldberg (1982)	Navy Districts	Annual: 76-80	1-3A HSDG	0.98*	0.15*	0.72*	0.47*
	Goldberg (1983)	Navy Districts	Annual: 76-82	1-3A HSDG	1.19*	0.24*	0.52*	0.55*
	Cotterman (1982)	States	Monthly— 74:10-81:3	1-3A HSDG	0.59*	—	0.85*	—

* Statistically significant at 0.05 level.
† Refer to bibliography.

Table 5.18. Elasticities from Microdata Estimates

| Service | Authors† | Data Source | Pay | Elasticities | | |
				Unemployment	Recruiters	Population
Army	Daula, Fagan & Smith (1982)	NLS—1978	2.30*	3.36*	—	—
	Baldwin, Daula & Fagan (1982)	NLS—1978	0.93*	3.51*	—	—

* Statistically significant at 0.05 level.
† Refer to bibliography.

- *Combined cross-section and time-series analysis is a pooled analysis* of data from individual recruiting districts over a series of time periods. It combines the advantages of both the previous kinds of analyses and has only recently come into widespread use. The results from Goldberg's work in this area have become the basis for program and budget analysis in OSD. Data collection and measurement are also extremely important in this kind of analysis. In an ongoing study that Goldberg, Greenston, and I are doing for the air force, we have been able to achieve significant improvements in explanatory power through improved measurements of unemployment and eligible population. Because there is still much to be learned, no single study or series of studies on enlistment supply should yet be viewed as completely authoritative.

- *Microdata analysis,* based on very detailed longitudinal surveys of youth, is the latest method to be applied to enlistment supply analysis. The use of microdata sources, such as the National Longitudinal Surveys, has become the control thrust of labor economics in the past decade. Although sample sizes are frequently small, the data sources are incredibly rich in variables. A major task for researchers such as James Hosek, Thomas Daula, Thomas Fagan, and others is to be able to translate these variables on individuals into values that can be used for policy analysis.

The following section provides a brief look at our current understanding of the roles of pay, unemployment, educational benefits, recruiters, and population on military enlistment supply over the past ten years. Although I have tried to synthesize the results from a number of individual studies, it probably represents my personal opinion more than the weight of scientific evidence. My objective is to measure the contributions of these five variables to the precipitous decline in enlistment supply from 1976 to 1979 and to the equally sharp rebound since then.

Review of Enlistment Supply Factors

Relative Military Pay. Relative military pay is the ratio of first-term military pay to a measure of civilian earnings. Following the Gates Commission, most recent researchers have constructed variables based on the present discounted value of pay throughout the first term.

A large pay increase for military recruits was a centerpiece of the recommendations of the Gates Commission. The commission agreed that such an increase would produce enough volunteers to meet the demands of an all-volunteer force and was "called for on the ground of equity alone."[13] From 1950 to 1964 basic pay for recruits had increased only 4% while career personnel received increases compounding to 58% (and civilian wages increased 69%). The Gates Commission used an estimated pay elasticity of 1.25: an increase of 10% in the total (discounted) value of first-term military pay would produce a 12.5% increase in enlisted volunteers.

The Gates Commission's estimated elasticity was based on several econometric studies of first-term enlistment supply. The studies used draft-era data and attempted to sort out the effects of changes in relative military pay from the effects of the draft, a changing world situation, and other variables. The Gates Commission used a conservative estimate given the range of findings among the different studies.[14]

The Gates Commission results on the effects of pay have stood the test of time. The most comprehensive recent studies of enlistment supply have found supply elasticities in the range 1.0 to 2.0 (see Tables 5.15 - 5.18). The results appear to indicate a somewhat larger pay elasticity for the army than for the other services. However, if the Gates Commission work were being redone today, it is quite possible its pay elasticity assumption would remain unchanged.

Civilian Unemployment. The relative pay measure contains an estimate of civilian earnings, one measure of civilian labor market opportunities. The unemployment rate is another measure of these opportunities. Over the course of the business cycle civilian pay levels and unemployment rates are negatively correlated. Individuals who are unemployed would tend to find military service relatively more attractive. At higher unemployment rates, employers are also able to raise standards and attractive opportunities would be less available. Some of these would show up in the civilian earnings component of the pay variable, because measured earnings would decline. The unemployment rate would measure the effects of economic conditions not measured by the pay variable.

Unemployment may be the most critical economic variable for the success of the AVF. Yet the effects of unemployment on enlistment supply is our area of greatest ignorance. The Gates Commission found only a relatively small effect of unemployment on military enlistment supply.[15] Because unemployment is so much more volatile than pay, even a relatively small elasticity can have demonstrably large effects. Overall unemployment rates, for example, doubled between 1979 and 1983. At an elasticity of only 0.2, which is consistent with the Gates Commission's approach,[16] enlistments would increase by about 20% due to unemployment changes reported above.

Recent research suggests that unemployment may have a very strong effect on enlistment supply. These researchers have had the benefit of analyzing enlistment supply during a period covering two major recessions. Goldberg, for example, has found unemployment elasticities in the range of 0.25 to 0.5, depending on the service and the base unemployment rate. Dale and Gilroy find much larger elasticities, ranging from 0.8 to 1.3 for army enlistees in a monthly time-series analysis from October 1975 to March 1982. The latter estimates are exceptionally high, given the volatility of unemployment. At an elasticity of 1.0, reducing unemployment by one-half from its recent peak of 10.7% would cut enlistment supply in half. If true, it makes the success of military recruiting heavily dependent on the course of the economy.

Educational Benefits. At the end of 1976, new enlistees were offered a reduced and contributory educational benefit in place of the G.I. Bill. The G.I. Bill provided tuition payments and cash stipends for up to forty-five months at a total value of $14,000 for single veterans and $16,500 for married veterans.

The G.I. Bill was discontinued because of concerns over its lack of efficiency. High discount rates for new recruits would give a deferred benefit less recruiting effectiveness than a much smaller cash payment. It also carried high economic rent in that for many people it was not a strong drawing factor at the time of enlistment. Yet many took advantage of the benefit. Thus, it was not a cost-effective recruiting incentive. Moreover, it often was not cost-effective in the broader societal context. Because it was of benefit only to those who took formal training and education, persons who derived only a marginal benefit from this training would still make use of this generous benefit.[17] None of these arguments state that the G.I. Bill had no recruiting punch but rather that the punch was weak relative to the high cost. The annual cost of the G.I. Bill in a steady-state AVF was $1.5 billion per year.

The new Veterans' Educational Assistance Program (VEAP), begun for those signing enlistment contracts after January 1, 1977, is a benefit whereby the government matches the recruit's educational savings at a two-for-one rate. The maximum government matching contribution under this formula is $5,400. In addition, the secretary of defense is authorized to make additional contributions (VEAP "kicker") as may be necessary for accession and retention incentives. For the past two years the army has been authorized to make additional payments of up to $12,000 for category I-IIIA HSDG enlistees in critical specialties, particularly in the combat arms.

Hunter and I have previously calculated that the economic effect of a change from the G.I. Bill to the basic VEAP programs was equivalent to a 5% to 10% reduction in first-term military pay and allowances.[18] More recently, Goldberg's studies have suggested that the decline was considerably larger. He showed enlistment declines of about 25% for the army and navy and about 15% for the air force and the Marine Corps attributable to the loss of the G.I. Bill. My personal view is that these estimates are unrealistically high. Yet, even at this higher effect, G.I. Bill benefits are not cost-effective because of their high cost and because the existence of the G.I. Bill provided a negative incentive for reenlistment.[19] And none of this evidence addresses whether the G.I. Bill affects the representativeness of the military force. Nevertheless, the loss of the G.I. Bill provided a major loss of benefit and contributed to the decline in enlistments.

Recruiting Programs. The AVF is as much a management problem as an economic problem. The services each conduct recruiting programs designed to contact and enlist qualified recruits. Recruiters must be trained, assigned to stations, and given management direction in terms of goals and objectives. The services engage in advertising programs to improve awareness among youth of military employment opportunities and to develop specific enlistment leads for recruiters. Under the AVF, recruiting programs have received considerably more resources and management attention than under the draft.

The Gates Commission recognized the importance of recruiting programs and suggested "that the armed services devote an increased proportion of their resources to recruiting and especially Army recruiting."[20] While the commission did not call for a specific increase in the recruiting effort, more recent studies have shown a strong positive relationship between enlistment supply and production recruiters. This is important because it indicates that the services are not merely subject to the vicissitudes of the labor market, but through their own efforts can affect the number and quality of their recruits.

The results from the cross-section studies and joint cross-section and time-series studies show strong positive effects due to increases in the number of recruiters. Although the results vary, the preponderance of studies show recruiter elasticities of 0.50 or larger. Thus, at this elasticity a 10% increase in recruiters would produce a 5% increase in enlistment supply. It is understandable that supply is not proportional to recruiters. As the services add recruiters, they are assigned to smaller communities where the yield is not as great, or they are used to augment an office in a large community. Diminishing returns are inevitable, but we have not reached the point where investment in greater numbers of recruiters is uneconomic. In fact, studies typically show that increased recruiters is the most cost-effective method of increasing enlistment supply.

A particularly interesting new approach in the area of recruiters and enlistment supply is the work of James Dertouzos at Rand. He has modeled the interaction between enlistment supply functions and management goals, quotas, and incentives. Dertouzos's work provides a systematic basis for taking account of recruiting goals and quotas on production.

Eligible Population. Gates Commission researchers and other analysts of military enlistment supply have assumed that enlistment supply was strictly proportional to population. Hence a 10% increase or decrease in eligible population produces a corresponding 10% change in enlistment supply (hence an elasticity of 1.0). The existence of recruiting programs may change that underlying relationship and make enlistment supply less sensitive to swings in population. If eligible population were to decline 20% as forecast, but numbers of recruiters remain unchanged, the population would be smaller but the ratio of recruiters to eligible population would increase. Because the recruiters could work the existing population more intensively, the decline in enlistment supply would not be as great as the population decline.

Empirical results have shown that the sum of the recruiter elasticity and the population elasticity is 1.0. That is, if recruiters and eligible population both decline 10%, enlistment supply declines 10%. However, a 10% decline in population alone would probably produce at most a 5% decline in high-quality recruits.

The fundamental issue is whether the military services are limited by the existing population or by the level of recruiting resources. If population-limited, additional recruiting resources would not help. If recruiter-limited, the size of the population is relatively less important because the existing population is not being fully exploited. The results suggest that there are not enough recruiters to contact and recruit all who would be willing to serve in the military and consequently, the use of additional recruiters would be productive. Thus, the military services are not population-limited; and the projected decline in population could be offset by increases in recruiting resources.

Summary of Contributions to Enlistment Supply

Supply-limited enlistments declined sharply between FY1976T and 1979 and rebounded equally dramatically by FY1982. The discussion under "Review of Enlistment Supply Factors" (p. 43) provides a basis for estimating the contributions to enlistment supply of the individual supply factors.

Three factors appeared to contribute to the decline in enlistments from 1976T to 1979. The index of relative military pay declined 13%; civilian unemployment declined 34%; and the G.I. Bill was replaced with a less valuable educational incentive. Table 5.19 shows the possible contributions to the decline in enlistments of five different factors. I have assumed high and low estimates of the effects of changes in relative military pay, unemployment, and the loss of the G.I. Bill, reflecting the uncertainties in our estimates. I have assumed that both recruiter and population elasticities are 0.5. The actual decline in high-quality enlistments (41.6%) lies midway between the high and low estimates of the table. Thus, a pay elasticity of 1.0, an unemployment elasticity of 0.3, and a lower estimate of the loss of the G.I. Bill are not sufficient to explain the decline that actually occurred. Other factors could certainly have affected enlistment supply during this period. The norming problem, for example, may have misled the service's recruiters to believe they were doing better than they actually were.

Table 5.19. Contributions to the Decline in DoD Enlistment Supply, FY1976T to 1979

Factor	Change in Factor 1976T-1979	More Conservative Assumptions		Less Conservative Assumptions	
		Elasticity[a]	Contribution	Elasticity[a]	Contribution
Pay	-13%	1.0	-13%	2.0	-24%
Unemployment	-34%	0.3	-11%	1.0	-34%
G.I. Bill	Delete	—	-7.5%	—	-21%
Recruiters	0	0.5	0	0.5	0
Population	+7%	0.5	+3.5%	0.5	+3.5%
	Overall Effect[b]		-26.6%		-59.2%
	Actual Change[c]		-41.6%		-41.6%

[a] In some cases effects are weighted averages.
[b] Does not add; takes account of compounding.
[c] Change in total DoD male HSDG contracts, category I-IIIA, renormed data.

Figure 5.8. Trends in Enlistment Supply and Supply Factors, FY1976T-1982

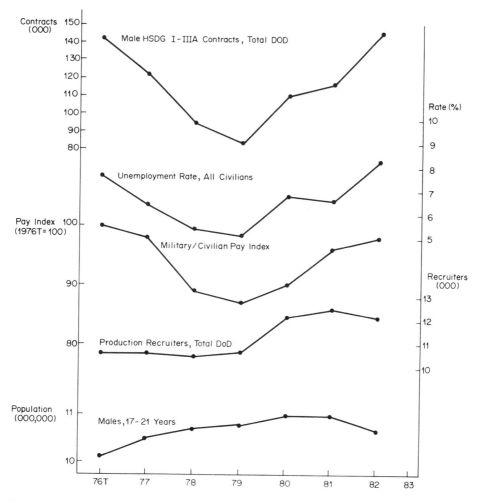

Source: Lawrence Goldberg, "Analysis of Enlistment Supply in FY1976T-1982," Unpublished paper, June 1983, p. A-5.

Table 5.20 traces the contribution of individual factors to the increase in total DoD enlistment contracts from FY1979 to 1982. There is one fewer factor shown, because the G.I. Bill had already been eliminated. Even with fewer potential factors, there is a far greater range in estimated response because of the large amount of uncertainty about the effects of unemployment on enlistment supply.

Other factors that could have contributed to the enlistment supply increase are potentially quite significant:

- The use of ultra-VEAP benefits for the army for high-quality enlistments in selected occupations.
- The increased targeting by recruiters, particularly in the army, on HSDG recruits in upper mental categories.
- The use of a correctly-normed ASVAB beginning in FY1981.

Table 5.20. Contributions to the Increase in Enlistment Supply, FY1979 to 1982

Factor	Change in Factor 1979-1982	More Conservative Assumptions		Less Conservative Assumptions	
		Elasticity[a]	Contribution	Elasticity[a]	Contribution
Pay	+13%	1.0	+13%	2.0	+28%
Unemployment	+61%	0.3	+15%	1.0	+61%
Recruiters	+14%	0.5	+7%	0.5	+7%
Population	-1%	0.5	-0.5%	0.5	-0.5%
	Overall Effect[b]		+38.4%		+118.4%
	Actual Change[c]		+75.1%		+75.1%

[a] In some cases effects are weighted averages.
[b] Does not add; takes account of compounding.
[c] Change in total DoD male HSDG contracts, category I-IIIA, renormed data.

Because of these factors and other factors shown in Table 5.20, it appears unlikely that the supply elasticity of unemployment could be as large as 1.0. If that were the case, unemployment alone could explain nearly all the change observed. It is equally unlikely that the unemployment elasticity is as low as 0.3. A range of possible values of 0.5 to 0.8 is more consistent with the actual results both in the downturn ending in 1979 and in the recruiting rebound of the past three years.

LESSONS LEARNED

The story of the AVF in its first ten years is rich in the lessons needed to sustain it for the next ten years. In particular, the following points appear to be of value:

- In the last major decline, lags in military pay, decreases in unemployment, and the replacement of the G.I. Bill combined to produce a large decrease in enlistment supply. These three factors are unlikely to occur together in the future. However, if unemployment elasticities are 0.5 or higher, as seems likely, a rapid economic recovery could produce a major rupture in high-quality enlistment supply.
- Recruiting and advertising resources are the best short-term instrument to offset a downturn in recruiting. While both involve lags, they are flexible programs that have a significant effect on enlistment supply and are considerably less expensive than military pay increases.
- The future decline in the youth cohort is not nearly the threat to the AVF as commonly thought. Available estimates suggest that a 20% decline in the youth population could be substantially or completely offset by a proportionate increase in recruiting resources. Moveover, population changes are predictable while economic changes frequently are not predictable.
- The AVF is a volatile program, different in characteristics from the draft system it replaced. The AVF is far more sensitive to the movements of the business cycle, to relatively small but sudden changes in the demand for NPS enlistees, and to unexpected developments like the misnorming of entry-level test scores. It requires far better management than the draft.

  The management process by which the federal government responds to a decline in enlistment supply is totally inadequate to the problem at hand. The program-budget and appropriations process is two years from start to finish. We could go from surplus to disaster in that period of time—and in a much shorter period if there were a surge in demand.
- To manage the AVF requires two factors that are not present today. The first is an early warning system, different from the econometric models I have referenced here. It would be designed to predict future downturns,[21] using leading economic indicators as well as activity

levels within the recruiting system that may serve as a barometer of future recruiting conditions.

- The second critical factor is for DoD to develop an ability to respond quickly to possible downturns in recruiting. It took two years for DoD to respond to the last major downturn partly because the problems were not recognized immediately and partly because the DoD program budget process is simply not attuned to react to short-term (or even medium-term) changes in recruiting programs. From formulation of the service's program objectives memoranda[22] to the execution of the program may take in excess of two years, which is far too long to account for cycles in recruiting. Some new management process should be defined and put in place.

In summary, to manage the AVF properly, DoD needs accurate and current information on recruiting, an early warning system to forecast problems, a set of plans to counteract downturns, and a set of management procedures to speed up response. It must be able to shorten the response time from two years to six months. If the AVF is to provide the military manpower required by national defense in the decade ahead, DoD must meet and overcome these management challenges.

NOTES

1. The table compares the annual accessions into the military with the size of a single year group of youth (18-year-olds). In the long run, this ratio does approximate the percentage serving in the military.
2. Even with pre-Vietnam demands for manpower, the percentage entering military service would only be about 30% of the eligible pool.
3. Statement of President Nixon announcing creation of the Commission, printed in *The Report of the President's Commission on an All-Volunteer Armed Force* (New York: Macmillian Co., 1970). Hereafter referred to as "Gates Commission Report."
4. Voluntary enlistees had higher reenlistment rates than either draft-motivated enlistees or draftees. Consequently, in the early years of the AVF turnover was high, because draftees and draft-motivated enlistees were still in the military.
5. An interpolated value between the projections of 2 million and 2.25 million.
6. An excellent discussion of the ASVAB and the AFQT appears in *Profile of American Youth*. Office of the Assistant Secretary of Defense (Manpower, Reserve Affairs and Logistics) March, 1982.
7. Figures for youth aged 18-23. Source: *Profile of American Youth*, p. 25.
8. This problem of inter-service equity for new recruits could also occur during the draft era. Such concerns have led the Association of the U.S. Army to propose that, if the draft were reinstated, voluntary enlistments be prohibited and draftees be allocated randomly across the services. This would give each service an equal share of top-quality recruits.
9. *Military Manpower Task Force: A Report to the President on the Status and Prospects of the All-Volunteer Force* (Washington D.C.: Government Printing Office, November 1982).
10. Personal correspondence.
11. Female enlistments have been under definite contraints in the number of enlistment slots available and number of occupations open. Non HSDGs are clearly a less preferred group, as are category IV enlistees. Category 3B (percentile range 31-49) have shown some signs of being demand-limited in econometric studies of this period.
12. October 1, 1975 to September 30, 1976 includes portions of FY1976 plus the transition quarter.
13. Gates Commission Report, p. 6.
14. See particularly, Harry J. Gilman, "The Supply of Volunteers to the Military Services," in *Studies Prepared for the President's Commission on an All-Volunteer Armed Force* (Washington, D.C.: Government Printing Office, 1970) Vol. I, pp. II-1-1-90.
15. The commission's researchers, chiefly Burton C. Gray, used the percentage employed in formulating the civilian earnings variable. Hence estimated earnings were C(1-u) where C represented observed earnings and (1-u) was the unemployment rate. A separate variable measuring unemployment was not statistically significant. See Burton C. Gray, "Supply of First Term Military Enlistees", in *Studies Prepared for the President's Commission on an All-Volunteer Armed Force* (Washington, D.C.: Government Printing Office, 1970), Vol. I, pp. II-2-1-40.

16. See Richard W. Hunter and Gary R. Nelson, "The All-Volunteer Force: Has It Worked, Will It Work?" in Martin Anderson, ed., *Registration and the Draft* (Stanford, CA: Hoover Institution Press, 1982) pp. 229-298.
17. Hunter and Nelson, "Supply of First Term Military Enlistees", pp. 280-281.
18. The estimate assumed 20% discount rates and that only about 25% of available dollars would be used.
19. The benefits of the G.I. Bill were of greatest value to those who left military service.
20. Gates Commission Report, p. 83.
21. Existing econometric studies have largely focused on analyzing what policy variables and other factors affect enlistment supply, not on predicting downturns in enlistment supply.
22. Program Objective Memoranda is a document from the service secretary to the secretary of defense proposing a five-year program of spending and resources.

BIBLIOGRAPHY

The Report of the President's Commission on an All-Volunteer Armed Force, (New York: Macmillan Co., 1970.)

Studies Prepared for the President's Commission on an All-Volunteer Armed Force, Vols. 1 and 2. (Washington, D.C.: Government Printing Office, 1970). See especially Harry J. Gilman, "The Supply of Volunteers to the Military Services," Burton C. Gray, "Supply of First-Term Military Enlistees," Alan E. Fechter, "Impact of Pay and Draft Policies on Army Enlistment Behavior," A.A. Cook, "Supply of Air Force Volunteers," A.A. Cook and John P. White, "Estimating the Quality of Airmen Recruits."

America's Volunteers: A Report on the All-Volunteer Armed Forces. Office of the Assistant Secretary of Defense (Manpower, Reserve Affairs and Logistics) December 31, 1978.

Profile of American Youth. Office of the Assistant Secretary of Defense (Manpower, Reserve Affairs and Logistics) March 1982.

Military Manpower Task Force: A Report to the President on the Status and Prospects of the All-Volunteer Force. (Washington, D.C.: Government Printing Office, November 1982).

Barmor, David J., Richard L. Fernandez, Kathy Bess, Donna Schwarzbach et al. *Recruit Aptitudes and Job Performance*: *Setting Entry Standards for Infantrymen* Santa Monica, CA: Rand Corporation, 1982.

Bash, Colin, Bernard Udis, and Robert F. McNown. "Enlistments in the All-Volunteer Force: A Military Personnel Supply Model and Its Forecasts" *American Economic Review,* 73, (1983):145-155.

Baldwin, Robert H. Jr., Thomas V. Daula, and Thomas W. Fagan. "Some Microdata Evidence of Enlistment, Attrition, and Reenlistment." Manuscript. (West Point, N.Y.: Army Center for Economic and Manpower Research, 1982.)

Daula, Thomas V., Thomas W. Fagan, and D.A. Smith. "A Microdata Model of Enlistment in the Armed Forces." Paper presented to the Econometric Society, June 1982, Ithaca, NY.

Fechter, Alan E. "The Supply of Enlisted Volunteers in the Post-Draft Environment: An Evaluation Based on Pre-1972 Experience." in R.V.L. Cooper, ed., *Defense Manpower Policy* (Santa Monica, CA: Rand Corporation, 1978) R-2396-ARPA.

Fernandez, Richard L. "Forecasting Enlisted Supply: Projections for 1979-1980" (Santa Monica, CA: Rand Corporation, 1979) N-1297-MRAL.

Goldberg, Lawrence. "An Econometric Model of the Supply of Enlistments: Estimates and Application." (McLean, VA: General Research Corporation, 1975.)

Goldberg, Lawrence. "Recruiters, Advertising, and Navy Enlistments (Alexandria, VA: Center for Naval Analyses CRC, 1979) 409.

Goldberg, Lawrence. "Enlisted Supply: Past, Present and Future." (Alexandria, VA: Center for Naval Analyses) CNS 1168, 1982.

Goldberg, Lawrence. "Analysis of Enlistment Supply in FY1976T-1982" Unpublished paper, June 1983.

Greenston, Peter M., and R.S. Toikka. "The Determinants of Navy Recruit Quality: Theory and Evidence, 1970-1977" (Washington, D.C.: The Urban Institute, 1978) No. 1168.

Grissmer, David W. "The Supply of Enlisted Volunteers in the Post-Draft Environment: An Analysis Based on Monthly Data, 1970-1975." In R.V.L. Cooper, ed., *Defense Manpower Policy* (Santa Monica, CA: Rand Corporation, 1978) R-2396-ARPA.

Hooper, Larry T., and C. Beswick, "Recruiting Resources and Goal Allocation Decision Model." Air Force Human Resources Laboratory, TR-79-55, 1980.

Huck, Daniel F., and Jerry Allen, *Sustaining Volunteer Enlistments in the Decade Ahead: The Effect of Declining Population and Unemployment* (McLean, VA: General Research Corporation, 1977.)

Hunter, Richard W., and Gary R. Nelson. "The All-Volunteer Force: Has It Worked, Will It Work?" In Martin Anderson ed. *Registration and the Draft* (Stanford, CA: Hoover Institution Press, 1982.)

Hunter, Richard W., and Gary R. Nelson, "Eight Years with the All-Volunteer Force" in Brent Scowcroft, ed. *Military Service in the United States* Englewood Cliffs, NJ: Prentice-Hall, 1982.)

Jehn, Christopher, and William F. Shughart III. "Modeling Recruiting District Performance." In R.V.L. Cooper, ed., *Defense Manpower Policy* (Santa Monica, CA: Rand Corporation, 1978) R-2396-ARPA.

Moore, D.S. et al. "An Econometric Analysis of Volunteer Enlistments by Service and Cost-Effectiveness Comparison of Service Incentive Programs" (McLean, VA: General Research Corporation, 1974).

Morey, Richard C. "The Impacts of Various Types of Advertising Media, Demographics, and Recruiters on Quality Enlistments--Results from Simultaneous and Heteroscedastic Models" reviewed by F.M. Bass in *Department of Defense and Navy Personnel Supply Models*, edited by J. Cirie, J.J. Miller, and H.W. Sinaiko, Smithsonian Institution, TR-9, 1981.

Saving, Thomas W., et al. "Air Force Enlisted Personnel Retention-Accession Model" Air Force Human Resources Laboratory, TR-80-12, 1980

6 The Enlisted Career Manpower in the All-Volunteer Force*

C. ROBERT ROLL, JR.
JOHN T. WARNER

INTRODUCTION

Our charge is to examine the trends in enlisted force manning during the All-Volunteer Force (AVF) era, to identify the problems and successes in career force manning and the external factors that have most affected career manning during the last ten years, and to discuss the major issues in career force management. The key theme is to compare what *The Report of the President's Commission on an All-Volunteer Armed Force*, popularly known as the Gates Commission Report, predicted would happen in an AVF environment with what has actually happened. Remarkably, the Gates Commission had very little to say about career force manning and management. Several staff studies for the Commission estimated the effect of bonuses on first-term reenlistment rates and the Commission expressed the beliefs that (1) career force manning would increase under a volunteer system because of improving first-term reenlistment rates, and (2) a more career-intensive, and possibly an even smaller volunteer force would be more productive than a draft-induced force. Other than that, the Gates Commission had very little to say on the subject. This is not too surprising, given its primary concern with getting personnel in the front door, instead of keeping them. Luckily, a significant body of research has evolved in the last ten years concerning careerist supply and careerist productivity. We make substantial use of these studies in our discussion.

*Revised version of a paper presented at the AVF Conference at the U.S. Naval Academy on November 3, 1983. We wish to thank members of the Defense Manpower Data Center, particularly Bob Brandewie and Monty Kingsley, and the Quadrennial Review of Military Compensation, particularly Maj. Roy Smoker, for most of the data collected and reported.

We begin by examining the major trends in career force manning and retention during the AVF era. We attempt to interpret these trends and identify the major factors explaining them. We then discuss what is known about the supply side of the military manpower market by reviewing the results of studies which have analyzed the relationship between retention and economic factors as well as other contributing factors. Next we turn to the demand side of the market. We examine the services' stated requirements for personnel and compare those requirements with current personnel inventories. We then address issues of personnel effectiveness or productivity and issues surrounding the mix of personnel by experience level as well as other factors. Finally, since the military compensation system is a major tool for equating the supply of personnel with the demand for personnel, we discuss the various policy issues surrounding the military compensation system.

CAREER FORCE TRENDS

In examining several of the major trends that have shaped the enlisted career force over the last ten years, we begin with a broad-brush look at aggregate career force retention rates and manning levels, and then examine more detailed trends within one-digit DoD occupation groups.

Table 6.1 displays retention rates by term of service and branch of service for FY1975-1982. Here, retention rate is defined as the percentage of personnel at the expiration of term of service (ETS) who reenlist or extend their contract. The first term includes personnel with between one and six years; terms two, three, and four include year of service (YOS) intervals seven to ten, eleven to fourteen, and fifteen to nineteen, respectively. We also show retention rates of YOS twenty. Retention rates show considerably different patterns by term of service. The trend in first-term rates has been generally upward, with the largest increases coming after FY1979. The increases came earlier in the army and have been more pronounced in that branch of service. As we shall discuss in more detail below, these first-term trends reflect a variety of influences, including the lack of draft pressure bringing in many "reluctant volunteers," the changes in personal attributes of first-term personnel, variations in the reenlistment bonus program and other service-specific factors, and fluctuations in civilian employment opportunities.

Second and third-term retention rates reveal a more cyclical pattern. Retention rates in these career zones fell over the period FY1975-1979. The drop in second-term rates was especially precipitous, and it sparked much debate in the late 1970s about the sustainability of adequate career forces. Fortunately, second and third-term rates rebounded, and by FY1982 they were generally higher than they were even in FY1975. Again, this pattern may be explained by a variety of factors, in our view the most important of which are trends in the economic factors of compensation and civilian unemployment.

One may glean from Table 6.1 the pronounced influence of the military retirement system on career retention patterns. Retention rates are low at the first-term decision point, where personnel are farthest away from retirement vesting, and they rise steadily as personnel get closer to retirement vesting. Fourth-term retention rates are very high and much less sensitive to changes in active duty compensation than earlier rates. Finally, retention rates fall sharply at the twentieth year of service, when personnel become eligible for immediate annuities. We will have more to say later about the policy issues posed by this career retention pattern.

We now examine what has happened to the stock of careerists and the percentage of the force made up by careerists. Careerists are here defined as personnel with more than four years of service (even though some careerists are still under an initial enlistment contract). Table 6.2 displays total careerist end strength in each service for FY1974, 1978, and 1982 and careerists as a percentage of the total force. We see that the total number of army careerists and the careerist percentage both rose steadily over the period. The navy career force actually dropped between FY1974 and FY1978 but increased rapidly between FY1978 and FY1982 (with most of the increase coming only after FY1980). The marine career force shows almost the same pattern as the navy force, with only slight growth between FY1974 and FY1978, but rapid growth later. The air force is the only service to have reduced the size of its career force. The decline has not been the result of any "failure" on the part of the air force to retain people. Part of the decline has been due to a total end strength reduction of about 50,000 personnel since FY1974. Further, the air force has also pursued policies aimed at reducing the size of the career force, as its career force has been consistently above that called for in its career force objective plan, especially in the more senior enlisted grades. To summarize, then, the army, navy, and marines have substantially increased the size of their career forces over the period FY1974-1982. The army has been the most successful. The significant jumps in the navy and marine career forces came only after FY1980.

Not only have the careerist percentages changed, but the distribution of careerists by experience level has shifted considerably. These distributions are shown in Table 6.3. In every service, the fraction of careerists with between five and ten years of service has increased and the fraction with more than ten years has declined. This shift should have been expected, given the fact that first-term retention rates were rising during the period, but rates in subsequent terms were falling prior to FY1980.

Table 6.1. Retention Rates by Term and Branch of Service FY1975-1982

	75	76	77	78	79	80	81	82
1st Term								
Army	21.4	25.0	30.7	30.2	29.6	32.9	41.6	43.8
Navy	23.0	23.3	24.6	24.9	24.3	26.3	32.4	38.6
Air Force	26.0	28.4	29.2	32.0	25.4	32.3	39.0	49.2
Marine Corps	22.0	19.8	24.3	24.2	23.6	29.0	33.3	39.2
2nd Term								
Army	63.5	59.5	59.6	59.1	52.2	55.5	65.8	71.6
Navy	64.8	62.8	59.4	54.1	51.0	55.6	63.9	71.1
Air Force	67.9	64.8	65.1	56.5	52.8	52.6	62.5	70.1
Marine Corps	57.8	59.4	55.6	55.9	58.5	65.6	68.9	71.2
3rd Term								
Army	84.4	79.6	79.0	79.7	78.3	80.9	83.6	86.2
Navy	89.3	87.3	84.2	81.0	80.6	81.2	85.2	88.3
Air Force	93.1	91.7	90.9	88.2	82.8	83.3	88.0	86.9
Marine Corps	84.0	82.0	82.4	80.8	81.9	82.9	88.0	86.9
4th Term								
Army	92.8	90.9	92.0	93.4	93.5	92.7	93.8	93.8
Navy	92.6	92.1	93.6	94.1	93.9	94.6	94.8	96.4
Air Force	98.5	98.4	98.5	98.5	97.3	97.4	97.3	98.0
Marine Corps	91.3	91.9	93.4	94.8	94.8	94.1	96.1	95.1
YOS 20								
Army	33.2	28.8	31.8	37.0	35.4	35.1	41.2	41.2
Navy	29.9	26.9	30.9	33.1	33.1	30.4	33.7	38.5
Air Force	32.1	34.7	35.3	33.4	30.4	34.8	40.7	39.5
Marine Corps	39.1	38.8	35.5	40.4	45.3	46.0	53.4	54.5

Table 6.2. Careerist End Strength and Careerists as a Percentage of
Enlisted End Strength, Selected Years

	Army	Navy	Air Force	Marine Corps	DoD
	End Strengths %				
1974	219,691	191,971	271,416	42,894	725,972
	32.6	40.4	51.3	25.2	39.3
1978	255,535	190,331	250,804	44,008	740,678
	38.2	41.2	53.4	25.5	41.8
1982	300,282	218,160	250,961	57,623	827,026
	44.7	45.5	52.6	32.9	45.8

Table 6.3. Percentage Distribution of the Career Force by YOS,
1974 and 1982

	YOS	Army	Navy	Air Force	Marine Corps	DoD
1974	5-10	47.1	43.0	37.7	54.7	42.9
	11-20	44.5	51.7	49.1	37.5	47.7
	21-30	8.4	5.3	13.3	7.8	9.3
1982	5-10	61.4	57.6	47.5	66.9	56.6
	11-20	32.6	35.8	42.4	27.6	36.0
	21-30	6.0	6.7	10.1	5.4	7.4

Trends by Occupational Category

We will examine some of the career force trends in more detail by examining trends by skill area, first by looking at the distribution of personnel by one-digit DoD occupation category. We have adopted the following abbreviations throughout for each of the nine one-digit DoD occupation categories:

One-Digit Code	Title	Abbreviation
0	Combat & Seamanship	CS
1	Electronics Equipment Repair	EE
2	Communications and Intelligence	CI
3	Medical & Dental	MD
4	Other Technical	OT
5	Administrative & Clerical	AC
6	Mechanical & Electrical Equipment Repair	ME
7	Craftsmen	CR
8	Supply & Service Handlers	SS

Note that many personnel, primarily those with only one or two years of service, have no occupation code. We apportioned the personnel with unknown occupations into the nine one-digit categories based on the frequency distribution of personnel with known codes and the calculated distributions displayed in Table 6.4.

Table 6.4. Percentage Distribution of Personnel by
1-Digit DoD Occupation Category, FY 1974 and FY1982

	Fiscal Year	CS 0	EE 1	CI 2	MD 3	OT 4	AC 5	ME 6	CR 7	SS 8
Army	1974	25.5	5.5	7.5	6.2	.7	21.9	15.6	3.0	12.9
	1982	26.1	5.2	11.7	6.1	2.6	18.9	15.9	2.6	11.7
Navy	1974	4.7	15.0	10.3	7.9	1.7	15.1	32.2	7.5	5.6
	1982	4.2	16.0	11.4	6.9	1.3	12.6	33.7	7.1	6.7
Air Force	1974	.8	16.2	6.4	4.5	2.6	23.7	24.7	6.7	14.5
	1982	7.1	14.0	7.3	4.5	3.7	21.7	26.1	5.8	9.8
Marine Corps	1974	29.9	7.8	7.2	0.0	1.6	17.2	17.3	3.2	15.7
	1982	28.3	5.6	8.4	0.0	2.2	17.0	18.7	3.1	16.5

As expected, the skill distribution of personnel in the four services varies considerably. Over a quarter of army and marine jobs are in the CS area, while the two largest areas in the navy and the air force are the two equipment maintenance categories, EE and ME. The important point from Table 6.4 is that despite a perception that the military has become more technical, the more highly skilled areas, EE, CI, and ME do not appear to have grown in relative importance. In fact, there appears to have been very little change in the occupational distribution since 1974. Of course, this is not to argue that significant changes will not occur in the future with the introduction of more complex weapons systems.

Now, examine the trend in the first-term/career mix of personnel in each one-digit category. The data are displayed in Table 6.5 for FY1974 and FY1982. Several interesting conclusions can be drawn from this table. First, there is weak evidence that the more skill-intensive areas have higher proportions of career personnel. For instance, in the army and navy in FY1974, over half of the personnel in the EE area were careerists, while most other areas were under 50%. In the army and the marines, the CS category was the least career-intensive category in both FY1974 and FY1982. In the navy, the CS category is the most career-intensive of all categories, but many navy ratings in the CS area are in fact very skill intensive (e.g., missile technicians [MT] and gunner's mate missiles [GMM]). The very high careerist fraction in CS jobs in the air force in FY1974 appears to be an anomaly due to the very small number of personnel in CS jobs in that year (see Table 6.4).

Table 6.5. Careerists as a Percentage of Enlisted End Strength,
by 1-Digit DoD Occupation Category, FY 1974 and FY1982

	Fiscal Year	CS 0	EE 1	CI 2	MD 3	OT 4	AC 5	ME 6	CR 7	SS 8
Army	1974	24.9	52.3	34.9	30.5	30.4	42.9	37.6	33.1	33.8
	1982	37.1	53.6	40.4	40.7	53.1	56.4	42.8	41.9	42.9
Navy	1974	57.4	54.0	41.0	29.0	40.9	35.5	40.6	43.5	65.8
	1982	58.2	49.2	40.5	38.6	48.5	51.0	41.8	43.4	53.0
Air Force	1974	86.4	50.0	56.1	38.1	64.9	60.4	48.7	50.9	40.3
	1982	44.8	50.3	57.9	51.0	57.1	62.7	46.8	54.4	50.1
Marine Corps	1974	15.7	32.9	29.8	0.0	39.7	37.5	28.0	25.1	19.5
	1982	19.1	46.2	31.6	0.0	48.5	48.6	37.1	29.5	29.4

A second point is that in the "softer" skill areas, AC and SS, and the high-skill CI area, the careerist percentage varies substantially across the four services. Why such variation should exist is not clear. Two competing explanations seem most likely. One is that even with one-digit occupation categories, there are considerable differences in skill requirements across the four services, and the data simply reflect this fact. The second explanation is that the services have not attempted to actively control the first-term/career mix in these areas and allowed the mix to be governed by retention behavior.

The third point, which lends some credence to the latter hypothesis, is that the largest gains in the careerist percentage have been made in the softer skill areas. With the exception of the EE category in the Marine Corps, the gains in the careerist percentage have been much smaller in the higher skill occupational areas.

Trends by Mental Group

We turn now to another important trend: the mental group characteristics of the career force. There has been a perception that the services, particularly the army, have failed to adequately retain upper mental group personnel, so that the career forces are becoming more and more diluted with less able personnel. We begin examining this issue by looking at the retention rates in YOS one to four by mental group for the years FY1974, FY1978, and FY1982. These rates were generated by the Defense Manpower Data Center (DMDC), which categorized each person on its data files by mental group according to a very recent renorming of the various versions of the Armed Forces Qualification Test (AFQT) and Armed Services Vocational Aptitude Battery (ASVAB) tests. The rates are displayed in Table 6.6. To save space, we do not display the rates in later years of service because the patterns are very similar to those shown in the table.

Retention rates do, in fact, vary by mental group and in the direction expected. Lower mental group personnel reenlist at a greater rate than higher mental group personnel. However, the differences between mental groups I-II, IIIa, and IIIB are not large. The large difference appears

Table 6.6. Retention Rate in YOS 1-4 By Mental Group,
FY1974, FY1978, and FY1982

	Mental Group	FY1974	FY1978	FY1982
Army	I-II	13.3	26.4	34.5
	IIIA	14.8	25.0	38.1
	IIIB	16.2	29.2	41.0
	IV	18.6	33.3	43.1
Navy	I-II	15.0	20.9	36.7
	IIIA	14.8	21.3	35.9
	IIIB	16.8	23.0	38.2
	IV	32.8	28.0	41.7
Air Force	I-II	14.5	28.5	44.7
	IIIA	16.3	30.4	46.3
	IIIB	18.0	32.6	48.7
	IV	22.9	28.9	50.1
Marine Corps	I-II	14.8	21.5	36.9
	IIIA	15.1	21.1	36.6
	IIIB	16.2	21.1	35.4
	IV	18.2	29.0	36.8

to be between all other groups and mental group IV. The important point from these data is that first-term retention rates have increased across the board, and the increases have been the largest among higher mental group personnel. This is surprising, and it casts some doubt on the perception that the services have failed to retain higher-quality personnel in recent years.

To continue this investigation, we calculated the percentage of the first-term force and the percentage of the career force in mental groups I-IIIA in FY1974, FY1978 and FY1982. These percentages are displayed in Table 6.7, and they illustrate the much discussed drop in high-quality accessions during the AVF era. The decline has been most severe in the army. Yet, while the percentage of first-termers in mental groups I-IIIA has been declining, the percentage of careerists in these categories remained fairly constant in all four services. What is even more interesting, however, is that the fraction of the career force in mental groups I-IIIA is now higher than the fraction of the first-term force in these mental groups in all services except the air force. At least as measured by entry test scores, these data suggest that the services' career forces are, if anything, more qualified now than they were at the start of the AVF era.

Table 6.7. Percentage of Force in Mental Groups I-IIIA,
FY1974, FY1978, and FY1982

		FY1974	FY1978	FY1982
Army	First-Term	56.7	43.7	33.9
	Career	52.0	56.4	50.3
Navy	First-Term	68.1	65.7	61.2
	Career	70.8	72.9	70.9
Air Force	First-Term	70.0	75.8	66.9
	Career	68.0	68.5	70.2
Marine Corps	First-Term	59.0	58.5	51.1
	Career	66.5	67.0	65.0

Trends by Sex

During the AVF era, women have comprised an increasing share of accessions (see also chapter 7). As Table 6.8 shows, the percentage of the first-term force made up by women has more than doubled since FY1974. The increases have been particularly large in the army and air force. This increased share has spilled over into the career force, where the percentage of females has grown at an even faster rate than in the first-term force. Women currently make up a smaller portion of the career force than they do the first-term force, but the difference is diminishing due to the significantly higher first-term retention rates of females. The first-term retention rates in FY1982 for males and females are compared in Table 6.9.

One common perception is that female accessions during the AVF era have been of much higher quality than male accessions. At least as measured by mental group, this perception is not entirely true, as Table 6.10 illustrates. At the start of FY1982, the percentage of female first-term personnel in mental groups I-IIIA was only marginally higher than the percentage of male first-term personnel in these mental groups in the army and navy, and no different in the air force. The percentage was substantially higher only for the marines. This lack of difference is probably explained by the fact that, in the wake of the extreme shortfalls of high-quality male recruits in the late 1970s, the services resorted to accessing so many more females that they had to lower standards even for them. However, most female accessions are still required to be high school graduates, so mental group is not the only basis upon which to compare male and female accession quality.

Table 6.8. Females as a Percentage of End Strength,
FY1974 and FY1981

		FY1974	FY1981
Army	First-Term	5.3	13.0
	Career	1.1	5.0
	Total	4.1	9.6
Navy	First-Term	4.4	10.2
	Career	.6	3.6
	Total	2.8	7.3
Air Force	First-Term	6.6	16.9
	Career	.9	7.1
	Total	3.8	11.6
Marine Corps	First-Term	1.6	4.9
	Career	.7	2.2
	Total	1.4	4.1

Table 6.9. First-Term Retention Rates By Sex and Mental Group, FY1982

		I-II	IIIA	IIIB	IV
Army	Male	33.6	36.3	39.3	42.3
	Female	39.4	47.1	50.4	53.0
Navy	Male	36.1	35.0	41.3	37.7
	Female	44.5	49.9	49.3	48.1
Air Force	Male	44.0	45.1	47.4	48.5
	Female	48.9	52.5	55.3	59.6
Marine Corps	Male	36.0	35.2	35.0	36.8
	Female	47.6	55.6	55.3	60.0

Table 6.10. Percentage of Personnel in Mental Groups I-IIIA
By Sex, FY1982

	YOS	Males	Females
Army	1-4	33.4	38.5
	5-10	45.9	87.2
Navy	1-4	61.0	63.7
	5-10	70.2	92.4
Air Force	1-4	67.0	66.7
	5-10	72.4	91.9
Marine Corps	1-4	49.4	84.9
	5-10	62.9	96.0

Even though it does not appear that the females in the first-term force today have significantly higher mental ability than the males, there are substantial differences in the career force percentages again, illustrated in Table 6.10. In all four services, among personnel with five to ten years of service, the percentage of females in mental groups I-IIIA is substantially higher than the male percentage.

THE RELATIONSHIP BETWEEN RETENTION AND CAREERIST COMPENSATION AND OTHER FACTORS

The data in Table 6.1 reveal substantial variation in retention rates during the AVF era. We now examine the extent to which this variation is due to economic factors, demographic factors, and service-specific factors. The data in Table 6.11 suggest that much of the variation has been due to economic factors. The drop in post first-term retention rates over the period prior to 1980 and the subsequent rise mirror the movements in military pay relative to civilian wages and the civilian unemployment rate. While the rise in first-term retention rates throughout the AVF period might give one the impression that economic factors are less important at the first-term point, we must keep in mind the fact that important changes were occurring in the demographic composition of the first-term force and the fact that more recent cohorts entered service voluntarily. Because of the multitude of factors influencing retention during the AVF period, we cannot derive estimates of the effect of factors such as pay and unemployment from a comparison of Tables 6.1 and 6.11. However, a series of studies, which we attempt to summarize, have used regression analysis to estimate the separate effects of economic, demographic and other factors on retention.

Table 6.11. Trends in Military Pay, Civilian Pay, and Civilian Unemployment Since 1974

	Regular Military Compensation Index	Base Pay Index	Civilian Wage Index	(1)/(3)	(2)/(3)	Unemp. Rate for Males Age 20+
1974	100.0	100.0	100.0	100.0	100.0	3.3
1975	109.4	105.5	109.3	100.1	96.5	5.5
1976	114.7	110.8	118.1	97.1	93.8	6.3
1977	119.6	114.8	128.5	93.1	89.3	5.5
1978	128.3	121.9	139.6	91.9	87.3	4.4
1979	135.8	128.6	151.4	89.7	84.9	4.0
1980	147.6	137.6	164.5	89.7	83.6	5.5
1981	167.8	153.7	180.5	93.0	85.2	6.3
1982	191.3	175.2	194.9	98.1	89.9	7.3

Note: Unemployment rate is a fiscal year average of monthly unemployment rates.

Even prior to the AVF era, many studies examined the relationship between military compensation and enlisted retention. Three studies for the Gates Commission by Nelson, by Grubert and Weiher, and by Wilburn analyzed the effects of pay on the first-term reenlistment decisions of army, navy, and air force enlisted personnel, respectively. These studies were followed by Kleinman and Shughart (1974) and Enns (1977). These studies all used draft-era data, and they were fairly simple in approach. To estimate the retention effects of changes in military compensation, they usually employed data for different military occupations in a single year to correlate differences in bonuses with differences in reenlistment rates. A drawback of these studies was that the effects of other factors usually could not be estimated. Despite this, the studies provided statistically significant estimates of the first-term reenlistment pay elasticity ranging from about 2.0 to 4.0, with a central tendency of about 2.5. That is, a 10% increase in real military pay would raise the first-term reenlistment rate by between 20% and 40%, with a mean increase of 25%.

Because these studies were done with draft-era data and because the effects of other factors could not be estimated, a series of more recent studies has reexamined the relationship between pay and retention using AVF-era data. These studies include Chow and Polich (1980), Daula and Fagan (1982), Goldberg and Warner (1982a, 1982b, 1983), Cylke et al. (1982), Rodney et al. (1980), and Zulli (1982). The Chow and Polich study, which utilized a cross-section of first-term, reenlistment decision makers who were also in the 1975 DoD personnel survey, is interesting because of the very rich information on service-specific factors other than compensation. The other studies, except those by Daula and Fagan and Goldberg and Warner (1982b) analyzed navy reenlistment decisions. These various studies differ considerably in terms of data and methodology, and we do not intend to discuss their technical details here. But taken together, they provide considerable evidence for the following conclusions.

Military Pay

First, military pay has a strong influence on first-term reenlistment decisions. The average first-term pay elasticity is surprisingly similar to those found in previous studies using draft-era data. However, the elasticity appears to be lower in more arduous occupations and higher in less arduous occupations. Second and third-term retention are also sensitive to changes in military pay.

Second, lump-sum bonuses have a larger retention impact than equivalent installment bonuses, and they induce personnel to reenlistment for longer periods.

Third, larger bonuses serve to increase the length of reenlistment. However, bonuses are now limited by law to $16,000 for nonnuclear trained personnel and $20,000 for navy nuclear-trained personnel. When it becomes effective, this legal limit on the size of the bonus serves to reduce the length of reenlistment. The length of reenlistment also increases with the civilian unemployment rate, but the effect is small.

Fourth, holding second-term bonuses and other items of military pay constant, an increase in first-term bonuses has a negative effect on the second-term reenlistment rate. However, the total flow of personnel through the second-term reenlistment point will be increased.

Demographic Factors

First, higher mental group personnel and more highly educated personnel reenlist at a lower rate than others. Second, married personnel reenlist at a higher rate than single personnel. Third, nonwhites reenlist at a somewhat higher rate than whites.

The State of the Economy

Several recent studies have estimated the effect of changes in the civilian unemployment rate on retention rates. Due to high collinearity between this variable and movement in relative pay, the estimates are highly variable. However, the central tendency appears to be that each one percentage point increase in the unemployment rate of males aged twenty and over raises the retention rate by about .015 to .020. The elasticity of first-term retention rates with respect to the civilian unemployment rate is approximately 0.3. While this elasticity appears low compared with the elasticity of retention with respect to pay, note that over the course of the business cycle, unemployment varies much more than pay. From these results, the increase in the unemployment rate of males age twenty and over from 4.0 in FY1979 to 7.3 in FY1982 explains about .050 to .066 of the increase in first-term retention rates over this period, or about one-third of the actual increase in Table 6.1.

Service-Specific Factors

Several studies have focused on the effects of service-specific environmental factors such as family separation, hours of work, duty outside the United States, etc. The data utilized by Chow and Polich (1980) contain the most detailed information on such factors. Holding pay and other factors constant, they find that service-specific environmental factors "have very little detrimental effect on reenlistment rates." Rodney et al. (1980) and Goldberg and Warner (1981,1982) found the extent of sea duty to be significantly negatively related to navy first-term retention rates, but the elasticity is only about 0.3. Neither study could find an impact on second-term retention rates. Taken together, these studies suggest that the retention effects of service-specific factors are minor relative to the impact of changes in pay and unemployment. Further, they suggest that the services are not likely to be able to improve retention rates significantly by altering such factors as the extent of sea duty or the length of overseas tours, at least not within the feasible range of adjustment of these controls. The major policy implication of this research is that the compensation system is, and will remain, the major tool for controlling retention patterns.

While research has established that the factors discussed above are significantly related to retention rates, a substantial "random component" influencing retention rates remains. This random component incorporates all of the factors that are difficult to measure or for which no data exist. In the military setting, factors like morale, leadership, public attitudes toward military service, and involvement in a popular or unpopular war may exert a substantial influence on retention rates. Indeed, some of the recent increase in retention may reflect the waning influence of the Vietnam War and increased public support for a strong military. While these factors no doubt exert a significant influence on retention rates, it would be difficult to assess their separate effects or to determine how policymakers might alter such factors so as to improve retention. "More effective leadership" is easier said than done!

PERSONNEL REQUIREMENTS AND ACTUAL SUPPLY

We have discussed the major demographic trends that have shaped the career force since the early 1970s. We now turn to the services' statements of what they require, i.e., demand, and how well this demand is being met by the available supply of career personnel. To answer this question, we examine the services' objective forces, which depict their plans for their manpower force structure by length of service and occupational group.

Table 6.12. Percentage Distribution of Personnel
By 1-Digit DoD Occupation Category, FY1982 and Objective Forces

		CS 0	EE 1	CI 2	MD 3	OT 4	AC 5	ME 6	CR 7	SS 8
Army	82	26.1	5.2	11.7	6.1	2.6	18.9	15.9	2.6	11.7
	OBJ	25.3	5.6	12.3	6.0	2.6	17.6	16.1	2.5	12.0
Navy	82	4.2	16.0	11.4	6.9	1.3	12.6	33.7	7.1	6.7
	OBJ	6.2	16.3	11.8	5.8	1.3	14.0	32.3	5.9	6.4
Air Force	82	7.1	14.0	7.3	4.5	3.7	21.7	26.1	5.8	9.8
	OBJ	7.0	13.3	7.5	4.5	3.7	22.8	25.2	5.9	10.0
Marine Corps	82	28.3	5.6	8.4	0.0	2.2	17.0	18.7	3.1	16.5
	OBJ	26.2	7.5	8.3	0.0	2.4	16.7	20.0	3.4	15.4

First consider the data displayed in Table 6.12. The data show the services' objective forces and the actual FY1982 distributions by the one-digit DoD occupation category we discussed previously. The service's plans are almost identical to the actual FY1982 data, indicating no substantial differences between the actual mix of occupations and the desired mix. This is also true for absolute levels as well, as all objective force strengths are quite close to current strengths. In terms of total personnel and the distribution of personnel by one-digit occupation category, demand closely matches supply

The data in Table 6.13 examine the match between the actual FY1982 aggregate careerist percentage and the desired percentage as indicated by the services' objective-force profiles. Here we see the army and air force FY1982 career forces actually exceeding their objectives, the navy close to its objective, and the marines considerably below its objective. Across services, the match between the demand for careerists and the supply of careerists is not as good as the match between demand for, and supply of, total personnel.

Table 6.13. Actual Versus Desired Careerist Percentages FY1982, Aggregate

	Army	Navy	Air Force	Marine Corps
FY1982	44.7	45.5	52.6	32.9
OBJ	40.0	46.2	47.2	38.6

Within one-digit occupation categories, the disparities between demand and supply are larger, as the data in Table 6.14 illustrate. Consider first the army. Army plans call for a less career-intensive force that it currently has, with six out of nine categories showing planned declines, two of which are over seven percentage points. Even the more highly skilled areas, EE, CI, and ME, all show planned declines. The army at least presents the picture of a service in which the very high careerist retention rates for the last several years have produced a surplus of careerists across the whole spectrum from low to high skill occupations.

Table 6.14. Careerists as a Percentage of Enlisted End Strength
By 1-Digit DoD Occupation Category, FY1982 and Objective Forces

		CS 0	EE 1	CI 2	MD 3	OT 4	AC 5	ME 6	CR 7	SS 8
Army	82	37.1	53.6	40.4	40.7	53.1	56.4	42.8	41.9	42.9
	OBJ	37.6	45.0	38.3	42.9	49.2	49.1	34.5	36.1	36.2
Navy	82	58.2	49.2	40.5	38.6	48.5	51.0	41.8	43.4	53.0
	OBJ	28.5	61.5	50.3	50.0	50.4	52.5	42.8	36.0	45.5
Air Force	82	44.8	50.3	57.9	51.0	57.1	62.7	46.8	54.4	50.1
	OBJ	44.0	41.3	40.1	44.2	43.9	54.3	47.0	43.1	51.9
Marine Corps	82	19.1	46.2	31.6	0.0	48.5	48.6	37.1	29.5	29.4
	OBJ	30.4	40.0	37.7	0.0	46.1	52.6	41.2	33.5	33.7

The navy, on the other hand, has stated careerist shortfalls in some areas and surpluses in others. The navy has stated careerist shortfalls in the EE and CI categories but substantial surpluses in the CS, CR, and SS categories. Generally speaking, navy careerist shortfalls are occurring in the high skill occupations while the surpluses appear in the low skill occupations.

The air force, with very high career percentages, shows substantial surpluses in all occupation groups except three: CS, ME, and SS.

The Marine Corps reveals a mixed pattern. It has a substantial shortfall in the CS category and smaller ones in the CI, ME, AC, CR, and SS categories. Curiously, there appears to be a surplus in the EE category. Although EE is planned to decline, CI and ME are planned to increase.

In summary, at the aggregate level, the services' actual career forces deviate somewhat from their desired career forces. However, the deviations at the aggregate level mask substantially larger deviations at the one-digit occupation category level. But the comparisons we have made give a general impression of forces that are currently too rich with respect to experience, although this is a situation which may disappear as the economy improves. This discussion begs the question of whether careerist requirements as stated in the services' objective-force profiles in any sense represent an optimal mix based on comparisons of the relative productivities of first-term and career personnel and their costs.

EFFECTIVENESS AND PRODUCTIVITY ISSUES

What is the optimal mix of first-termers and careerists—a mix that provides a force of given effectiveness at the least cost? How closely do the services' objective-force profiles approximate an optimal force based on such considerations? The answers to these questions are difficult, but we first argue that the services' objective-force profiles tend, in general, to be based less on a consideration of the cost and productivity of personnel at different experience levels than upon a combination of factors including personnel management considerations such as a desire to maintain adequate promotion opportunities, the retention pattern generated by the current compensation system, and external constraints such as a congressional limitation on the number of personnel in the top two pay grades.

In principle, economic considerations of the relative costs and productivity of first-term and career personnel should guide force-structure planning. In carrying out its analysis, the Gates Commission itself relied upon a notion of equal effectiveness forces and discussed in qualitative terms the substitution possibilites that might be present. For instance, a draft force and a volunteer force could be of different sizes but of the same effectiveness. Specifically, the reduction in turnover in the AVF would allow for the same "effective" labor units as a larger draft force. In this context "effective" simply meant that fewer personnel would be assigned to training and transient positions. The conclusion was drawn that an AVF could be about 5% smaller than a draft force. The commission further stated that it is without question that a more experienced force is more productive than a less experienced force, but did not attempt estimates of these relative productivities. Some frustration with its inability to deal with the productivity issue seems to be implied by the Gates Commission's discussion of this issue: "Military officers agree that one career enlisted man is worth more than one first-term serviceman, but few officers are willing to indicate the precise trade-offs" (Gates, pp. 41-42). Despite the inability to measure accurately substitution possibilities between first-termers and careerists, the Gates Commission viewed a career-intensive force as more efficient as well as more effective precisely because its recommendation about the level of first-term pay would significantly lower the relative cost of careerists.

A degree of effort, less than that focused on supply, has centered on the requirements issue since the Gates Commission first raised the question in an economic framework. Unfortunately, this research area has been one of the hardest in which to reach generally accepted empirical results. One set of studies has attempted to assess the productivity of first-term personnel relative to career personnel, and how that measure changes as the skill mix changes. These studies include Albrecht (1977), Cooper (1977), Gotz and Roll (1979), Horowitz and Sherman (1977), and Marcus et al. (1982). It is not our intention to provide a detailed survey of the data and methods of these studies, but simply to indicate their major conclusions, as well as the conclusions of other studies where appropriate.

First, studies indicate that experience is a major determinant of productivity. This result has also been found in analyzing the task performance data of Project Utility and Skills Qualifications Test (SQT) data (Armor et al., 1982). The estimates suggest that productivity grows quite rapidly with experience on the job. Depending on the occupation, career personnel are found to be about 1.2 to 2.5 times as productive as average first-term personnel. The higher-skilled occupations have higher productivity ratios.

Second, it is clear that these relative productivities vary with unit mix. As the career mix increases the relative productivity of first-termers rises. The speed with which this occurs seems to depend on the occupation. In some cases it can change more than twice as fast as the percentage change in the unit mix.

Third, changes in formal training can change relative productivities, primarily by increasing the level and rate of growth of productivity in the first term (Gay and Albrecht, 1979).

Fourth, the quality of first-term personnel is a determinant of relative productivity when quality is measured by mental ability and educational level. The effects of these factors are probably larger in higher-skill occupations (Cooper, 1977). However, these effects do not appear to carry over to the second and later terms probably due to the screening process and self-selection at reenlistment (Armor et al., 1982).

Fifth, although very little has been done on unit performance, occupations contribute differentially to such performance (Horowitz and Sherman, 1977).

Sixth, these studies generally focus on the first term/career distinction. Few studies have gotten good estimates of the trade-offs among second, third, and later-term personnel, although the study by Marcus (1982) finds a very high relative productivity for senior enlisted personnel. Implicitly, however, the services behave as if personnel productivity begins to diminish after a certain age, as their objective plans do not call for any more post twenty-year personnel than they currently have, and they have consistently stated that they do not want more post twenty-year personnel even if more would stay. While the productivity of personnel in certain "youth and vigor" jobs (e.g., infantry) may in fact diminish after a certain age, one would not expect productivity to diminish with age across the board. The idea that personnel productivity diminishes with age seems particularly incongruous given the fact that the group being discussed includes people in their late thirties and early forties.

Part of the military's treatment of older personnel arises from the fact that personnel are generally required to become supervisors as they advance in rank and experience. Since the number of supervisory positions is limited, personnel who fail to advance to such positions must leave upon reaching retirement vesting (i.e., "up or out"). Interestingly, the army's chief enlisted advisor has recently proposed a two-track system that will enable technicians to stay as technicians and be paid for their skills on a basis other than rank.

Finally, even given all the problems with measurement of productivity, most studies suggest that more career-intensive forces may be more efficient as well as more productive. We illustrate this with data from Gotz and Roll (1979). Making conservative assumptions about the relative productivity of careerists—conservative in comparison with the results of Albrecht (1979) and others—they derived the optimal mix of first-termers and careerists in three army and three air force specialties. Each service contained a low-skill, a medium-skill, and a high-skill specialty. Their derivations of the optimal mix considered the whole range of personnel costs from initial accession to retirement costs. Their derivations assumed the retention pattern and compensation levels in existence in FY1977, and they varied the experience mix by varying reenlistment bonuses. By grouping all of the various army and air force occupations into the three skill levels listed above, they were able to estimate the optimal first-term/career mix at the aggregate service level as well. Their results are displayed in Table 6.15.

Army calculations show a direct relationship between skill level and the optimal careerist percentage. For the air force, the relationship is not as direct. The optimal careerist percentage in

Table 6.15. Optimal Careerist Percentages
as Estimated by Gotz and Roll

Army	
Infantryman (L)	41
Auto Repairman (M)	48
Field Radio Repairman (H)	61
Aggregate	44
Air Force	
Fuel Specialist (L)	57
Aircraft Maintenance (M)	60
Ground Radio Repairman (H)	49
Aggregate	53

army low-skill jobs is much lower than it is in the air force. The situation reverses itself in high-skill jobs, where the optimal careerist percentage is much higher in the army. These reversals appear to be due to supply side considerations, where (relative to the air force) the marginal cost of increasing the careerist percentage in the army is higher in low-skill jobs but lower in high-skill jobs.

The data in Table 6.13 and Table 6.14 can be compared with the optimal percentages estimated by Gotz and Roll in Table 6.15. At the aggregate level, the current army and air force careerist inventories are close to the optimal aggregate percentages calculated by Gotz and Roll. The aggregate objective-force percentages are below the optimal percentages they estimated. Note that Gotz and Roll allowed force size to vary in their calculations of the optimal force mix. If their assumptions about substitution possibilities between first-termers and careerists are close to reality, any action by the army or the air force to move their careerist percentages toward those called for by their objective-force profiles would require an increase in end strength in order to hold effectiveness constant.

We expect the optimal navy careerist percentage to be close to the optimal air force percentage in Table 6.15, and the optimal Marine Corps percentage to be close to the optimal army percentage. These various comparisons suggest that despite the substantial improvements in careerist manning over the last several years, the services are, in general, still below the optimal level of careerist manning, not above it as the comparisons of current inventories and objective-force percentages suggest. Further, the understatement is probably largest in the high-skill areas. (In several of the low-skill occupational areas, on the other hand, the services may be above the optimum.)

In any event, whether or not current forces are at their most efficient levels, there is no doubt that the current career forces are more effective than early AVF or draft-era forces simply because of the reduced turnover and the data we have just presented. Namely, the career mix has increased and there is no evidence of a decline in mental category among those reenlisting. In addition, the career mix itself has changed, with more personnel concentrated in the second term of service than previously. This suggests that more operational work, as compared to supervision, is being performed by more experienced personnel. This may also give rise to more effective on-the-job training of first-term personnel.

Because it will be addressed in chapters 8-10, we will not explore the theme of how technology will shape future manpower requirements, and whether it will drive the services toward an even richer manpower mix in the coming decade.

ISSUES IN USE OF COMPENSATION TO CONTROL CAREER FORCE RETENTION PATTERNS

An earlier section briefly examined empirical evidence regarding the effect of compensation (and other factors) on career retention rates. By and large, the evidence suggests that retention rates are strongly influenced by compensation. This section examines the policy issues surrounding careerist compensation. What are the apparent strengths and weaknesses of the current compensation system? Could the system be restructured so as to provide a better (i.e., more productive) force than today's force at the same (or even less) cost? These questions are explored in this section.

The current compensation system has several distinctive features. First, over 90% of compensation is in the form of nondiscretionary items received by everyone, including basic pay and allowances, retirement benefits, and other entitlements. Though large in total dollar value, reenlistment bonuses and other special and incentive pays make up less than 10% of total outlays for personnel. Second, retirement benefits are a key element of total compensation. The accrual cost of the retirement system, that is, the amount that would have to be set aside each year to fund fully the further retirement liabilities of active-duty personnel, is over 40% of yearly outlays for basic pay.

On the positive side, this compensation system produces a very stable mid-length career force. By about the tenth year of service, the availability of twenty year retirement becomes the predominant factor in retention decisions. The level and stability of these benefits have served to produce very high ten to twenty year retention rates, even during the latter 1970s when other elements of compensation were deteriorating. Because much of the compensation of careerists has been in the form of entitlements, less of total careerist compensation has been exposed to the budget-cutting pressures on Congress than might have otherwise been the case.

Even though the current compensation system has produced a very stable mid-length career force, one may ask several questions about it. First, is too much of active duty compensation in the form of entitlements and too little in discretionary items, bonuses, and other special incentive pays? Second, what is the proper mix of discretionary items between bonuses and other special and incentive pays? Third, are retirement benefits an inordinate share of total compensation? Does the current retirement system produce a desirable pattern of careerist retention? Should the retirement system be restructured and, if so, how?

Active Duty Compensation Issues

Because most active duty compensation is in the form of entitlements received by everyone, there is little occupational variation in military pay. Failure to compensate according to occupation is an outgrowth of a philosophy that stresses equal pay for equal responsibility. This philosophy holds that pay should vary by rank and experience, not by occupation; it views as unfair the notion that personnel of similar rank and experience should receive different pay just because they are in different jobs. Its proponents also contend that too much variation in compensation is undesirable because it leads to lower performance and to morale problems, at least among those in the lesser-paid occupations. A corollary to this philosophy is that general pay raises must be used to solve recruiting and retention problems.

Such an approach is expensive. As the data in Table 6.14 indicate, careerist supply varies considerably in relation to stated requirements, while some occupations may be experiencing shortages at the same time others are experiencing surpluses. General pay raises are a costly solution to shortages that exist in only some occupations. Increased used of discretionary items of compensation, which can be targeted at specific occupations, offers a much more efficient mechanism for controlling careerist shortfalls. The question is, which items should be expanded the most?

Bonuses

Many analysts prefer simply expanding the use of reenlistment bonuses because they are the most flexible of the options available and need only be paid at career points where retention is a problem. Moreover, unlike general pay raises, bonuses minimize the superfluous money (or "rents," in the economist's jargon) paid to those who would have stayed without a pay raise.

Many analysts favor lump-sum bonuses because they have a greater impact on retention than installment bonuses. Recent work by Cylke et al. (1982) finds the lump-sum method of payment to be cost-effective. A recent policy change to award bonuses half in lump-sum and half in installments may be expected, therefore to have a negative impact.

Although expanding the use of bonuses is a simple remedy with much merit, several arguments may be advanced against this approach. Bonuses, especially lump-sum bonuses, are not a very visible element of compensation; surveys show that personnel tend to forget about their bonuses when asked about their compensation level. Also, there is the somewhat paternalistic fear that most lump-sum bonus recipients will squander the money on a new car and then spend the next several years starving and regretting that they reenlisted. This argument suggests that lump-sum bonuses may have a detrimental effect on subsequent job performance. There is also a problem of recoupment of bonus payments to those who fail to complete their obligations successfully, although this problem appears to be a minor one.

Another major problem with the bonus program occurs when the ceiling on bonus payments is effective and it induces personnel to reenlist for shorter periods. While this ceiling appears to exist to reduce the cost of the bonus program and to prevent the pay differentials among personnel in different skills from becoming "too large," recent work by Goldberg and Warner (1983) shows this ceiling to be inefficient.

Other Special and Incentive Pays

Some analysts prefer expanded use of other special and incentive pays. Some of these other special and incentive pays, shortage specialty pay, for example, are just bonuses in disguise, but others are awarded for reasons other than retention shortfalls. An example is sea pay, which is awarded to sailors to compensate for the arduous nature of sea duty and the added expenses due to family separation. The major argument for greater reliance on special and incentive pays is that they offer inducements that bonuses do not. Bonuses, for example, provide no extra incentive for personnel to accept less desirable assignments or to perform and advance as would a well-structured system of incentive pays. Special pays like sea pay encourage personnel to accept more arduous assignments. Indeed, the navy has experienced significant increases in voluntary extensions to sea duty in the wake of the new sea pay rates. The recent sea pay increase is especially important because voluntary extensions to sea duty, coupled with the higher retention brought about by sea pay, should prove to be a much more cost-effective way of improving ship manning than what appears to be the navy's desired policy: to increase retention rates of careerists by reducing the extent of sea duty.

The primary argument against increasing the use of special and incentive pays is that, unlike bonuses, they too are entitlements that cannot be reduced if retention gets too high. Yet occupations that would benefit the most from higher special pays are already high-bonus occupations. Therefore, any tendency for retention to rise too much in these categories could be offset by reducing bonuses.

The Pay Adjustment Mechanism

One final problem exists which deals with the way yearly pay adjustments are made. Military pay should be linked to an index of civilian wages that is reflective of the jobs performed by military personnel and should then be adjusted yearly on the basis of this index without interference from the executive or legislative branches. The substantial swings in relative military pay during the last ten years were quite disruptive, causing substantial swings in retention rates and force structure. By adding to the uncertainty about future compensation, these fluctuations may in fact raise the pay personnel require to remain in service and hence add to manpower costs in the long run.

THE MILITARY RETIREMENT SYSTEM

Finally, we turn to the military retirement system. This system, which offers an immediate, lifetime, inflation-protected annuity to those who complete twenty years of service, is the focal point of the military compensation system. Because the military annuity is significant in size (from 50% to 75% of basic pay, depending on length of service) the decisions of members to remain or separate from the military are heavily influenced by retirement pay considerations. As the data in Table 6.1 indicate, the retirement system exerts an increasing "pull" effect on personnel as they approach the twenty year point, but a substantial "push" effect thereafter. The retirement system is clearly the dominant determinant of the whole pattern of careerist retention and force structure.

Whether this particular system produces the most desirable pattern of retention and whether it does so at the least cost has been a long debated issue. In the view of the military services, the system is desirable—indeed almost sacrosanct—on several grounds. First, it helps ensure a stable supply of mid-length careerists, whose retention rates are less affected by fluctuations in the private sector than they would be under a system more reliant on active duty pay. Second, by providing a voluntary inducement to leave upon achieving retirement vesting, the system facilitates military personnel management. It maintains "youth and vigor," provides more rapid promotion opportunities for younger personnel, and prevents "grade stagnation." Because retention rates past the ten year point are so predictable, the current compensation system in general makes manpower planning and personnel management much easier than they might be under a system in which the retirement system plays a less dominant role. Finally, applying the ideas of Lazear (1979), because military retirement benefits represent a form of deferred compensation and because continued good job performance is required to become eligible for retirement benefits, the existing system may in fact provide a stronger inducement to productivity enhancement than would a system more reliant on up-front compensation. For example, because of the substantial cost of leaving during mid-career, many personnel will accept duty assignments that they might not under a system where the penalty for leaving is not so severe. (For a strong defense of the current system, see the statement by LTG Benjamin O. Davis, Jr., USAF [Ret.] in *The Report of the President's Commission on Military Compensation* [Washington, DC: Government Printing Office, 1978] pp. 175-190).

Despite these perceived virtues, at least six different commissions or study groups have criticized the present system and have offered alternatives to it in the past fifteen years. These groups include the First Quadrennial Review of Military Compensation (1967); the Interagency Committee (1971); a DoD study group that recommended the Retirement Modernization Act (1973); the Defense Manpower Commission (1976); the President's Commission on Military Compensation (1978); and a second DoD study group which reviewed the report of the President's Commission. The Fifth Quadrennial Review of Military Compensation (QRMC) has performed yet another review and analysis of the military retirement system.

The current system has been criticized on both equity and efficiency grounds. The equity argument centers around the fact that those who leave prior to twenty years receive no retirement benefits, which is seen by many as "inequitable." The study groups mentioned would rectify this inequity by offering earlier vesting of retirement benefits, usually after ten years. In some proposals, the benefits would take the form of an old-age annuity. In others, the benefits would take the form of immediate cash payments. The efficiency argument centers around a belief that a restructured retirement system would be more efficient, that is, it would generate a more productive force for the same total system cost or a force of equal effectiveness at lower total system cost. Although varying considerably in detail, the proposals advanced by the study groups would restructure the system by reducing twenty year retirement annuities and putting some of the money thereby saved into either earlier retirement benefits or into active duty compensation, and by increasing the rate at which retirement benefits increase for those who remain beyond the twenty year point. These changes would tend to produce a force with more five to ten-year careerists, fewer eleven to twenty-year careerists, and more twenty-one to thirty-year careerists. (See Gotz and McCall [1977, 1980a, 1980b] and Enns, Nelson, and Warner [1983] for details of retention analyses of several recent proposals.)

Many analysts believe that such a restructuring would produce a more efficient force because the force would have more five to ten-year careerists and this is the group that should have the highest productivity relative to cost, and because the additional post twenty-year personnel would counterbalance the reduction in eleven to twenty-year personnel. Note however that the move to a more senior force would probably require a considerable change in the paygrade structure, and it would require the services to alter their concept of what more highly experienced personnel should do to include more technician work and less supervisory work.

While these arguments for change appear plausible, the caution flag has been raised. First, the estimated impact on retention of a change in the system is shaky at best. Second, we do not know for sure the rates at which careerists at different experience levels substitute for one another, so it is not clear that a force restructured along the lines outlined above would be better than the current force. Finally, because personnel now in service would most likely be grandfathered, any change to the system would require a long phase-in, during which time manpower outlays would probably increase. These problems, the last one especially, make any radical restructuring less likely than changes which basically maintain the twenty year system but with, say, a more graduated structure of post twenty-year annuities. It will be interesting to see what the Fifth QRMC concludes on the subject.

CONCLUSIONS

We began this chapter by reviewing trends in enlisted career force manning during the AVF era. Except for the air force, careerists now make up a considerably larger fraction of the total force than they did at the start of the AVF era. The growth in careerist manning has been greatest in the low and medium-skill occupations. Measured on the basis of mental group, today's career forces appear just as capable as those of the early AVF. Today's career forces have more females, although females still comprise a smaller fraction of the enlisted career force than they do of the total enlisted force.

We then reviewed existing evidence concerning the effects of changes in economic and other factors on career force manning. Pay and unemployment have by far the largest effects. A policy implication is that the compensation system is, and will remain, the most important tool for controlling careerist manning levels.

We then compared the services' demand for careerists as measured by their objective-force profiles with their current personnel inventories. These comparisons seem to indicate that, if anything, the services have an excess supply of careerists. However, a review of the existing literature concerning personnel effectiveness and cost casts doubt on whether, from a cost-benefit perspective, an excess supply exists. If anything, this literature suggests that current careerist manning levels are less than optimal, at least in high-skill occupations.

Finally, we discussed the major issues surrounding the military compensation system and how it should be used to balance careerist demand and supply. We hope that our discussion has contributed to an understanding of the issues and that it will contribute to the formulation of more effective career force management in the coming decade.

BIBLIOGRAPHY

Albrecht, Mark J. "Labor Substitution in the Military Environment: Implications for Enlisted Force Management"(Santa Monica, CA: Rand Corporation, November 1979). R-2330-MRAL.

Armor, David J. et al. "Recruit Attitudes and Job Performance: Setting Entry Standards for Infantrymen" (Santa Monica, CA: Rand Corporation, 1982).

Ash, C., B. Udis, and R.F. McNown. "Enlistment in the All-Volunteer Force" American Economic Review, 73(1) March 1983 pp. 145-55.

Binkin, Martin, and Irene Kyriakopoulos. *Paying the Modern Military* (Washington, D.C.: The Brookings Institution, 1981).

Chow, Winston K., and Michael J. Polich. "Models of the First-Term Retention Decision" (Santa Monica, CA: Rand Corporation, September 1980). R-2468-MRAL.

Cooper, Richard V.L. "Military Manpower and the All-Volunteer Force" (Santa Monica, CA: Rand Corporation, September 1977). R-1450-ARPA.

Cooper, Richard V.L. "Military Compensation Policy" (Santa Monica, CA: Rand Corporation, 1980). WD-159-MRAL.

Cylke, Stephen C., Matthew S. Goldberg; Paul F. Hogan; and Cdr. Lee S. Mairs, USN. "Estimation of the Personal Discount Rate from Military Reenlistment Decisions" Professional Paper 356 (Alexandria, VA: Center for Naval Analyses, April 1982).

Daul, Thomas, and Thomas Fagan. "Modelling the Retention Behavior of First-Term Military Personnel: Methodological Issues and a Proposed Specification." Paper presented at the American Economic Association meetings, December 29, 1982.

De Vany, A.S., and T.W. Saving. "Life-Cycle Job Choice and Supply of Entry Level Jobs: Some Evidence from the Air Force." *Review of Economics and Statistics* 64(3) August 1982, pp. 457-65.

Enns, John H. "Reenlistment Bonuses: Their Impact on First-Term Retention" (Santa Monica, CA: Rand Corporation, September 1977). R-1935-ARPA.

Enns, John H., Gary R. Nelson, and John T. Warner. "Retention and Retirement: The Case of the U.S. Military" *Policy Sciences*, (17) Spring 1984, pp. 101-121.

Gay, R.M., and M.J. Albrecht. "Specialty Training and the Performance of First-term Enlisted Personnel" (Santa Monica, CA: Rand Corporation, November 1979). R-2330-MRAL.

Gilman, Harry J. "Supply of Volunteers to the Military Services" In vol. 1 of *Studies Prepared for the President's Commission on An All-Volunteer Armed Force* (Washington, D.C.: Government Printing Office, November 1970).

Gilman, Harry J. "Determinants of Implicit Discount Rates" (Alexandria, VA: Center for Naval Analyses, September 1976).

Goldberg, Lawrence. "Enlistment Supply: Past, Present, and Future." Study 1168 (Alexandria VA: Center for Naval Analyses, September 1982).

Goldberg, Matthew S., and John T. Warner. "Determinants of Navy Reenlistment and Extension Rates." Research Contributions 476 (Alexandria, VA: Center for Naval Analyses, December 1982).

Goldberg, Matthew S. and John T. Warner. "Determinants of Reenlistment and Extension Rates in the United States Marine Corps." Memorandum 82-1733 (Alexandria, VA: Center for Naval Analyses, November 1982).

Goldberg, Matthew S., and John T. Warner. "On the Length of Navy Reenlistment Decisions." Manuscript, July 1983.

Gotz, Glenn A., and John J. McCall. "The Retirement Decision: An Analysis of a Dynamic Retirement Model" (Santa Monica, CA: Rand Corporation, March 1977). WN-9628-AF.

Gotz, Glenn A., and John J. McCall. "Estimating Military Compensation and Retention Rates: Theory and Empirical Method" (Santa Monica, CA: Rand Corporation, June 1980). R-2541-AF.

Gotz, Glenn A., and John J. McCall. "Estimation in Sequential Decisionmaking Models: A Methodological Note." *Economic Letters*, 2(6) December 1980, pp. 131-136.

Gotz, Glenn A., and C. Robert Roll. "The First-Term Career Mix of Enlisted Military Personnel." A supporting paper prepared for the Defense Resource Management Study, February 1979.

Grissmer, David W. "The Supply of Enlisted Volunteers in the Post-Draft Environment: An Analysis Based on Monthly Data, 1970-1975." In Richard V.L. Cooper, ed., *Defense Manpower Policy*. (Santa Monica, CA: Rand Corporation, December 1978). R-2396-ARPA.

Grubert, Harry, and Rodney Weiher, "Navy Reenlistments: The Role of Pay and Draft Pressure." In vol. 1 of *Studies Prepared for the President's Commission on an All-Volunteer Armed Force*, Vol. 1 (Washington, D.C.: Government Printing Office, November 1970).

Horowitz, Stanley, and Rodney Weiher. "The Relative Costs of Formal and On-the-Job Training for Navy Enlisted Occupations." (Alexandria, VA: Center for Naval Analyses, November 1971).

Horowitz, Stanley A., and Cdr Allan Sherman, USN. "Crew Characteristics and Ship Condition." CNS 1090 (Alexandria, VA: Center for Naval Analyses, March 1977).

Jaquette, David L., and Gary R. Nelson. "The Implications of Manpower Supply and Productivity for the Pay and Compensation of the Military Force: An Optimization Model" (Santa Monica, CA: Rand Corporation, July 1974). R-1451-ARPA.

Kleinman, Samuel, and William F. Shugart. "The Effects of Reenlistment Bonuses." CRC 269 (Alexandria, VA: Center for Naval Analyses, September 1974).

Lazear, Edward. "Why Is There Mandatory Retirement?" *Journal of Political Economy*, 87(5) December, 1979, pp. 1261-84.

Marcus, A.J. "Personnel Substitution and Naval Aviation Readiness." Professional Paper 363 (Alexandria, VA: Center for Naval Analyses, October 1982).

Marcus, A.J. et al. "Advances in the Measurement of Personnel Productivity." CRC 466 (Alexandria, VA: Center for Naval Analyses, June 1982).

Nelson, Gary R. "Economic Analysis of First-Term Reenlistments in the Army." In vol. 1 of *Studies Prepared for the President's Commission on an All-Volunteer Armed Force* (Washington, D.C.: Government Printing Office, November 1970).

Reame, David, and Walter Oi. "Educational Attainment of Military and Civilian Labor Forces," In vol. 1 of *Studies Prepared for the President's Commission on An All-Volunteer Armed Force* (Washington, D.C.: Government Printing Office, November 1970).

Rodney, David et al. "The Impact of Selective Reenlistment Bonuses upon First and Second-Term Retention." (Falls Church, VA: The Rehab Group, July 1980).

Sullivan, John A. "Qualitative Requirements of the Armed Forces." In vol. 1 of *Studies Prepared for the President's Commission on An All-Volunteer Armed Force* (Washington, D.C.: Government Printing Office, November 1970).

Warner, John T., and Matthew S. Goldberg. "The Influence of Non-Pecuniary Factors on Labor Supply: The Case of Navy Enlisted Personnel." *Review of Economics and Statistics*. 66(1), February 1984, pp. 26-35.

Wilburn, Robert C. "The Impact of Income, the Draft, and Other Factors on Retention of Air Force Enlisted Men." In vol. 1 of *Studies Prepared for the President's Commission on an All-Volunteer Armed Force* (Washington, D.C.: Government Printing Office, November, 1970).

Zulli, David M. "Zone C Recommitment Elasticity Estimates" (Santa Monica, CA: The Assessment Group, September 1982).

7 Women and Minorities in the All-Volunteer Force*

MARTIN BINKIN
MARK J. EITELBERG

One of the most conspicuous, controversial, and from the standpoint of the Gates Commission, unexpected changes in the U.S. armed forces since the end of conscription has been in their social composition. Indeed, over the last ten years, the traditional image of the military establishment as a white male preserve has been substantially altered as unprecedented proportions of minorities and women have entered the ranks. This chapter traces the trends in race and sex in the armed services since the end of the draft, identifies the issues left in their wake, and examines the implications that demographic and technological trends are likely to have on the social configuration of the armed forces of the future.

LOOKING BACK: A DECADE OF CHANGE

The first year of the modern volunteer military was a year marked by bickering and strife both at home and around the world. If the United States could have chosen an ideal time and situation to end over three decades of conscription, it would not have been the year 1973. There was enough turmoil in the world to worry even the most eternal of optimists. The war in Vietnam and the unfolding events of Watergate had split the nation and its people at their patriotic seams. Young men and women were now being asked to display their confidence and pride in the country, to heed their nation's call, and to demonstrate their civic duty, once again, by signing on to serve in a rejuvenated, peacetime force.

*The authors express their appreciation to the Defense Manpower Data Center (DMDC) for help in obtaining statistical information for this chapter. In particular, the assistance of Les W. Willis and Helen T. Hagan is gratefully acknowledged. The views and interpretations expressed here are those of the authors and should not be ascribed to the Brookings Institution or to the U.S. Naval Postgraduate School.

A great deal was happening around the time of the volunteer "experiment" and even more, needless to say, has happened since. Among the many changes in our political, social, and economic life was the continually shifting social configuration of the American work force. Since 1973 young women have been entering the civilian labor force in unprecedented numbers, constituting a relatively greater proportion of those working or seeking work each year. Between 1974 and 1982 the civilian labor force participation rate of white females in their late teens increased from 60% to 65%, and the comparable rate for those between twenty and twenty-four jumped from 64% to 72%. In 1974, about 51% of white women who were between thirty-five and forty-four held a job; by 1982, the proportion had grown to over 63%. In contrast, the civilian labor force participation rates and employment-to-population ratios for males of any race or age group declined.[1]

"During the past decade," one study points out, "record numbers of women, of young people, and of legal and illegal immigrants have been added to the U.S. labor force, which, as a result, grew from 82.8 million in 1970 to 108.7 million in 1981 at an annual rate of 2.5%—more than twice as fast as in the 1950s."[2] Yet, unemployment in the United States and other Western industrialized nations today stands at levels unparalleled since 1940 and unemployment among minority youths, now at record levels, more than doubled over the past ten years. Even as the average level of education for young blacks has increased, black high school graduates in 1983 still have a higher unemployment rate than their white counterparts who dropped out of high school.[3]

Concurrently, as the racial and ethnic configuration of the general population changed, economically disadvantaged minority youths began to form an increasing proportion of the work force. This trend is expected to continue as the population of black young men and women in the labor force will probably rise by 7% by the year 1990, with even greater increases among Hispanics and "based on labor-market developments in the 1970s, the Bureau of Labor Statistics estimates that up to one-million women, constituting two of every three new entrants, will enter the work force each year for the balance of the decade."[4]

Against this background, it is not surprising that the nation's armed forces underwent a transition of their own. Indeed, between 1972 and 1983, the social composition of the military was recast in a manner never planned or contemplated by the architects of all-volunteer recruitment. At the end of FY1972, the last full year of conscription, over 82% of all personnel on active military duty were white males. Today they constitute only 67% of the total.

Increased Black Participation

Critics of the decision to abolish military conscription warned that an armed force that raised its manpower solely by voluntary means would become increasingly unrepresentative of the society it was established to protect and defend; of major concern was the prospect of racial imbalances.

The Gates Commission had attempted to allay these fears, concluding that "the composition of the military will not be fundamentally changed by ending conscription."[5] The commission's "best projections for the future" were that blacks would comprise 14.9% of enlisted males in all services, and that the proportion of black enlistees in the army would be just under 19% by 1980.[6] Moreover, the commission left little room for doubt: "To be sure, these are estimates, but even extreme assumptions would not change the figures drastically."[7]

Table 7.1. Blacks as a Percentage of Total Active Force by Officer/Enlisted Status and Service for Selected Fiscal Years, 1942-1983[a]

Fiscal Year	Army			Navy			Marine Corps			Air Force			All Services		
	Enlisted	Officer	Total	Enlisted	Officer	Total	Enlisted	Officer	Total	Enlisted	Officer	Total	Enlisted	Officer	Total
1942	6.2	0.3	5.8	n/a	n/a	n/a	n/a	n/a	n/a	b	b	b	n/a	n/a	n/a
1945	9.3	0.8	8.4	4.8	0.0	n/a	n/a	n/a	n/a	b	b	b	n/a	n/a	n/a
1949	11.1	1.9	10.1	4.4	*	4.0	2.5	*	2.3	6.1	0.6	5.3	7.5	0.9	6.7
1964	11.8	3.3	10.9	5.9	0.3	5.3	8.7	0.3	7.9	10.0	1.5	8.6	9.7	1.8	8.7
1968	12.6	3.3	11.5	5.0	0.4	4.5	11.5	0.9	10.7	10.2	1.8	8.9	10.2	2.1	9.2
1970	13.5	3.4	12.1	5.4	0.7	4.8	11.2	1.3	10.2	11.7	1.7	10.0	11.0	2.2	9.8
1971	14.3	3.6	12.9	5.4	0.7	4.8	11.4	1.3	10.4	12.3	1.7	10.5	11.4	2.3	10.2
1972	17.0	3.9	15.0	6.4	0.9	5.7	13.7	1.5	12.5	12.6	1.7	10.8	12.6	2.3	11.1
1973	18.4	4.0	16.3	7.7	1.1	6.8	16.9	1.9	15.4	13.4	2.0	11.5	14.0	2.5	12.4
1974	21.3	4.5	19.0	8.4	1.3	7.5	18.1	2.4	16.5	14.2	2.2	12.1	15.7	2.8	13.9
1975	22.2	4.8	19.9	8.0	1.4	7.2	18.1	3.0	16.7	14.6	2.5	12.5	16.1	3.1	14.3
1976	24.3	5.3	21.9	8.1	1.6	7.3	17.0	3.5	15.6	14.7	2.8	12.7	16.9	3.5	15.1
1977	26.4	6.1	23.9	8.7	1.9	7.9	17.6	3.6	16.2	14.7	3.2	12.7	17.9	4.0	16.0
1978	29.2	6.4	26.3	9.4	2.2	8.5	19.0	3.7	17.6	14.9	3.6	13.0	19.3	4.3	17.3
1979	32.2	6.8	28.9	10.7	2.3	9.7	21.5	3.9	19.8	15.8	4.3	13.8	21.2	4.7	19.0
1980	32.9	7.1	29.6	11.5	2.5	10.4	22.4	3.9	20.6	16.2	4.6	14.1	21.9	5.0	19.6
1981	33.2	7.8	29.8	12.0	2.7	10.8	22.0	4.0	20.2	16.5	4.8	14.4	22.1	5.3	19.8
1982	32.7	8.4	29.5	12.4	2.9	11.2	21.4	4.0	19.7	16.9	5.0	14.3	22.0	5.6	19.8
1983	31.4	8.6	28.3	12.7	3.0	11.5	20.5	4.3	18.8	16.8	5.2	14.8	21.4	5.8	19.2

Source: Data on 1942 and 1945 are from Ulysses G. Lee, Jr., *The United States Army in World War II. Special Studies: The Employment of Negro Troops* (Washington, DC: Office of the Chief of Military History, United States Army, 1966), p. 415. Data on 1949 through 1970 are from U.S. Department of Defense *The Negro in the Armed Forces: A Statistical Fact Book* (Washington, DC: Office of the Deputy Assistant Secretary for Defense for Equal Opportunity, September 15, 1971). Data on 1971 through 1983 were provided by the Defense Manpower Data Center, Office of the Assistant Secretary of Defense for Manpower, Reserve Affairs, and Logistics.

n/a = Not available.

* Less than 0.05%.

a Percentage computations are based on the total active force as of the month of June for years 1942, 1945, and 1970 through 1975; as of December for years 1964 and 1968; and as of September for years 1976 through 1983.

b Army computations for years 1942 and 1945 include Air Force personnel.

Strength Trends[8]. As matters turned out, however, the commission's predictions were off by a substantial margin. In fact, one of the most striking trends during the post-draft era has been the growth in black participation. Whereas just before the end of the draft, black membership in America's armed forces was roughly in line with the military-age population (about 12%), today the proportion stands at approximately 19%. The rank and file in the nation's ground forces have been the most noticeably affected: blacks comprise just over 31% of army enlisted personnel and about 21% of enlisted marines. Growth in the black membership of the air force and navy enlisted ranks has been far more modest. At last count, black representation in the navy was about equal to, and in the air force slightly over, the proportion of blacks in the military-age population. At the same time, the proportion of black officers in the armed forces has remained noticeably out of balance, even though it more than doubled over the period, from 2.3% in 1972 to 5.8% twelve years later.

The trend in the proportion of blacks can be tracked in Table 7.1, which shows that the growth in the enlisted force actually predated the end of conscription, increasing from 11% in 1970 to 14% in 1973. This initial increase was the result of a higher retention rate among blacks during the post-Vietnam drawdown. It wasn't until the draft ended, however, that the percentage of black recruits started to climb considerably, especially in the army (see Table 7.2). By FY1974, in fact, the percentage of army recruits who were black was almost double what it had been in FY1970. The percentage declined somewhat in FY1975 and FY1976, increased again during the Carter era, and reached unprecedented levels in FY1979 (26% overall and close to 37% in the army) before once again starting to decline. By FY1983, black recruits comprised less than 18% of all new enlisted entrants and about 22% of army recruits. In fact, in absolute terms,

Table 7.2. Black Enlisted Entrants to the Army, by Sex, Selected Fiscal Years, 1954-83[a]

Fiscal Year	Male		Female		Total	
	Number	Percent	Number	Percent	Number	Percent
1954[b]	34,617	9.9	N/A	N/A	N/A	N/A
1964[b]	30,534	14.0	N/A	N/A	N/A	N/A
1971	41,326	14.1	1,161	20.7	42,487	14.2
1972	26,599	15.1	1,055	17.7	27,654	15.2
1973	38,159	19.6	1,574	18.9	39,733	19.6
1974	46,250	28.0	2,987	19.8	49,237	27.4
1975	37,491	23.2	3,558	19.2	41,049	22.8
1976	40,710	25.0	2,810	17.8	43,520	24.3
1976[c]	14,619	30.1	955	22.4	15,574	29.5
1977	44,900	30.1	3,163	21.6	48,063	29.4
1978	36,624	34.9	5,239	30.3	41,863	34.2
1979	40,030	36.1	7,010	40.9	47,040	36.7
1980	37,790	28.0	8,775	39.6	46,565	29.7
1981	25,328	25.7	6,635	36.6	31,963	27.4
1982	24,515	23.7	4,439	29.9	28,954	24.5
1983	24,344	21.1	4,636	28.1	28,980	22.0

Sources: Data for 1954 and 1964 army accessions from Bernard D. Karpinos, *Male Chargeable Accessions: Evaluation by Mental Categories (1953-1973)*, SR-ED-75-18 (Alexandria, VA: Human Resources Research Organization, January 1977), pp. 33-35. All other years derived from data provided by the Defense Manpower Data Center.

N/A = Not available.

a Enlisted entrants include inductees and enlistees without prior service.

b Data for 1954 and 1964 include blacks and other (nonwhite) racial minorities who entered military service between January and December of each of those years.

c Fiscal 1976 transition quarter (July through September).

substantially fewer blacks entered the army in 1982 and 1983 than in any year since the end of conscription, and fewer black males than since the early 1960s.

This pattern has been the result of a variety of factors. While black youths may find many aspects of the military appealing, the common factor that influences its overall attractiveness, particularly to young black males, is the dismal civilian labor market that confronts them. They have been more likely to be unemployed and, when employed, to earn less on average than their white counterparts. While unemployment rates for black youths have typically been higher than for whites during the postwar period, the differences widened greatly in the 1960s, and by 1973 the unemployment rate among young blacks was two and one-half times the rate for whites (see Table 7.3).

Table 7.3. Unemployment Rates (Percentage) by Race and Age, Selected Years, 1955-1982

Race and Age	1955	1965	1973	1978	1981	1982
All workers 25 and over	3.6	3.2	3.1	4.1	5.4	7.4
White Males						
16-19	11.3	12.9	12.3	13.5	17.9	21.7
16-17	12.2	14.7	15.2	16.9	19.9	24.2
18-19	10.4	11.4	10.0	10.8	16.4	20.0
20-24	7.0	5.9	6.6	7.7	11.6	14.3
Black Males[a]						
16-19	13.4	23.3	30.7	36.7	40.7	48.9
16-17	14.8	27.1	35.7	43.0	43.2	52.7
18-19	12.9	20.2	23.0	32.9	39.2	47.1
20-24	12.4	9.3	13.2	21.0	26.4	31.5

Sources: 1955 and 1956, Bureau of Labor Statistics, *Handbook of Labor Statistics*; other years, unpublished figures from BLS, *Current Population Survey*.

[a] Figures for 1955 and 1965 include all nonwhite males.

The degree to which military recruitment patterns can be attributed to changes in the labor market is a contentious issue. Most estimates of unemployment elasticities have ranged from 0.2 to 0.5. These aggregate figures, however, mask important differences by race. Analysts who have attempted to distinguish between the enlistment responses of white and minority youths to variations in unemployment have consistently measured a significantly smaller response from blacks. In some cases, the changes in enlistment rates have been in an *opposite* direction. While a 10% increase in white youth unemployment, by one estimate, would result in roughly a 5% increase in high-quality white volunteers, a similar increase in black youth unemployment would yield a 6% *decrease* in black volunteers with similar qualitative characteristics.[9] This anomaly is probably a manifestation of the "substitution effect" that typically occurs during periods of rising unemployment. When the services are able to attract more high school graduates who have scores in the top Armed Forces Qualification Test (AFQT) categories, they are less inclined to accept volunteers from the bottom categories. The fact that white youths are more likely to be in the former group and blacks in the latter supports this explanation.

Young blacks who are able to find civilian employment can expect to earn less on the average than whites of similar age and education. In 1979, for example, black male high school graduates who were employed full time earned approximately 20% less than their white counterparts.[10] It is evident then why military pay scales, which are the same regardless of race, are relatively more attractive to blacks than to whites.[11]

It has also been contended that while economic considerations may have played a role in the expanded participation by blacks, "the main cause is the vastly larger number of blacks qualifying for military service."[12] According to this argument, the proportion of young black males estimated to possess aptitudes in the AFQT category I-III range (above the thirtieth percentile) jumped from 33% in 1972 to 42% in 1973, while the capabilities of nonblack youths remained virtually the same. This abrupt change in a single year was attributed to the changeover by the army to a new test (the Army Classification Battery) which eliminated "the 'cultural bias' that was presumably present in earlier tests."[13] This analysis therefore "suggests that the percentages [of blacks in the armed forces] would have been about the same whether or not the draft was ended . . . ."[14] It should be noted, however, that in contrast to the estimate that 42% of the young black male population in 1973 was in the AFQT category I-III range, more recent estimates indicate that only 27% of the current generation of black males would score in these categories.[15]

In any event, the importance of the military as an employer of black youths is vividly illustrated in Table 7.4, which shows that at least 20% of all black males born between 1957 and 1962 had entered the armed forces by September 1983, compared with only 13% of white males in the same age group. The contrast is even sharper when account is taken of the fact that blacks are two to three times less likely to qualify for enlistment. For example, by conservative estimate, over 46% of all potentially qualified black males had enlisted by the end of FY1983. The comparable "participation rate" for potentially qualified white males was less than 16%.[16]

Table 7.4. Military Participation Rates (Percentage) of Male Youths Born Between 1957 and 1962, By Racial/Ethnic Group and Level of Education[a]

Level of Education[b]	Racial/Ethnic Group[c]			
	White	Black	Hispanic	Total
Below High School Graduate				
All Youths	17.7	12.7	6.2	15.6
Qualified Youths	37.6	109.0[d]	43.2	42.6
High School Graduate and Above				
All Youths	11.5	25.6	12.0	13.2
Qualified Youths	12.0	38.7	13.5	14.2
All Levels				
All Youths	13.0	20.3	9.3	13.9
Qualified Youths	15.5	46.4	17.1	18.0

Source: Adapted from data appearing in M.J. Eitelberg, J.H. Laurence, L.S. Perelman, and B.K. Walters, *Screening for Service* (Alexandria, VA: HumRRO, September 1984); and special tabulations provided by the Defense Manpower Data Center.

[a] *Participation rates are shown for two base populations: 1. all male youths within the racial/ethnic and education category; and 2. all male youths who would be expected to qualify* for enlistment under current aptitude standards (by racial/ethnic and education category). The cross-sectional participation rates *understate* the true percentage of male youths who join the military since they do not include individuals who a) enlist after 30 September 1983; b) enter officer programs; and c) join the Reserves. Estimates of the number of youth qualified for military service were calculated on the basis of results from the "Profile of American Youth" (administration of the Armed Services Vocational Aptitude Battery to a national probability sample in 1980) and the 1981 education/aptitude standards used by the armed services. (Eligibility for enlistment would also depend on other factors—including medical and moral requirements.)

[b] For military personnel, education at time of entry (and initial qualification) into service. Approximately 1% of the male youth population could not be identified on the basis of education; and 1% of military personnel could not be identified on the basis of racial/ethnic group. These unknown cases were not included in the calculations of participation rates. Persons with equivalency certificates appear in the Below High School Graduate category.

[c] White category includes all racial/ethnic groups other than black or Hispanic. Black category does not include persons of Hispanic origin.

[d] This figure reflects the fact that during the FY1976-1980 period the armed services unknowingly accepted volunteers who did not meet eligibility standards because of errors in test calibration. Since these errors affected principally non-high school graduates with low aptitude scores, the services enlisted many more black male dropouts than would have been qualified in the relevant population group.

Perhaps an even more revealing aspect of youth participation is that potentially qualified young men who do not have a high school diploma regardless of race or ethnic group find military service an especially appealing job or education alternative. As shown in the table, approximately 43% of all high school dropouts who could probably pass the aptitude test standards had enlisted, compared with just over 14% of young men who were high school graduates. In fact, the image of the armed forces as a second chance, a place of equal acceptance and involvement despite prior social disadvantage or preexisting handicap, has helped to make the military a traditional channel for social mobility. The participation rates displayed in the table tend to confirm that both the image and the promise of opportunity are still quite strong.

Once in the military, blacks are more inclined than whites to choose it as a career. When allowed, blacks have reenlisted at greater rates than their white counterparts throughout the recent recorded history of the armed forces.[17] In the army, for instance, the reenlistment rates for both first-term and career blacks (who were eligible to reenlist) far exceeded the comparable rates for whites each year after the end of conscription (see Table 7.5). In fact, the proportion of blacks among all army reenlistments doubled between 1972 and 1981, to a point where more than one out of every three was black.

Table 7.5. Army Reenlistment Rates (Percentage), by Race and Career Status, and Racial Composition of All Army Reenlistments, FY1972-1981.

| Fiscal Year | Army Reenlistment Rates[a] | | | | Racial Composition of Army Reenlistments | |
| | First-Term | | Career | | | |
	White	Black	White	Black	White	Black
1972	12.6[b]	20.4[b]	42.6	61.3	79.8	18.8
1973	35.7[b]	46.1[b]	60.9	69.8	78.1	19.9
1974	26.6	43.3	70.4	80.5	77.6	20.9
1975	33.4	54.1	70.3	82.7	74.9	23.5
1976	29.4	42.2	69.1	82.0	71.8	25.9
1977	30.5	48.4	66.3	80.3	70.5	27.7
1978	27.8	47.5	63.4	78.0	68.7	28.7
1979	33.5	53.7	59.6	74.9	63.4	33.4
1980	45.1	65.1	66.3	79.6	60.2	36.1
1981	44.9	66.4	68.0	81.9	57.9	37.5

Source: Data provided by the Department of the Army.

[a] Reenlistment rates for first-term and career-eligible persons who are considered qualified and in specified categories for reenlistment are statistically adjusted to include only those scheduled to separate from active duty during the fiscal year.

[b] Reenlistment rates in 1972 and 1973 are for persons who originally entered the army as volunteers. In 1972 the reenlistment rates for white and black draftees were 11.8% and 14.8%, respectively. In 1973, 10.6% of all eligible first-term white draftees and 12.4% of all eligible first-term black draftees reenlisted.

Occupational Mix. The expansion in the number of black Americans serving in the armed forces has been accompanied by modest changes in the occupational mix. Because blacks perform relatively poorly on the military's entry tests and because the aptitude testing system is used to match individuals with jobs, a disproportionate number of blacks have always served in the so-called "soft," nontechnical jobs where training is minimal and advancement is often slow.

Since the Vietnam War, the armed forces (especially the army) have attempted to meet affirmative action goals for a more representative distribution among occupational groupings. Most efforts have been concentrated on reducing the number of blacks who serve in the combat arms specialties, that is, military jobs that are more likely to bear the burden of casualties in wartime. The army has been successful in reducing the relative proportion of blacks assigned to those jobs. At the close of FY1983, for example, 30.3% of the enlisted men in the army were black, and 28.5% of the enlisted men assigned to combat occupations were black (see Table 7.6). But the proportion of blacks in all the services assigned to the combat category (24.7%) still exceeded the overall percentage of black enlisted men (20.7%) by a slight margin, due principally to the occupational distributions in the navy and Marine Corps.

There is a definite pattern of black participation in major occupational areas. Blacks are overrepresented in administrative and clerical jobs and in the relatively unskilled service and supply handler categories. This is nothing new. Throughout World War I, blacks were assigned almost exclusively to service and supply jobs, and at the end of World War II blacks in the army were still predominantly in quartermaster, transportation, and engineer occupations.

A closer examination of the twenty most common occupational subgroups in the army reveals more about recent trends in black participation. In FY1983 over half of all army enlisted men assigned to supply administration (54%) and linemen (53%) occupational subgroups were black. Although blacks were slightly underrepresented in the infantry, 42% of all men assigned to artillery and gunnery skills (the second most common occupational subgroup) were black. Blacks also accounted for over 40% of army enlisted personnel in several other "soft skills": unit supply (47%), food service (45%), administration (40%), and personnel (45%). On the other hand, less than 14% of the law enforcement (military police) subgroup was black, and blacks were noticeably underrepresented in armor and amphibious, combat operations control, combat engineering, track vehicle repair, and aircraft jobs.

Table 7.6. Blacks as a Percentage of Male Enlisted Personnel Assigned to Major Occupational Areas in the Army and All Services, Selected Years 1964-1983[a]

Occupational Category	1964[b]		1972		1976		1983	
	Army	All Services	Army	All Services	Army	All Services	Army	All Services
Infantry, gun crews, and seamanship specialists	19.3	16.4	19.0	17.5	23.9	22.4	28.5	24.7
Electronic equipment repairmen	11.2	5.6	12.2	5.2	16.8	6.9	24.1	10.2
Communications and intelligence specialists	9.2	6.7	11.6	7.5	23.8	15.5	28.7	21.3
Medical and dental specialists	16.6	12.0	16.7	11.6	21.6	15.4	32.3	24.1
Other technical and allied specialists	9.3	7.1	10.4	8.2	13.5	12.4	25.3	18.1
Administrative specialists and clerks	11.7	10.4	18.3	14.8	31.7	22.4	43.2	30.7
Electrical/mechanical repairmen	11.3	7.2	14.3	8.9	20.4	12.1	27.7	16.3
Craftsmen	11.2	9.7	14.5	11.8	16.0	12.1	26.7	15.6
Service and supply handlers	17.1	17.1	22.2	20.6	24.2	20.9	32.6	27.0
Nonoccupational and miscellaneous[c]	5.0	6.2	16.2	15.4	28.4	19.0	20.6	16.5
Blacks as percent of all male enlisted personnel	11.8	9.7	17.0	12.6	24.4	16.8	30.3	20.7

Sources: Data for 1964 from Department of Defense, *The Negro in the Armed Forces: A Statistical Fact Book.* All other distributions derived from data provided by the Defense Manpower Data Center.

[a] Percentage distributions are based on enlisted force compositions as of December 1964, June 1972, and September 1976 and 1983.
[b] Data for 1964 include both males and females.
[c] "Nonoccupational" includes patients, prisoners, officer candidates and students, persons serving in undesignated or special occupations, and persons not yet occupationally qualified (service members who are in basic or occupational training).

Other Minorities

Nonblack racial/ethnic minority groups account for about 7.3% of total armed forces personnel, as shown in Table 7.7. Next to black Americans, Hispanics are the largest racial/ethnic group in the armed forces, accounting for about 3.7% of total personnel. Asian/Pacific Islanders (mostly Filipinos in the navy) constitute 2.0% of the total.

Table 7.7. Active Duty Military Personnel (Officers and Enlisted) by
Racial/Ethnic Group and Service, September 1983 (Percentage)

Racial/Ethnic Group[a]	Army	Navy	Marine Corps	Air Force	All Services
Black	28.3	11.5	18.8	14.8	19.2
Mexican	1.3	1.5	2.8	2.0	1.7
Puerto Rican	1.8	0.8	1.1	0.9	1.2
Cuban	0.1	0.1	0.1	0.1	0.1
Latin American	0.1	0.1	0.1	*	0.1
Other Hispanic Descent	0.5	0.6	0.5	0.6	0.6
Aleut	*	*	*	*	*
Eskimo	*	*	*	*	*
North American Indian	0.3	0.5	0.5	1.1	0.6
Chinese	*	0.1	0.1	0.1	0.1
Japanese	0.1	0.1	0.1	0.2	0.1
Korean	0.2	*	*	0.1	0.1
Indian	*	*	*	*	*
Filipino	0.4	3.6	0.4	0.7	1.3
Vietnamese	*	*	*	*	*
Other Asian Descent	0.3	0.1	0.1	0.5	0.3
Melanesian	*	*	*	*	*
Micronesian	*	*	*	*	*
Polynesian	0.1	0.1	0.1	*	0.1
Other Pacific Islander Descent	0.1	*	*	*	*
Unknown	1.0	1.5	0.3	0.3	0.9
Other[b]	65.4	79.3	75.0	78.5	73.5
Total					
Percent	100.0	100.0	100.0	100.0	100.0
Number (thousands)	775	564	195	588	2,123

Source: Derived from data provided by the Defense Manpower Data Center.

* Less than 0.05%
a Racial/Ethnic group is self-stated by the individual at time of entry into military service. Percentages are rounded.
b This group includes predominantly persons of European descent who are typically categorized as "Caucasian" or "white" for reporting purposes.

Compared with their numbers in the overall population, Hispanics are slightly under-represented and Asian/Pacific Islanders slightly overrepresented in the armed forces. It is difficult to track trends in the participation of these minority groups since definitions have changed over the years. The best estimate of the trend in Hispanic representation is depicted in Table 7.8, which shows a very slight growth during the early 1970s, then stabilizing at 4% for the rest of the decade, followed by a slight decrease in the early 1980s. While the variation is small, the decline since 1980 mirrors the black experience, no doubt reflecting the ability of the armed forces to attract higher-aptitude recruits, who are more likely to be white.

In terms of occupational mix, compared to 1972, Hispanics now make up a smaller portion of individuals assigned to the combat, craftsmen, and supply and service categories, and they constitute a larger part of the technical and administrative job holders. Compared with blacks, Hispanics are slightly more concentrated in technical and craftsmen jobs and less likely to be assigned to clerical or service and supply skills. Roughly one out of every five Hispanic males in the armed services is assigned to the general military skill category, which includes combat. This is identical to the proportion of black males in that category.

Table 7.8. Number and Percentage of Active Duty Military Personnel (All Services)
Who Are Hispanic, FY1971-1983

Fiscal Year[a]	Officer[b]		Enlisted Personnel		Hispanics as Percent of All Active Duty Personnel[c]
	Number	Percent of All Officers	Number	Percent of All Enlisted Personnel	
1971	4,750	1.3	78,382	3.4	3.1
1972	4,152	1.2	78,756	4.0	3.6
1973	4,046	1.4	83,434	4.6	3.9
1974	4,032	1.3	81,739	4.4	4.0
1975	3,858	1.4	81,887	4.6	4.1
1976	3,899	1.4	80,846	4.5	4.1
1977	4,133	1.5	78,970	4.4	4.0
1978	4,242	1.5	77.654	4.4	4.0
1979	4,529	1.7	75,425	4.3	4.0
1980	3,176	1.1	70,506	4.0	3.6
1981	3,541	1.2	72,376	4.1	3.7
1982	3,866	1.3	72,842	4.0	3.7
1983	4,226	1.4	72,330	4.0	3.6

Source: Derived from data provided by the Defense Manpower Data Center.

a Numbers and percentages are based on the total active duty force as of June for 1971-1975 and September for 1976-1983.

b Officers include commissioned and warrant officers.

c Between 1971 and 1979, persons of Hispanic descent were identified through a computerized match of Active Military Master Files with a file containing a list of Spanish surnames. The Spanish surname list was an augmented version of a list used by the Census Bureau, excluding names that occurred frequently in non-Spanish cultural groups. Beginning in 1980, new service members were required to categorize themselves according to their ethnic heritage. In general, the computerized method for identifying persons of Hispanic descent results in a slightly larger number than that attained through self-classification.

Women And The Military

Prior to the 1970s women's participation in the nation's peacetime military forces had been small and confined mainly to traditional occupations. In fact, from 1948, when the Women's Armed Services Integration Act was passed, until 1966, the number of enlisted women in the armed forces was not permitted to exceed 2% of total enlisted strength and the number of female officers (excluding nurses) could not exceed 10% of female enlisted strength.[18] Moreover, military women had been largely relegated to "women's work," mainly health care and clerical jobs. In the mid-1960s, "nearly 70% [of enlisted women] were performing clerical and administrative work . . . [and] another 23% were in medical facilities."[19]

In 1966, under pressures from the expanding role of women in the labor force and from the large manpower demands of the Vietnam War, the Pentagon established a task force to reassess the role of women in the armed forces, to include "the potential for greater employment, recruitment, and retention, especially in relation to current skill requirements of the buildup for Southeast Asia and other deployments."[20] Partly as a result of that study, legislation enacted the following year contained several significant changes in the status of military women, including the removal of the 2% limitation. Nevertheless, women constituted less than 2% of total military strength for the rest of the decade. Indeed, from 1948 to 1969 the percentage varied between 1.0 and 1.5%, averaging only 1.2%.[21]

The Gates Commission never considered the need for, nor the feasibility of, expanding the role of women in the volunteer military. In fact, the commission staff, in its background studies, assumed that the "baseline" for women would remain at around 1.2% of the post-Vietnam force. The commission staff even explored seriously the possibility of replacing females with civilians, as a way of reducing budget outlays, since most of the positions held by females were "believed to be included in the group identified as potentially substitutable."[22]

But this attitude concerning the place of women in the military soon changed when the nation finally moved to substitute volunteers for draftees. Early in 1972, a task force established by Secretary of Defense Melvin R. Laird set out "to prepare contingency plans for increasing the use of women to offset possible shortages of male recruits after the end of the draft."[23]

No sooner had the study commenced than the Equal Rights Amendment cleared Congress. Although the vague contours of the amendment left its specific impact on the military unclear, it served to reinforce the pressures for change. At the same time, a number of military women instigated legal challenges to a variety of military practices charging discrimination. The results of the litigation were mixed, but women achieved one major victory in *Frontiero v. Richardson*, when the Supreme Court struck down the law which denied military women certain dependency benefits that had been made available to similarly situated male personnel.[24]

The combined impact of the end of the draft, the women's rights movement, and feminist litigation can be measured both in terms of the growth in the number of women serving in the armed forces and in the jobs to which they have been assigned.

Strength Trends. In 1972, when the decision was made to increase the proportion of women in the military, some 45,000 women comprised 1.9% of all active-duty military personnel. Today the number stands at about 197,000, just over 9% of the total. As Table 7.9 shows, the rate of growth has varied over the years.

Table 7.9. Total Female Military Personnel, FY1972-1983 (In Thousands)

Fiscal Year	Army		Navy		Marine Corps		Air Force		Total	
	Number	Percent of Total Personnel	Number	Percent of Total Personnel	Number	Percent of Total Personnel	Number	Percent of Total Personnel	Number	Percent of Total Personnel
1972	16.8	2.1	9.4	1.6	2.3	1.2	16.5	2.3	45.0	1.9
1973	20.7	2.6	12.6	2.2	2.3	1.2	19.8	2.9	55.4	2.5
1974	30.7	3.9	17.0	3.1	2.7	1.4	24.2	3.8	74.7	3.5
1975	42.3	5.4	21.2	4.0	3.2	1.6	30.2	5.2	96.9	4.6
1976	49.6	6.3	23.0	4.4	3.5	1.8	35.7	6.1	111.8	5.4
1977	51.8	6.6	23.3	4.4	3.9	2.0	40.0	7.0	119.0	5.7
1978	56.8	7.4	25.3	4.8	5.1	2.7	47.1	8.3	134.3	6.5
1979	62.0	8.2	29.4	5.6	6.0	3.2	53.7	9.6	151.1	7.5
1980	69.3	8.9	35.0	6.6	6.7	3.6	60.4	10.8	171.4	8.4
1981	73.7	9.4	39.9	7.4	7.6	4.0	63.5	11.1	184.7	8.9
1982	73.3	9.4	42.8	7.8	8.4	4.3	64.0	11.1	188.5	8.9
1983	75.5	9.7	46.8	8.3	8.9	4.6	65.4	11.1	196.7	9.3

Source: Derived from data provided by the Defense Manpower Data Center.

During the initial period, 1972-1976, the number of women on active duty more than doubled, reaching close to 112,000, or just over 5% of the force, by September 1976. In that year, though, the relatively high growth rate started to abate as service plans called for more gradual increases in the future, and the number of new female recruits dropped for the first time since the start of the buildup (see Table 7.10). In contrast to the 67,000 increase that occurred in the previous five years, total female strength was scheduled to climb by only half that amount over the next five years.[25]

These plans, however, were soon challenged by the incoming Carter administration. In 1978, following an internal Pentagon review, Secretary of Defense Harold Brown directed that the military services approximately double the number of women by FY1983, at which time about 200,000 enlisted women would comprise just over 11% of the force.[26] In the following year the

Table 7.10. Enlistment of Female Recruits, FY1972-1983 (In Thousands)

Fiscal Year	Army Number	Army Percent of Total Recruits	Navy Number	Navy Percent of Total Recruits	Marine Corps Number	Marine Corps Percent of Total Recruits	Air Force Number	Air Force Percent of Total Recruits	Total Number	Total Percent of Total Recruits
1972	6.0	1.2	2.2	2.5	.7	1.3	4.7	5.4	13.6	3.3
1973	8.3	4.1	4.9	5.2	.7	1.4	6.3	6.7	20.3	4.6
1974	15.1	8.4	6.7	7.4	.9	2.0	8.2	11.2	30.8	7.9
1975	18.5	10.3	6.7	6.9	1.3	2.3	9.7	13.1	36.3	8.9
1976	15.8	8.8	5.1	5.6	1.3	2.5	8.6	12.0	30.8	7.8
1976[a]	4.3	8.1	1.2	3.9	.3	2.4	2.7	13.1	8.5	7.1
1977	14.6	8.9	4.8	4.8	1.4	3.3	9.5	13.5	30.3	8.0
1978	17.3	14.2	5.6	7.1	2.2	5.8	12.4	18.5	37.5	12.1
1979	17.2	13.4	8.7	11.2	2.1	5.4	13.3	20.0	41.2	13.3
1980	22.1	14.1	10.5	12.2	2.2	5.4	13.9	19.2	48.7	13.7
1981	18.1	15.5	9.6	10.7	2.2	5.5	10.6	13.8	40.6	12.6
1982	14.8	12.5	7.8	10.2	2.1	5.7	8.4	12.4	33.1	11.1
1983	16.5	12.5	8.1	11.4	2.0	5.5	8.5	14.3	35.1	11.7

Source: Derived from data provided by the Defense Manpower Data Center.

[a] Fiscal 1976 transition quarter (July through September).

goal for FY1984 was set at 236,000, or 12% of the armed forces.[27] Accordingly, the number of female enlisted recruits was increased each year during the rest of the Carter period, reaching almost 50,000 in FY1980, at which time there were over 170,000 women in the military; and what was to be the final Carter administration plan called for further increases to 265,000 by FY1986.[28] In early 1980, as the nation debated whether women should be required to register for the draft along with their male counterparts, *Newsweek* noted: "Amid all the controversy, what isn't generally realized is that women have already established a beachhead in the U.S. armed forces. In fact, the U.S. now has more women in service—and a greater percentage of women in service—than any other country."[29]

Coincident with the change of administration in 1981, the ambitious expansion plans of the Carter administration were put on hold, pending a review of the impact of women on force readiness.[30] This was justified by the Pentagon on the grounds that "the increase [during the 1970s] was spurred primarily by social pressures for equal opportunity with particular emphasis on utilization of women in nontraditional skills . . . [and] little effort was made during this period to empirically determine the best way to utilize women based on skill, mission, and readiness requirements."[31] Following the internal reviews, the goals were revised downward. According to the latest available projections, by FY1987 there will be just over 220,000 women in the military, approximately 24,000 more than FY1983, but some 45,000 below the level envisioned by the Carter administration, as shown in the FY1987 goals below:[32]

Service	Carter Program	Reagan Program
Army	99,000	83,100
Navy	53,700	52,200
Marine Corps	9,600	9,700
Air Force	103,200	76,000
Total	265,500	221,000

The downward revision in the army's goals for women was a result of the findings of the Women in the Army Policy Review Group, which concluded in 1982, based on the probability that soldiers filling particular jobs (including carpenters and plumbers) might find themselves in direct combat in fluid wartime situations, that sixty-one military occupations accounting for over 300,000 jobs should be closed to women. Included in the list were twenty-three occupations that previously were opened to them.[33] Subsequently, under pressure applied by the Pentagon's civilian leadership, the army announced that only forty-nine career fields would be closed.[34]

The rationale underlying the more substantial reduction in the air force goal for FY 1987 is more difficult to pin down. Presumably, the air force forecast considers the following factors: "propensity of women to enlist in the Air Force, propensity of women to enlist in a particular skill, and a projection of the number of women who will qualify by aptitude and physically (including strength measurement) in each skill."[35] But how these factors are calculated and how they translate into specific goals has not been made publicly available.

Occupational Mix. Substantial changes have taken place in the last decade in the kinds of jobs to which women can be assigned. Traditionally, in peacetime, women in the military performed nursing and clerical duties. In fact, prior to the 1972 expansion, only 35% of all military enlisted job specialties were "sex-neutral." Following an initial reassessment in 1972, over 80% of the specialties were opened to women, and by 1976 they could be used in all but the combat-associated specialties (although there is still no generally agreed-upon definition of combat).

The proportion of enlisted women actually assigned to nontraditional jobs has also increased dramatically. Compared to 1972, for example, when less than 10% of all enlisted women were in nontraditional jobs, the percentage of women assigned to scientific, technical, or blue-collar specialties had grown to over 40% by 1976, and today it stands at just under 45%. These changes are detailed in Table 7.11. In the nontraditional areas, the largest concentration of women is found in communications and intelligence (14%), service and supply (11%), and electrical/mechanical equipment repair (9%).

Table 7.11. Percentage Distribution of Female Enlisted Personnel by Occupational Category, End of Selected Fiscal Years[a]

	1972	1976	1983
Traditional	90.6	59.9	55.3
Medical and dental specialists	23.8	18.6	13.6
Administrative specialists and clerks	66.8	41.3	41.7
Nontraditional	9.4	40.2	44.7
Infantry, gun crew, and allied specialists	0.2	0.2	0.8
Electronic equipment repairmen	1.2	4.3	5.6
Communications and intelligence specialists	4.2	15.0	14.0
Other technical specialists	2.8	2.7	3.0
Electrical/mechanical equipment repairmen	0.0	6.7	8.7
Craftsmen	0.1	1.4	1.9
Service and supply handlers	0.9	9.9	10.7

Sources: Fiscal year 1972, Central All-Volunteer Task Force, "Utilization of Military Women" (Washington, DC: Office of the Assistant Secretary of Defense for Manpower and Reserve Affairs, December 1972; processed), p. 26; FY 1976 and 1983 derived from data provided by the Defense Manpower Data Center.

[a] Distributions do not include female enlisted personnel in "nonoccupational" status (for example, officer candidates, students, patients, prisoners, and persons in undesignated occupations).

Beyond the question of numbers and roles, many of the practices that discriminated against military women were also altered during the decade. Among the more important:

- women now command organizations composed of both men and women;
- women now enter aviation training and the military academies;

- pregnant women or those with minor dependents are no longer automatically discharged;
- family entitlements for married servicemen and servicewomen have been equalized;
- women have access to a wider range of training opportunities;
- except for the Marine Corps. the military services have formally established "sex-neutral" entry standards.[36]

CONTEMPORARY ISSUES

The changes in the social composition of American armed forces that have accompanied, if not resulted from, voluntary recruitment raised a number of issues during the 1970s, some of which remain unresolved today. While there are some areas of commonality in issues involving minorities and women in the armed forces, there are likewise important differences. Concerns about the expansion of blacks center on overrepresentation, especially in semi-and unskilled jobs, while concerns about women center on underrepresentation, especially in nontraditional jobs.

Overrepresentation Of Blacks

The expansion of the role of blacks in the armed forces has given rise to a number of worries—some held predominantly by whites, others held predominantly by blacks, and some shared by members of both groups. Much of the uneasiness may simply be a reaction to change from racial proportionality—a situation that is generally understandable and acceptable to all population subgroups. But there are specific concerns as well.

Some say fielding combat forces composed of an overproportion of blacks imposes an unfair burden on one segment of American society; a burden that seems decidedly inequitable because members of that group have not enjoyed a fair share of the benefits bestowed by the state. From this perspective, the possibility that blacks will die in disproportionate numbers—at least in the initial stages of a conflict—is immoral, unethical, or otherwise contrary to the precepts of democratic institutions. Indeed, if the United States becomes involved in another military conflict, the 20% casualty rate of blacks that provoked charges of racial genocide in the early stages of the Vietnam War could appear small. If black casualties were simply proportional to the number of blacks in the army's enlisted ranks, one of every three army combat deaths would be that of a black soldier. This estimate probably represents the lower bound; black casualties in the opening days of any military engagement are likely to be heavier than 30% in the army, depending on the specific units engaged in combat. If, for example, the Second Infantry Division had to fight on the Korean peninsula, black soldiers probably would suffer about 40% of the early casualties because of the racial mix in that division. The proportion could be larger, since blacks account for more than half the strength of some combat battalions.[37]

Many Americans, however, welcome the growth of black participation in the military because it can give young blacks educational, social, and financial opportunities not otherwise available to them. To this group, the fact that depressed minorities enlist in disproportionate numbers is a healthy sign, an indication that these individuals can and will receive help. "It is a good thing and not a bad thing to offer better alternatives to the currently disadvantaged," Milton Friedman has observed.[38] The Gates Commission concluded that "Government service has traditionally been a major source of employment for blacks. . . . The participation of blacks in municipal, state and national governments reflects the confidence blacks have in the government as a 'hirer of last resort.'"[39]

Others, nonetheless, view this trend as a mixed blessing. Some question the long-term value of military service to blacks, holding that they tend to be trained in skills that are of relatively little value in the civilian economy. In fact, although black males in the enlisted ranks are more likely

Table 7.12. Distribution of Male Enlisted Personnel, All Services,
By Major Occupational Category and Race, September 1983

Major Occupational Category[a]	White[b]		Black	
	Number	Percent	Number	Percent
White collar	*447,908*	*43.1*	*140,421*	*44.8*
Technical workers[c]	314,087	30.2	70,177	22.4
Clerical workers[d]	133,821	12.9	70,244	22.4
Blue collar	*591,682*	*56.9*	*172,944*	*55.2*
Craftsmen[e]	325,901	31.3	69,571	22.2
Service and supply workers	95,065	9.1	40,856	13.0
General military skills, including combat	170,716	16.4	62,517	20.0
Total[f]	1,039,590	100.0	313,365	100.0

Source: Derived from data provided by the Defense Manpower Data Center.

[a] Categories are based on the Defense Department occupational classification system.

[b] White category does not include Hispanics or other racial/ethnic minorities.

[c] Includes "electronic equipment repairmen," "communications and intelligence specialists," "medical and dental specialists," and "other technical and allied specialists" categories.

[d] Includes the "functional support and administration" category.

[e] Includes "electrical/mechanical equipment repairmen" and "craftsmen" categories.

[f] Totals do not include male enlisted personnel in "nonoccupational" status (for example, officer candidates, students, patients, prisoners, and persons in undesignated occupations).

than whites to hold a white-collar job, they are more concentrated in clerical positions and less likely than whites to receive technical assignments (see Table 7.12). Among male enlisted personnel with blue-collar skills, whites are more likely to be trained as craftsmen and blacks as service and supply workers or in general military skills (including combat). All in all, while the military clearly provides employment opportunities for black youths, whites tend to acquire training and skills that put them in a position to compete for better jobs in the civilian sector.

Equity issues aside, some fear that disproportionate black casualties could create social divisiveness at a critical juncture, possibly with adverse implications for national security. How black Americans would actually react to heavy military casualties, particularly among their most promising young men (those who qualify for the military), is hard to predict. "It is naive, if not duplicitous," according to Charles C. Moskos, Jr., "to state that disproportionately high black casualties will have no or only minor consequences on the domestic political scene."[40] "In the emotional climate aroused by combat deaths," Robert Fullinwider concludes, "attitudes and feelings are subject to volatile shifts and may suddenly crystallize into adamant opposition to the military action, especially under the stimulation of concentrated and graphic television coverage of a highly telegenic 'issue.'"[41]

The extent to which disproportionate black casualties would create social divisiveness, however, ultimately rests on the degree of public support for the particular military engagement. A more important ramification would be a possible reluctance on the part of national leaders, fearful of the consequences, to commit military units with a high proportion of minorities to certain contingencies. This would reduce both the flexibility of decision makers and the ability of the nation's military forces to meet national security commitments. That the specter of heavy black casualties may be on the minds of national leaders was suggested by former Secretary of Defense Harold Brown:

There is also concern about the racial composition of the Army, particularly of its combat forces. It is a negative comment on U.S. society, rather than on the Army, when the proportion of minority group members among enlisted personnel in those forces approaches 50 percent. This is a troubling trend, even though the educational qualifications of black soldiers are, on the average, as good or better than those of white soldiers. To the extent that an Army drawn significantly from conscription would reflect more closely the racial composition of society, that could ease the serious consequences, both for the cohesion of U.S. society and for the conduct of particular conflicts, if (as would be likely today) the first Army casualties and the first reinforcements would be heavily black.[42]

At bottom, the two powerful national principles, equal opportunity and equal representation, are in collision. The issue has been drawn vividly by William K. Brehm, a former assistant secretary of defense for manpower and reserve affairs:

> Does America prefer its army to represent a reasonable cross section of the American racial and social fabric, or will it be content to accept major departures from a representative force as a consequence of applying the principle of equal opportunity to a PMVF [Peacetime Military Volunteer Force] recruited largely through economic incentives? How long can the PMVF endure with this issue unresolved? Should not the Congress, representing the people, deal with it openly, with the aim of reaching a national consensus?[43]

Thus far, most discussions of this issue have been confined to a relatively small number of academics, commentators, and legislators. Americans in general, according to one survey, do not appear "concerned" about the overrepresentation of blacks in the military. "It may be that some military planners have questions about the current ethnic composition of the armed forces," the survey researchers write, "but the general population does not seem to find it a problem. Only about 12% say there are 'too many' blacks, and these respondents are outnumbered by the 19% who say 'too few' and overwhelmed by the 70% answering 'right number'."[44] Yet, "American enthusiasm" for a further increase in the proportion of blacks is "definitely less than for increases in the proportion of women and Hispanics."[45]

Underrepresentation Of Women

The principal issue involving women and the military is the extent to which remaining laws and policies that constrain further expansion are justified by valid national security concerns or whether they are instead anchored to sexual stereotypes of an earlier era. Some feel that the expansion of the 1970s went too far, claiming that the goals imposed during the Carter years were arbitrarily set, forcing the services to assimilate too many women too soon and to assign them to nontraditional jobs for which they were physically and aptitudinally ill-prepared. Moreover, the army, for its part, feels that it erred by assigning women to dangerous jobs that carry a high probability of direct contact with the enemy. These, in effect, are the arguments offered to support the lower goals for women in the military.

On the other side, critics claim the revised goals are also arbitrary and are merely elements of a "hidden agenda" by the armed forces to return to the draft.[46] Some have questioned the rationale underlying the army's "combat exclusion policy," claiming that it is needlessly restrictive to close jobs to women based on proximity to the battlefield. The principal arguments here center on the belief that, in an age of long-range smart weapons, casualties will not be restricted to the front areas. While most critics do not argue against the exclusion of women from jobs that are indisputably "combat" (such as infantryman, tank driver, etc.), a number object to policies that bar women from jobs based on probability estimates of direct physical contact with the enemy or risk of capture.

The armed forces may be reluctant to modify the traditional role of women in what has been one of the last of the male bastions, but there is evidence to suggest that many Americans feel otherwise. Recent survey results, for example, reveal that one in three Americans thinks that more women should be serving in the military. Better than half of the general population— whether in favor of the draft now or only in the case of national emergency—supports the conscription of women as well as men. At the same time even though a majority of people approve having women serve in such nontraditional military occupations as truck mechanic, jet fighter pilot, missile gunner, and crew member of a combat ship, only one in three Americans thinks that women should perform as soldiers in hand-to-hand combat.[47]

The conclusion here, as the authors of the study observe, is that "virtually no one is opposed to women in the military—in jobs and roles that have civilian counterparts."[48] There is "evidence here that traditional sex norms have not totally evaporated. To anyone brought up to hold the door open for females the finding that a third of the contemporary U.S. adult population endorses assignment of females to hand-to-hand combat is astounding because it is so high, not because it is so low." And "taken together, these items show strong national support for extensive feminine involvement in the military, including the 'military military.'"[49]

Skepticism also surrounds the current air force rationale for limiting the utilization of women. According to Maj. Gen. Jeanne Holm:

> Air force planners . . . have worried that if the Army were permitted to reduce its intake of women in the coming years, the Air Force could be required to take more than its "fair share" to meet overall DOD female strength requirements. They are well aware that their service is especially vulnerable in this respect because its capacity to absorb women without infringing on combat policies is, for all practical purposes, unlimited. The Air Force is hard pressed, therefore, to come up with any rationale for *not* using more women that will withstand objective analysis. Statements of concern about their impact on readiness and having "too many" women in traditional fields, etc., are thinly veiled attempts to give legitimacy to what is in fact an arbitrary decision on the part of Air Force planners to hold down the numbers of women.[50]

The issues will not be easy to resolve. In many ways, women in the military today seem as much concerned with protecting the hard-won status quo as with making further gains. Indeed, it has been observed that women may have reached "a threshold beyond which they cannot advance unless there is further social change in women's roles and in men's attitudes in American society."[51]

In any event, it seems safe to predict that any further change will come slowly, and the most radical of changes will only occur when necessity demands it. The nation, at various times and under various circumstances, has denied members of certain social categories entrance into military service when it was important to them to serve and has protected members of other groups when it was important to them not to serve. The black experience in the American armed forces, like the more recent experience of women, has been marked by policies of exclusion during periods of calm and expedient acceptance during times of trouble. Women, and minorities to a lesser extent, are perceived primarily as a supplemental source of manpower, a "filler" to be called upon and used sparingly when needed. The exigencies of war opened the doors of military service to blacks. The exigencies of war—or an extended effort to save all-volunteer recruitment—may one day flatten the barriers to "equality of service" for women as well.

THE OUTLOOK

The social composition of the U.S. armed forces over the next decade and beyond will be shaped by many forces, some of which are uncontrollable, others unpredictable, and most not well understood. In the end, much will depend on changes that affect the supply of and the demand for "choice" recruits: male high school graduates with strong aptitudes for military service in general, and for technical skills in particular. Changes in the size and composition of the nation's youth population will have an important bearing on the question as will anticipated increases in the technological complexity of the nation's military forces.

Changes In The Youth Population

Dwindling birthrates in the United States—a trend that started in the late 1950s and brought the baby boom to an end in the mid-1960s—are having a significant impact on many areas of public policy. As the "birth-dearth" generation passes through its formative years, the effects have already been felt, most notably by the nation's primary and secondary educational institutions. As the first cohorts of the generation completed high school, starting about 1983, institutions of higher education and the civilian labor force began to notice the effects, as did the armed forces, which have traditionally attracted eighteen to twenty-one-year-old volunteers.[52] The magnitude of the change can be seen in Table 7.13; compared to 1981 levels, there will be about 2.5 million fewer men and women in this age group by 1987 and roughly 4 million fewer by 1995.[53]

Table 7.13. Projected U.S. Population Aged 18 to 21, by Sex and Race,
Selected Years, 1981-95 (In Thousands)

Category	1981	1983	1985	1987	1989	1991	1993	1995
Male	8,618	8,356	7,821	7,356	7,404	7,197	6,702	6,608
White	7,281	7,010	6,509	6,085	6,098	5,864	5,405	5,331
Black	1,147	1,145	1,102	1,053	1,070	1,071	1,022	994
Other	190	201	210	218	236	262	275	283
Female	8,401	8,142	7,621	7,164	7,197	6,984	6,495	6,386
White	7,059	6,799	6,312	5,896	5,897	5,666	5,220	5,137
Black	1,168	1,161	1,116	1,067	1,081	1,076	1,022	990
Other	174	182	193	201	219	242	253	259
Total	17,019	16,498	15,442	14,520	14,601	14,181	13,197	12,994

Source: Bureau of the Census, *Current Population Reports,* series P-25, no. 704, "Projections of the Population of the United States: 1977 to 2050" (Washington, DC: Government Printing Office, 1977), pp. 40-60. Figures are rounded.

The sex composition of the smaller population of young Americans will change little through the projected period, as men continue to hold a slight edge, growing from 50.6% in 1981 to 50.9% in 1995. More noticeable is the shift that will occur in the racial/ethnic composition, as minorities make up an increasing proportion of the population. Compared to 1981, for example, when minorities comprised 15.7% of all eighteen to twenty-one-year-olds, in 1995 they will constitute 19.4%. Nonblack minorities will register the largest relative growth over the period: from 2.2% to 4.3%. Inasmuch as minorities have lower high school completion rates, a decline in overall high school graduation rates in the coming years seems likely. By one estimate, the number of high school graduates in 1991 will be roughly 25% smaller than in 1982, while the population of seventeen-and eighteen-year-olds will have declined by only 20%.[54]

The shrinking youth population, in itself, will have substantial implications for recruitment. The dimensions of the problem can be traced in Table 7.14, which shows the proportion of the "qualified and available" male youth population that would have to enlist if the active and reserve forces are to meet projected recruit requirements.[55] During the period 1984-1988, for example, about 1,827,000 young men will be turning eighteen each year. Of these, 552,000 who are institutionalized or who are expected to enter college and complete at least two years should not be considered available for all-volunteer service. Moreover, roughly 526,000 would not be expected to meet current mental, physical, or moral standards. During this period then, the pool of qualified and available manpower will be filling by roughly 750,000 a year, out of which the armed forces will need to attract 376,000, or about half of them, to meet total male recruit requirements.[56] To fulfill the recruiting needs of the active forces alone, 278,000 young men or

Table 7.14. Qualified and Available Males Required for Military Service, Selected Periods, 1981-1995 (In Thousands Unless Otherwise Indicated)

Category	Annual Average		
	1981-1983	1984-1988	1991-1995
Total eighteen-year-old males	2,049	1,827	1,637
Minus nonavailable	626	552	489
Minus unqualified	576	526	461
Equals: Qualified and available male pool	847	749	687
Total male recruit requirements	354	376	376
Active forces	270	278	278
Reserve forces	84	98	98
Percent of pool required	42	50	55

Source: Martin Binkin, America's Volunteer Military: Progress and Prospects (Washington, DC: The Brookings Institution, 1984), Table 8.

37% of the total will have to enlist. The situation will worsen in the early 1990s. As the table shows, about 60,000 fewer young men will be entering the qualified and available pool, and the armed forces will have to draw 55%, compared to 42% currently participating.

Whether the armed forces will be able to attract a larger proportion of the smaller male youth population is an open question, depending largely on how much the nation is willing to invest in the military payroll and on the extent to which the economy recovers. By most economic reckoning though, the number of male recruits with high school diplomas and high aptitude scores can be expected to decline from the unusually high levels of the early 1980s. The armed services can nevertheless expect to attract enough to meet congressionally mandated requirements at least through 1990, providing that military pay raises remain apace with those in the private sector and that economic recovery is not more vigorous than expected.

Should these forecasts prove to be overly optimistic or should the decline in quality be considered unacceptable, the military services would once again be under pressure to enlist more minorities and women. The merits of this strategy, however, would rest largely on the match between the aptitudes of the population subgroups and the military's occupational structure.

Technology And Aptitude Standards

The influence of technology on the military's skill mix during the postwar period can be measured in terms of the shift from work requiring general military skills toward tasks requiring special expertise. The sharpest increase has taken place in the technical skills (computer specialists, electronics technicians, medical technicians, etc.) at the expense of service and supply occupations and general combat skills.

These trends, which are discussed by the perspective of each service in chapters 8-10, are likely to continue into the future, as new generations of weapons systems enter the inventory. With a growing emphasis on computerized command, control communications, and intelligence functions, new systems are invariably more complicated than their predecessors and serve to increase the number of specialists in the military services. It is estimated, for example, that the air force's need for people with high aptitudes for electronics skills will increase by about one-third before the year 2000.[57] The additional sailors needed to man the expanded fleet will also have to meet higher standards since "highly technical" jobs are expected to increase disproportionally. By 1986, for example, "semi-technical" positions are expected to increase by 13% over 1981, "technical" billets by 16%, and "highly technical" jobs by 31%.[58]

The impact that emerging technology will have on the army's occupational mix and personnel standards is more difficult to identify. Unofficially, concerns have been expressed that, given the present course, the technologies that will be embodied in the army's weapons systems of tomorrow may well be beyond the abilities of its manpower.[59] The issue is under study within the army, but results are unlikely to be available before the middle of the decade. It has been suggested that, pending those findings, the army adopt manpower standards that would provide an enlisted population with a qualitative profile similar to that being recruited by the air force in the early 1980s.[60]

As the roster of technical skills grows, the number of jobs for which blacks and women can qualify can be expected to shrink since, by current standards, a large fraction of these jobs require a traditionally "white male" aptitude.

Each military service currently applies its own aptitude standards in determining eligibility for enlistment. These aptitude standards reflect the diverse requirements for the separate services, and they typically vary according to educational attainment (high school graduation status) and, at times, sex. For example, high school graduates wishing to enlist in the army are presently required to achieve a minimum AFQT percentile score of sixteen and a standard score of at least eighty-five on any one of the army's nine aptitude composites; high school dropouts with equivalency certificates are required to score no less than the thirty-first percentile on the AFQT and obtain a standard score of at least eighty-five on any one of the aptitude composites; and nongraduates who do not have equivalency certificates are required to achieve a minimum AFQT percentile score of thirty-one along with a standard score of eighty-five on any two aptitude composites.

In contrast to the army, the air force requires that male and female high school graduates achieve a minimum AFQT score of twenty-one; in addition, prospective recruits are required to attain a score of at least 120 on a combination of the mechanical, administrative, general, and electronics composites, along with a score of no less than thirty on the general composite alone. Nongraduates who do not have equivalency certificates must score at least sixty-five on the AFQT and also meet the various aptitude composite standards. The other services likewise apply their own separate standards for basic eligibility. All services except the Marine Corps currently use the same education and aptitude standards for both male and female applicants. In the Marine Corps, female high school graduates are required to have higher AFQT scores than their male counterparts, and women who do not have high school diplomas are formally barred from enlisting.

The varied effects of education and aptitude standards on the enlistment eligibility of the youth population (between the ages of eighteen and twenty-three) can be seen in Table 7.15. In general, proportionately more young men and women, within each racial/ethnic group, would be able to qualify for enlistment in the army than in any other service. Overall, about three out of four young men could probably qualify for the army (77%) or the navy (75%) under current standards, compared with about two out of three (68%) in the Marine Corps and even fewer (63%) in the air force. About four out of five women would be able to meet the minimum requirements in either the army (80%) or the navy (78%). Approximately three out of five (60%) women could probably qualify for enlistment in the air force, while less than one out of two (46%) could meet the minimum aptitude and education requirements in the Marine Corps.

Even more striking, however, are the effects of qualitative standards on the enlistment eligibility rates for the three major racial/ethnic groups. For example, over four out of five (86%) white youths would be expected to qualify for enlistment in the army. Just over half (55%) of all Hispanic youths, and just under half (48%) of all black youths, could probably pass the minimum education and aptitude standards established by the army. And the disparity between racial/ethnic groups is even wider in the other services. About three out of ten white youths

Table 7.15. Percentage of American Youth Population (18-23 Years) Eligible for Enlistment Based on FY1984 Education and Aptitude Standards, by Sex and Racial/Ethnic Group[a]

Sex and Racial/Ethnic Group[b]	Percent Eligible for Enlistment			
	Army	Navy	Marine Corps	Air Force
Male				
White	84.3	82.3	76.0	71.3
Black	43.8	41.4	32.2	21.3
Hispanic	54.5	51.3	45.0	37.5
Total	77.1	75.0	68.3	62.6
Female				
White	87.1	85.3	54.4	69.6
Black	52.3	48.1	13.1	21.7
Hispanic	54.8	51.2	18.0	27.9
Total	80.3	78.1	46.4	60.4
Total				
White	85.7	83.8	65.4	70.5
Black	48.1	44.8	22.6	21.5
Hispanic	54.6	51.3	31.7	32.7
Total	78.7	76.5	57.5	61.5

Source: Adapted from data appearing in M.J. Eitelberg, J.H. Laurence, L.S. Perelman, and B.K. Waters, *Screening for Service* (Alexandria, VA: HumRRO, September 1984).

[a] Estimates of the percent of youths qualified for enlistment were calculated on the basis of results from the *Profile of American Youth* and the FY1984 education and aptitude standards used by the armed services. (It should be noted that eligibility for enlistment would also depend on other factors—including medical and moral requirements.)

[b] White category includes all racial/ethnic groups other than black or Hispanic. Black category does not include persons of Hispanic origin.

(30%), for instance, probably would fail to qualify for entry into the air force, based on FY1984 minimum education and aptitude standards; in sharp contrast, almost four out of five (79%) black youths would most likely be rejected by the air force.

In addition to meeting basic eligibility standards, candidates for enlistment must often pass through a prescreening phase even before they are allowed to take the standardized entry test. Then, they must meet the military's requirements for medical, physical, and moral fitness. In the navy, applicants must also attain a minimum "SCREEN" score indicating that they have the personal characteristics, background, and ability that correlate highly with successful service. Finally, applicants must be able to fill an occupational vacancy. Indeed, an applicant may be able to meet the minimum criteria for enlistment, but if he or she cannot pass the requirements for placement in an available occupation (or an area in which the yearly quota of openings or training "school seats" has not been filled), or is unable to qualify for any career field he or she is willing to enter, enlistment may be postponed indefinitely or ruled out entirely. For all intents and purposes, then, an applicant who is able to pass the minimum entry criteria but unable to qualify for the "right" job is rejected. (Although the services do have a system for granting waivers for occupational assignment to candidates who may be otherwise qualified.)

The influence of aptitude test scores on job assignments and the general opportunities for technical training is illustrated in Table 7.16. The percent of young men and women, by racial/ethnic group, who could qualify for assignment to occupations in four major areas (mechanical, administrative, general, and electronics) was estimated using *Profile of American Youth* results and the minimum aptitude standards applied during FY1983. The "eligibility rates" are shown in Table 7.16 for two populations: *all* persons (eighteen to twenty-three) and

Table 7.16. Percent of American Youths (18-23 Years) Who Would Qualify for Selected Occupations in the Army and Navy (Arranged According to Occupational Area), by Sex and Racial/Ethnic Group

Sex and Racial/Ethnic Group	All Persons	Persons Eligible for Basic Enlistment	All Persons	Persons Eligible for Basic Enlistment
	Mechanical Occupations			
	Army: Heavy Construction Equipment Operator		Navy: Machinist's Mate	
Male				
White	82.2	97.5	76.0	92.3
Black	29.8	68.1	20.5	49.4
Hispanic	47.4	87.1	38.5	75.0
Total	73.1	94.8	66.3	88.4
Female				
White	71.3	81.8	51.9	60.8
Black	21.0	40.1	12.6	26.2
Hispanic	26.3	48.0	17.7	34.5
Total	61.6	76.7	44.4	56.8
	Administrative Occupations			
	Army: Administrative Specialist		Navy: Yeoman	
Male				
White	63.6	75.5	35.5	43.1
Black	19.4	44.3	6.5	15.7
Hispanic	34.4	63.1	14.6	28.5
Total	56.0	72.6	30.4	40.5
Female				
White	74.2	85.2	48.9	57.4
Black	27.3	52.3	10.9	22.7
Hispanic	37.1	67.8	15.7	30.6
Total	65.4	81.5	41.6	53.3
	General Occupations			
	Army: Military Police		Navy: Mess Management Specialist	
Male				
White	78.3	92.9	78.0	94.8
Black	27.4	62.6	30.1	72.8
Hispanic	44.3	81.3	44.8	87.3
Total	69.5	90.1	69.7	92.9
Female				
White	77.7	89.3	79.1	92.7
Black	29.1	55.6	32.0	66.5
Hispanic	37.6	68.6	37.7	73.6
Total	68.5	85.4	70.0	89.7

Continued

(Table 7.16. Continued)

| | Electronics Occupations | | | |
	Army: Satellite Communications Equipment Repairman		Navy: Electronics Technician	
Male				
White	29.7	35.2	50.7	61.6
Black	3.4	7.7	8.4	20.3
Hispanic	9.2	16.9	21.4	41.7
Total	24.9	32.3	43.3	57.8
Female				
White	11.7	13.4	30.4	35.6
Black	0.4	0.7	3.4	7.1
Hispanic	2.2	4.0	7.0	13.7
Total	9.5	11.9	25.2	32.3

Source: Department of the Navy, *Enlisted Transfer Manual,* NAVPERS 15909C, pp. 7-11, 7-12; Department of the Army, *U.S. Army Formal School Catalog,* Pamphlet 351.4, 1 April 1983; and data (*Profile of American Youth*) provided by the Defense Manpower Data Center.

those who could first meet the requirements for basic enlistment within selected occupations in the army and the navy. The selected occupations are representative of a wide variety of similar occupations within the services. (For example, the minimum eligibility requirements for training as a navy electronics technician are the same for at least fifteen other navy ratings, including aviation technician, data systems technician, missile technician, and training devicemen.)

The remarkable differences between racial/ethnic groups in their ability to meet minimum aptitude standards are vividly depicted in the "eligibility rates" for assignment in the selected occupations. Generally, minorities are far less likely than their white counterparts to qualify for any of the jobs shown in Table 7.16, regardless of the particular service or occupational area. The relative difference in qualifying rates between racial/ethnic groups varies somewhat from job to job. However, in the highly technical or "hard skill" areas where a reduced, but still ample proportion of whites are potentially qualified, minorities stand little or no chance of passing the test score standards. In the electronics field, for instance, about 50% of all white young men (and 62% of those who could pass the navy's basic enlistment standards) would probably qualify for training as a navy electronics technician. In contrast, fewer than one out of ten black males, and one in five Hispanic males nationwide could probably qualify for this rating. Only about 3% of all black young men and 9% of Hispanic males could qualify for training as a satellite communications (SATCOM) equipment repairman in the army, compared with just under 30% of all white males.

Sharp differences are also seen in the "eligibility rates" for training assignment among males and females within the same racial/ethnic groups. Approximately three out of four (76%) white young men, for example, could probably qualify for training as a navy machinist's mate. For white females, however, the "eligibility rate" in this occupation is substantially lower at 52%. Lower qualifying percentages for females than males are likewise seen in another "mechanical" occupation, army heavy construction equipment operator, where 73% of all males and 62% of all females could meet the test score standards. Conversely, the ability of females to qualify for positions in the administrative field consistently surpasses that of their male counterparts. Overall, about 65% of young women could probably qualify for administrative specialist in the army, compared with 56% of young men, and almost 42% of all women, compared with 30% of men, could probably pass the aptitude requirements for assignment as a navy yeoman.

Females and males tend to have similar "eligibility rates" for jobs within the "general" occupational field, such as mess management specialist and military police. On the other hand, wide differences are again observed for jobs within the "electronics" area. Among those women qualified for enlistment in the army, for instance, just over one out of ten could probably meet the aptitude standards for assignment to training as a SATCOM repairman. The comparable "eligibility rate" for males in this "high-tech" occupation is considerably greater, at around 32%.

It does not appear that the trend in the occupational placement of minorities will change very much in the near future. The margin of difference in the average educational level of whites and blacks nationwide and the test score differences revealed in the *Profile of American Youth* imply that, unless the services modify their classification criteria, blacks (as well as Hispanics) may be disproportionately relegated to the military's "soft skills" for some time to come.

Current selection and assignment practices, in concert with testing trends, will likewise influence the future participation of women in the military. Historically, female superiority on verbal tasks has been "one of the more solidly established generalizations in the field of sex differences."[61] Females have also demonstrated, in the past, an advantage in rote memory, perceptual speed, numerical computation, dexterity, and tasks involving the mechanics of language. Males, on the other hand, for whatever reason, have tended to excel on tests of mathematical reasoning, visual-spatial tasks, and science.[62]

The results of a nationwide administration of the Armed Services Vocational Aptitude Battery (ASVAB) correspond with the pattern of sex differences observed in the history of mental testing. As seen in Table 7.17, of the ten ASVAB subtests, six "favor" (in the statistical sense) males, three favor females, and no difference between the sexes is observed on one subtest.

The consequences of these sex differences on selection and occupational classification can be perceived best when the subtests are examined within the context of the services' aptitude composites. The AFQT includes a combination of verbal and quantitative subtests in approximately equal proportion. This balance reduces the likelihood of sex-related differences in performance on the AFQT composite. Nevertheless, sex differences surface on the aptitude composites used for matching prospective recruits with military jobs. And, as shown in Table

Table 7.17. Comparative Means and Standard Deviations of Percentile Scores of 18 to 23-Year-Olds on Armed Services Vocational Aptitude Battery (ASVAB) Subtests, by Sex

	Mean		Standard Deviation	
ASVAB Subtests	Male	Female	Male	Female
Difference Favors Males				
General Science	51.3	47.9	10.1	8.9
Arithmetic Reasoning	51.7	48.9	10.5	9.8
Auto & Shop Information	51.4	40.9	9.8	6.8
Mathematics Knowledge	52.6	51.1	11.1	10.3
Mechanical Comprehension	51.2	43.9	9.7	7.8
Electronics Information	51.5	44.3	9.9	8.5
Difference Favors Females				
Paragraph Comprehension	50.6	52.4	10.0	9.2
Numerical Operations	47.6	49.6	10.8	10.4
Coding Speed	49.9	54.1	9.8	10.0
No Difference				
Word Knowledge	50.8	50.9	10.3	9.8

Source: Department of Defense, *Profile of American Youth: 1980 Nationwide Administration of the Armed Services Vocational Aptitude Battery* (Washington, DC: Office of the Assistant Secretary of Defense [Manpower, Reserve Affairs, and Logistics], March 1982), p.91.

Table 7.18. Common Aptitude Composites and Their Component ASVAB Subtests
Arranged According to Male and Female Score Differences

Common Aptitude Composites	Component ASVAB Subtest		
	Difference Favors Males	Difference Favors Females	No Difference
Mechanical (M) (Air Force version)	Mechanical Comprehension Auto & Shop Information (weighted twice) General Science		
Administrative (A)		Coding Speed Numerical Operations Paragraph Comprehension	Word Knowledge
General (G)	Arithmetic Reasoning	Paragraph Comprehension	Word Knowledge
Electronics (E)	Arithmetic Reasoning Electronics Information General Science Mathematics Knowledge		

7.18, certain composites (such as mechanical and electronics) overwhelmingly favor males over females.[63]

A number of surveys suggest that women who enlist in the military are "tradition oriented" and they desire to be in the administrative-clerical positions and other jobs that are traditionally associated with female workers. "American women, it turns out after one year of experimenting," writes a *Washington Post* reporter, "are not wild about joining the Army or doing the jobs formerly restricted to men if they do sign up."[64]

If a majority of women were interested in serving in the technical or "nontraditional" occupations that are characteristically occupied by men, however, they would be hard-pressed to overcome the aptitude screens set before them. The tests that "favor" males are the same tests used to place new recruits in traditionally male jobs; and conversely, the tests that "favor" females are the same tests used to place new recruits in traditionally female jobs. It is a circle of cause and effect, underpinned by complex social and psychological factors, that will effectively limit the prospects for integrating females in male-dominated military jobs. Assuming that the current job classification standards do not change drastically over the next several years, it is highly unlikely that women will by employed to any greater extent in the "nontraditional" areas. With questions of philosophy and politics aside, many manpower managers and military leaders see this as a welcome prospect for the future effectiveness of the force. Aptitude composites used to assign new recruits to occupational training, they note, are established on the basis of solid empirical analysis. These composites and the minimum qualifying scores are validated against successful performance in training. It follows, then, that a person who does not achieve the appropriate test score for assignment to a particular specialty probably will not do very well (or well enough) in training. So unless training is modified or the job is revamped, women, like minorities and everyone else, will have to remain in those jobs that experience and careful study have demonstrated to bring the most economical and productive return for the military.

If the doors to military service are ever opened fully for women and a vigorous attempt is made to achieve complete integration of the sexes in the armed forces, it is perhaps ironic that minorities might end up as the true losers. Women may not do as well as men on the aptitude composites for technical training, but white women achieve far higher scores on the average than any minority group. Indeed, as seen in Table 7.16, white females outperform black males on the aptitude composites used to decide who will be an army SATCOM repairman or a navy electronics technician. And, from the basic "eligibility rates" depicted in Table 7.15, it is apparent that black males, as a group, have the *lowest* probability of meeting the military's enlistment requirements. In all services except the Marine Corps (which has more restrictive standards for female applicants), women, regardless of racial/ethnic group, stand a much better chance than black men of being accepted for enlistment on the basis of education and aptitude. In numerical terms, there are over nine million more women (eighteen through twenty-three years) than black men who are at least minimally qualified (in terms of education and aptitude) for enlistment in one of the armed forces (including about 150,000 more black women than black men), and many of the women have more formal education and higher test scores.[65] (In light of this, it is somewhat remarkable that, at the conclusion of FY1983, there were approximately 160,000 more black men than women of all races or ethnic groups in the entire active-duty military.)

Numbers also help to place the problems and issues surrounding the future use of minorities and female "manpower" in proper perspective. For instance, in the many discussions that deal with the declining pool of eligible males, reference is frequently made of the opposite trend (a relative and absolute increase) for minorities. In this respect, attention is focused especially on the increasingly important role of Hispanics in the military. The fact of the matter is that when any particular subgroup is singled out for study as a military manpower resource, it must be subdivided into males only who (a) have a high school diploma and (b) can meet the minimum aptitude criteria for enlistment. Presently, it is estimated that there are approximately 370,000 males of Hispanic origin (eighteen through twenty-three years) in the United States who hold a high school diploma and can also qualify for enlistment in the army. That is not a very large number (or proportion of the general population) to begin with, and it certainly will not grow to any great extent over the coming decade. The numbers "gap" of the late 1980s may be closed somewhat by recruiting more minorities, but the role of Hispanics will still be quite limited as a consequence of their relative size and representation in the general population.

In summary, over the next decade the nation's armed forces will be squeezed between a shrinking supply for potential recruits and a swelling demand for people who are trainable in technical skills. If the military services are unable to encourage a higher participation rate among white males, who by present measures are more likely to have the aptitudes for these jobs, they will be pressured to expand the opportunities for females and minority youths. The rub, however, is that proportionately fewer females and minorities possess the aptitudes considered necessary today to absorb the training required in a large and growing share of military jobs. Furthermore, there is some question whether most women can meet the physical standards currently deemed essential for a number of military occupations.

By most accounts, the military services tapped the mother lode of qualified volunteers during the past two years, and this under practically peak conditions. It is doubtful that recruiters can continue to attract as many or more white males as the economy shifts gears and certain incentives for enlisting slip away. If the All-Volunteer Force is to weather the demographic depression over the next decade, then the services will have to find new ways to utilize minorities and women, perhaps by reassessing entry standards, altering training strategies, or redesigning weapons systems. This assuredly is a tough task, considering the sluggish pace of change as well as the many personal and institutional barriers that lie embedded within the nation's profession-in-arms. But the alternatives, it would seem, are either a reduction in force levels or a return to conscription, both of which carry a good deal of unwelcome freight.

NOTES

1. Ford Foundation, *Not Working: Unskilled Youth and Displaced Adults* (New York: Ford Foundation, August 1982), p. 12.
2. Ibid., p. 7.
3. Ibid., p. 18
4. Ibid., pp. 9-10
5. President's Commission on All-Volunteer Force, *The Report of the President's Commission on an All-Volunteer Armed Force* (New York: Macmillian Co., 1970), p. 15.
6. Ibid., p. 147.
7. Ibid., p. 15.
8. This chapter focuses exclusively on the active-duty military. Nevertheless, it should be noted that trends in the active force have been mirrored, more or less, in the reserves. At the end of FY1976, women made up about 5% of the total selected reserves ranging from 2% in the Marine Corps reserve to about 10% in the army reserve and 8% in the air force reserve. By the start of FY1983, the proportion of women in the selected reserves had grown to 9.4%. The Marine Corps still had the smallest proportion of women (3%), while the proportion in the army reserve and air force reserve had increased to 16% and 15%, respectively.

    In 1972, less than 3% of the total selected reserves was black. By 1976 the proportion of blacks in the selected reserves had jumped to 11%, with highest concentrations in the army and marine components (both at 16%). At the start of FY1983, the proportion of blacks in the selected reserves was just under 17%, and the proportion of Hispanics was about 5% (from 3.5% in FY1976). Blacks were most likely to be found in the army reserve (23%) and Marine Corps reserve (19%), and least likely to be in the naval reserve (8%). The highest proportion of Hispanics was in the Marine Corps reserve (5.4%), and the lowest was in the naval component (1.3%).
9. David W. Grissmer, "The supply of enlisted volunteers in the Post-Draft Environment: An Analysis Based on Monthly Data, 1970-75," in Richard V. L. Cooper, ed., *Defense Manpower Policy: Presentations from the 1976 Rand Conference on Defense Manpower* (Santa Monica, CA: Rand Corporation, 1978), R-2396-ARPA, p. 111. Estimates for the relation between enlistments and black youth unemployment are particularly shaky, given the quality of available data on the earnings and employment of black teenagers and young adults. Most researchers have expressed misgivings about the size of the sample data and the statistical reliability of census surveys of the minority population.
10. Martin Binkin and Mark J. Eitelberg with Alvin J. Schexnider and Marvin M. Smith, *Blacks and the Military* (Washington, DC: The Brookings Institution, 1982), p. 72.
11. All members of the armed forces who hold the same rank and who have served the same amount of time receive the same basic pay, regardless of sex, race, or other dissimilarities. To the extent, however, that race enters into occupational differences and hence into bonus eligibility and promotion opportunity, the average earnings profiles will differ.
12. Richard V. L. Cooper, *Military Manpower and the All-Volunteer Force* (Santa Monica, CA: Rand Corporation, September 1977), R-1450-ARPA, p. 221.
13. Ibid., p. 213.
14. Ibid., p. 221.
15. Office of the Assistant Secretary of Defense (Manpower, Reserve Affairs, and Logistics) *Profile of American Youth: 1980 Nationwide Administration of the Armed Services Vocational Aptitude Battery* (Washington, DC: Government Printing Office, March 1982), p. 71.
16. If physical standards were taken into account, it is estimated that the historical military participation rate for "qualified" blacks would be at least 56%, and somewhat higher if service in the officer corps and reserves were included.
17. See, for example, Department of Defense, "Retention Rates and Composition of the Male Enlisted Force by Race and Year of Entry to Active Service as of 30 June 1973," Manpower Research Note 73-13 (Washington, DC: Office of the Deputy Assistant Secretary of Defense for Equal Opportunity, September 1971), pp. 174-229.
18. 62 Stat. 357, 358.
19. Jeanne Holm, *Women in the Military: An Unfinished Revolution* (Novato, CA: Presidio Press, 1982), p. 184.
20. Ibid., p. 190.
21. Department of Defense, *Selected Manpower Statistics* (Washington, DC: Office of the Assistant Secretary of Defense [Comptroller], Directorate for Information, Operations and Control, May 1975; processed), pp. 22, 46.

22. Ames S. Albro Jr., "Civilian Substitution," *Studies Prepared for the President's Commission on an All-Volunteer Force*, vol. 1 (Washington, DC: Government Printing Office, November 1970), p. I-5-19. It was also observed here that "there may be sufficient political or other noneconomic grounds to preclude civilianization of positions normally filled by women service members, although they are substantially more costly than civilian employees." (The authors express their appreciation to William H. Meckling, executive director of the commission staff, for pointing this out.)

23. Central All-Volunteer Task Force, "Utilization of Military Women" (Washington, DC: Office of the Assistant Secretary of Defense for Manpower and Reserve Affairs, December 1972; processed), p. i.

24. 411 U.S. 677 (1973).

25. Department of Defense, "Use of Women in the Military," background study (Washington, DC: Office of the Assistant Secretary of Defense for Manpower and Reserve Affairs, May 1977; processed), pp. 32, 40.

26. Department of Defense, *Annual Report: Fiscal Year 1979* (Washington, DC: Government Printing Office, February 1978), p. 328.

27. Department of Defense, *Annual Report: Fiscal Year 1980* (Washington, DC: Government Printing Office, January 1979), p. 300.

28. Holm, *Women in the Military*, p. 381.

29. "Women in the Armed Forces," *Newsweek*, 18 February 1980, pp. 34-42.

30. Holm, *Women in the Military*, p. 381.

31. Department of Defense, *Military Women in the Department of Defense* (Washington, DC: Office of the Assistant Secretary of Defense [Manpower, Reserve Affairs, and Logistics], April 1983), p. 1.

32. Carter administration goals appear in Holm, *Women in the Military*, p. 381. Reagan administration goals provided by Office of the Assistant Secretary of Defense for Manpower, Reserve Affairs, and Logistics.

33. Department of the Army, *Women in the Army Policy Review* (Washington, DC: Office of the Deputy Chief of Personnel, November 1982), pp. 2-17 2-37.

34. News Release No. 522-83, Office of the Assistant Secretary of Defense (Public Affairs), October 20, 1983.

35. Memorandum, "Methodology for Determining Number of Enlisted Women," Office of the Assistant Secretary of Defense (Manpower, Reserve Affairs, and Logistics), March 17, 1983.

36. In the case of entry standards, however, formal regulations do not always tell the full story of what may be happening at the operational level. Standards may be altered occasionally to keep pace with fluctuations that occur in the recruiting market, in retention, and in strength requirements. Fiscal year 1983 was an exceptionally good recruiting year for males, and an even better year for females. To "regulate the flow" of female applicants, all services treated females who did not possess a high school diploma as ineligible for enlistment. Thus, in 1983 a total of only 107 female high school dropouts were permitted to enlist (probably with special waivers) compared with 23,515 male dropouts in those military services that supposedly had "sex-neutral" entry standards.

    In the Marine Corps, the formal entry standards during FY1983 required that male applicants have an AFQT percentile score of at least twenty-one, if they were high school graduates, and a score of thirty-one, if they were nongraduates or recipients of a high school equivalency certificate. Male high school graduates were also required to score at least eighty (standard score) on the general-technical composite, while nongraduates could score no lower than 105. Women who did not have a high school diploma were ineligible for enlistment in the Marine Corps during 1983. And those who were high school graduates were required to score in the upper 50th percentile on the AFQT.

37. Binkin and Eitelberg, *Blacks and the Military*, pp. 179-183.

38. Milton Friedman, "The Case for Abolishing the Draft—and Substituting for It an All-Volunteer Army," *New York Times Magazine*, 14 May 1967, p. 118.

39. *The Report of the President's Commission on an All-Volunteer Armed Force*, p. 150.

40. Charles C. Moskos, Jr., "Symposium: Race in the United States Military," *Armed Forces and Society* (6) Summer 1980: 589.

41. Robert K. Fullinwider, "The AVF and Racial Balance," Working Paper MS-1 (College Park, MD: University of Maryland, Center for Philosophy and Public Policy, March 1981), p. 16.

42. Harold Brown, *Thinking About National Security: Defense and Foreign Policy in a Dangerous World* (Boulder, CO: Westview Press, 1983) p. 257.

43. William K. Brehm, "Peacetime Voluntary Options," in Andrew J. Goodpaster, Lloyd H. Elliott, and J. Allan Hovey, Jr., eds., *Toward a Consensus on Military Service: Report of the Atlantic Council's Working Group on Military Service* (Elmsford, NY: Pergamon Press, 1983), p. 163.

44. James A. Davis, Jennifer Lauby, and Paul B. Sheatsley, *Americans View the Military: Public Opinion in 1982*, Report No. 131 (Chicago: National Opinion Research Center, University of Chicago, April 1983), p. 43.

45. Ibid., p. 44.

46. Holm, *Women in the Military*, p. 385.

47. Davis et al., *Americans View the Military: Public Opinion in 1982*, pp. 32-33. It is interesting to note that support for women in the military is strongest among persons with more formal education, younger adults, persons from the northern regions of the country, and those who express a relatively weaker religious preference. In addition, working women and working men were the greatest supporters of women in the military—as opposed to housewives, who were consistently less supportive.

48. Ibid., p. 33.

49. Ibid., p. 35.

50. Holm, *Women in the Military*, p. 392.

51. Mady Wechsler Segal and David R. Segal, "Social Change and the Participation of Women in the American Military," in Louis Krierberg, ed. *Research in Social Movements, Conflicts and Change*, Vol. 5 (Greenwich, CT: JAI Press, 1983) p. 256

52. Although both fertility rates (live births per 1,000 women aged fifteen to forty-four) and the number of births began a gradual decline in 1958, demographers seem to agree that the end of the baby boom did not occur until 1965, when the decline in both measures became more conspicuous.

53. Cohort size will begin to increase again after 1995, since the annual number of births began to rise in 1976. This is a result of a delayed "echo effect": there are more women, born during the baby boom, who are now of childbearing age. Once this generation passes that age, starting in the 1990s, the annual births will decline once again, barring substantial increases in fertility rates.

54. Martin M. Frankel and Debra E. Gerald, *Projections of Educational Statistics to 1990-91*, vol. 1 (Washington, DC: National Center for Education Statistics, March 1982), p. 69.

55. The "qualified and available" pool excludes those who cannot volunteer and those who are unlikely to volunteer for military service. The former are individuals who would not be expected to meet minimum mental, physical, and moral standards. The latter includes college students who continued beyond the second year and individuals confined to various training, curative, or correctional institutions. The calculation here is confined to male youths since, under present policies, they will continue to constitute roughly 90% of all military personnel. Obviously, if the armed forces expanded the role of women beyond current goals, a smaller proportion of the male population would have to be attracted. This possibility is discussed later.

56. For the relevance and mathematical basis for expressing the manpower supply problem in terms of annual accession requirements as a percent of one representative age cohort, see Martin Binkin and John D. Johnston, *All-Volunteer Armed Forces: Progress, Problems, and Prospects*, prepared for the Senate Armed Services Committee, 93 Cong. 1 sess. (Washington, DC: Government Printing Office 1973).

57. Tidal W. McCoy, "U.S. Armed Forces Ill-Prepared for Today's Super-Sophisticated Weaponry," *Human Events*, October 21, 1982.

58. David Roehm, "The Developing Market for Military Manpower: Challenge," in *Conference Proceedings, Naval Manpower Research in the 1980s*, (Alexandria, VA: Center for Naval Analyses, July 1, 1982), p. 15. According to this analysis, the semi-technical jobs require an equal mix of AFQT category IIIA and IIIB groups, technical jobs call for two-thirds category III and one-third category II people, and highly technical positions require, on average, those who score in category II.

59. Juri Toomepuu, *Soldier Capability-Army Combat Effectiveness (SCACE)*, vol. 1 (Fort Benjamin Harrison, IN: U.S. Army Soldier Support Center, Training and Doctrine Command, April 1981). See also J. Richard Wallace, "The Gideon Criterion: The Effects of Selection Criteria on Soldiers' Capabilities and Battle Results," USAREC Research Memorandum 82-1 (Fort Sheridan, IL: U.S. Army Recruiting Command, January 1982); Thomas A. Horner, "Killers, Fillers, and Fodder," *Parameters*, vol. 12, September 1982; Dave Griffiths, "Incompetent GIs Man Army's Missile Posts," *Defense Week*, March 29, 1982.

60. Toomepuu, *Soldier Capability*, pp. 50-51.

61. E. E. Maccoby and C. M. Jacklin, *The Psychology of Sex Differences* (Stanford, CA: Stanford University Press, 1974), p. 75.

62. Mark J. Eitelberg, "Subpopulation Differences in Performance on Tests of Mental Ability," Technical Memorandum 81-3 (Washington, DC: Office of the Secretary of Defense, August 1981), pp. 1-4.

63. The aptitude composites shown here are the so-termed "common" aptitude composites used by the armed services. The administrative, general, and electronics composites are the same for all four services. The air force version of the mechanical composite is presented in Table 7.18, but it is illustrative of composites used by the other services to assign new recruits to mechanically-oriented occupations.

It is worth noting here that the relatively smaller difference (shown in Table 7.16) between the "eligibility rates" of males and females in the army's "mechanical" occupation, as compared with the navy's, is partially due to the construction of the specific aptitude composites used by these services in this instance. The test composite used by the army (mechanical maintenance) includes one subtest (numerical operations) on which women score higher than men. Most men, however, outscore women on all of the subtests that are included in the navy composite.

At the same time, the mechanical composite used by the air force applies a double-weighting to the auto and shop information subtest. It is the subtest on which women achieve their lowest mean percentile score (40.9 compared with a score of 51.4 by men).

64. George C. Wilson, "Army Programs for Women Falter During Fiscal-Year Test," *Washington Post*, 23 April 1979, p. A-6.

65. If women were allowed to serve in the army's combat specialties, about 62% (78% of those qualified for army enlistment) could meet the education and aptitude standards for assignment to the infantry. Only one in four (26%) black young men (and 58% of those who could pass the basic entry standards) are currently able to qualify for infantry training. Overall, 72% of all males and 93% of males qualified for enlistment would be expected to pass the classification requirements for the army infantry.

Commentary

Gus C. Lee

There are four points that I would like to make that, in a sense, represent "lessons learned" during the first ten years of the AVF:

1. The Gates report on the volunteer force is an important public document that provides the rational and intellectual basis for the All-Volunteer Force.
2. The way that we manage the volunteer force, particularly the policy decisions that we make, is a critical factor in sustaining the volunteer force.
3. The army performance under the volunteer force will be the determining factor in whether we return to the draft.
4. We can probably sustain the peacetime force on a volunteer basis during the remainder of the 1980s provided sufficient resources continue to be made available.

The Gates report is a landmark document that was a major catalyst in bringing about the change to a volunteer force. Although its economic projections were over-optimistic, the significance of the report in bringing about the actual change in national policy is a more important consideration. During the 1960s the writings of Milton Friedman, William H. Meckling, Walter Oi, and other economists repeated over and over the theme that a volunteer force could be accomplished by making military pay competitive with pay in the civilian sector. The Gates report made this message available to a much wider audience and helped create a climate conducive to change in military manpower policy.

It is easy to forget the widespread skepticism concerning the feasibility of the volunteer force that prevailed in the Pentagon building in 1970. I used to say that there weren't a dozen people in the Pentagon at the time who were convinced the volunteer force would work, and we would have to discount most of these because they worked for Assistant Secretary Roger Kelley. As late as 1969, 62% of the respondents in public opinion polls favored continuance of the draft over the volunteer force. By arguing the feasibility and the desirability of a volunteer force the Gates report helped to change opinion both in the press and among the general public. The report remains a landmark in the history of the volunteer force.

The econometric analysis of the report was considerably on the optimistic side. If you recall, the recommended pay increase of about 50% was estimated to be the increase needed to maintain a force of 2.5 million. The report concluded that no pay increase was needed for a force of 2 million and only a small increase for a force of 2.2 million. It simply has not been as easy as the report suggested to maintain the force at about the 2.1 million level during the past ten years.

One reason for the over-optimistic slant to the Gates projections is inherent in econometric models: the future management problems are uncertain and unpredictable. Who could have forseen the management problems that have occurred throughout the AVF time period so far?

The way that we manage is a critical factor in sustaining the volunteer force. We have not only demonstrated that we are capable of maintaining the supply in the numbers and kinds of people needed for a force of over 2 million but that we are also capable of sufficient management "glitches" to make sustaining this size force very uncertain from time to time. We have allowed relative military pay to lag behind civilian pay. At times, we have let the number of recruiters decline. We also, at various times, have neglected to instruct recruiters clearly as to the qualitative attributes we expected among enlistees. We have even misnormed the entry test. All of these unfortunate policy decisions and management occurrences happened during the later years of the 1970s.

The misnorming of the entry test makes it difficult, if not impossible, to evaluate market capabilities under the conditions that existed from 1977 to 1980. The services, particularly recruiters, initially thought they were enlisting only 9 or 10% mental group IVs among their total accessions. After this misnorming of the 1976 version of the Armed Services Vocational Aptitude Battery was discovered, the corrected scores showed that 45% of the accessions were mental group IV's. It is not likely that this unusually high proportion of new enlistees who scored below average on the mental test accurately reflected recruiting capabilities. The substandard recruiting performance more likely resulted from the inflated scores of the misnormed test.

While management problems have caused us difficulty from time to time the results during the first decade, on the whole, are impressive. As chapter 6 by Roll and Warner points out, the drop in first and second-term reenlistment rates that followed the lag in relative military pay in the late 1970s has apparently been corrected. The proportion of experienced career personnel in the force is at an all-time high. I mention this point because it is appropriate, after ten years, to base the evaluation of the AVF on measures of retention and of the condition of the personnel inventory, as well as on accession results. From our mistakes, as well as our successes, we have accumulated a body of experience in managing the AVF that will serve us well, if we apply it in the future.

During the decade of the volunteer force, all services have met their numerical accession requirements with few exceptions. In the army particularly, this is a considerable accomplishment because the army's demand for new recruits is much higher. After the end of the draft, the army was the only service that had a sharp drop in the quality of accessions, as measured by the percentage of high school graduates. It is very likely that army performance in the future will determine whether or not we return to the draft. On the average, the army's accession requirements have been three times those of the Marine Corps, double the accession requirements of the air force, and 50% higher than the navy's. The disparity is even greater in the recruiting objectives for the reserve and National Guard components. The Gates Commission recognized this difference among the services by observing that pay scales that were adequate for the army to meet its enlisted accession requirements would surely be adequate for the other services.

The army has accomplished a remarkable turn for the better in the 1980s. Throughout most of the 1970s youth preferences were higher for the other services that for the army. More recently, the army has narrowed this gap. Under the favorable recruiting conditions of the past three years, the army, as well as the other services, has demonstrated a remarkable recruiting performance. This momentum will be needed as we face higher navy and air force accession requirements and a smaller manpower pool of military age youth during the last half of this decade.

We can probably sustain the volunteer force at planned force levels, in peacetime and throughout the remainder of the decade, if sufficient resources continue to be made available and if we manage wisely. We must maintain competitive pay and we must provide adequate recruiting resources. In the first decade we have survived the "up" curve of the business cycle and relatively low youth unemployment rates. We need to learn to size the recruiting services for the long pull, not to overreact to the ups and downs of the business cycle and unemployment rates by cutting back too much in the favorable recruiting years.

In summary, the volunteer force has proved to be a viable manpower policy. I have mentioned only a few lessons to be learned from the experience so far. There is one final point: The All-Volunteer Force is a peacetime force. We cannot afford to knock the draft or neglect the standby draft system because, in this uncertain world, we simply do not know when the national security needs of the United States will require that we use the draft system again.

John D. Johnston

I would like to comment on the quantity, quality, and the management of the force. First, let me address quantity. One thing I discovered when I was a Federal Executive Research Fellow at The Brookings Institution in 1972 was a surprising statistic: in order to achieve and sustain the All-Volunteer Force (AVF) in the 1970s, the services had to recruit one out of three of the qualified and available youth (an amazing number). I didn't think it was possible; however, it turned out to be quite possible, for the AVF was achieved and sustained.

Even more challenging, in the 1980s, the services must recruit one out of two of the qualified and available population in order to sustain the AVF. You might ask why has the ratio changed? All the authors thus far have alluded to it; the baby boom is over. From 1979 to 1985, the youth population will decrease in absolute numbers by 15%, and from 1979 to 1992, by 25%. Quantity is, and should be, a major concern in the 1980s. However, Gary Nelson indicates one lesson learned: "the future decline in the youth cohort is not nearly the threat to the AVF, as commonly thought." Available estimates suggest a 20% decline in youth population could substantially, or completely, be offset by proportional increases in recruiting resources. I take issue with this observation. While I believe recruiting resources are quite important, I doubt if they could completely offset the projected 15% to 25% population decline in the 1980s and 1990s time frame. I believe this is especially true when coupled with the state of the U. S. economy. As the economy recovers, the higher-quality supply pool will shrink. More youth will go into civilian jobs and more families will be able to afford to send their sons and daughters to college.

Another by-product of an improved economy will likely be a decline in reenlistment rates especially among high-tech skill areas that are transferable to the private sector. Programs must now be enhanced to avoid this problem. If we have lower reenlistment rates, we will then have a higher recruitment requirement which will further strain the 1980/1990s recruitment challenge.

I believe flexible management actions must now be identified to deal with these quantity and quality challenges. Increasing recruiting resources would be an important part of the plan. However, other options must be identified, developed, and placed on the shelf ready to go. I don't want to gamble with sustaining the AVF. The bureaucracy is cumbersome and may not be able to react quickly enough to severe quantity or quality problems unless we plan ahead and place coordinated options on the shelf.

With respect to the quantity of minorities, there really were not many surprises. Given the issue of equal opportunity versus equal representation, the country has chosen equal opportunity. We find that there is a 20% representation of blacks in the armed services and maybe one in three in the combat arms. What I did find surprising were the results of the public survey Binkin and Eitelberg presented in chapter 7. Of the public at large, 12% thought there were too many blacks in the armed services and 19% thought not enough. But 69% felt the mix was about right. So the public at large is very satisfied with their current perception of the minority mix. I found that extremely interesting. With regard to women, we have seen a doubling of their numbers in all services from 1974 to 1981. In the army, the increase is from 5% to 13%, the navy 5% to 10%, the air force 7% to 17%, and the Marine Corps 2% to 5%. This is an amazing growth. When I was in the air force in 1970, we projected a 20% increase in women's representation. We're almost there. The public view, and again out of Binkin and Eitelberg's chapter, is that 60% believe there should be more women in the military. In addition, 50% believe that if conscription returns, women should be drafted. The other statistical finding that surprised me was that 33% of the public at large believe women should serve in combat jobs. I still believe women are viewed as a supplementary source of manpower. However, I think in good recruiting times constraints are placed on the skills women serve in, and in hard times, they are waived. Binkin and Eitelberg cite that 53% of the women are serving in jobs in which the army claims that only 8% of the women could qualify. In conclusion, major progress has been made, but it appears that still more progress can be made.

Increases in technology and the complexity of the nation's military generate the perception that higher-quality recruits are essential to sustain the force. Roll and Warner found that from 1974 through 1982 the occupational distribution of the career force had not changed much. Despite the perceptions, the services have become more technical. The highly skilled areas of electronic equipment repair, communications and intelligence, and mechanical and electronic repair have not grown in relative importance. Actually, the gains have occurred in the softer skill areas. That was a surprise to me. A brief examination, which I did with Joe Silverman at the Naval Personnel Research and Development Center, looked at the navy skill area of aviation mechanics. We were curious about job complexity—has it increased or decreased? We went back to 1970 and found that in order to qualify to be an aviation mechanic, one had to take out the engine and disassemble it. What's required in that job skill today? We found that one yanks out a "black box" and puts in another one. The equipment appears to have been designed for a less qualified person. I'm not saying it's been that way across the board and I'm not suggesting that standards be lowered because aboard ship you may have to repair the black box. However, it's an area that needs closer examination. Exactly which quality is really required today and will be required in the next decade? The baby boom period of the AVF allowed a high-quality recruit to be brought into the force across the board. Standards were often determined by what the market would bear, not necessarily what the job required. Recognizing the quantity challenge in the 1980s and 1990s, now may be the time to validate quality standards. What jobs are simpler due to design? What jobs are more complicated due to high-tech weapons? Let's make sure the right jobs get the quality people.

Finally, I believe that management of the force is the key to sustaining the AVF. We must have flexible options on the shelf to deal with quantity and quality short falls in recruiting, as well as in first-term enlistments. I agree wholeheartedly with Gary Nelson's view that the options have to be flexible. We have a two-year lag because of the budget system. We need to design the options and have some appreciation of when it would make sense to use them. Hopefully we will have a contingency fund available so we will be ready to follow through with these options when they are required.

In sum, I think we may have serious problems. The issues are quantity as well as quality. Quality drives the problem in terms of particular jobs, but with a shrinking quantity and with improvement of the economy, I believe sustaining the force by volunteers will require alert monitoring and responsive management.

Curtis W. Tarr

Looking back over a decade of progress, I wish to express my respect for the splendid manner by which the leaders of the armed services have made a success of the All-Volunteer Force. What the nation has achieved is a tribute to the imagination and industry with which these people have worked.

The panelists have summarized in their presentations some of the findings that I had an opportunity to study before coming here. I compliment the authors on their research and the way they have presented their findings.

We had an interesting colloquy on registration for a possible future draft and whether the process should continue. As I consider this question I wonder how well I can predict what form a future war might take. Although we can make assumptions about a short nuclear war or a more lengthy conventional conflict, we cannot be at all sure that any of our assumptions will be valid. We cannot forsee clearly the weapons that will be used or the nations that will use them.

I recall that Napoleon once judged that wars are won by the last battalion. Recently I have been reading again about the campaigns of the Civil War, and certainly Napoleon spoke correctly for those battles, decided so often by the arrival of fresh reserves. If a nation can win a war by providing the strength at last to top the scale, then we as national leaders must be careful to preserve the process that will bring people to the armed services in a manner commensurate with our national potential.

We have heard the argument that wars stimulate enlistments. This is true and we have seen that phenomon frequently. But this momentum of eagerness cannot be sustained in a long war. Recently, I heard a report on television that many people had volunteered to become marines just after the invasion of Grenada. One of these was a seventy-three-year-old woman; I presume her enlistment would have been a unique expression of lateral entry! But typically when reports come back to the home front about the extent of battle, the casualties, and the terror of combat, then enlistments dwindle. Were this not so, we would recommend to the Marine Corps that they use a documentary account of the Battle of Tarawa for a recruiting film.

Registration will not provide trained people for the armed services. Only forces in being can do that. But it will hasten the supply of people to begin training, eliminating the turbulence that would be required to initiate selective service at a time of general mobilization. It can be helpful, particularly in replacing combat losses. And registration will assist in the preparation of forces to sustain the nation if ever we face the horrible prospect of a global war.

Gary R. Nelson, Robert Roll and John Warner have argued convincingly for the adoption of means by which the Department of Defense can employ the management tools required to anticipate difficulties in recruitment. Presumably giving our defense managers the option to improve pay or bonuses before recruitment ebbs or reenlistment falls would provide a more stable force and improve readiness. I would not disagree. But politically it probably will not be possible to accomplish. Congress will not permit that flexibility, and were I a member of

Congress I am not certain that I would favor it. Furthermore, I suspect that if money were appropriated to provide that option to the services it would be allocated to the procurement of weapons systems in advance of the time that it could be used for these other purposes. Frankly I believe that the best means to assure a stable force is to do what is needed to provide a stable economy.

We have heard arguments about the level of quality required by the services for various positions. I do not disagree with most of what has been said. Some jobs require people in lower mental categories because those who are more able would find the tasks boring and probably they would perform poorly as a consequence.

But there are two factors that I urge us to consider. The first relates to survivability on the field of battle. I am not sure what work has been done on this subject during the last decade. But when I left the government I recall that what little study had been given to survivability indicated that the brightest had the best chance of survival. If that is true, then we should consider that when we formulate the desiderata for qualities of combat soldiers. I recall well one day when I received a call from an important official in the White House. He knew that I worked on statistics related to enlistments while we sought to eliminate the draft. He asked about progress, and I told him we had encouraging numbers but some loss in quality. "Oh that's ok," he replied, "they'll make good infantrymen." To stimulate his thought in a harmless way, I asked him what men he would select if he had to go on patrol in Vietnam. He admitted that he did not know and asked my advice. "I would pick the men most likely to return." "Who would they be," he wanted to know. "From all the evidence we can gather, the ones most likely to return are the brightest." That is a sobering thought.

Similarly, we are witnessing a profound change in our society in the way we must manage people. I understand that the services already have encountered this shift in attitudes. People no longer wish to do something simply because someone in authority has directed them to do it. Increasingly people ask to be a part of the process of decision where their lives and their welfare are at stake. Thus we hear a great deal in America about participative management. Handled well it can accomplish wonders of performance in a working group. Those who respond best to participative management and who help best to formulate constructive ideas are those who are brighter. So quality is something that we must consider in dimensions larger than the minimal requirements of a job.

We have looked at the quality of life in the services. Someone here advanced the argument that the conditions one faces have had little to do with retention and that economic incentives are much more important. My own experiences with service people do not corroborate this conclusion. I remember the afternoon I visited with a young man as we cruised underwater in a Poseidon submarine. He took care of the nuclear power plant on that boat, and he was preparing to leave the service in a few days. I asked him why he wanted to leave his job. He answered that his wife recently had called him to say that his son needed a father, not a sailor who spent so much time on cruises, and that he had to come home to assume his parental responsibilities or their family would suffer the consequences. I heard similar objections from people elsewhere—on a destroyer in the Gulf of Tonkin, a carrier in the Mediterranean, and at Thule Air Force Base. My warning is that unless we take these quality of life factors into account we will pay the price in lower retention.

We have talked about monetary factors, and certainly I do not deprecate the value of these incentives. The success of the AVF indicates that these tools have been used well. But my observation is that the people who have contributed most to the service were not "economic people." They needed money to care for their personal and family needs. But with that assured, they were motivated by a desire to serve the nation. We must keep that in mind or we may attract a force composed of people seeking inappropriate goals.

Finally, I would like to refer to Binkin and Eitelberg's final paragraph in which they discuss how the nation should face the demographic depression of this decade and then the next. Let me discuss a few of the items they set forth.

I agree completely with those who have argued that recruitment is somewhat more difficult when youth unemployment is low. As our economy recovers somewhat, we hope for opportunities for young people. But I am not sanguine that these openings will appear as quickly as the economy improves. Business leaders have looked carefully at their costs and have resolved that they will not hire back the force that they maintained in better times. Those they do recall often will be the more experienced people. So I expect youth opportunities to lag behind the recovery, and thus I believe that we will continue to enjoy successful recruitment of both numbers and quality even while the economy improves. Only later will the strong economy dampen enlistments.

We have talked about opportunities for women. Again we see profound changes in our society. Women are accepting positions previously taken only by men, and they are doing well. This should be no surprise. One of the problems in utilizing women in the armed forces rests with the restriction on combat jobs. I believe this should change. I am not arguing for placing women in ground combat jobs where they might be forced to accept taxing physical demands. But I do not see why a woman could not operate a transport plane in a combat zone or carry out repairs on sophisticated equipment just behind the lines. Soon we should alter our conventional thinking in this regard.

Many talk about the reinstitution of conscription. We do not need it now, most admit, but we may someday. I do not deny this. But as one who had considerable experience with the draft in its last days, let me remind you that we had problems we never solved, difficulties we never overcame. We would have them again. Conscription is not a process shorn of difficulties. We must recognize this lest we consider it too quickly as a remedy for recruitment problems.

An alternative to reinstituting the draft would be to reduce force structure. I refer here to a situation without a war but with enlistment and retention problems. Rather than considering the size of our forces to be fixed, I would prefer that we evaluate force reduction prior to a return to conscription. Perhaps careful study would indicate that we could not reduce our commitments or the forces that guarantee them. But I have never seen such a careful study to justify our force levels during the last decade.

Another alternative in the situation I described is to lower quality in order to maintain forces through enlistments. We did too much of this in the 1970s. I believe we have a much more effective and ready military force when we maintain the quality of accessions, even when that force is smaller.

Finally let me say that in a democracy no program works well, for any extended time, without public acceptance and support. The great lesson of Vietnam, to me, is that our leaders cannot accomplish national plans, however noble, without the full endorsement of our people. The American people now believe in the All-Volunteer Force. That is largely the reason for its success. We must continue maintaining our forces with volunteers as long as the public believes that this is the appropriate manner of doing so. If ever again our leaders decide that we must return to conscription, we must act only when the public is convinced that we must do so or we court a national disaster. Public opinion can be influenced by leadership, but the preparation of our people must be the prelude for change.

Stephen E. Herbits

In looking back, primarily to the Gates Commission, but also to the few years of debate before that, we shouldn't forget some of the great accomplishments of the All-Volunteer Force.

We have brought into being a government policy that is consistent with, and enhances the basic principles of, what we as a nation are. That's no small achievement. We have brought substantial benefit to the readiness of the military in many ways.

Two that have intrigued me most are the highly reduced turnover in small units of the military and the implications for people working together when they actually get into combat. Also of importance is the higher proportion of people actually operating in skills for which they've been trained.

We have reduced the economic distortions across the country caused by a draft. And we've reduced the personal distortions. Higher education seems to have been able to survive without the inducement of the draft.

Let's take a look back at the management issue which is a polite name for the political issue. When Assistant Secretary of Defense (M&RA) Roger Kelley left the Pentagon in 1973, he was quoted frequently as having said that there is a potential problem of sabotage to the AVF program. It was a stern warning. It received a lot of attention. I'll be somewhat more direct and say that in the nine months that followed his departure from the Pentagon, I tracked and found such a pattern.

Many new policies were established and many of them in the army. Each one was justifiable in its own right but interestingly enough, when collected together into a pattern, there was what I would call a deliberate attempt by some people in senior management to undermine the viability of the All-Volunteer Force and to stimulate a political environment for the return of the draft. That was repeated to some degree in the early years of the Carter administration. The only problem is that the Carter administration agreed with it and through various actions, including reducing pay comparability, managed to do to the military what the military couldn't have done to itself. It will take us several years yet to recover from that damage. Interestingly, there was another flutter just after the new Reagan administration took office. While I won't cite specifics, some in the services attempted to adopt programs which would gradually erode and undermine the effectiveness of the volunteer force. Another presidential commission was established to review and rededicate the entire administration to the issue.

I think we can predict with some certainty that the next administration will face a similar problem. This is a political and a management problem; a management problem that is going to be considerably more complicated in the 1980s than it was in the 1970s. We've gone over in some detail the demographics, the numbers of people, the very tough relationship of recruiting to unemployment, and a history of attempts within the military to adopt programs which are not necessarily consistent with the long-term benefits of the volunteer force. Management is going to be difficult; we must keep it in front of us.

Let us look at some of the specifics. One is quality standards, which we've discussed. I want to look at it from a management point of view. I get nervous when I look at the army's nonprior-service category I-III high school graduate requirement projections from now through 1989. I think they are irresponsible, inflated, and need to be looked at again. I think outsiders have to watch them.

We have to watch attritions, for instance, programs on how we handle drug abusers or how we handle people who don't read as well as others. We have to watch when we continually reduce the level of military responsibility as to who can dismiss a soldier outright without recourse. It's getting lower. There has been a flurry of discussion about such programs just in the last few months.

John Johnston has talked briefly about validating the specific qualification requirements for jobs. This is something we have yet to do although we all know it is the fundamental issue. Because it is difficult, we've shied away from it. But we really have not perfected the concept of attracting and assigning the right quality for each kind of job. We're still shooting in the dark and doing more shooting than managing.

I saw an article the other day in which a longtime reenlistment counsellor said that he was losing a lot of people because those individuals simply were not checking early enough on what they had to do to stay in. That's a management issue. That's not a philosophical issue. Somebody's got to pay attention to those things. Where is our communication with these people? Are we reaching out to them to discuss what they need to do if they want to stay in rather than forcing them to appeal to a general board to beg to stay in because they were unaware of what they needed to do?

A second issue is the timing of accessions or subtitled; when are the numbers available? We've heard of the concept of flexibility. I would like to see Congress enact a provision that would allow the Defense Department to go 10% over its mandated accession ceilings if eligible and desirable recruits are available. Let's take them even when we may not need them in the ensuing months.

An interesting corollary came up not long ago with the basic skills education program. The General Accounting Office reported that a substantial proportion of the people in that program were ineligible because they were in the program while on duty and they were supposed to be bettering themselves off duty. I think that's the wrong way of looking at the problem.

If people in the service have a desire to take advantage of the benefits of training and education for self-improvement for their future careers, then we ought to give it to them. If it means extending the payback period of their enlistment in order to get into certain curricula, let's do it. To deny it doesn't serve anyone's purpose. It's simply a matter of managing it, rather than cutting out the program.

A third issue is the capital-labor trade-off. It is a problem which is very difficult to manage because our Pentagon structure doesn't connect the manpower staff with the weapons development staff. We've never really gotten to the root of this problem. It's going to get more complex as we send more complex weapons into the field, yet we are producing a whole generation that will start entering the military in the next several years who went through high school pushing buttons, first on calculators, then on Pac-man games, and now on computers. How are we going to take advantage of those skills? How are we going to make that interface much easier in the field rather than more difficult? We must adjust to the quality that civilian society is producing, rather than the other way around.

Finally, there is the issue of women. The services have made extraordinary progress in accepting and assimilating women; perhaps, and I can't speak of this authoritatively, better than industry itself. But are we ready for the next generation? Are we ready to press again for a new level of assimilation and comfort and emotional acceptance (because this issue is more emotional than anything else) of the role that women can play in the service? A new major push, talking about 20% levels, not 9 or 10 or 11% levels, is what we should be seeking if we really want to keep the primary goal in mind of manning and "womaning" the armed forces in a way which will optimally serve our defense needs.

These issues I've mentioned are, of course, a sprinkling of the vast numbers of opportunities facing the armed forces. These are management issues. The policy has been decided. All ranks of the armed forces in the United States will be filled with volunteers—not just the career force. Only in the most dire circumstances will we revert to the draft in peacetime. Is the army willing to destroy itself to create those dire circumstances? Failure to manage the problem is a political decision of significance.

William H. Meckling

I must echo the sentiments of my colleagues that it is nice to get together with people who were intimately involved with the work of the Gates Commission. It is worth noting at the outset that it has been much longer since the Gates Commission sat than is implied by the tables which have been used. Most of the data presented dates from the time the All-Volunteer Force went into effect. The Gates Commission did most of its work in the fall of 1969, fourteen years ago rather than ten years ago. The data the commission had to work with were even older than what's implied by these tables. I believe the commission and its staff would have been very comforted to know in 1969 that the course of the All-Volunteer Force would approximate their predictions as well as it has. I also think, however, that this happy state of affairs has not been entirely due to our predictive abilities. The efforts that were exerted in ensuing years to make the system work contributed importantly, even though there were elements in the Department of Defense and elsewhere in the government busy trying to undermine the basic policy. There were also many in the Defense Department and elsewhere trying hard to make voluntarism succeed.

While I am on the subject of the commission's work, I must note that Martin Binkin and Mark Eitelberg's adverse assessment of two aspects of the commission's work is correct. We did underestimate what would happen to black accessions as a consequence of the pay schedule we recommended. I'll have some more to say about what should be inferred from that later.

When I first read Binkin and Eitelberg's presentation, I was shocked to find their allegation that we gave no consideration to increasing the number of women in the military. I assure you, we were searching everywhere for a potential supply. My shock led me to canvass my files in search of contradictory evidence. I could find no record anywhere that we seriously considered the question of expanding the number of women in uniform. We did look at civilianization, that is, the possibility of transforming military billets into civilian billets. In fact, as an outcome of that exercise, we recommended abolishing many military billets that were then filled by females. Our performance on that front was perhaps even worse than Binkin and Eitelberg reported. On the other hand, I can't feel very badly about our neglect. The increase in supply represented by females will soften the impact of the cohort shrinkage over the next ten years.

I want to raise some questions regarding certain research results presented. I'm not convinced yet of the importance of unemployment for accessions. The commission pondered this issue at length fourteen years ago. One question is whether what we observe is simply an enlistment timing phenomenon or whether unemployment actually increases accessions over a longer period. It is clear that increased unemployment would make a difference in the total number of accessions.

I have a second problem, however, of a more fundamental sort. Unemployment figures have ceased to mean what they meant heretofore and the implications of that for drawing inferences about enlistments and reenlistments from unemployment data seem to me to have been neglected. Normal peacetime unemployment rates are now on the order of 8 or 9%. Much of the increase that has occurred has nothing to do with cyclical unemployment. The basic unemployment rate has risen for a variety of reasons. Some of the increase is simply due to changes in reporting, such as requiring those who receive food stamps to register as unemployed. Part of the increase is due to the fact that some unemployed, such as second and third workers in a family, are not eagerly seeking reemployment. Substantial increases in the level and duration of unemployment benefits have also reduced the incentives to job search. To the extent that factors such as these explain the increased unemployment over the past decade, we would not expect that increase to lead to higher levels of enlistments or reenlistments.

I would like to turn now from the discussion of specifics to a more general problem I see stemming from the way people view the volunteer force; a phenomenon which affects the choice of research topics by a tendency to identify problems of personnel management or personnel policy with voluntarism. For example, there's a presumption that voluntarism is necessarily accomplished by an increase in the number of blacks in the military. A more subtle example is provided us by John Johnston's discussion of the decline in the size of the eighteen to twenty-one-year old cohort, and the implications of that fact for choosing between an all-volunteer force and conscription.

The decline in the size of the eighteen to twenty-one-year old population, will occur no matter what method is adopted for recruiting manpower. Nothing can be done about this. A range of options is available as reactions to that development, but reducing costs by reintroducing conscription is not one of them. Military manpower costs are (like all costs) what we have to give up in order to get whatever military manpower we employ. If we, as has been suggested here, want one-half of the eighteen-year-old cohort to join the services each year, the cost is (to a first approximation) independent of whether we conscript the eighteen-year-olds or get them to volunteer. The real question is whether we impose a very large tax on the subgroup who happens to be conscripted or whether we tax society as a whole to pay for that portion of our defense. The perennial (entirely false) claim that conscription reduces costs is the classic example of tarring voluntarism with a black mark it does not deserve.

The same comment applies to many of the military manpower topics which get so much attention, including the quality of military manpower, the fraction of the force which is black, and the number of women in uniform.

We can have any quality of career force we want, at least up to the quality of the population of the United States, but higher quality inevitably will mean higher costs: costs that cannot be avoided by conscription. The quality of a career force is a matter of personnel policy, largely compensation policy. Similarly, there are a variety of ways to control the number of blacks in the army under a voluntary regime. The simplest is to impose quotas. The imposition of such a quota would increase costs again, if the size of force is to be maintained, but control of black participation is perfectly consistent with all all-volunteer force, and the same is true of increasing female participation. Voluntarism cannot be blamed for black participation rates, a dearth of females, or the quality of military manpower. Personnel policies can be blamed.

I also want to make it clear that neither the military nor civilians in the Defense Department are involved in most of what I'm calling personnel policy, but I mean policy that is invoked by Congress and the administration. More and more, however, it is really congressional policy.

The truth is that the military and civilian defense establishments are given very little freedom to manage military affairs. Compensation policy is a classic example. The Gates Commission itself did not feel free to consider any compensation revisions it might want. For example, they were unwilling to consider proposals which would violate the sacrosanct policy that pay by grade had to be equal across the services, even though that policy was more costly than it would have been to raise pay only where first-term enlistments were a major problem, namely, in the combat forces, especially the army. Another example of such constraints is the congressional policy, not only of specifying pay scales and personnel budgets, but also of dictating manpower quotas by service. This set of policies deters the Defense Department from considering substitutions of capital for labor when relative costs shift. One would hope that in a period when the pool of persons best suited for military service is shrinking by 25%, one reaction would be to reduce manpower demands. If a 2.1 million-man force makes sense when the cohort of eighteen-year-olds is 4 million per year, it probably doesn't make sense when the cohort is only 3 million per year. In the private sector we would expect that phenomenon to be accompanied by some substitutions economizing on the scarce manpower. In the case of the military, however, we go on talking about "requirements" as if the size of the services ought to be independent of costs. In no small part this is due to congressional control. If the services were given budgets, and then evaluated and monitored on the basis of the military effectiveness they produce, they would be more cognizant of shifts in costs. If I had my most radical wishes granted, one would be to have

Congress turn over a bundle of money to the military each year to spend almost as they see fit. Congress would do much better spending its time evaluating the military effectiveness produced by the services, then adjusting budgets for their performance, than it does trying to make all the decisions itself. I realize that my wish is a wild dream, of course, but movement in that direction is something which researchers ought to have under consideration. Taking such constraints as given in doing research fosters perpetuation of the status quo.

Despite all of these critical comments, I want to make it clear that I am delighted and amazed at both the quantity and quality of ongoing military manpower research. I believe such research means we will continue to improve the management of military manpower. Not only will that improve our security, it will help us preserve freedom by nurturing the All-Volunteer Force.

AUDIENCE

Question for C. Robert Roll, Jr. and John T. Warner (from Stanley A. Horwitz): Most research suggests that we get more for our money in terms of training costs and productivity gains from a larger career force. Why do you only say *maybe* we should have more senior people.

Roll: I agree with the research and your general conclusion. The issue I was trying to raise is that we do not know what the specific career content should be and perhaps we never will. However, despite the lack of the consensus, most agree that the general direction should be toward more careerists.

Warner: In the paper we reach a stronger conclusion than "maybe." Existing cost benefit analyses indicate that even with the historically high career content of today's force, the services may not have enough careerists. One note of pessimism is that some of the services' objective force plans call for smaller career content in high-school areas than in low-skill areas. This is curious. It almost looks as if the system is being driven by supply, and we plan needs around what we can get not what is efficient from a cost benefit perspective. We shouldn't let what we can get dictate what our plans are.

Question for Gary R. Nelson (from Fred Suffa): In Stephen Herbits' comments he mentioned a very important factor which I haven't seen in econometric models, and that is the management function. In the management of the recruiting program the services tell the recruiters how many and what type of people to get. Yet, the services use different goaling techniques and some of them have historically been pretty unsophisticated. Given that recruiters tend to recruit the easiest targets, they will get the lower-quality groups unless there are incentives to do better. What assurance do you have that your supply estimates are supply-constrained rather than reflect demand constraints?

Nelson: The econometric equations are as close as we can get to a measure of supply. As you suggest, there are periods when we were trying to do less well than we could have done by different goaling of recruiters, or by different management of recruiters. It's a very fertile research area. Some work has been done at Rand in the past year in that area that suggests that indeed there are benefits to goals. You can achieve a higher-quality mix through management of the goaling process. At the same time, I don't see anything that suggests the "V" shaped curve of enlistments between 1976 and 1983 was primarily demand constrained, although there may have been demand components and a management factor. Clearly misnorming had an effect, but I think it is generally indicative of supply at that time.

Question for Martin Binkin (from Cdr. Lee Mairs, USN): One thing that has been irritating me for a couple of years is the argument that one of three and then one of two *qualified* people must be recruited for the AVF to work. In order to get these numbers, a large group of people must be excluded from the denominator: all those who are in colleges, all those who are in junior colleges, and in fact all those who are in the services. I think there is a terrible and largely incorrect scare factor involved in the continued propagation of numbers like these.

Binkin: What you say is true. The "qualified and available" pool excludes college students beyond the second year. That seems to be appropriate because the proportion of kids that the services are attracting out of college is very small. (So, I don't see why one would consider in the normal qualified and available supply pool those kids who go into college when typically they have not been interested in the enlisted status military.) Some who finished college do go on to become officers. One of the current issues is the extent to which the services could attract more of the community college population. Some people feel that may be a fertile field. But as long as policies are in effect whereby you discourage lateral entry, whereby you don't target colleges, and whereby you're not attracting many college youth, I think it is appropriate to exclude that part of the population.

Nelson: I'd like to comment on and support what was said in the audience. Basically, when you remove the college population from the denominator, you're saying that people do not make a decision between going into the military and going to college. That's just plainly wrong. Every person who graduates from high school in this country can be admitted to college. People make trade-offs all the time. Every person that we take in who is in the supply-limited category is one who had the option of going to college and chose to go into the military. To somehow take the college population out of that pool is a mistake.

John Johnston: I think there is also interest in diverting the college population into the military via the GI Bill, or some similar program. After service they go on into a college program. I feel it's a meaningful alternative. The army, principally, is going after that pool and being successful.

Question for William H. Meckling (from Richard Lieberman): You appear to be upset because quality manning constraints are placed on the military by Congress. The only one that I can remember that Congress imposed on DoD was in 1973 when a certain requirement, I think 55% high school diploma graduates, was fought very strongly by everyone in DoD and in the military. It was very important at that time to get the AVF off the ground without filling it up with the wrong kind of people.

Meckling: I didn't mean that the military themselves never suggest things like bonuses. While those kinds of examples are of interest, the fact is that those big numbers, and the budgets themselves, are really determined by Congress. Just take the issue of pay and grade. Does anybody really believe that the military could have much impact if they went to Congress and said they wanted to have a different set of pay and grade relationships for the army than for the air force or the navy? What if they wanted to change the whole basic pay structure? That, in fact, would be a sensible compensation solution to the problem of attracting combat people to the army. It's very simple—the army ought to have a whole different base pay system than the rest of the services. I don't think there's a chance you could sell that, and that's what I mean by things that are imposed by Congress. I think both researchers and people in the business don't look carefully enough at the potential for changing the ability to react to things such as what is going to happen over the next ten years to the size of the eighteen-year-old pool.

Question (from Gen. Jeanne Holm): Would someone address the impact of having available the entire population, including women, on the factors we're talking about here?

Binkin: The cohort analysis is intended to present the issue in a way the general public can understand it, or get scared by it, depending upon who is talking about it. Its purpose is to show, given the present policies, what the magnitude of the task might be, holding everything else constant. What it says is, "if that looks too formidable, there are a lot of options one can look at in order to alleviate the task." Certainly the obvious one, and the one General Holm is raising, is to attract more women. There are other possibilities: substitute more civilians, go to a larger career force, or substitute reserves for active forces. There's a whole list you can go through, but first you must get the attention of policymakers. If we continue doing things the way we're doing them now under current policy, then the number is about right. I should mention, though, that it includes reserve nonprior service-accession requirements as well. Some people would argue that we don't really take the reserves seriously and the calculation should consider active requirements only; in that case it becomes about one in three. The purpose in using this type of analysis is to bring into focus the need for examining alternatives that would make the task less awesome.

Question (from Frank D. Margiotta): One concern I have is that I think there is a national security interest which is a more important determinant of our manpower requirements than pure economics. The second thing that distresses me is that nobody has mentioned the return of the legitimacy of military service. I think this administration has helped that greatly, beyond pay, because they say they care. Psychological aspects may be more important than pay and benefits.

Nelson: I'd like to broaden those comments even further to say that the other major input to national security, at least to combat-ready military forces, is material. We've just gone through an interesting experiment of increasing the defense budget, and we had some increases in end strength, but basically the money has been spent for material rather than people. Money has been spent in terms of higher pay; I think it's well merited and a good decision. But the question is, if you made the defense budget 10% larger, would we have 10% more people in uniform or would we simply have a more modern force with greater sustainability and readiness? I think the vote might well be for the latter.

Question for Stephen E. Herbits (from William Clark): You indicated concern that sabotage of the AVF has taken place over a period of time. I take exception to that, although I clearly acknowledge that there are people who would prefer to have a draft army over a volunteer army, but the proof is that the army has made its AVF goals. Then you went on to comment that you felt the qualitative objectives of the army are irresponsible. My question is, how did you come to that conclusion? Is it a conclusion drawn by your concern about its achievability and therefore perhaps another form of sabotage of the AVF, or is it based on some evaluation of what our qualitative requirements are, particularly in view of some of the comments that Mr. Tarr made earlier?

Herbits: Let me deal with the second part of your question first. What I was talking about was irresponsible projections of quality needs for 1984 through 1987, or perhaps 1989, because they are based on conjecture by the military without the proper validation by skill for what is really needed. The requirements go up disproportionately to any need demonstrated over the last twenty years, and that's why I say the numbers are out of line.

Let me try to answer the first question with a couple of stories. On Friday afternoon the day before the Gates Commission was to present its report to the president, the commissioners had agreed to embargo the report until it was released by the White House after the meeting with the president. I got a call from Dan Rather about two o'clock saying that he had just been handed a draft of the report and he was going to go with it that night (the night before it was to be released), and did I have any comments. I said I couldn't imagine where he got it and was he sure it was a valid report. He said he wasn't, so I asked him to read me the summary of the recommendations, which he did. When I calmed down, I said, "If the only way to stop you from releasing that report is for me to come down to the White House now and give you an exclusive interview as a commissioner and break the embargo, and go and get myself into trouble with everyone, including the president of the United States, I will do it. But what you have been handed is an incredibly outrageous attempt to discredit the Gates Commission." He didn't go with the story. We subsequently had some talks about that afterwards because he and I were both intrigued by what happened. The minor fact that it was delivered by a person in uniform began the inquiry. I won't go into the details of how we found out or who we found out submitted that report, but that kind of activity contributes to the belief that there are people who take actions that are inconsistent with proper behavior and therefore can be called sabotage.

A more dramatic example was when I was privileged to attend a meeting, called in February or March of 1974, with Secretary Clements, the Secretary of the Army, and the Chief of Staff of the Army, then General Abrahams. Many of you may know that Secretary Clements is a rather colorful man and, in the confines of his own office, uses little restraint. That meeting was for one purpose only: to tell those gentlemen that the analysis done for the secretary had revealed a substantial pattern of decisions that demonstrated to him that the senior management of the army was not behaving itself. And he wasn't talking only about people in uniform, but within the Department of the Army. He put a substantial amount of pressure on them to get the AVF back on track and to reverse many of the policies that he termed, mildly, irresponsible. His language was much more colorful than I would dare to repeat, but it was based on a document that was prepared, studied, and analyzed by a number of people in the building. The document exists—whether it is classified or not I don't know—but it exists and it demonstrated what Roger Kelley was most fearful of. It is history and perhaps it is time history became unveiled. If you look at that pattern of behavior, it comes and goes. It is consistent with the beginning of each new administration. The fact is, some people must monitor that behavior because I think we can expect it to continue. There are people who will take active steps to undermine, whether short term or long term, the viability of the AVF by adopting policies that over time, gradually erode the base of how well an AVF will work.

Part III

TECHNOLOGY AND MANPOWER DEMANDS

Introduction

ISSAC C. KIDD, JR.

One of the important, difficult to quantify, and often overlooked aspects of military manpower planning and projection is the actual quality mix needed to efficiently man existing systems. During the next decade, this problem will be made even more perplexing and critical by the scope and magnitude of the new, complicated, and sophisticated weapons systems which are being planned, developed, and added to the inventory.

Chapters 9 through 11 discuss the manpower impacts of the new systems that will become operational in the next decade and attempt to predict the effect of these systems on the number and type of people needed in the enlisted force. In general, the authors predict a very modest need for more manpower (less than 5%) despite a much larger (percentage wise) increase in new systems. However, the new systems and those being developed do imply a major shift toward occupations which require higher test scores and more training, i.e., higher personnel quality. Gen. William E. DePuy makes a convincing argument that the most cost-effective way for the army to improve system effectiveness is to invest in a higher-quality force, not enhanced equipment performance. Robert J. Murray makes similar comparisons for the navy and points out that the military services build rather than hire their technicians. Thus a large part of the problem posed by more sophisticated, complex systems must be addressed by the training commands. Gen. John W. Roberts, who addresses the air force quality requirements, expresses concerns about changing institutional values and assuming that the reserve force, with its part-time status, could be expected to perform the same missions as the active force. He also suggests that DoD should be training generalists who would be more able to adapt and learn instead of pursuing the current trend toward more narrow specialty-specific training.

There appears to be the growing appreciation that personnel quality and training are as important to operational effectiveness as hardware capabilities. Closer integration is needed. There is, additionally, a general consensus that not enough attention is being paid to the likelihood that new training technologies can markedly assist in bridging the gap between the quality of the force and the operational requirements of our systems.

8 Technology and Manpower: Army Perspective

WILLIAM E. DEPUY

STRENGTH, STRUCTURE, AND HIGH TECHNOLOGY

Projections of the overall strength of an all-volunteer army show that, short of hostilities, it is not expected to change much in the next few years. In the event of hostilities a draft will be required. Although its size will remain about the same, the internal structure of the army will change as new systems arrive and as their impact and opportunities are translated into new or modified tables of organizations and equipment (TO&E). The external structure of the army in terms of the number of divisions and their types may also change somewhat, but the major impact on personnel requirements will stem from support and operation of new weapons and equipment.

In the discussion below, three major dimensions to the manning of new systems are explored: effects on operators, maintainers, and tactical and technical leaders. While it is not necessary to itemize all of the new systems being introduced to convey the personnel-requirements impact in the army, some of the systems which portend enormous effect on certain categories of soldiers are shown below:

Name	System
M-1	Tank
M-2	Infantry fighting vehicle
AH-64	Attack helicopter
PATRIOT*	Air Defense Missile System
TPQ-37*	Artillery locating radar
Battery Computer*	Artillery fire direction
MLRS	Multiple rocket system
DIVAD*	Self-propelled air defense
ASAS*	All source intelligence fusion
SIGMA*	Automated C3
JSTARS*	Airborne MTI radar

Those systems with an asterisk are characterized by their utter dependence upon electronic data processors. Some, like ASAS and SIGMA, are 80% to 90% software-intensive. All the systems listed place heavy requirements on maintenance and other support and they will have major effects on the quality and quantity of soldiers needed to fill the demand for operators, maintainers, and tactical and technical leaders.

We are now beginning to see the impact of these systems on the manning requirements. Table 8.1 shows the expected increases and decreases by function over the period from FY1983 to FY1990. The combat requirements are contracting and the combat support is expanding. These changes will alter the relative sizes of the three groups during this time period as is illustrated by Figure 8.1.

Figure 8.1. Relative Size by Army Functions, FY1983 and FY1990

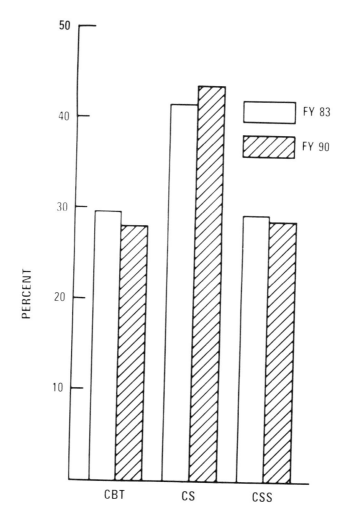

Additionally, Figure 8.2 shows that over the seven year period, combat support is expected to increase at over 1% a year, a rate much faster than other groups. One result is that the Signal Corps, the second largest group in the army after the infantry, is projected to become the largest by 1990.

Table 8.1. Changing Nature of the Army Manning Requirements, FY1983-FY1990

| Area | Total Increment/Decrement FY1983-FY1989 | | | |
	OFF	WO	ENL	Total
Air Defense	− 28	+ 26	− 1031	− 1033
Armor	− 17	—	− 2376	− 2393
Aviation	+ 393	+ 714	+ 1007	+ 2114
Field Artillery	+ 269	+ 33	+ 3296	+ 3598
Infantry	− 68	—	− 5845	− 5913
Spec Opns Forces[1]	(+ 600)	(+ 227)	(+ 3046)	(+ 3873)
Combat Arms (CBT) Subtotal	1149	1000	− 1903	+ 246
Commo/Elec	+ 248	+ 26	+ 4336	+ 4610
Engineer	+ 131	+ 39	− 1369	− 1199
Military Intel	+ 560	+ 198	+ 2852	+ 3610
MP	+ 87	—	− 613	− 526
Ordnance	+ 263	+ 129	+ 6240	+ 6632
Combat Support (CS) Subtotal	1289	392	11446	13127
Quartermaster	+ 300	+ 124	+ 4217	+ 4641
Soldier Spt	+ 104	+ 3	− 3653	− 3546
Transportation	+ 72	+ 2	+ 1999	+ 2073
Chemical[2]	—	—	—	—
Medical	—	—	—	—
Combat Service Support (CSS) Subtotal	476	129	2563	3168
Total[3]	2914	1521	12106	16541

[1] 600 commissioned officer and 227 warrant officer increases in special operations has not been decremented from other areas.
[2] Change is not available as of this date.
[3] Total overstated by 827 commissioned officer/warrant officer positions as stated above.

Figure 8.2. Percentage Change in Manning Requirements by Army Functions from FY1983 to FY1990

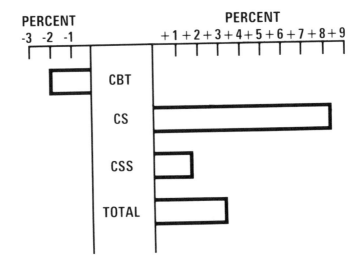

ANALYSIS—QUALITY VERSUS SCHOOL PREREQUISITES

When the movement from combat to combat support is examined in terms of the military occupational specialities (MOS) required, the primary impact noted is a shift toward occupations which necessitate higher prerequisite aptitude area scores for school training. While it may be fair to ask whether school prerequisites are a reasonable measure of on-the-job performance, the frank answer, at this time, is that we can only assume there is a positive correlation because hard data are limited. Meanwhile, we accept school prerequisites as an indicator of success in training because they have been established by the Training and Doctrine Command (TRAOC) on the basis of course attrition data.

Further, if we assume that training tasks, conditions, and standards have been developed through competent front-end analysis, one may expect a meaningful connection between training and later on-the-job performance. Thus, in the following analysis and discussion Armed Forces Qualification Test (AFQT) categories and aptitude area scores are used as surrogates for quality when we investigate relationships between quality and performance.

Table 8.2. Prerequisites Aptitude Area Scores

MOS	Title	Aptitude Area Prereq.	Authorizations FY83	Authorizations FY90	Deltas No.	Deltas %
11C	Indirect Fire Infantryman	CO 85	11261	8243	-3019	- 27
11H	Hv Anti-Armor Infantryman	CO 85	7573	6491	-1082	- 14
19D	Cavalry Scout	CO 85	9847	9434	- 413	- 4
19E	M48-M60 Crewman	CO 85	15014	5295	-9719	- 65
19K	M1 ABRAMS Crewman	CO 85	2772	10822	8050	290
35C	Automatic Test Equip Rpr	EL 110	60	256	196	327
05C	RTT Operator	SC 100	7559	8906	1347	18
26Q	TAC SAT Microwave Syst Opr	EL 95	1150	2042	892	78
31V	TAC COM Syst Opr/Mech	EL 95	5721	6190	469	8
26Y	SAT Com Equip Rpr	EL 120	672	896	244	36
31Z	Comm-Elect Opns Chief	Non Acc*	1862	1961	99	5
32D	Station Tech Controller	EL 105	1049	1364	315	30
36H	Dial/Manual Central Office Rpr	EL 100	1084	1244	160	15
36L	Electronic Switch Syst Rpr	EL 110	283	470	187	66
34Y	FA Computer Rpr	EL 95	228	358	130	57

*Non Accession MOS

Table 8.2 shows the aptitude area prerequisites for a set of combat MOSs in the top portion and combat support MOSs in the bottom part. Authorized manning levels for FY1983 and FY1990 by MOS are shown here and depicted graphically in Figure 8.3. Cursory inspection of the table and figure reveals that decreases are expected in MOSs with low prerequisites (that is, easy to fill positions) and increases are expected in MOSs with high prerequisites (that is, hard to fill positions). Not included in Table 8.2 are a number of military intelligence MOSs with prerequisites as high as 120 in electronic (EL) and skill technical (ST) aptitudes. During the period up to FY1990, there is a requirement for 3,610 soldiers in this category. The difficulty in meeting these prerequisites is made clear by the fact that in 1983 they were manned at only 66% of authorized strength.

Figure 8.3. Effects of Selected MOS Quantity Increases on Quality Requirements

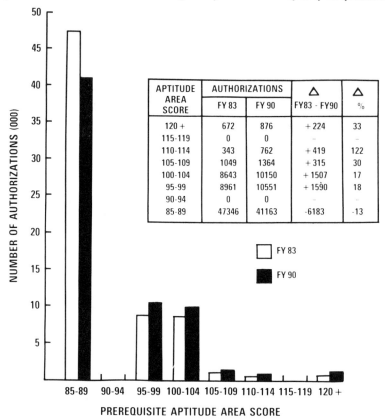

| APTITUDE AREA SCORE | AUTHORIZATIONS | | Δ | Δ |
	FY 83	FY 90	FY83 - FY90	%
120 +	672	876	+ 224	33
115-119	0	0	-	-
110-114	343	762	+ 419	122
105-109	1049	1364	+ 315	30
100-104	8643	10150	+ 1507	17
95-99	8961	10551	+ 1590	18
90-94	0	0	-	-
85-89	47346	41163	-6183	-13

Table 8.3. Relationship of AFQT to Other Measures*

Mental Category	AFQT Percentile	General Technical	Reading Grade Level	Level of Trainability
I	93-99	129-155	12.7-12.9	Well Above Average
II	64-92	110-128	10.6-12.6	Above Average
IIIA	50-63	100-109	9.3-10.5	Average
IIIB	31-49	90-99	8.1-9.2	Average
IV	16-30	75-89	6.6-8.0	Below Average
V	3-15	52-74	3.4-6.5	Well Below Average

*By law, no mental category Vs and no more than 20% mental category IVs in an accession year.

Historically we have used the AFQT as a means of qualifying individuals for military service and for dividing soldiers into mental categories for the purpose of assignment to schools and MOSs. Table 8.3 illustrates how mental categories are related to percentiles and to other quality measures including general technical aptitude scores, reading level, and trainability.

A portrayal of mental category requirements based not only on school prerequisites, but also on quality requirements for higher skill levels (leaders or supervisors in the same or derivative

MOS), is contained in Figure 8.4 in which current quality requirements and those projected for FY1990 are compared with the current inventory. Notice that current shortfalls in the upper mental categories (I-IIIA) are over 30% and, considering structure changes, approach 40%. In the lower mental category (IV) the inventory exceeds the requirement by over 60%.

Figure 8.4. Present Versus Future Total Army Quality
Requirements, FY1983 and FY1990

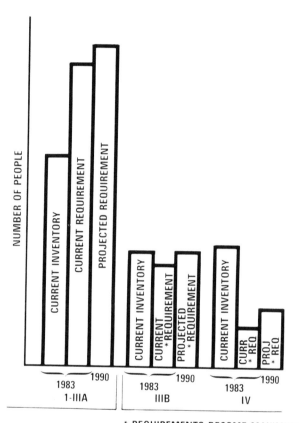

* REQUIREMENTS BECOME MAXIMUM
ACCEPTABLE LIMIT

The obvious question, and one addressed in chapter 11, is whether the future inventory will match future requirements. In order to assess the magnitude of the problem, Figures 8.5, 8.6 and 8.7 compare FY1983 inventory with expected FY1990 requirements in the component categories of combat (Figure 8.5), combat support (Figure 8.6), and combat service support (Figure 8.7). The pattern, and hence the relative magnitude of the problem, generally is the same in each area. But there is one apparent anomaly: the combat category shows a decreasing requirement for quality in 1990. This anomaly results from a quantity decrease in combat arms as a whole which masks an actual quality requirement increase.

A major reason for the imbalances shown in the figures is that the new systems and product improvement of existing systems are creating a boom in the communication-electronics (COMM-ELEC) maintenance area. Increases are not just in the number of systems but in the density of equipment within systems. An example of the potential problem can be gleaned from

Table 8.4, which indicates that some 249,000 major items of COMM-ELEC equipment will be added by FY1989. These equipment additions, of course, will drive personnel requirements. For example, Figure 8.8 shows the present inventory and future requirements in one important COMM-ELEC area, career management field 29 (communication and electronic maintenance). Note the small requirement for people in the lower mental categories.

Table 8.4. Introduction of Major Items of Comm-Elect Equipment

Functional Area	FY83	FY84	FY85	FY86	FY87	FY88	FY89	Total
Data	142	1,309	1,483	1,634	1,630	698	1,116	8,012
Avionics	927	2,539	2,638	4,836	4,264	3,542	1,982	20,728
Comsec	25,855	177	4,158	3,759	3,167	3,867	3,688	44,671
TMDE	121	71	311	137	4	1	0	645
Control	1	3	29	13	13	30	0	89
Trucking	656	785	3,769	6,485	13,766	22,963	20,169	68,593
Terminal	1,040	3,576	5,461	5,249	4,424	4,893	5,137	29,780
Switching	15	32	15	56	72	278	389	857
Miscellaneous	3	11,325	11,480	6,544	3,518	20,346	22,684	75,900
Total	28,760	19,817	29,344	28,713	30,858	56,618	55,165	249,275

Figure 8.5. Present Versus Future Combat Arms Quality Requirements, FY1983 and FY1990

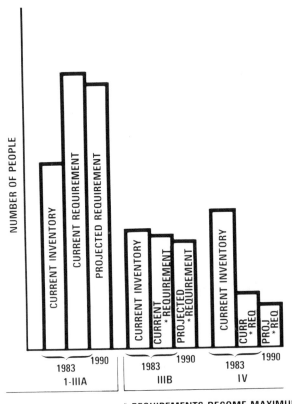

* REQUIREMENTS BECOME MAXIMUM
ACCEPTABLE LIMIT

Figure 8.6. Present Versus Future Combat Support Quality Requirements, FY1983 and FY1990

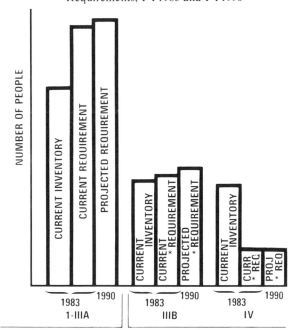

Figure 8.7. Present Versus Future Combat Service Support Quality Requirements, FY1983 and FY1990

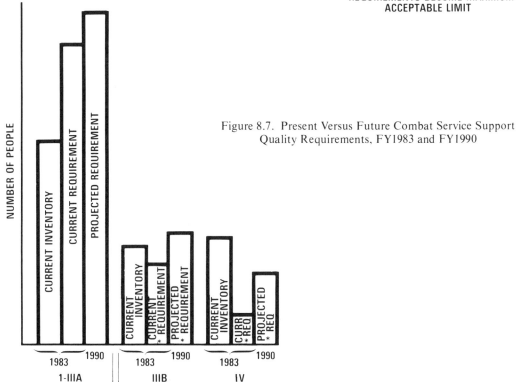

Figure 8.8. Career Management Field 29
(Communications and Electronic Maintenance)

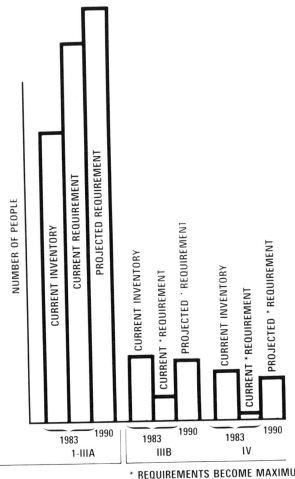

* REQUIREMENTS BECOME MAXIMUM
ACCEPTABLE LIMIT

Parallel with increased requirements in COMM-ELEC maintenance has come a realization that "Face Plate" diagnostics (BITE [built in test equipment], etc.) haven't worked very well. Faults arrive in pesky combinations which defeat the diagnostic algorithms. Trouble shooting by the repairman then is required. A return to "theory based" maintenance training would be shockingly expensive and probably would move the AFQT prerequisites up another 10 to 15 points. Unfortunately, the variety of equipment also overwhelms the training base. In the case of MOS 31J (teletypewriter repairer) the school course covers only 13 items of equipment while the MOS covers 153 items.

In summary, we have said or implied that in the future:

- Fewer soldiers will be required in combat areas, and more in combat support and combat service support;
- Combat operator jobs will not be much more difficult, and sometimes will be easier (e.g., laser range-finders);
- More and more difficult electronic maintenance will be required.

ANALYSIS—QUALITY VERSUS EXPLOITATION OF NEW SYSTEMS

Even if recruiters are able to meet the prerequisites set by the trainers and meet the MOS requirements by aptitude and mental category, how closely will we exploit the full potential of the new weapons and equipment we are building? The short-term answer is not very close.

Let us assume that system performance P_s is the product of equipment performance, P_e, and human performance, P_h. That is $P_h \times P_e = P_s$. We may also note that operational testing often measures only operability and suitability instead of the performance of the system in the hands of the typical operators and maintainers. Figure 8.9 shows the relationships between P_e (inherent performance of the equipment) on the ordinate and P_h (performance of the operators) on the abscissa together with P_s (performance of the whole man/machine system) shown as a series of performance curves which are convex to the origin and pertain to the system as a whole.

Figure 8.9. Graphic Display of System Performance Equation

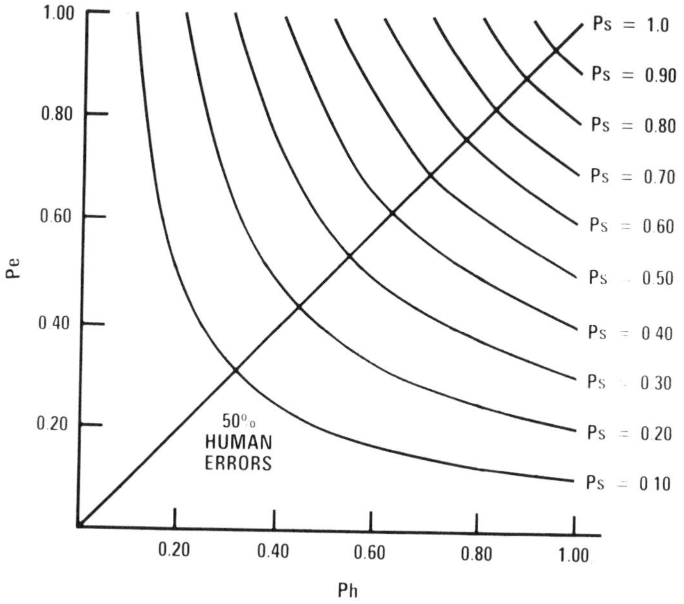

$P_e \times P_h = P_s$

P_s = SYSTEM PERFORMANCE
P_e = EQUIPMENT PERFORMANCE
P_h = HUMAN PERFORMANCE

Consider the STINGER as an example using the approach above. The design P_e for STINGER was .80 while the design P_s was .64. From the curves, we find that a P_h of .80 would be required to reach a system performance level of .64. It turns out however, that the P_h of a tested cohort of MOS 16P (air defense short range missile crewmen) averaged .55 instead of the required .80 (Table 8.5). Human performance at the .55 level drags the system performance down to .44 (P_e of .80 × P_h of .55 = P_s of .44), a 30% decrease in expected system effectiveness. Parenthetically, the added cost of STINGER over REDEYE is about $1.7 billion. A 30% loss of expected performance implies a $500 million decrease in the return on investment (ROI). We will not dwell on the fact that the P_e also came down 30%, further decreasing P_s and ROI.

Table 8.5. STINGER Human Performance Characteristics

Mental Category	Performance of TRASANA Sample	MOS 16P Current Force	Human Performance Factor
I-IIIA	.67	.29	.19
IIIB	.52	.28	.15
IV	.48	.43	.21
Total			.55

Unfortunately we do not have human performance data on many current or projected systems. Therefore we instinctively turn to skill qualification tests (SQT) as a surrogate for on-the-job performance. In the case of STINGER we have been able to compare actual data on critical task performance collected by TRASANA using SQT data. That comparison is depicted in Figure 8.10. The SQT pass rate plotted by AFQT mental categories is the top curve. Note that a soldier can pass the SQT by correctly answering (or performing) 60% or more of the questions/tasks. Therefore the raw score curve is more meaningful. Notice also that the median spread between the SQT raw score and TRASANA task performance score (actual operational tasks) is 10 to 15 points and that the SQT is higher. Obviously there is no precise numerical correlation but there is numerical symmetry.

With the STINGER example in mind, and although it is based on the narrowest of samples, we can look at some additional SQT scores and performance relationships. Recall that all SQTs are based on critical task analysis and are administered under controlled conditions against common standards at the various skill levels for each MOS. To the extent that the front-end task

Figure 8.10. MOS 16P Performance Data

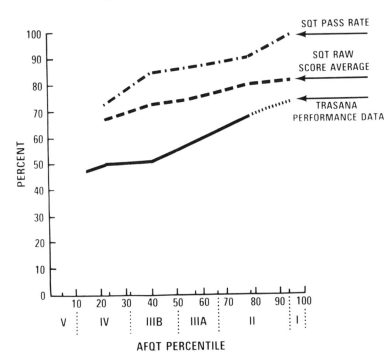

analysis has been done competently and the tests fairly represent the tasks, the SQT should stand alone as a rough measure of expected performance. The STINGER example, however, tells us that actual performance on the system may fall below SQT scoring by 15-20%.

One interesting and critical MOS is TOW gunners (MOS 11H). Table 8.6 shows their SQT raw score averages and a weighted average score based on the current force. Using the calculated P_h of .70 multiplied by an estimated P_e of .90, the estimated P_s is .63. Most war game models have used a single shot kill probability (SSKP) of .90 for TOW. If our data are correct, we could never exceed a system performance level of .77 even if we assigned only mental category I soldiers as TOW gunners. This is tantamount to putting a lieutenant on each weapon.

Table 8.6. TOW Performance (MOS 11H)

Mental Category	Average SQT Raw Score	Composition of Current Force	Weighted Average
I	.86		
II	.75	.48	
IIIA	.71		
IIIB	.67	.28	
IV	.63	.24	
			.70

Two additional examples are presented and they can be abbreviated. The raw SQT scores of armor crewmen (MOS 19E) in the current force can be averaged and weighted giving a figure of .66 (Table 8.7). With human performance at .66, even if equipment performance were in the 90% bracket, battlefield effectiveness (P_s) would be around a .60 or a 30% shortfall when compared to equipment potential. Last, looking at maintainers, consider the case of TOW/DRAGON Repairers (MOS 27E). Table 8.8 shows human performance weighted by SQT raw scores averages in the current force to be .54. Thus, in our limited examples, we find human performance in the current force of operators ranges between .55 and .70 while maintainers appear to be on the low end of the range.

Turning to leadership positions, and first to tank commanders (MOS 19E-Skill Level 3), we find that the assumed level of system performance is approximately .80. SQT averages in the current force are .68 (Table 8.9). It is obvious that in order to reach the assumed P_s level, the required P_e would have to be over 100%. (An interesting challenge!)

A second leadership position that we can examine is that of infantry squad leader. Table 8.10 shows an expected human performance figure of .80 for these individuals. Compounding the human performance findings for both leadership positions and operators (above), is the STINGER example which suggests that all of these weighted values derived from SQT's may be 15% to 20% too high!

Table 8.7. Armor Crewman Performance (MOS 19E)

Mental Category	Average SQT Raw Score	Composition of Current Force	Weighted Average
I-IIIA	71	.42	
IIIB	65	.27	
IV	61	.31	
			.66

Table 8.8. TOW/DRAGON Repairer Performance (MOS 27E)

Mental Category	SQT Raw Score Average	Composition of Current Force	Weighted Average
I-IIIA	59	.54	
IIIB	49	.27	
IV	48	.19	
			.54

Table 8.9. Tank Commander Performance (MOS 19E)

Mental Category	Raw Scores	Composition of Skill Level 3 (E6) Current Force	Weighted Average
I-IIIA	.71	.54	
IIIB	.65	.30	
IV	.61	.16	
			.68

Table 8.10. Infantry Squad Leader Performance (MOS 11B)

Mental Category	Sample SQT Average Score	Composition of Skill Level 3 (E6) Current Force	Weighted Average
I-IIIA	82	.49	
IIIB	80	.32	
IV	74	.19	
			.80

What could this mean to force performance even if we assume the most optimistic view of human performance? Relying on the data available from this very rough analysis and the limited examples shown here, plus some others, we find human performance ranges between .53 and .63 for operators, .44 and .64 for maintainers, and .64 and .74 for leaders. These three measurements of human performance could logically be multiplied together to arrive at an estimate of human performance for the system. The total effect is enormous. For example, the higher range of P_h would multiply out to a $P_h = .25$ thus degrading a .90 for equipment performance to a system performance level of .23. Whether these numbers are precise or not is beside the point. From the standpoint of force performance, P_h is the driver. The best leverage available for increasing force performance lies in the selection (recruiting), training, assignment, and retention of high quality personnel.

OVERALL CONCLUSIONS

1. With the current inventory of personnel the army cannot meet the training prerequisites established by its schools.
2. The MOS requirements for quality personnel are not being met either for skill-level one tasks or for skill-level two and three selection and training.
3. Operator performance falls substantially below the levels assumed and required to produce and man/machine system performance expected during development and acquisition.

4. Operator performance falls below the levels required to exploit the potentials inherent in the systems being deployed.
5. By internalizing operator functions in electronic processors, complexity at the maintenance level has increased. The required number of maintainers and their required skill levels have increased well beyond the quantity and quality inventory.
6. Leader/supervisor quality has not been measured in this analysis except tangentially (tank commanders and squad leaders), but we know intuitively that full tactical and technical exploitation of new system capabilities (e.g., M-1 tank—intelligence fusion) will be even more difficult to reach than operator/maintainer performance.
7. Man/machine system performance is very sensitive to personnel quality and so too, therefore, is force performance. Raising force quality through selection and training probably equals or surpasses the leverage of improved technology on the battlefield.
8. The best leverage available for increasing force performance lies in the selection (recruiting), training, assignment, and retention of high-quality personnel.

One of the important, difficult to quantify, and often overlooked aspects of military manpower planning and projection is the actual quality mix needed to efficiently man existing systems. During the next decade, this problem will be made even more perplexing and critical by the scope and magnitude of the new, complicated, and sophisticated weapons systems which are being planned, developed, and added to the inventory.

9   Technology and Manpower: Navy Perspective*

ROBERT J. MURRAY

This chapter assesses future manpower requirements of the navy and Marine Corps as a result of force-structure changes and the impact of technology and new systems. Also, this chapter examines the history of the last twenty years in force structure and technology for clues to this next decade.

Force structure establishes the broad parameters of manpower demand. The much-advertised 600-ship goal of the present naval building program, up from about 478 ships in 1978, carries with it an inevitable additional increment of manpower. This is particularly so because the 600-ship navy being built is a navy in which, on average, the individual ships are larger than their predecessors, and also because it is a navy formed around fifteen aircraft carriers, rather than the thirteen carriers of 1978, and modern carriers, despite occasional hopes to the contrary, are big ships.

In less obvious but still fundamental ways, technology is creating its own manpower demand. The navy relies increasingly on technological advantage for war-fighting success, and maintaining technological advantage is requiring increasing numbers of higher-skilled people.

A discussion of naval missions will follow, for it is missions that shape, or ought to shape, the force structure, technology, and manpower demand, and missions which provide the criteria for judging their adequacy.

---

*In preparing this chapter, the author has been helped by the information kindly provided by the Department of the Navy, and by conversations with thoughtful and experienced navy and marine officers and civilian officials. Responsibility for the use of the information, however, and for errors of omission or commission, lie exclusively with the author.

NAVAL FORCES IN NATIONAL STRATEGY

There are four missions for naval forces in support of national strategy. The first mission is comparatively new, the remaining three are traditional naval missions.

The first mission is to contribute to nuclear deterrence by deploying ballistic missile submarines of a quality sufficient to prevent them from being targeted by Soviet weapons systems. This is a responsibility of enormous consequence and increasing importance as land-based ICBM systems lose their relative invulnerability.

The second mission is flying the flag and signaling American readiness to act in those areas of the world in which the United States has interests and commitments but where other kinds of forces—army and air forces—are politically inappropriate or practically inconvenient. Among recent examples are U.S. naval presence in the Indian Ocean in 1979-1980 and in the Caribbean today.

A third mission is responding to crises and smaller-scale combat, the "short-of-war" actions such as the Cuban missile crisis in 1962, the Lebanon crisis in 1982-1983, or the Grenada intervention in 1983. Of course, naval forces are not the only forces to be used in a crisis, nor are they appropriate for all crises, but history is replete with examples of their use for this purpose. They are used in this way more than other forces, and such use influences navy and marine force structure and weapons systems.

The fourth mission is to employ naval forces in helping deter or, if necessary, fight a general war. The "proper" role for naval forces in general war is controversial outside the navy, and it is not the purpose of this chapter to debate that role, only to state what, in the author's opinion, are the underlying premises in naval planning for this mission.

Naval forces in war have two main tasks, both of an offensive character: to sink the enemy navy wherever it is to be found, in this way to protect the sea lines of communication and, to permit no threatening naval force at war's end; and to help achieve a favorable outcome in key land-air battles, particularly on NATO's flanks and in the Pacific. Both tasks would be accomplished in conjunction with other U.S. forces and with the Allies.

In addition, there would be at least three other important war tasks: (1) assuring the continuing security of the ballistic missile submarine force; (2) safely transporting the equipment and supplies of deployed combat forces, which would be crucial for the land combat (90% of all war material would move by sea, and as an equipment-poor alliance, we could not afford to lose much); and (3) maintaining forces for the unexpected contingencies that could still arise in a condition of general war.

From this general discussion of naval missions, we may draw two conclusions for the purposes of this chapter. First, the need for technological superiority is indispensable for success in the nuclear deterrent and general war missions, but also important for the other missions where the possibility arises of combat against less powerful but still dangerous opponents. This was illustrated by Great Britain, the Falklands and by numerous Arab-Israeli engagements and, in a more modest way, even by the brief encounter between U.S. Navy and Libyan aircraft in 1981.

Second, the four missions overlap in their consequences for force structure. The peacetime and wartime tasks merge, and it is difficult to separate the force-structure implications of one mission from the other. We do not decide on numbers of aircraft carriers, for example, solely on the basis of what would be needed in general war. The shortage of aircraft carriers noticed in 1979-1980 was not caused by general war considerations, but by the breadth of our peacetime commitments and concerns—in Admiral Hayward's phrase, "a one-and-a-half ocean navy to meet a three-ocean commitment." Assessments of naval force need necessarily take into account all four missions.

NAVY FORCE STRUCTURE

From the end of World War II, when the active fleet numbered more than 8,000 ships, until 1964 when there were just under 1,000 ships in active service, the U.S. Navy was without naval peer. Since 1964, the Soviet Navy has been visibly improving, and the signs of serious competition are unmistakable if not overwhelming. These improvements in Soviet naval capabilities were occurring, moreover, while the U.S. Navy was shrinking in ship numbers, if not equally in capability. Table 9.1 shows the changes in ship force levels occurring in the last two decades.

Table 9.1. Active Navy and Early Mobilizing Reserve Ships

	FY1964	FY1978	FY1983
Warships	484	295	338
Amphibious Ships	133	67	65
Auxiliary Ships	251	110	78
Mine Warfare Ships	85	3	3
Patrol Combatants	6	3	6
Total Active and Early Mobilizing Ships	959	478	490

Note: Table includes all active ships and reserve ships in Mobilization Forces Category A.

Sources: For 1964 and 1978 data, Department of the Navy publication, "Ship Forces of the U.S. Navy—Historical Force Levels by Category Type," December 6, 1982; for 1983 data, Department of the Navy publication, "Listing of U.S. Naval Ship Battle Forces (as of 31 August 1983)," August 31, 1983. In addition, in FY1983 there are twenty-seven civilian-manned ships of the Naval Fleet Auxiliary Force in support of the active fleet.

The growing Soviet naval capabilities and the shrinking American fleet were not enough, by themselves, to win support for an expanded naval force structure. Support for a larger navy grew out of the Middle East melee of 1976-1980: Soviet and Cuban military support for revolution in Ethiopia, the consistent bellicosity of Libya's Khaddafi, the fall of the Shah of Iran, the seizing of American Embassy staff in Tehran, the attack by South Yemen on North Yemen with its implicit threat to Saudi Arabia and potential consequences for Persian Gulf security, and the Soviet invasion of Afghanistan. These events reminded Americans of wider interests and dangers and brought American naval forces to the Indian Ocean in strength for the first time, overtaxing the force structure and shaping the Reagan campaign promise to build a 600-ship navy, a program on which the administration is now embarked.

Ship numbers do not tell the whole force-structure story, however. At least two other factors are important. The first factor is the mix of ship types. The number of warships, for example, is usually more significant for measuring fleet capabilities than the total number of ships, for while one can imagine pressing civilian ships into military service to provide logistic support in an emergency, as the British did for the Falklands, it is not similarly possible to acquire additional warships quickly. And, as Table 9.1 shows, warships decreased less markedly than other ships (39% compared to 63%) from 1964 to 1978.

Ship displacement is the second important factor, for, in general, larger ships pack more combat punch than smaller ones. Ship displacement trends are shown in Table 9.2.

We see from Tables 9.1 and 9.2 that, while ship numbers were reduced more than 50% between 1964 and 1978, fleet tonnage fell only 17% and warship tonnage only 10%. Also by 1983, warship tonnage exceeded (by 11%) the 1964 tonnage.

What of future force structure? What can we anticipate about the 600-ship navy? Well, we know the administration intends the 600 ships to be in place by 1990. We know also it is being constructed along present lines, that is, no new philosophies of warfare are envisaged (it will not,

Table 9.2. Ship Tonnage, Active Navy Ships (In Thousands of Tons)

	FY1964	FY1978	FY1983
Warships	2,170	1,950	2,400
Amphibious Ships	700	600	650
Auxiliary Ships	1,110	800	680
Mine Warfare Ships	67	2	2
Patrol Combatants	1	1	1
Total Ship Tonnage	4,048	3,353	3,733

Source: Author's estimates based on sources listed in Table 9.1 and published design displacement for each class ship in the active force. (Table 9.2 does not include reserve ships or civilian-manned ships.)

for example, emphasize frigates or small carriers or surface effects ships, or other low cost variants occasionally recommended). We know it will be built around fifteen large aircraft carriers, and will include four modernized battleships. We know from construction programs already authorized by Congress that it will include additional Trident ballistic-missile submarines, more *Los Angeles*-class nuclear attack submarines, further new *Ticonderoga*-class cruisers, the beginning increment of a new class of guided-missile destroyers, more FFG-7 frigates, a new class of mine warfare ships, and additional amphibious and auxiliary ships of types already under construction. We may assume it will also include the early-mobilizing reserve mobilization forces category A ships (of which there are nine ships in FY1983), even though these are not part of the active fleet, and also the twenty-seven civilian-manned support ships under Military Sealift Command direction that service the active fleet. So, while we do not know the precise composition of the 600-ship navy, we do know a lot about it; enough, in fact, to estimate the approximate additions to fleet composition between now and 1990 (see Table 9.3).

Thus, in the quarter-century between 1964 and 1990, navy force structure will have been transformed from a large number of ships of relatively smaller individual size, to a smaller number of ships of greater total capacity. Specifically, there will be about one-third fewer ships in 1990 than in 1964, but fleet capacity (tonnage) in 1990 will exceed by 15% to 20% the capacity of 1964. In the process of transition, the lingering effects of World War II technology, so prominent a part of the 1964 fleet, will have disappeared by 1990.

Table 9.3. Changes in Fleet Composition, 1984-1990

	Additional	
	Ships	Tons (in Thousands)
Warships	43	600
Amphibious Ships	10	250
Auxiliary Ships	22	125
Mine Warfare Ships	10	10
Patrol Combatants	0	0
Total Additional Ships/Tons	85	985

Source: Author's estimates.

TECHNOLOGY AND THE NAVY

The navy is a technical service, and the importance of technology to the success of naval forces grows steadily in importance. Gone is the day when the order of battle is the principal measure of a navy. Now it is much less the ship itself than what is in the ship that counts; and increasingly, what is in the ship that counts is electronic.

There has been occurring for much of this century, but especially in the last quarter-century, another of those periodic technological revolutions that cause fundamental change in the character of naval warfare and naval forces, comparable in significance to the replacement of sail by steam, and the introduction of the airplane and the submersible ship. It is the electronic revolution.

The electronic revolution, particularly through advances in high-speed data processing, has increased the effectiveness of defending forces and improved the penetrability of attacking forces. The U.S. Navy is ahead of its Soviet opposite number in both areas, and the competition to retain this technological edge is intense.

The electronic revolution, by vastly increasing the speed of communications, has altered the relationship between political superiors and military subordinates, and between higher military commands and lower echelons. Decisions about naval operations are now much more a matter of central determination, and fleet commanders now have available a far fuller brief of relevant intelligence and other information important to their tactical planning and maneuvering than was ever the case before.

Technology has also changed the scale of naval warfare. Increasingly, naval forces can bring power to bear at longer ranges, and are influential over wider and deeper portions of the prospective battlefield. Examples of this are the greater range and durability of combat aircraft and the fighter/tanker combination, the changed role of submarines as a result of nuclear propulsion, and the consequences for tactical forces of rapidly received intelligence from long-distance detection systems. Battle can now be joined at distances far from the ship, as targets are first identified at hundreds, and in certain instances, through cooperative systems, at thousands of miles away, and engaged entirely by electronic eye and ear. Off-board systems, such as land or air-based radar, satellite communications systems, and fixed-wing aircraft, are now able to make influential contributions to the maritime campaign.

Technology imposes on the navy in two interacting ways: first, in the many environments in which naval forces must operate—on the sea, under the sea, in the air, on land and over land, in space—the physics of which are often different in each case; and second, in the countertechnology mounted by the Soviet Union—the speed and quietness of Soviet submarines and torpedoes, the range and other characteristics of their aircraft and missiles, the quality of their targeting systems, etc. Both nature and the potential foe must be mastered.

Maintaining the technological edge is not simply a matter of ensuring better individual systems such as better missiles, farther-seeing radar, or quieter submarines, although these are essential. It is also a matter of linking the individual systems in a way that achieves a synergistic result and improves battlefield performance. In addition, for the commander, there is a dimension beyond technology: he must combine new technology with new and imaginative tactics. New technology must be a cause for rethinking existing tactics. This in itself is an intellectual and organizational challenge of considerable proportion.

Technology only occasionally descends on the navy, like Moses from the mountain; mainly it creeps into the navy: constantly, persistently, and inexorably, it moves into the training base, into the force structure, into daily operations. Outwardly, ship and aircraft appear the same, but inwardly they are always changing. The navy's technological pot is always boiling, and the cumulative effects are great, including a new model helicopter with new anti-submarine warfare (ASW) systems, a new towed array behind the destroyer, a new computer to link the several sonar systems, a new communications system that lessens the consequences of battle damage, a new data link between radar and gun, a new aircraft engine that increases fighter range, a new carrier landing system that reduces aircraft loss rates, a new black box that provides an improved antijamming capability, a more accurate missile system, a quieter submarine, a new satellite down link. The list is lengthy, and additions frequent.

The march of technology is so steady, involves such a wide variety of separate technologies over the whole range of naval activities, and occurs during such a prolonged period, that estimating its consequences for manpower at any given moment is an uncertain undertaking.

MANNING THE FUTURE NAVY

Both technology and force structure are affecting manpower demand. Is technology pushing ahead faster than the navy's ability to man the force with qualified people? Does technology at least reduce the total manpower needed, even if it requires more highly skilled people? What is the level of additional manpower required by the force-structure increases? These are the questions examined in this section.

Expansion of the force structure, or the filling out of the 600-ship navy, is naturally adding to total manpower requirements, and technology is requiring people of higher skills. Table 9.4 illustrates both points in comparing estimates of FY1984 and FY1990 manpower requirements.

As seen in Table 9.4, highly technical ratings are growing at a faster rate than is the total force (9% compared with 5%). This is a trend that has been underway at least since World War II. Figure 9.1 demonstrates the point with respect to the destroyer and frigate force.

Table 9.4. Navy Manpower Requirements (In Thousands)

	FY1984	FY1990	% Increase
Officers	76.5	79.9	4
Petty Officers	381.4	401.4	5
Highly Technical	(75.4)	(82.5)	9
Technical	(207.0)	(217.0)	5
SemiTechnical	(99.0)	(101.9)	3
Other Enlisted	195.3	204.1	5
Total Requirements	653.2	685.5	5

Source: Office of the Chief of Naval Personnel, from data in the Naval Manpower Planning System (NAMPS).

Figure 9.1. High Tech Manning of Destroyers and Frigates

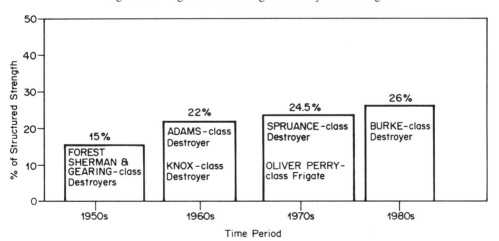

Source: Office of the Chief of Naval Personnel.

But Figure 9.1 also suggests that the process has slowed over time. This slowing process is confirmed in Table 9.4, in which the relationship of highly technical personnel to total personnel changes only modestly (an increase of 1%) between 1984 and 1990.

Table 9.5 shows the distribution of highly technical ratings among the warfare communities. As shown, about 50% of the ratings in the warfare communities are in aviation, about 30% in surface warfare, and 20% in submarines. (Although not mentioned in the table, within each community the need for highly technical ratings varies: 20% of total enlisted billets in the submarine community, 15% in the aviation community, and 10% in the surface community require highly technical ratings.)

Table 9.5. Highly Technical Manpower Requirements
by Warfare Community (In Thousands)

	FY1984	FY1990
Submarine	10.9	11.0
Surface	14.0	16.8
Aviation	23.8	26.1
Subtotal	48.8	53.9
All Other*	22.0	22.6
Total	70.8	76.5

Source: Chief of Naval Personnel, from data in the Naval Manpower Planning System (NAMPS).

*Includes other sponsors and the individuals account.

These highly technical ratings are filled by people with performance abilities usually ascribed to the upper mental groups (mental groups I - IIIA). People with these characteristics exist in relative abundance within the navy now. They are reenlisting at the end of their first and subsequent terms at reasonably impressive rates, and 65% to 70% of all new recruits now entering the navy are in these mental groupings. There are more than sufficient Americans of ability able to man the force and, so far, willing to serve. Provided recruiting and retention goals continue to be met, the navy should be well placed to meet its long-term requirements for highly technical ratings.

Navy recruiting is based on tested ability, not on technical skill. The navy trains technicians, it does not hire them. Thus, the impact of technology falls heavily upon the training establishment. There is no accounting system which documents the historical changes occurring in navy training, but the evidence that does exist suggests that the impact of technology is very large.

The chief of naval education and training recently examined a highly technical naval rating, the surface sonar technician, to determine the impact of technology upon training. The results are interesting.

Sonar, a British invention, was introduced into the U.S. Navy before the Second World War. It was an important but, relative to today, limited device for locating submarines by the transmission and receipt of high frequency sound waves. The sonar consisted of the transducer, with its associated transmitting and receiving equipment located in the hull of the ship. The training requirements for its operation were modest.

Advances made in sonar technology since the war have created more capable but also more complicated sonars, and a wider variety of sonars that are useful on greater numbers of ships and also now on aircraft. Today's challenge is to electronically integrate the signals of several different sonar systems. It is a bigger task than the original and is applicable across a wider range of naval activities. In consequence the numbers of technicians needed to operate the systems are increased, as is the quantity and quality of the training. The job today requires an upper mental group person.

For example, in 1971, the number of surface sonar technicians authorized throughout the navy was 3,174 petty officers and 645 strikers; in 1982, it was 4,121 petty officers and 942 strikers, a growth in the decade of 33% notwithstanding that the fleet was shrinking for most of these years. Changes occurring in the training base showed similar tendencies, as would be expected. (See Table 9.6.)

If Table 9.6 were expanded to include other ratings for which roughly comparable information is available, similar changes would be seen in those ratings. (See Table 9.7.)

As is apparent from these data, the building of technicians is increasingly more complicated, more expensive, and more manpower-consuming, as the complexities of modern technology, which are essential to the successful operation of the fleet, are introduced into the navy.

It is often suggested that technology allows the man to be replaced by the machine. Is technology helping the navy economize on manpower? There is convincing evidence that technology is helping economize on ship crew size. The navy has been designing ships in such a way that more capacity is being put to sea with fewer men. Table 9.8 shows the trends since 1964 and makes an estimate for 1990. Thus, the 1990 fleet will put to sea with the same crew strength as the 1978 fleet, but with 40% more capacity. Obviously, this will be a more powerful and, in manpower terms, a more economical fleet. This is an impressive accomplishment. Table 9.9 provides examples for selected ship classes.

Table 9.6. Increases in Navy Technical Training: I (Manweeks per Unit)

	1950s	1960s	1970s	1980s
Sonar Technician, Surface (STG)	63	504	718	827

Source: Office of the Chief, Naval Education and Training.

Table 9.7. Increases in Navy Technical Training: II (Manweeks per Unit)

	1950s	1960s	1970s	1980s
Data Systems Technician (Surface)	0	0	500	622
Machinery, Electronics, and Weapons Technicians (Surface)	810	3367	4671	6534
Aviation Maintenance Ratings	573	785	1050	1140
Submarine Technical Ratings	1675	4300	6400	16846

Source: Office of the Chief, Naval Education and Training

Table 9.8. Crew Requirements Per Ship Ton

	FY1964	FY1978	FY1984	FY1990
Total Ship Tonnage (000s)	4048	3346	3733	4716
Total Design Crew Strength (000s)	327	237	204	237
Crew Required per Ton	.08	.07	.05	.05

Source: Athor's estimates based on published design data.

Technology has so far been less useful in economizing on other, "noncrew" personnel. Table 9.10 shows these trends. "Noncrew" includes people who go to sea, even though not part of the ship's crew, such as aviators and fleet staffs, but the majority are the shore establishment. Can technology be applied to the shore establishment with the same vigor as it has been applied to ship design? It is a worthy objective.

Table 9.9. Ship Displacement and Crew Size (Selected Classes)

Ship Class	Year Launched	Tons	Crew Size	Mpr. per Ship Ton
Destroyers				
Fletcher	1942	2050	249	.12
Spruance	1973	7300	353	.05
Destroyers				
Charles Adams	1959	3370	396	.12
Kidd	1979	8140	332	.04
Frigates				
Brooke	1963	2640	325	.12
Perry	1976	3000	200	.07
Cruisers				
Albany	1945	13700	1000	.07
Ticonderoga	1981	8910	349	.04
Carriers				
Midway	1944	51000	2522	.05
Nimitz (nuclear)	1972	81600	3177	.04
Submarines				
Guppy	1944	1870	84	.04
Los Angeles (nuclear)	1974	6000	132	.02
Amphibious				
LST-511	1943	1653	115	.07
LST-1179	1969	4500	259	.06

Source: Author's estimates, based on published design data.

Table 9.10. "Non-Crew" Requirements Per Ship Ton (In Thousands)

	FY1964	FY1978	FY1984
Total Active Manpower	668	530	572
Less: Design-Crew Strength	327	237	204
Equals: "Non-Crew" Navy Strength	341	293	368
Total Ship Tonnage	4048	3346	3733
"Non-Crew" Required per Ton	.08	.09	.10

Source: Author's estimates, based on published ship design data and active navy personnel strengths.

In general, the navy is mastering technology, rather than the other way around. The 600-ship navy need not founder on the rock of technology. There are sufficient numbers of people available who are able to learn the skills needed to serve successfully.

But the navy does not run on high technology alone. Can the navy achieve the total manpower strength required? Here, the answer is less certain.

Table 9.4 shows a requirement for 685,000 people in 1990, when the 600-ship navy is to be in place. This is admittedly the ideal from the point of view of filling all billets; navy manpower managers do not expect to reach this level in practice. They do hope to achieve 640,000-650,000 by 1990.

Table 9.4 also shows a 1984 requirement for 653,000 people. Congressional authorizations for FY1984, however, fell short of this number by 81,000, or 12½%. If congressional authorizations in 1990 were below requirements by the same percentage, navy end strength would only be 600,000 people. Would that be enough to man the 600-ship navy? An examination of certain historical trends suggests it would not.

Table 9.11. Ship and Manpower Strengths

	FY1939	FY1945	FY1964	FY1978	FY1983
Active Ships	346	8628	917	453	479
Active Manpower (In Thousands)	125	3381	668	530	572
Average Manpower per Ship	361	391	728	1170	1194

Sources: Ship data (excluding mobilizing reserve ships) from navy historian (1939 and 1945) and Table 1 (1964-1984); Manpower data from navy comptroller.

Table 9.11 shows that, over the past half century, an increasing number of sailors is needed to man a given number of ships.

If the average in 1990 were not to exceed the present average of about 1,200 men per ship, then the required 1990 force would number about 675,000 people (600 ships minus nine reserve ships minus twenty-seven civilian-manned ships equals 564 active ships x 1200).

If we look not at ship numbers but at displacement, which is a better measure, we see from Table 9.12 that for the navy as a whole there has been a trend toward greater manpower efficiency.

Table 9.12. Manpower Requirements Per Ship Ton (In Thousands)

	FY1964	FY1978	FY1983
Total Ship Tonnage (000s)	4048	3353	3733
Total Active Manpower (000s)	668	530	572
Manpower per Ton	0.17	0.16	0.15

Sources: Manpower: navy comptroller, tonnage: author's estimate.

If we assume the trend toward greater efficiency continues until 1990, and manpower per ton will then average approximately 0.14, and assuming displacement then to be 4.7 million tons (Table 9.3), then 1990 manpower needs would on this basis be about 658,000 people.

Yet another perspective on the same point is provided by the ratio of ships' crew to other "noncrew" navy personnel. ("Crew" in this instance, as in earlier tables, is defined as the sum of the design-crew strength of all active ships.) Table 9.13 shows the changes occurring since 1964, and, in particular, the relative growth in the noncrew portion of the navy earlier remarked upon.

The design-crew strength of the 1990 fleet was estimated in Table 9.8 to be 237,000 people. If the ratio of noncrew to crew were to remain at the 1984 level, the noncrew share of total 1990 strength would be 421,000 people, and total strength in 1990 would be, again, 658,000 people.

These several ways of looking at navy manpower trends are illuminations of the past and not predictors of the future. They do suggest, however, that congressional authorizations far below likely requirements will jeopardize the effectiveness of the 600-ship navy. While a certain

Table 9.13. Ships' Crew as a Percent of Total Manpower (In Thousands)

	FY1964	FY1978	FY1984
Total Active Manpower	668	530	572
Total Design Crew Strength	327	237	204
Percent Crew	49	45	36
NonCrew	341	293	368

Sources: Manpower data: navy comptroller. Crew strength: author's estimates, from published design data.

percentage of manpower shortages can be overcome by alternative methods, i.e., civilian substitutions, contracting, it seems unlikely that the 600-ship navy can be manned at the 600,000 level. A level of around 650,000 is more realistic. Of course, it is desirable that the 1990 force be manned as modestly as practical because every additional 25,000 men adds about $500 million in annual payroll costs alone. The Congress should look for incentives to help the navy economize on manpower; it should not simply cut end-strength requests each year.

MARINE CORPS DIMENSION

United States Marine Corps force structure has remained more or less constant since the Korean War: three active divisions and three active air wings, with a fourth division-wing in the reserves. Excluding the manpower effects of the Vietnam War, which caused considerable expansion in marine strength for the period of the war, end strength has been remarkably consistent over time. (See Table 9.14.)

Table 9.14. USMC Active Duty Personnel (In Thousands)

	FY1964	FY1978	FY1984	FY1989
Officer	18	18	20	20
Enlisted	172	172	176	184
Total	190	190	196	204

Source: Office of the Deputy Chief of Staff for Manpower, HQMC.

Similarly, as shown in Table 9.15, there has been a consistent allocation of billets across combat and support functions. The relative shares of total-force effort assigned to combat, combat support, and combat-service support are not changing significantly, although support jobs are increasing at a greater rate than combat jobs.

Table 9.15. Enlisted Billets By Function (In Thousands)

	FY1978	FY1984	FY1989
Combat	41.4	40.8	41.4
Combat Support	27.8	28.5	30.0
Combat Service Support	91.5	94.9	102.8
Other	11.7	12.2	9.8
Total	172.4	176.4	183.9

Source: Office of the Deputy Chief of Staff for Manpower, HQMC. Totals may not add due to rounding.

Examining enlisted billets by skill level indicates anticipated growth in the highly technical jobs and reduction in jobs of low technical skill levels. But again, the anticipated changes are modest, as shown in Table 9.16.

Table 9.16. Enlisted Billets By Skill Level (In Thousands)

	FY1978	FY1984	FY1989
High Tech	35.5	37.0	41.5
Technical	70.2	72.8	77.3
Low Tech	55.0	54.4	55.3
Undesignated	11.7	12.2	9.8
Total	172.4	176.4	183.9

Source: Office of the Deputy Chief of Staff for Manpower, HQMC.

Finally, ranking the current force by AFQT percentile and comparing that with estimated FY1989 requirements to meet school quotas, we see that the aim is to eliminate the mental group IV accessions and to seek a higher-quality force to match the expected growth in sophisticated equipment that will be entering the force in quantity beginning in FY1986. (See Table 9.17.)

The marines are tied to the navy for aviation and to the army for ground force equipment. Thus, many of the problems of adapting to new technologies common to those services are also common to the marines. They have kept pace with the technological demands of naval aviation, but the challenge ahead is for the ground forces, as they adjust to an increasingly automated battlefield. These challenges are cogently discussed in chapter 8 by Gen. William E. DePuy, USA (Ret). Many of the difficulties facing the army are, no doubt, also on the marine horizon. The question of scale is, however, a mitigating factor. The marines do not operate either the numbers or the variety of equipment available to the army, and appear to have been generally conservative in seeking out new equipment that taxes their ability to absorb, maintain, or employ it. Still, the automated battlefield is approaching, and the issues raised by General DePuy are worthy of examination by the marines.

Table 9.17. Percent Enlisted Billets By AFQT Percentile

AFQT Percentile	Current Force	Required FY 1989
Above 92	3.0	--
65 - 92	32.3	40.0
50 - 64	24.1	29.7
31 - 49	28.7	30.3
21 - 30	11.9	--

Source: Office of the Deputy Chief of Staff for Manpower, HQMC.

CONCLUSION

The navy is embarked on a substantial shipbuilding program that conditionally promises that the U.S. Navy will be, for the foreseeable future, sufficiently numerous to meet peacetime commitments and cope with contingency situations and sufficiently powerful to dominate potentially opposing navies in most circumstances. The condition on which the promise depends is that the navy stay technically ahead of potential foes. Technology more than force structure will decide who is number one. Similarly, the Marine Corps is approaching an automated battlefield that, in the very near future, will demand a higher-than-usual level of technical skill.

Thus, force structure and technology are both tending in the same manpower direction: toward more and more capable people. Whether or not the additional people, and the people of higher technical potential, will be available for naval service is the subject of other chapters. But the answer for both the navy and Marine Corps, barring unforeseen changes in public attitudes, is almost surely "yes" if we pay the price of competitive wages and benefits.

In the end it comes down to cost: the cost of recruiting and paying young people with potential, the cost of training them, the cost of losing experienced people versus the cost of keeping them, and the opportunity costs associated with higher personnel costs—fewer new ships and aircraft, fewer new weapons, and lower readiness rates. Thus, much hangs on the ability of the navy, in particular, to man the growing force with as small an increase in manpower as is practical; and this, in turn, suggests a scrutiny of the shore establishment that is as rigorous in effort and as productive in results as the scrutiny of ship manning that has already occurred.

10 Technology and Manpower: Air Force Perspective

JOHN W. ROBERTS

INTRODUCTION

Remember 1973? The B-52 celebrated its eighteenth birthday. The F-15, whose initial contract had been awarded in 1969, became operational. The B-1A airframe, with 244 purchases planned, was being developed by Rockwell International. Less than 200,000 computers were in use in the private sector, while the air force itself operated or leased approximately 1,300 general purpose computers valued at $866 million. As part of preliminary studies to determine future strategic systems that might eventually augment or even replace the family of Minuteman or Titan ICBMs, the air force conducted exploratory studies of the Experimental Missile, or the MX, the missile system for the year 2000. Secretary of the Air Force Robert C. Seamans, Jr. wrote in a March 1973 *Air Force Magazine* article: "The decade ahead will undoubtedly be one of tight defense budgets. We must attract and hold capable people and at the same time cut to a minimum the costs of training and maintaining our organizations."[1]

Plans to make technical training more effective included revisions of requirements and course content plus the use of improved techniques, including simulation in technical and flying training. Average Scholastic Aptitude Test (SAT) scores continued their nationwide decline, which had begun ten years earlier. External and internal struggles concerning resource allocation, the future course of technology, compensation, and retirement continued. The air force began, with the other services, an undertaking which was truly a revolutionary development in military manning—the All-Volunteer Force.

Now it's 1983! The B-52 is thirty years young. The F-15 has assumed a prominent role that enhances tactical air capabilities. The on-again/off-again B-1B airframe, with only 100 purchases planned, is on again and will be introduced into the Strategic Air Command inventory beginning in 1986. As the largest single user of computers in the federal government, the air force

148

has spent more than $647 million in FY1983 alone just to replace its base-level computers, not to mention its enormous investment in computers embedded within new weapons systems. One hundred Peacekeeper missiles will be placed in existing Minuteman silos beginning in December 1986. Secretary of the Air Force Verne Orr and Chief of Staff General Charles A. Gabriel, in their *Fiscal Year 1984 Air Force Report to the 98th Congress of the United States of America* in February 1983, stated:

> Air Force people are the foundation of our war-fighting and readiness capability. The need for high quality, trained and experienced people crosses all mission areas and programs. Strong and modern strategic nuclear forces, improved readiness and sustainability, enhanced mobility forces and more modern tactical forces give the Air Force the hardware—the tools it needs to carry out the mission. However, our people give life to those systems, and history has shown, ultimately determine the course of battle.[2]

Future technical training challenges can be generalized into three broad areas: (1) the ability to adapt limited resources to meet student training requirements; (2) the ability to respond to the most extensive modernization of weapons systems in air force history; and (3) the ability to improve efficiency in all phases of training. Each challenge will be discussed in more detail later within the context of the future environment which we anticipate will differ significantly from that experienced during the first decade of the AVF. Therefore, while not unique in themselves, these areas will continue to offer significant challenges for the technical training community. In 1982, after reaching an all-time low, average SAT scores finally reversed their previous decline, reflecting a modest increase. However, in 1983, there were no further improvements in SAT scores. Increasing concern with the scientific illiteracy of American youth and the overall quality of American education and teachers has surfaced as a national problem. Compensation and entitlement issues, as reflected in recent pay caps and current congressional hearings on the military retirement system, continue to be areas of great concern for all military personnel.

In retrospect, the first decade of the AVF, while controversial in some aspects, has been a successful period for the air force. It has been my experience that our success is directly attributable to our ability to balance the various forces which compete internally—between various air force agencies (logistics, R&D, operations, manpower, and personnel) and even within some manpower and personnel directorates (manpower and organization, personnel programs, and personnel plans) themselves—for scarce resources. In addition, we worked hard to modify the important external factors (demographic, socioeconomic, budgetary, support of the American people, and interaction with other services and the Office of the Secretary of Defense) that impact either directly or indirectly on mission priorities. None of the internal, or for that matter external, forces are mutually exclusive. In fact, their complex interaction requires daily confrontation and problem solving.

As the air force looks ahead to the second decade of the AVF, it does so with a cautious optimism; an optimism for the future success of all services' manpower and personnel programs. This optimism is based not only on the extremely successful recruiting and retention achievements of FY1982 and 1983, but perhaps more importantly on the belief that the services, the Congress, and the American people learned some valuable lessons from the traumatic recruiting and retention experiences of the late 1970s. We hope these experiences, which impacted directly on personnel quality and ultimately the readiness capability of all services, will provide a sound foundation for a realistic assessment of future military personnel needs that will enable the AVF to continue to function successfully.

To recap briefly, the air force's FY1983 nonprior-service (NPS) recruiting results included the highest high school diploma graduate rate, 98%, not only since the advent of the AVF, but in the entire history of the air force; a combined mental category I and II (above average) rate of 49%; and a mental category IV (below average) rate of only 2%. Prior-service (PS) recruitment, targeted toward the direct duty assignment of fully-trained chronic critical skill (CCS) air force personnel, achieved significant inroads to reduce midlevel NCO shortages which resulted from the low retention rates of the late 1970s. The FY1983 entry of 928 engineer officers into officer training school by our recruiting service, was particularly noteworthy as it represented a 378% increase relative to our FY1980 achievement. This successful recruitment of many engineers provided significant impetus to reduce the total engineering shortage of 850 which existed at the beginning of the year. This success will be difficult to duplicate, however, because we anticipate that the primary engineering skills needed (electrical, aeronautical, and astronautical) will also be those most sought after in the private sector. Of perhaps even more importance are FY1983 reenlistment rates which, through the third quarter, were also excellent: first term-71%; second term-85%; and career-96%. While I certainly applaud these most recent achievements, I'm concerned that they may be perceived as representative of normal recruitment and retention patterns these past ten years by persons new to the congressional budget process. In fact, they're not.

While fully recognizing the increasing ability of air force manpower analysts to model future manpower requirements and force-structure trends for planning purposes, I don't believe a presentation that only considers the demand side of our requirements accurately reflects the reality of the world in which the air force operates. As a matter of fact, the on-again/off-again nature of major weapons-systems acquisitions such as the B-1 bomber or the MX missile serves to vividly illustrate the turbulent nature these external factors have had, and will continue to have, on future requirements and force-structure trends. As a matter of fact, dynamic requirements are the rule, not the exception. Analysis by the air force has indicated that on the average, program instability is a key factor in escalating costs, with the current average program taking twelve years from concept to initial operating capability. In its development, then, a typical system will have been through the administrations of two or three different presidents and a dozen federal budget debates. In addition, air force concepts, strategies, and priorities will almost certainly have shifted in response to changing requirements and strategies.

Furthermore, based upon my thirty-five years of air force experience, the demand side of the manpower model must always be considered in conjunction with key supply factors in order to enable assessment of the so-called "big picture." Some recent examples of the interaction and impact these factors can have on each other will better illustrate my point. The air force recently wanted to change its current policy of an unaccompanied one-year overseas tour to three-year accompanied tours in preparation for the implementation of the Ground Launched Cruise Missile (GLCM) at Comiso, Italy. However, a lack of congressional funding for housing, schools, and other support items did not allow implementation of this plan. Accordingly, planned personnel requirements and assignment patterns relative to this base will be significantly different than the air force had originally planned, although requirements remain the same. Other examples of the difficulty associated with personnel requirements and force planning include the two major weapons systems previously mentioned. The determination of the MX basing mode which was up in the air for several years is essential to accurate planning and programming of future requirements for enlisted skills such as security police and maintenance, to name a few. Likewise, total manpower requirements for the B-1 bomber have changed dramatically in the last decade, particularly since the current program involves the purchase of only 41% of the bombers the air force initially planned for ten years ago. In both cases, the necessary personnel procurement and training requirements designed to achieve the appropriate skill levels for both systems to enter the operational inventory successfully would have benefited from earlier implementation decisions.

As the air force plans for the decade ahead, the ability to achieve a balance between the various external and internal pressures previously mentioned will once again be instrumental to the enhancement of our future war-fighting capability. To provide a perspective for my discussion of these factors, as I believe they may occur in the future, five broad assumptions have been made. First the air force's future demand for people will be determined by the roles, mission strategies, and support structure necessary to carry out a national security strategy that emphasizes the global nature of U.S. interests and commitments. Second, long production lead times, coupled with high costs, will preclude the introduction of major new weapons systems not currently under development or presently in being. Third, the discussion will be limited to the enlisted force, although I fully recognize that officer and civilian requirements are essential to our future. Fourth, air force end strength will continue to grow, but at a rate that can only be estimated due to the interaction of various competing factors which causes imprecision in any attempt to predict the future. Thus, while current planning documents such as the Program Objectives Memorandum (POM) and Extended Planning Annex (EPA) indicate significantly higher manpower requirements to support expanded strategic, space, general purpose, airlift, R&D, training, intelligence, and communications missions, the recent countervailing mood of the Congress, combined with increasingly larger budget deficits, tends to indicate these documents may be somewhat optimistic. Fifth, new weapons systems such as the B-1B bomber, Air-Launched Cruise Missile (ALCM), Peacekeeper missile, Ground-Launched Cruise Missile (GLCM), and Advanced Tactical Fighter (ATF) will progress to operational reality as the air force continues its drive toward force modernization.

With these assumptions as a backdrop, my discussion will concentrate on three broad, countervailing components, whose interaction will in large part determine the future readiness of our air force. These components are: (1) future manpower requirements and force-structure trends; (2) internal (demand) factors; and (3) external (supply) factors. It is through the interaction of these three areas that we hope to achieve a balance to maximize the air force's future war-fighting potential. The external/internal subdivision is purely for the sake of this discussion alone and with the full realization that shifts in one area can, and most probably will, cause reactions in other areas.

My initial discussion of future requirements and force trends provides a baseline for conjecture about the impact competing factors may have on future decisions. My discussion is not intended to produce any firm conclusions, for I certainly realize the folly in attempting to be clairvoyant. Rather, I would like to surface the issues as I see them with the hope that recognition of these competing interests can be an important first step toward their ultimate resolution.

FUTURE MANPOWER REQUIREMENTS
AND FORCE STRUCTURE TRENDS

Air Force 2000: Air Power Entering the 21st Century, which includes some definitive statements concerning future air force requirements, anticipates an overall moderate growth in enlisted end strength through the end of the century. This growth is required to support new weapons systems such as those mentioned in the previous section and to support added requirements such as R&D for future aircraft and support systems, and expanded airlift capability. Since 1976, air force manpower has grown nearly 3% or at an annual rate of about one-third of 1%. Assuming similar gradual growth, air force end strength will be 10% to 15% larger by the year 2000 than it is today.[3] While I believe this estimate is consistent with current budgetary constraints and the prevailing mood of the congress, manpower planners must also be flexible and able to react to other scenarios as times and conditions change quickly. To illustrate, what if large budget deficits and a slower than anticipated economic recovery result in virtually no end strength increases from now until 1988-1989? And then let us suppose that as we enter the

1990s an improved economy, reduced budget deficits, lower unemployment, a growing concern about the Soviet threat, and continuing escalation of tensions in areas such as North Africa, Central American, and the Middle East result in a decision to authorize rapid "catchup" end strength increases just as the declining youth population reaches its nadir. My point is clear; manpower and personnel planners must always be prepared to deal with scenarios which range the full spectrum from unduly pessimistic to conservative to very optimistic. They also must be prepared for changing war-fighting strategies and new system developments.

While our best estimate is for a moderate, steady increase in enlisted end strength, we believe requirements for personnel with electronic and mechanical aptitudes will grow at a faster rate. The development of air force space operations, continued expansion of computerization in support functions, and the use of digital, reprogrammable, self-testing equipment that features remove/throw-away/replace maintenance parts will require people who can work with software and computer-based systems. *Air Force 2000* anticipates that requirements for people with high electronic aptitudes will increase by one-third, while requirements for people with mechanical aptitudes will increase by about 12%. However, these increases will be partially offset by general aptitude requirements which remain relatively constant and lower requirements for people with administrative skills (Figure 10.1).[4]

Figure 10.1. Enlisted Aptitude Requirements

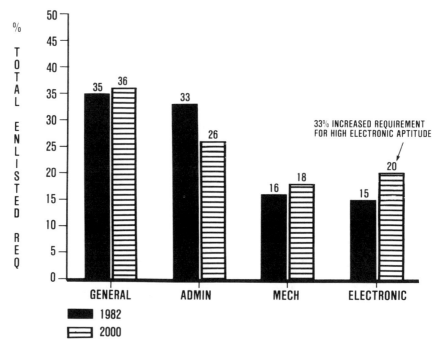

Source: Air Force 2000: Air Power Entering the 21st Century (Washington, DC: Government Printing Office, 1982). Declassified 1982.

These projections are reasonably consistent with those of air force logistics planners who emphasize that the vulnerability of air force aircraft at large main-operating bases will be the most critical support issue facing the air force for the rest of the century. Vulnerability will require a modification of our current support strategy and the dispersal of aircraft and resources away from main-operating bases to improve their survivability. Adoption of this strategy will require the deployment of small units and create increased requirements not only for people with technical skills, but also for those who are multiskilled (generalists).[5] This strategy will resurface the traditional conflict as to what exactly is the proper mix of "specialists" and "generalists." Its resolution will have far-reaching implications for the entire manpower, personnel and training (MP&T) community and will significantly impact the air force's successful implementation of a global war-fighting strategy utilizing the small-unit approach. To offset these increased manpower requirements, the air force must utilize the latest technological advances to develop its weapons systems and initiate management actions that insure that MP&T requirements receive consideration at the earliest point possible in the development and acquisition process.

Significant federal budget deficits will increase pressure on the air force to find offsets, i.e., dollars and manpower within existing programs, to fund increases in future programs, particularly in the near term. Of specific importance will be increasing pressure to expand the mission of reserve forces and contracting out.

Air Reserve Forces (ARF)

Plans for rapid deployment, sustainability, and survivability rely heavily on the selected reserve's ability to deploy with and reinforce the active force. Although the Air National Guard and Air Force Reserve contain only about 15% of total force personnel resources, they are responsible for nearly 25% of all flying missions and in selected missions such as tactical airlift and fighter interceptor, they contribute approximately 60% of total capability (Figure 10.2). This capability is due in part to active force responsibility for a large portion of base support, staff, and overhead functions. I believe the ARF will continue to modernize through the introduction of new aircraft and continue to share many operational missions with the active force.[6] In addition, I anticipate growing congressional pressure to increase the size of the ARF mission as a supposedly cost-effective method to provide manpower in support of new mission requirements.

Figure 10.2. Air Reserve Contribution to Total Force, FY1983

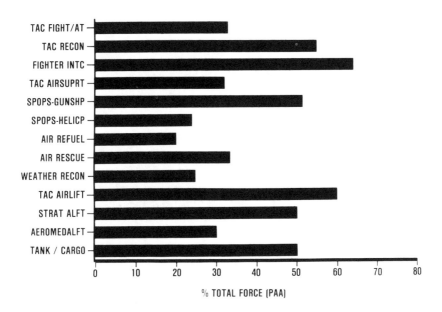

% TOTAL FORCE (PAA)

Source: Air Force 2000: Air Power Entering the 21st Century (Washington, DC: Government Printing Office, 1982). Declassified 1982.

However, potential declines in the quantity and quality of the prime recruiting market will adversely affect the selected reserve as well as the active force. Can MP&T planners develop new uses for the ARF, and will Congress accept and fund these increases in areas such as training and possibly basic support missions that require a seven-day work week? Will congressional and budgetary pressures attempt to force expansion of the ARF mission beyond its demonstrated capabilities?

Contracting Out

The air force is the largest user of contractors for commercial activities within the Department of Defense. Future contracting requirements are expected to remain stable as a percentage of the total force (8%) and its role will be determined, as always, by military imperatives.[7]

In summary, the trends of a growing demand for people are already apparent. The exact size and specific mix of personnel requirements can be estimated, but only imprecisely. Consistent with our experience during the first decade of the AVF, we believe future success hinges largely upon our ability to influence satisfactorily those factors we can impact directly. In addition, our ability to formulate plans and options that mitigate those factors beyond our direct control, but whose outcome is essential to our war-fighting capability, is crucial. In the next sections, both external and internal factors most important to the future of the AVF will be discussed. The purpose of the discussion is not to propose solutions, although in the course of considering certain factors, possible solutions are plainly evident. In most instances, consideration of an issue will illustrate the complexity and interaction of the factors which make solutions speculative at best.

INTERNAL FACTORS

Resources and Technology: Proactive Involvement

Within the air force, internal decisions that result in changing strategies, reprioritized mission requirements, and the allocation of resources within our total obligation authority (TOA) will determine the course of future MP&T activities. Several recent studies suggest that MP&T involvement should be more "proactive" in internal air force decisions, particularly at the action officer level. One study concluded that MP&T requirements are not being effectively determined during the early states of the weapons systems acquisition process (WSAP) and that MP&T considerations are not being effectively included in early design trade-off decisions or in the development of operational scenarios and maintenance concepts.[8] Another, dealing with the ATF, which is scheduled for deployment in the mid-1990s, stressed the need to compress the number of specialists and tasks associated with aircraft turnarounds. This study concluded that to achieve a reduction in the number of maintenance personnel would require changes not only in the way maintenance procedures are implemented, but also in the way senior maintenance career personnel are trained.[9] The implication is clear—increased MP&T involvement at the earliest possible time in the design, development, and acquisition process is vital. Will the MP&T community be able to exert its influence at the appropriate time to insure that proper consideration is given to the MP&T perspective?

Another example of a key area which will require early MP&T involvement is in the extensive planning required for air force participation and leadership in space operations. And yet, the future role of man in space has not yet been determined. Gen. Robert T. Marsh, Commander, Air Force Systems Command, in a recent *Air Force Magazine* article corroborated this uncertainty:

Some maintain that man is simply excess baggage in an on-orbit system. Others believe manned systems have great potential to increase our capabilities, provide flexibility and do more with less. The fact is that we do not yet have the requisite programs under way to determine which view is correct. We simply do not know the military-related limitations of man in space, nor do we know enough about additional capabilities that might result from man-machine interface aboard space systems.[10]

The crucial point is that future decisions concerning systems and strategies will require a corporate determination of priorities and require the early involvement and integration of MP&T personnel with other air force agencies in the decision-making process. Resolution of internal difference, such as the one mentioned by General Marsh, is essential to insure that MP&T activities and policies are geared to support air force requirements. Even beyond the determination of man's future role in space are human factor considerations, e.g., the physical and even mental requirements which will be necessary to use space as our nation's leaders determine appropriate. No matter what the outcome, it is people who make it happen.

Notwithstanding our future role in space, the MP&T community will certainly have to confront the traditional challenges of requirements, recruiting, training, retention, compensation, and retirement with innovative solutions. It's possible that the answer to some of these challenges will require reconsideration of concepts which have been previously rejected, e.g., lateral entry, extended age limits, and relaxed physical standards, to enable further expansion of the manpower market. However, I also believe that methods now being developed to include all items associated with a military weapons system in the original purchase decision may offer some of the most significant avenues to gain leverage and balance the impact of certain external and internal factors.

Although the air force has significantly increased the war-fighting capabilities of its current weapons systems, we have not yet achieved the same improvements in reducing the associated manpower "tail." For example, the F-4 of 1950s vintage requires approximately twenty-seven maintenance technicians. The F-15 of 1970s vintage requires twenty-six people. Future plans for small-unit operations, combined with external and internal constraints, demand that we pay attention to this issue. When a unit deploys to a bare base environment, logistically we just can't support 600 people to keep twenty-four F-15s in the air. Nor can we take along complete maintenance shops as they currently exist at our main-operating bases. A positive side benefit of reducing our manpower requirements per airplane in a forward operating area would be a similar reduction in war zone combatants, resulting in fewer casualties. To achieve this reduction requires the application of advanced technologies that maximize the manpower-hardware interface. Through full development of this interface, the potential exists to not only improve the effectiveness of weapons systems, but also to mitigate potential manpower problems.

Application of advanced technologies need not imply increased complexity. A primary objective should also be to improve the system's reliability in wartime, while at the same time reducing manpower costs for training, maintenance, and logistics. An example of what can be accomplished is the air force's insistence on new standards which have been increased significantly, for mean-time-between-failure (MTBF) on aircraft electronic components. Immediate benefits include the increased amount of time the equipment is available for combat, plus the ability to simplify maintenance strategies. Improved reliability of other aircraft systems, combined with throw-away components, could completely eliminate repair requirements in a forward area. Potential long-term benefits include reduced technician requirements, reduced training programs, reduced demands for spare parts, and a major improvement in our ability to maintain technologically sophisticated equipment within future constraints. Another example of technology's potential is the modular unit. As currently conceptualized, this unit would conform to the shape of the fuselage and contain munitions, fuel, or parts. Immediate benefits could be quick turnaround times combined with spectacular savings.

However, as with most new technologies, there are also trade-offs which must be considered. Cost trade-offs associated with this strategy would include higher design, development, and engineering costs plus slightly more expensive, robust parts. However, overall life cycle costs would be significantly reduced. To make the strategy really work, a more precise way to predict the numbers and mix of people needed to operate and maintain these systems would be needed. The bottom line is that we must continue to increase the capability of our weapons, while at the same time making them simpler to operate and maintain.[11]

In an environment which is constrained by both manpower and the increasing costs of weapons systems, the advancement of technology has served to reshape the nature and role of people in combat. Reliance on advanced technology has served not only to depersonalize warfare with standoff weapons systems, but also to place more emphasis on the individual by stressing specialization in individual skill knowledge. Increased emphasis on strong, dynamic leadership within the officer and NCO ranks, plus a rekindling of traditional institutional values, must go hand in hand with future technological advances to insure the most successful employment of air power.

In addition to the development of improved man-machine interface, selection/classification and training technologies also offer significant possibilities for future advances. Accordingly, the final section of this discussion of internal factors will concentrate on these areas.

Selection, Classification and Training Technologies

Flexible selection/classification and training strategies will be required due to technological advances and anticipated war-fighting trends required in future conflict environments. As indicated earlier, technical training challenges can be generalized into three broad areas: (1) changing student resources, (2) equipment modernization, and (3) improved efficiency. All areas present resource management problems and can be further broken into subelements of students, equipment, training management, and technology application.

Students. The potential exists for the air force to face a future training environment which could have an insufficient student resource in terms of sheer numbers as well as individual quality. Compounding this problem is the fact that several career fields currently have wide variations in annual requirements which follow a four-year cyclical pattern of high requirements one year with relatively low or stable requirements the other three. This cycle creates significant training turbulence both for formal schoolhouse and on-the-job training (OJT) requirements at a time when the experience level of the career field may least be able to deal with it. In a high-quality recruiting market, we have been able to endure this condition. However, future constraints combined with unprogrammed changes in program requirements will require better overall management of student flow, particularly in these skills.

Efforts to reduce both basic and technical training attrition offer a significant potential for future improvement. Improvement of the selection and classification process through use of state-of-the-art technologies can be used to counter negative demographic and socioeconomic trends. Improved person-job-match techniques, through the use of specific ASVAB subtest scores to predict more accurately technical school performance, updated strength aptitude testing (X-Factor), and use of the Vocational Interest Career Examination (VOICE), which allows an objective assessment of an individual's interest relative to air force skills, all offer significant potential for improving the process of matching applicants to jobs through the application of advanced technology. Use of these techniques may become even more feasible if the operational paper and pencil ASVAB is replaced with computerized adaptive testing (CAT). CAT can reduce the average length of enlistment testing by approximately 50%, provide more precise measurement of aptitude at the high and low-ability levels, and also reduce the potential for test compromise. The ability to develop job performance measures and, if feasible, establish their link to enlistment standards, while a high risk venture, may offer another avenue to improve the selection/classification process. A device which may reduce attrition in the selection process is a written adaptability screening questionnaire, such as that currently under research by a joint service committee, that uses biographical information. This test could be administered at military entrance processing stations (MEPS). Another possibility is to utilize experience gained from the Air Force Reading Aptitude Test (AFRAT) and remedial reading courses. If the deficiencies in our public school system's math and science curricula continue, the use of tests and remedial programs in mathematics and science courses may provide an additional option to qualify candidates for electrical and mechanical courses. Finally, tying personnel to specific weapons systems and equipment for longer portions of their careers offers a potentially high payback; however, its cost in terms of training equipment will require skill by skill consideration.

Equipment: The full spectrum of air force equipment from fighters, bombers, airlift, and missile systems to communications, intelligence, and data automation is undergoing change. Compounding this problem are highly concurrent acquisition programs, such as GLCM and the B-1B, which force the identification of training equipment requirements before the operational, maintenance, and logistical support concepts of these systems have been finalized. Proactive MP&T involvement in the weapons design and acquisition process plus strong operating command support of the air training command's budget submissions are essential to insure the inclusion of high priority training items in the POM process.

Training Management. The internal development of training programs, from initial skills basic courses through advanced courses to career development courses (the knowledge basis of our OJT programs), offers a significant challenge to the training community. Establishment of a training development service (TDS) that provides an integrated set of training courses, preplanned to guide an individual from initial introduction through a full career in a specific skill, has the potential to be the greatest innovation in managing training development. Better balancing of loads among training centers, combined with an increase in total capacity within the technical training system, require consideration of congressional concerns, along with practical concerns for handling increased student loads.

The ability to manage contingencies in full-scale mobilization will require the alteration of course content. Unnecessary peacetime programs will be reduced to enable task qualification in skills necessary to do battle in an abbreviated time frame. The involvement of training personnel in the air force wartime manpower and personnel requirements team is necessary to improve training planning in a contingency environment.

Technology Application. As computer application explodes across the country, there will be increased pressure to take advantage of the obvious gains to be made from the use of various computer systems. Experience with current systems has provided a solid background to guide future modifications. The fact that small changes in current instructional programs are both time consuming (120 man-hours to convert one hour of traditional instruction) and expensive reinforces the point that there may be practical limits to computer application in technical training. However, the long-term gains realized from these conversions may well be worth far more than the initial time and cost involved.

Judicious applications where computers make sense and are cost-effective must guide future decisions. Innovative use of mini and microprocessors which employ inexpensive technology currently appears to offer the best chance for expanded utilization. These newer systems offer quicker and less expensive change capability which is the key ingredient when dealing with an environment that requires flexibility in the face of extensive modernization of operational weapons systems.

The requirement for flexibility, mobility, and sustainability, combined with the increased technological complexity of weapons and support systems, raises the traditional question as to the preferred mix of "specialists" versus "generalists" for enlisted, officer, and civilian personnel. Because of the different kinds of training required, a shift in either direction could have a serious impact not only on recruitment but also on training capabilities and resource requirements. On the one hand, specialization requires more people to accomplish specialized tasks, but it is also cost-effective and timely. On the other hand, increased generalist requirements reduce the demand for people but require increased training time at a higher cost. Resolution of this issue must again result in a balance that maximizes our war-fighting potential. Significant shifts from our current posture toward multiskilled personnel must be accompanied by more innovative applications of technology, simplified yet longer training programs, and the creation of weapons systems that can be maintained by fewer people. Once again the need for earlier involvement in weapons system development is evident.

Overall, there are several advanced technologies that can be used to upgrade training and in addition have the potential to keep pace with the increasing complexity of weapons systems. Those associated with computers appear most promising, because we cannot afford the high costs associated with the use of real training equipment and must increasingly rely on simulation. Benefits include low-cost, high-fidelity simulation of many maintenance and support functions with rapid collection, reduction, and retrieval of data. There are also new input and output methods such as voice synthesis and recognition. These technologies allow the student or user to interact with the computer or computer-based device by speech rather than using a keyboard or touch panel. The key advantage is that the user's hands are free to perform the task at hand. Finally, OJT can be an extremely "high-cost" option because it requires the individual unit to utilize its most experienced personnel for the training function, while at the same time drawing NCO experience away from the primary unit mission, with a possible negative impact on overall unit readiness.[12]

Quality. Although the services certainly didn't plan it that way, the results of the Armed Services Vocational Aptitude Battery (ASVAB) norming error between 1976 and 1980 reinforced the air force's constant emphasis on quality personnel as the key ingredient in mission capability. Higher attrition rates, increased disciplinary problems, reduced productivity, and a reduction in the overall readiness of the force are the byproducts of lower-quality personnel. In a supply-constrained environment such as that of the late 1970s, the benefit of the doubt in recruiting and retention decisions tended to go to the individual. In a demand-constrained environment such as the one we are currently experiencing, increased emphasis on the recruitment and retention of only the "best-qualified" people has resulted in a fine-tuning or "honing" of the force, tending to shape the force structure to the air force's benefit and thus insure a more capable and therefore mission-ready force. It is absolutely imperative that all services continue to emphasize quality and that quality will continue to attract quality since the most crucial period for all services will be from 1986 to 1988 when the current bumper crop of high-quality enlistees complete their first term of enlistment. Strong retention results during this period will pay extra dividends for the future war-fighting capability of our nation's armed forces. Further, the FY1983 basic military training attrition rate, which is currently running lower than previous years, appears to indicate that our emphasis on high school diploma graduates is paying dividends.

EXTERNAL FACTORS

Declining Youth Market

Certain demographic factors, e.g., the well-publicized declining youth market, can be estimated with a reasonable amount of precision. We know for instance that what is normally considered the prime recruiting market, eighteen-year-old youths, will continue to decline, reaching its lowest level in 1992 (Figure 10.3). What impact will this decline have on the future of the AVF? Because of its interaction with many other factors, I do not believe we can determine its future impact with any great precision. In anticipation of this continued decline, adequate recruiting and advertising budgets, enlistment bonuses, pay comparability, and strong internal retention programs that emphasize the use of selective reenlistment bonuses should be planned and budgeted. As previously discussed, the air force anticipates increased requirements for high-aptitude electronic and mechanical personnel. Nevertheless, it is possible that the development of remove/throw away/replace electronics/avionics equipment could lead instead to increased requirements for multiskilled personnel, particularly in forward operating areas, with requirements for high-aptitude electronics personnel confined to central maintenance or depot level functions. In fact, it could be that the ability of air force enlisted personnel to operate built-in test equipment and read and follow checklist instructions in small-unit environments may be more important than the ability to perform sophisticated on-the-spot repairs. Perhaps the technological development of aircraft electronics equipment will pattern advances in the American automotive industry so that routine maintenance is not a frequent requirement. Can technological advances in computational technology lead to fault-tolerant (self-healing) electronics systems with a decreased requirement for high-aptitude electronics personnel and a significant reduction in the potential strain from the declining youth market?

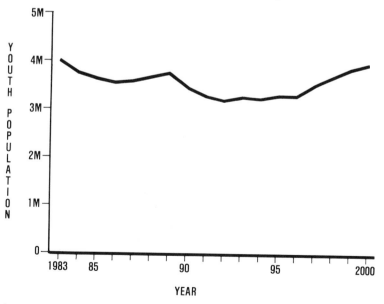

Figure 10.3. Eighteen-year-old Youth Population

Source: U.S. Census Bureau.

Minorities/Internal Population Redistribution/Women

Minorities (primarily blacks and Hispanics), who currently represent 19% of the U.S. population, are anticipated to increase to over 25% by the year 2000.[13] In addition, minorities will be distributed disproportionately in particular areas of the country as the population's statistical center of gravity continues to shift.

A potential solution to the declining youth population would be for the air force to access minorities in increasing proportions. However, if we accept either premise mentioned earlier, i.e., that an increasing number of jobs will require higher-technology skills to operate increasingly more sophisticated equipment, or that more multiskilled people will be required, then this solution may not be feasible. Qualification requirements of the services, particularly the Armed Forces Qualification Test (AFQT) of the Armed Services Vocational Aptitude Battery (ASVAB), which measures basic math and verbal skills as an indicator of general trainability, could prove an insurmountable barrier for a large percentage of minority populations. The *Profile of American Youth*, which resulted from administration of the ASVAB to a representative sample of about 12,000 young Americans, clearly points out the disparity between the performance of minority and white youths on the enlistment test used by all services (Figure 10.4). These results are similar to those obtained on other tests such as the SAT. Given the sensitivity of the Congress to lowering entry standards for enlistment, as reflected in annual minimum male high school diploma graduate percentages for the army, and maximum AFQT category IV (below average) percentages together with a requirement for a high school diploma, increased recruitment of minorities may not be possible. However, what if the immigrant population provides a valuable labor resource for less technical skills in both the public and

Figure 10.4. 1980 Youth Population AFQT Score by Racial/Ethnic Group

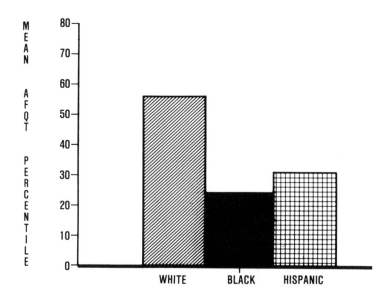

Source: Profile of American Youth Office of the Assistant Secretary of Defense (Manpower, Reserve Affairs, and Logistics) (Washington, DC: Government Printing Office, March 1982) p. 35.

private sectors and in a sense "frees" the higher-quality market for military recruitment? Overall, I believe the severity of the potential problems associated with this expansion may ultimately outweigh the potential benefit to the services.

The new federalism, which has reduced federal intervention in local affairs and increased the autonomy of states and local communities, will force local jurisdictions to manage their population growth or decline, however well or ill-equipped they may be to do so. For example, all states are trying to stimulate economic growth in high-technology industries through new initiatives in three areas: improving elementary and secondary education, strengthening research and higher education, and promoting economic revitalization through technical innovations. While recruiting new firms in microelectronics and other sophisticated fields will certainly be important, of equal importance will be the ability to modernize traditional industries. The key point is that the success of individual states to maximize the potential of their own high-tech resources will influence future migration patterns and directly determine the economic development and the employment and unemployment patterns of the future. These patterns will be important for manpower planners and for the determination of recruitment goals.

The air force has been the leader among the services in the recruitment of women and plans to continue to increase the representation of women in the active force commensurate with future requirements. However, other problems such as pregnancy and motherhood, upper body strength limitations, single member parent (which currently make up about 15% of all households nationwide), policy restrictions, legal and policy restrictions on women in combat, and lower aptitudes and propensity for nontraditional electrical and mechanical jobs in which we currently forecast increased requirements, may combine to limit their utilization. As an aside, some contend that the flood of white women into the work force has had a negative impact on jobs available for black men. Openings that might have gone to young black men now have been taken by women. Finally, if the limitations of the labor supply require increased recruitment of women and minorities, what impact will their concentration in certain traditional career fields, administration, for example, have on readiness and mobilization?

Limitations of the Nation's Educational System

Of increasing concern, and in direct conflict with our need to recruit and retain more high-quality, technically oriented people, are recent reports of serious deficiencies in our education system. At a time when America is trying to build a strong economy and compete internationally in a world that is becoming increasingly more technical, we face the possibility of growing shortages of trained or trainable personnel. Many critics allege that a number of schools are emphasizing "soft" subjects at the expense of basics, particularly in math and science courses. As Secretary of the Air Force Verne Orr wrote in the January 1983 edition of *Air Force Magazine*:

> . . . the requirement for a scientifically literate citizenry, able to master the implications of the new technologies, grows ever more important. Indeed, our nation's very technological advantage in defense and the future ability of our economy to compete in world markets may eventually be at stake.[14]

Comprehensive national efforts are being undertaken to assess the implications and find solutions. Causes for these deficiencies appear to have resulted in large part from a shortage of math and science teachers, which has been linked to salary differentials between teaching and other professions, plus a shift in the 1970s to "balanced" programs which emphasized vocational education. Internal air force discussions have centered around the role the air force should play in dealing with this issue. Traditional personnel planners argued for support of national efforts, but also argued that the primary focus should be to solve air force specific problems. Proactive planners argued that the air force should lead, along with the academic, business, and scientific communities, the search for solutions. In concluding his article, Secretary Orr supported the proactive position:

> The Air Force has an obligation both to itself and to the nation to do all that we can to assist efforts to improve the scientific literacy of our young people. Among the keys to success are closer cooperation between academia, the private sector, government and the military. Innovative solutions will be needed to solve potential Air Force recruiting and retention problems downstream. With a clear understanding of the trends and their implications, I am certain the Air Force family will respond to this challenge . . . .[15]

Of perhaps equal importance to the future air force may be the reading ability of air force enlistees. In conjunction with emphasis on math and science skills, a return to the basics in verbal ability may be of equal importance, particularly to meet the anticipated increased need for generalists. The decline from 1975 to 1982 in SAT scores reveals that verbal skills actually declined more rapidly than did math (Table 10.1). Crucial to improvement in both areas are innovative techniques such as merit pay for teachers, scholarships or incentives for prospective math and science teachers, and, most importantly, money to support new educational programs. As Dallas school official Rod Davis recently indicated: "That's how we're hurting, money for new programs. Trying to teach computer literacy without computers is like teaching geography without a globe."[16]

Table 10.1. Mean Scores, Scholastic Aptitude Test (SAT)

School Year	Verbal	Math	Total
1975	434	472	906
1976	431	472	903
1977	429	470	899
1978	429	468	897
1979	427	467	894
1980	424	466	890
1981	424	466	890
1982	426	467	893

[a] The SAT is taken by almost one million college-bound high school seniors annually.

Economy. Economic forecasts, which due to the complicated interaction of many factors normally tend to be somewhat imprecise, increase in imprecision the further into the future they are made. Current short-term (FY1984) forecasts predict a continuation of the recent boom in consumer spending, increases in business spending, and lower unemployment rates. However, risks to these forecasts center around the financial market's expectations concerning future levels of interest rates and inflation. Sustained economic recovery and growth, which are certainly essential to the national interest and a strong defense, will be accompanied by lower unemployment and have negative impact on recruiting and retention. While mid and long-term economic forecasts admittedly are imprecise, it is imperative that advanced economic analyses, forecasts, and models be incorporated into future MP&T projections and budget requests. Not only must these analyses be incorporated, but their efficiency must be sold to both the Office of Management and Budget and the Congress.

The transformation of the economy from manufacturing to a service orientation will be accompanied by greater degrees of technological application in all sectors. This evolution should stimulate total labor requirements and also sharpen the need for highly skilled technical workers. As the total labor supply and demand for labor converge, competition for quality employees will surely intensify. Air force personnel, already trained in technical skills, will find themselves increasingly more marketable. In addition, as the percentage of work force employed in service occupations continues to increase, I believe the impact of future economic downturns on unemployment rates must be much less dramatic than in the past. As a consequence, military recruiting and retention may become increasingly less sensitive to economic factors than they traditionally appear to have been.

Technology. Planners who predict a moderate rate of growth in end strength and significant increases in electronic aptitude requirements are confident that this growth is achievable, because the total increase equates to only about 29,000 people by the year 2000 or an annual increase of about 1,700. Even these moderate increases raise differences of opinion concerning the impact technological progress may have on future requirements. On the one hand, advances in computerization, telecommunications, etc., could reduce task complexity and increase productivity. The rapid growth of microcomputers in the home and computer education programs in elementary and secondary schools could produce a generation of young people who are well versed in computer operations with a basic understanding of computer programming. A survey by the National Assessment of Educational Progress, a program of the National Institute of Education, found a rapidly increasing use of computers by thirteen-year-olds between 1978 and 1982 (Table 10.2). This trend could alleviate some of the concern mentioned earlier about scientific illiteracy and lead to an adequate pool of young people capable of operating and supporting advanced computer systems. Furthermore, most air force computer systems are contractor-maintained, and computer maintenance is on the more skill/technology-intensive side of the technology issue.

Table 10.2. Computer Use by 13-Year-Olds

	Percent Answering Yes	
	1978	1982
Do you have access to a computer terminal in your school for learning mathematics?	12.2	22.7
Have you ever used a computer to solve a mathematical problem?	55.9	65.6
Do you know how to program a computer?	8.2	19.9
Have you ever written a program to solve a math problem?	28.4	39.6

Source: *Scientific, Engineering, Technical Manpower Comments,* Scientific Manpower Commission, July-August 1983.

On the other hand, it may well be that factors such as the increased technical requirements of the other services (Table 10.3) dramatically increased employment opportunities in the civilian electronics industry (which plans to double its recruitment of military technicians by 1985), plus significant expansion in the telecommunications industry (in which growth will more than triple by 1990), will cause skill shortages far worse than those recently experienced. It may well be that contracting out is not a panacea for critical skill imbalances which exist now, in sortie-generating skills such as avionics. Can the air force develop programs that emphasize technology to replace manpower or find uses for robotics to meet future requirements? Will technology work

Table 10.3. Military Requirements for Numbers of Technical Skills
Where Math/Science Background Is Desirable

	Number of Occupations	# Enlisted Jobs	% of Enlisted Force
Army[a]	359	130,696	22
Navy[b]	37	271,420	45
Air Force	183	313,147	72

[a] Army experienced a 34% growth in technical skill aptitudes between 1980 and 1982. This will continue to increase with ongoing force modernization.
[b] Navy anticipates 16%-17% increase in need for people with math/science/technical aptitudes by 1987.

for the air force or the air force for technology? An interesting sidelight to the computer issue is that the cost of home computers may limit their purchase to middle - and upper-income families. This limitation could preclude a large number of lower-income minorities from gaining a foothold in advanced technology and perhaps limit their ability to compete for jobs created by new technologies.

In times such as these, which are characterized by rapid technological advances, there is always the possibility of an enemy breakthrough in weapons capability. Our R&D communities work very hard to prevent this. However, recent reports indicate that our national technological edge in certain areas is being challenged by other nations. For example, the United States share of the world high-tech market has declined by 15% in recent years, while Japan's share has increased by 25%. While the United States holds the lead in the research and design of robotics, Japan is far ahead in production and use with about 3.5 times as many in use as we have.[17] Our flexibility and ability to apply innovative ideas that counter possible enemy breakthroughs are crucial under any future scenario.

Commitment of American People/Congressional Support

Perhaps the single most important factor that will determine the continued success of the AVF is the commitment of the American people as expressed through their elected representatives, the Congress. Solid support for the AVF will depend on many factors such as: the public perception of the Soviet threat, world political tensions, and the national and world economic situations. A strong commitment will be translated into congressional action which will be expressed in terms of: a stable, predictable pay system to insure relative pay comparability; adequate recruiting resources; support for bonus and incentive programs to meet total force critical skill needs; full reimbursement for reasonable expenses associated with a government-directed permanent change-of-station move; stability in the military retirement system; and implementation of a new noncontributory educational incentive with both recruiting and retention features. Our concern is that recent congressional and/or administration actions, e.g., pay caps, Civilian Health and Medical Program of the Uniformed Services (CHAMPUS) and recruiting resource reductions, etc., are reminiscent of actions taken in the mid-1970s and again could interact with other key factors in the mid to late 1980s that would allow a repeat of recruiting and retention problems of the late 1970s. The fact that we are in a force-building mode now rather than the force drawdown of the 1970s will further magnify the impact of these actions. The ability of the Department of Defense and the air force to make a strong case for future requirements will be crucial to obtain the appropriate resources necessary to balance competing interests.

Other Services. While the recent past has witnessed increased cooperation among the services in the development of roles to complement each other's missions, I foresee increased competition for a declining youth market compounded by technological advances in all services. Air force surveys of new recruits over the years have consistently indicated that only about 20% of our recruits would have joined another service if they had not enlisted in the air force. However, the increasing technological attractiveness of other services' missions (Table 10.3), the army's significant "competitive edge" in recruiting resources, plus all services' recent success in obtaining and retaining quality enlistees, have created a favorable recruiting and retention picture which is to the benefit of DoD.

In the area of mobilization, I foresee continued policy conflicts concerning the accession of volunteers versus nonvolunteers, the distribution of quality, and the acceptance of conscientious objectors. The air force intends to meet enlisted mobilization manpower requirements through the recruitment of volunteers, utilizing the same standards and procedures as during peacetime and believes the acceptance of conscientious objectors should be a service prerogative. While continuing to respect and defend each service's rightful individual prerogatives in areas such as enlistment standards, our continued exploration of methods that exploit new developments and technologies for common interests must be supported.

I have always been concerned with the perception that the success of the AVF is measured only in terms of the army, when in fact the true criterion should be the success of all services. While fully acknowledging and appreciating the extremely positive nature of the services' current relations with the Office of the Secretary of Defense (OSD) staff and recognizing OSD's responsibility for oversight, future disagreements may be inevitable. Specifically, competing interests in a more difficult recruiting and retention environment could again rekindle previous areas of conflict. While recognizing that conflict may be inevitable, strong OSD support on issues such as increased special duty assignment pay for recruiters and noncontributory educational incentive with both recruiting and retention features will be necessary to help secure the future success of the AVF.

Again, I believe consideration of these external factors, in conjunction with the demand issues, is necessary to provide a more complete perspective concerning the possible future direction and success of the AVF.

CONCLUSION

The air force is equipped with the most advanced, sophisticated, and complex weapons systems ever devised. The key to our war-fighting capability is to recruit, train, and retain high-quality, motivated people to operate and maintain these systems. Yet as we look forward to this decade and beyond, developments that are at once exciting and promising, yet disquieting and challenging, appear to dominate the horizon.

We face monumental challenges in the way people work, handle information, and wage wars. The industrial age is being replaced by the information-processing age. The ability to compress large amounts of information and provide only the key data necessary for decision making would be a key advance. Military activity in space and travel beyond our atmosphere are realities. Every aspect of air power is changing rapidly and dramatically. The events and conditions of the wars that threaten us now, and those we may have to fight in the future, forge an inseparable link between MP&T and the entire air force — active, reserve, and civilian.

Some trends are already known. Their impact and interaction must be assessed and flexible programs and policies developed to counter, or at least mitigate, the factors we can influence most. The air force must come to grips with the complex interaction of these trends and the diminishing ratio of resources available to meet requirements. The use of available and emerging technologies must be brought to bear in those areas where it can have its most positive effect.

Increased involvement in weapons systems development and acquisition plus flexibility in personnel management will be critical. Answers which seemed reasonable during the period of force drawdown and a relatively abundant surplus of young talent in the 1970s may no longer be valid. The standard answers "It just won't work" or "We've tried it before" will not be adequate.

Trained, experienced personnel are the foundation upon which the effectiveness of American airpower rests. The issues of recruitment, attrition, retention, training, morale, and, ultimately, readiness are closely interlinked. Both these and the other factors I've discussed have secondary impacts in a variety of areas other than their immediate focus. Our challenge is clear; the issue of manpower availability and trainability may be the most limiting factor on the amount of air *force* truly available in the future. *Forewarned is forearmed*!

NOTES

1. Robert C. Seamans, Jr., "How USAF Plans to Meet Its Personnel Needs," *Air Force Magazine*, March 1973, p. 45.
2. Verne Orr and Charles A. Gabriel, "Fiscal Year 1984 Air Force Report to the 98th Congress of the United States of America," Washington D.C. February 1983, p. 47.
3. *Air Force 2000: Air Power Entering the 21st Century*, (Washington, D.C.: Headquarters, U.S. Air Force, June 1982) p. 254.
4. Ibid.
5. Ibid., p. 255.
6. Ibid., p. 258.
7. Ibid., p. 259.
8. Ackman Associates, Inc., "Enhancing Manpower, Personnel and Training Planning in the USAF Acquisition Process," USAF Contract Delivery Order 12, Silver Spring MD, 12 April 1983.
9. M. B. Berman and C. L. Batten, "Increasing Future Fighter Weapons System Performance by Integrating Basing, Support and Air Vehicle Requirements." *Rand Note, N-1985-1-AF*, (Santa Monica, CA: Rand Corporation April 1983) p. 13.
10. Gen. Robert T. Marsh, "R&D Works up the Options," *Air Force Magazine*, August 1983, p. 40.
11. Tidal W. McCoy, "Military Technology: The Complexity Issue," *Policy Review*, 1983, pp. 74-77.
12. Lt. Col. John Dwyer, "Technical Training in the 1980s" (Washington, D.C.: Headquarters, U.S. Air Force, MPPTS, 1983) pp. 1-6
13. *Air Force 2000*, p. 262.
14. Verne Orr, "Scientific Illiteracy in the High Tech Age." *Air Force Magazine*, January 1983, p. 73.
15. Ibid., p. 76.
16. David Fink, "Rush to Make Our Schools Better Faster," *USA Today*, 24 August 1983, p. 2.
17. Jack Anderson, "America Losing High-Tech Race to the Japanese," *Washington Post*, 25 August 1983, p. 19.

Commentary

DISCUSSANTS

Jesse Orlansky

The services, except for the army which plans no personnel increases, believe they will need from 3 to 5% more personnel by FY1990, an increase less than the projected growth in weapons over the same period (e.g., 26% increase in ship tonnage). The modest increase in the need for personnel is attributed to greater efficiency in manning weapons and platforms and to greater use of more advanced computers. It is probably also realistic not to expect public support for large increases in the size of the military forces in the near future.

The services, however, do anticipate a significant change in the aptitude levels of personnel needed for military service. The need for personnel qualified to handle advanced electronic equipment will increase by 10 to 30%; the need for high-level mechanical aptitudes will increase by 10 to 20%; the need for semi-technical, administrative aptitude levels will stay the same in some areas and decrease in others by as much as 20%. The shift to higher aptitude levels will stay the same in some areas and decrease in others by as much as 20%. The shift to higher-aptitude levels is related directly to existing plans for more complex equipment and the need to operate and maintain them at high levels of performance; there is less need for lower-skilled personnel.

The greater need for high-quality personnel can lead to a serious problem for all services. Some relevant data, taken from *Profile of American Youth* 1980, are shown in Figure 1.

The distribution of the male youth population age eighteen to twenty-three in 1980, according to the Armed Forces Qualification Test (AFQT) category and percentile scores, is shown in column three; the distribution of young males who entered the military services in FY1981 is shown for all services and for each service separately in other columns. It is clear that, for the

Figure 1. Male Youth Population in 1980 and Nonprior-Service Accessions for FY1981

AFQT		DISTRIBUTION OF MALE YOUTH, PERCENT					
		POPULATION 18-23 YEARS, 1980	NON-PRIOR SERVICE ACCESSIONS, FY 1981				
CATEGORY	PERCENTILE SCORE		TOTAL DoD	A	N	MC	AF
I	93-100	5	3	2	3	3	3
II	65-92	35	30	21	35	29	39
III	31-64	29	47	43	48	53	50
IV	10-30	23	20	34	14	15	8
V	1-9	8	0	0	0	0	0
TOTAL PERCENT		100	100	100	100	100	100
MEDIAN SCORE		53	52	41	56	52	59

Source: Profile of American Youth Office of the Assistant Secretary of Defense (Manpower, Reserve Affairs, and Logistics) (Washington, DC: Government Printing Office, March 1982).

entire Department of Defense, accessions in categories I and II were below the proportions available in the population at large; they were above that for category III. The services were more successful in recruiting high-quality personnel in FY1975, 1976, 1982 and 1983 and so far in FY1984 than is shown in this table.

The facts that pose difficulty are that only 5% of all men are in the highest AFQT category and 35% are in the next highest category. In the past, competition between the military and nonmilitary sectors as places for young people to start careers has made it more difficult to enlist personnel in the higher AFQT categories. The increased use of new technology by virtually all industries and thus a greatly increased need for technically qualified personnel in the private as well as public sectors will increase the difficulty of the services to acquire higher-aptitude personnel. To put it simply, the improved market choices available to high-aptitude personnel will force the services to compete in areas in which they have not performed as well in the past as they are doing now.

People and Military System Performance

We are indebted to Gen. William E. DePuy for reminding us that the purpose of military service is to be prepared to fight effectively when and where it may be required. Issues related to acquiring and retaining manpower tend to dominate discussions of the All-Volunteer Force, but these are only part of the problem of military readiness. As Robert J. Murray (chapter 9) puts it: "The Navy builds technicians, it does not hire them. Thus, the impact of technology falls heavily upon the training establishment." The acquisition of manpower is a necessary but not sufficient condition for an effective military force. In addition to manpower, we need competent training, equipment, and management to assure an adequate level of military readiness.

General DePuy showed that system performance (P_s) is a product of equipment performance (P_e) and human performance (P_h), that is $P_s = P_e \times P_h$. The equation is shown graphically in Figure 2.

General DePuy described the results of recent field trials for STINGER, a missile operated by one person: system performance, P_s, was 0.44 rather than 0.64 specified by the design goal.[1] The 30% decrease in system effectiveness occurred because human performance, P_h, averaged 0.55 rather than 0.80 as required. Similar results were found from skill qualification tests (SQT)

Figure 2. Graph for System Performance Equation

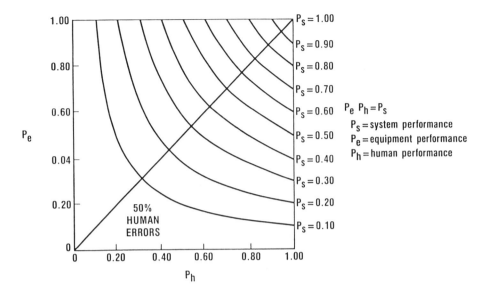

where average P_h's were about 0.7, 0.6, and 0.5 for leaders, operators, and maintainers, respectively. The findings are attributed to an interaction of AFQT category and training, i.e., observed human performance P_h declines as aptitude level declines from category I to IV.

Serious consequences follow if actual human performance is significantly less than that required by the goals set for weapons and support system performance. For STINGER, it may be expressed as a 30% decrease in return on an investment of $1.7 billion for military equipment. Another way of saying the same thing is that our weapons and support systems might not perform as required on a battlefield. The United States relies on high technology in order to cope with an adversary who possesses a greater quantity of weapons and people. Improvements in technology are generally hard to achieve and are also very expensive because they are at the limits of the state-of-the-art. Thus, even if accession goals are satisfied, the impact of training and personnel quality on readiness can hardly be exaggerated. In fact, it may well be that the success of the AVF will open our eyes to the enormous importance of excellent training for the personnel we are able to attract in the next ten years.

Training the Force

The Report of the Defense Science Board 1982 Summer Study Panel on Training and Training Technology,[2] cochaired by Adm. Isaac C. Kidd and Dr. Walter LaBerge, points out that a variety of advances in training technology can be used to improve the performance and readiness of our armed forces. Some significant findings, shown in Figure 3, are that new technology (e.g., flight simulators, computer-based instruction, and maintenance simulators) are as effective for training as the conventional methods they can replace; in addition, they also save significant amounts of training time and acquisition, operating, and life cycle costs. Investments in new technology for training in these areas can be amortized, within two to four years.

We should contemplate the fact that, over the last ten years, the services have used new training technology to reduce training costs rather than to improve the effectiveness of training or to increase the achievement level of students. There is no reason to quarrel with the use of new technology to save student time and money. However, the increasing need for higher-quality

Figure 3. Summary of Findings of Studies on the Cost-Effectiveness of Flight Simulators, Computer-Based Instruction and Maintenance Simulators

EFFECTIVENESS	FACTOR	SAVINGS OR COST		
		FLIGHT SIMULATORS	COMPUTER-BASED INSTRUCTION	MAIN-TENANCE SIMULATORS
	EFFECTIVENESS ⟶	22	48	14
ABOUT THE SAME	STUDENT TIME	50% OF SIMULATOR TIME 22	30% 48	20-50% 3
	ACQUISITION COST	30-65% 4	?	20-60% 13
	OPERATING COST	8% 42	?	50% 1
	LIFE-CYCLE COST	65% 1	?	40% 1
	AMORTIZA-TION	2 YEARS 4	?	4 YEARS 1

NUMBER OF STUDIES

Source: Orlasky, J., J. String, P.R. Chatelier; 1982. "Cost Effectiveness of Military Training." *Proceedings of the 4th Interservice/ Industry Training Equipment Conference.* Washington, DC: National Security Industrial Association.

personnel to operate and maintain more advanced equipment should lead us to reconsider our training strategy. Is it possible to use new training technology to improve the effectiveness of training rather than to save student time? Some recent findings on the use of computer-based instruction in secondary schools and in colleges suggest that this is indeed possible.[3]

These studies compared student achievement (i.e., scores on final examinations) at the same schools in the same courses administered either by conventional instruction or by computer-based instruction. An index, called Effect Size, was used to measure the magnitude of the difference between final examination scores of those who used computer-based and those who used conventional instruction. The difference is expressed in standard deviation units, that is:

$$\text{Effect Size} = \frac{\text{Difference Between Mean Score, Final Exam} \quad \text{CBI} - \text{Conventional}}{\text{Standard Deviation, Conventional}}$$

In secondary schools, the effect size was 0.32 standard deviation units. This means that the average exam score of those in computer-based instruction classes was at the sixty-third percentile of those in conventional instruction classes (Figure 4). In colleges, the effect size was 0.25 standard deviation units. That puts computer-based classes at the sixtieth percentile of those in conventional classes (see Figure 5).

How can we explain these different findings, i.e., that in military training computer-based instruction provides effectiveness equal to that of conventional instruction while in secondary schools and colleges, computer-based instruction provides greater effectiveness. The explanation that follows is called a speculation because it has not been tested directly, either in military or in nonmilitary schools. Nevertheless, we believe that there is a plausible explanation for the differences in effectiveness in the two environments.

Figure 4. Effect Size for Computer-Based Teaching in Secondary Schools, Based on 48 Studies

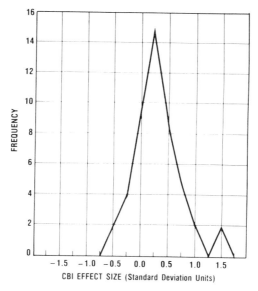

Source: Kulik, J.A., R.l., Bangert, and G.W. Williams. "Effects of Computer-based Teaching on Secondary School Students," in *Journal of Educational Psychology* 75 (1983): 19-26.

Figure 5. Effect Size for Computed-Based Teaching in Colleges, Based on 54 Studies

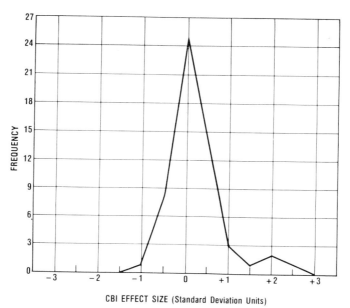

Source: Kulik, J.A., C.C. Kulik, and P.A. Cohen. "Effectiveness of Computer-based College Teaching: A Meta-Analysis Finding," in *Review of Educational Research* 50 (1980): 525-544.

Military training courses are generally designed to prepare students to perform particular jobs. In fact, a procedure called Instructional System Development is used to specify what a student should know and be able to do in order to complete a course; this is called the "criterion." With computer-based instruction, each student proceeds at his own pace and graduates whenever he can demonstrate that he has achieved criterion-level performance. The time savings found with computer-based instruction are due largely to the faster learners, i.e., those for whom the pace set in conventional classroom instruction (a pace that meets the needs of average and slower learners) is too slow. Since all students must achieve criterion performance in order to graduate, they all achieve about the same amount. The criterion level set for computer-based instruction is generally about the same as that for conventional instruction; hence, equal effectiveness and student time savings.

Computer-based instruction is used differently in secondary schools and colleges where it produces greater student achievement when compared to conventional instruction. Here again, there are faster and slower learners. However, the length of the school term is fixed and all students must stay for the same amount of time. With computer-based instruction, faster learners learn more than slower learners; hence, greater effectiveness and no student time savings.

Because students vary in their rates of learning (i.e., as shown in the normal distribution) we believe that computer-based instruction can be used either to save student time (with equal achievement) or to increase student achievement (with fixed time in the course). This hypothetical relationship is illustrated in Figure 6. For the sake of simplicity, the learning curves are shown as straight lines rather than as reaching some asymptote. The "choice" between increased achievement or reduced time need not be an arbitrary one because, with appropriate data for a particular application, there is probably an optimum trade-off between student achievement and time in the course.

Changing the way of using computer-based instruction in military training from saving time to increasing student achievement at school—which we believe is possible and which should be tested—can make a significant contribution to the increasing need of the military services to improve the performance of their personnel. The services should obviously try to recruit the

Figure 6. Hypothetical Relation Between Student Achievement and Student Time for Computer-Based Instruction and for Conventional Instruction.

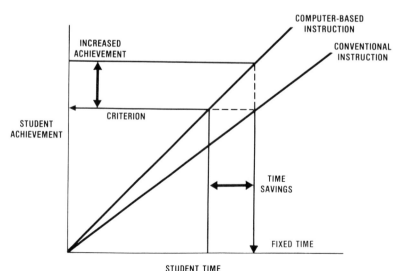

highest-aptitude level personnel they can attract. When that is achieved, it will still be necessary to train these people to higher levels of performance. And it seems clear that new training technology can be used to achieve that goal. Improved training to achieve readiness is the next milestone in the process started with the AVF.

NOTES

1. Nelson, A., E. Schmitz, and D. Promisel. *The Impact of Personnel Quality on STINGER Weapon System Performance*. Technical Area Working Paper 83-32. (Alexandria, VA: Army Research Institute, 1983).
2. *Defense Science Board 1982 Summer Study Panel Report on Training and Training Technology*. (Washington, D.C.: The Pentagon, Office of the Undersecretary of Defense for Research and Engineering).
3. Kulik, James A., Chen-lin C. Kulik, and P.A. Cohen. "Effectiveness of Computer-based College Teaching: A Meta-Analysis of Findings," 50 (1980): 525-544, and Kulik, J.A., R.L. Bangert, and G.W. Williams. "Effects of Computer-based Teaching on Secondary School Students," *Journal of Educational Psychology* 75 (1983): 19-26.

R. Dean Tice

I will attempt to introduce one single new dimension on how we might arrive at meeting some of the challenges presented. Dr. LaBerge stated that training technology could probably help us overcome many obstacles. Admiral Kidd supported that statement with the findings of the Defense Science Board which concluded that we can probably take lesser-quality individuals and use training technology to bring them up to speed so they can assimilate the training and perform better on the job. However, we are shortchanged because we have no incentive to entice the industry to come forth and offer a training technology that might help us accomplish the mission.

General DePuy pointed out, and I wouldn't disagree with him at all, that human performance, in the final analysis, is what determines the effectiveness of the weapons system. Robert J. Murray also discussed the growth of technology and force-structure growth with lesser increases in technology. But if you add those two together, there's still an increase in the demand for technically qualified people. General Roberts stated that the mission drives the force structure, and it probably does. I would suggest that at the time we were recruiting and training the two ranger battalions and were training the marines who would land on Grenada, we had no idea that we'd have that special kind of commitment for them or that we would be serving in five parts of the world today to accomplish our mission. I don't know anybody who is sage enough to anticipate all challenges fully, so you develop a force structure that would meet those contingencies. Perhaps the bottom line is this: if you have high-quality people who can maximize the effectiveness of the weapons systems, then you might do the job with fewer people. I do want to give credit for the things the weapons systems people have done to help the manpower people work through some of the toughcially using technology to reduce the number of individuals required to perform the mission. For example, in the air defense system we were able to increase greatly our kill probability when we changed from the Nike system to the improved Hawk. But in the process, we almost doubled the number of highly skilled individuals (electronics technicians) needed to operate and maintain that new system. However, in the design of the Patriot, we have been able to reduce the number of electronics specialties in an air force battalion by thirty-nine. Today, the total manning of an air defense battalion has been reduced from 1,000 to 799. That is progress! All our services have made similar headway in selected weapons systems.

For example, I recently reviewed the F-15 system. We changed to a single commander/weapons officer in the cockpit. This system replaced much of the F-4 series aircraft and each cost three times as much. The spares to maintain the same sortie rate went up five times. These two examples are useful. I'm not sure from a cost basis that the increased cost of spares was a balanced trade-off for fewer people. But I think such options should be examined by our weapons systems developers and project managers. General Roberts stressed increased involvement in the weapons systems development and in the acquisition process, plus flexibility in personnel management. I know Gary Nelson suggested that if we put more resources in the people business, he is not sure that it would buy more quality or more people—it might even go to readiness. I would suggest that if we accept the preliminary research done by the army on human performance, then there's a great payoff for buying higher quality in order to man our complex weapons systems.

If you approach the problem from the standpoint of the people involved in the weapons systems or acquisition process, you must realize it wasn't until 1978 (on Robert Pirie's watch) that we even had anyone from Manpower, Reserves and Logistics (MRA&L) sitting in judgment or as a participant in the Defense System Acquisition Review Council (DSARC) process. I'm not sure if they would have had any greater influence had they been invited earlier. Obviously, we haven't done so well since we have been on DSARC. We still have less than 1% of the R&D budget going to research on the people side. Even if there is a 4% or 5% growth in that area, I am not sure we would make the progress needed. Certainly we ought to use technology and we ought to insure that the manpower people participate in the decision process. I think the weapons system project managers need an incentive, and industry also needs to have some incentive, so that through improved design with built-in diagnostic capability the average soldier can be trained to identify and troubleshoot systems maintenance. They should develop and understand the cost trade-off for making the system more capable of being operated by the average person responsible for its maintenance. We need to design towards using manpower with average intellect.

I want to read an evaluation based on a mock-up of a prototype piece of hardware that got to the developmental stage. An average infantry soldier looked at the mock-up and made a quick assessment. He uncovered some horrible deficiencies in the design with respect to human engineering factors and he drew conclusions about the kind of individual who would operate it. His evaluation read:

1. The night site is positioned directly in front of the gunner where it should be. A standard gunnery control similar to the M60A1 system is at waist level.
2. The day site, however, is positioned 18-20 inches to the left and 8 inches forward. It also has a cover for the right eye when you move into the head rest.
3. The pillar for the gear control for manual rotation of the turret is directly to the left of the gunner.
   Now the foregoing has the following effect. When you strain forward to the left to site the weapon, the gear pillar is in the way and puts a strain on the left shoulder. And, when you lean forward and to the left the gun controls are jammed up against your stomach, and are almost impossible to operate.
   We know that when you have shoulder and neck stress it is difficult to acquire a target, see clearly, maintain eye control, and have effective mental functioning. All this stress and strain destroys your visual acuity.

When the contractor representative was asked about human engineering factors in the design of the system he said, "We put the switches where they were easy to reach."

When the problems with the firing position were pointed out he said, "Well, you just sort of have to make him fit the machine—and we build the best we can at the cheapest cost. If the army wants it changed, then they can pay for it."

This is another example of failing to incorporate human elements into the hardware design and acquisition process. Unless we're going to adopt the soviet T62 philosophy, then we'll need 20,000 right-humped, left-eyed, dwarf hunchbacks to shoot the improved TOW vehicle.

I agree with Robert Murray, and I want to give the weapons systems people credit for making great headway. For example, for a given tonnage afloat in the navy, we have been able to reduce significantly the number of people aboard ship. In addition, we have increased the lethal capability against the enemy. I saw a statistic that showed that 3,000 sorties of the F-16 could deliver the same iron bomb tonnage on an enemy as the 30,000 Army Air Corps troops did in the invasion of Normandy.

There is also an example contained in the development guidance for the remotely piloted vehicle (RPV). The evaluation and award factors given to the contractor with reference to what we wanted in design characteristics included eight major characteristics. Noteworthy is the fifth factor. That is effective support for training—minimize the number of military personnel, and minimize the amount of training required to make them proficient. I felt good that guidance on manpower considerations was included as one of the characteristics. Then I turned over the page and noticed that the guidance provided to the contractor stated that the first four characteristics are significantly more important than the remaining four characteristics. Obviously the priority of effort was cut just above the manpower requirement.

As we have increased the need for quality, I think we have some ability to influence the outcome if somehow we can become more involved in the weapons systems developmental process. It wasn't until about five or six years ago that we even did a very good job of having an accurate inventory of the skills required during the design of a system so that by the time the weapons systems was introduced and came on line, we could operate and maintain it. In my thirty-eight years of service I saw many pieces of new equipment come into the army which, in spite of the judgment of some who said there would be little retraining needed, required that we do major retraining in order to accept the system into the unit.

I would like to leave you two final questions to ponder. Can we allow the four services to operate in the manpower marketplace without OSD at some time stepping in and saying there are not enough quality people to go around? And, how can the manpower allocation process determine the proper share of the available quality?

W. B. LaBerge

The technology/manpower problem is one that I've had an opportunity to look at, first as a technician at China Lake and then as a person in various jobs in the Pentagon who subsequently went to NATO and looked at it from the outside. Very clearly, the manpower interface with increasingly sophisticated weapons systems has several sides and none of these sides is being done very well at all. Let me address why those of us in the technical implementing business are not doing our part very well. It's for the rest of you to understand why the manpower acquisition business isn't doing very well itself. As I sit and listen to you, it is more like Cassandra saying that the Greeks are inside the horse, or the tragedy where everybody stands around wringing their hands, rather than anybody having some specific proposals. As discussed by General DePuy, we collectively have a major potential problem in that we're fielding in the army, as in all of the services, a set of very capable equipment which needs to be handled and maintained by very capable people.

It is absolutely clear that the equipment we're putting in the field must in fact be operated by people who are trained or are able to be trained. Somehow or other, we are avoiding the problem for reasons that are not very clear to me. The issue of how you get the skilled people is one that all of you are more qualified to address than I. The issue of how you train the people using current technology is one that I think I'm reasonably qualified to talk about and I'm probably even more qualified to talk about why industry is not addressing the problem. I had the chance to work with Admiral Kidd on the Defense Science Board study on training and training technology. It was very clear to all participants that both the size of the problem and the size of the opportunity were evident. Current technology is revolutionizing the dimensions of the weapons systems which we can field. The same technology has the capability of helping to train and maintain the skills of the people and the capabilities of the equipment, but very, very little is being done to cause that to happen. Current technology has a great opportunity to cause the pieces to work together. But that doesn't happen either. There's a bit of a sociological problem in making things work together because we have a Pentagon system based on individual projects which have no relationship, necessarily, to the outcome of a war. If they had a relationship, you would in fact tie a bunch of things together which are not tied together as they should be today. But with respect to the application of the technology to training people and maintaining the skills, I would argue we have a very significant problem.

Let me put it in the context of the company that I now represent. I am the technical director, vice president of technology, for Lockheed Missiles and Space Company with an annual budget in the order of 2.5 billion dollars. This accounts for approximately 4% of our company-oriented research and development for bidding and proposing. Of that, about 2% goes to independent research and development. Therefore, we get about $100 million to work on the important things of the future. But we have to survive, and that means doing things we like to do, are capable of doing, and that someone will pay for. This latter element is as important in our free enterprise system as the other two. Lockheed would like to work on training and training devices. Lockheed is competent at working on training and training devices. But there is in fact no market for that. That's the same for Hughes and TRW and all of the major people in the business. From the major equipment suppliers' standpoint, working on the technology of training people, retraining of skills, and the application of these skills in the field by the presentation of information is, in fact, not related to the winning of any major program. If you concentrate on a new high-powered laser, or how to point that laser, or how to correct its wavefront, you can in fact win the next generation space age laser. If you describe the training and training technology supporting it, it will make no difference at all. And hence, we put our money on how you point and track. Thus training and training technology are not important to the winning of contracts because they're not related to profits. In the end one's success is not measured in terms of how well things work in the field. It is measured by how well you deliver them through an army office or a navy office, and there is no warranty on how well the system works in the field. Accordingly, very little customer research and development is paid for and consequently there is no economic reason to do it. As far as I can see, this basic trend is continuing. System performance is related to the ability of the people to perform, but we measure only the performance of hardware, and under the most optimum conditions. It's not related to the independent research and development scoring system, which in the end says how much recovery you get. The independent research and development is scrutinized by a group of technicians, most of whom have never thought through the issue of training or training technology and therefore, screwy things happen.

Currently we have the ability to renegotiate the independent research and development programs based on how they affect readiness in the reliability and maintenance area, or in several other areas, but not in the training area. What I'm saying is that we have an economic system where we are very much like Darwin's finches. We have a survival adaptation which requires that we survive in the business which is available. We grow the large beaks or the platypus beaks, depending on what our business area is. Until the system makes it economically important for imbedded training to be in systems and creative manpower systems to be implemented, we're going to continue to emphasize abstract performance systems; systems having nothing related to the issue of whether the young man you might get for the military can operate the equipment.

In conclusion, I'd like to suggest to the DoD that it might be really useful to get a small, ad hoc group of people at the vice president level in the major companies together to determine changes required to induce the business world to put emphasis on the kinds of technology which are important for knowledge-based systems and to provide incentives to develop systems which can help us better use the people we get, better train them, better maintain their skills, and better help them do the jobs that they have. I think if you changed the incentive system a bit, you would get industry swinging around. Right now, my point is that of the two sides of the problem, the one which supplies people is not changing a great deal. The technology opportunity, which is very substantial, isn't being worked because there is no constituency and no incentive to produce that work. We ought to be able to change. If there is a single thing the DoD should do, it would be to understand Darwin and the finches and look at industry as "finches" because all of us, whether we are Lockheed or Hughes or TRW, are the "finches," trying to honorably dig the worms where the worms are. You cannot expect us to devote our money or our attention to an area where there are no worms.

C. E. Mundy, Jr.

Let me say, as has been said by Robert J. Murray, that we marines, as soldiers and airmen of the sea, represent something of a microcosm of the three services, and much of what has been said by General DePuy is most applicable to the marines. I would agree that smarter and higher-quality soldiers, sailors, and airmen and marines, will tend to enhance any system's effectiveness. This tends to conflict with some of our historical and more popular perceptions of what, in particular, a soldier, a marine, sometimes a sailor, and perhaps less frequently, an airman, are or have been throughout our history. We have adopted the term "grunt" in association with marine infantrymen. We have often heard the statement made that anybody can carry a rifle, swab a ship deck, paint, peel spuds, and that sort of thing; therefore, this would seem to make a case for perhaps an overrepresentative number of mental category IVs in our ranks as opposed to those with more sophisticated skills.

I can remember people saying in my hometown, "He wasn't too good at arithmetic, but he sure could shoot straight!" That made him a good soldier when he went off to World War II or Korea. A lot of these people have served honorably and loyally; and they have been the heroes of many a movie and many a fictitious or actual circumstance in our history. Because of their loyalty, because of their dedication, because their shoes were always brightly shined and their brass polished (all "soldierly" virtues with which we can identify) they have tended to be promoted within the system.

Such qualities are part of the institution's recognition of excellence and reward for performance. Unfortunately, though, when these individuals become NCOs they are unable to relate to and effectively lead the caliber of young marines that we are bringing into the corps today. So, as Dr. Robert Murray has pointed out, the marines have not specifically identified a significant need for category IVs because we need NCOs who can lead, regardless of occupational field, and leadership (just like technical competence) takes intelligence. I gather from General DePuy that the army still has a representative number of category IVs forecast into the 1990s. I'm not certain whether that is really an analyzed and identified need or whether it's just a recognition of the reality of manpower supply, or what the market can bear.

In the minds of some, it may be possible to make a case for larger numbers of lower mental groups in the infantry or similar, perceived, lower-skill type organizations. We have tended always to think we can assign lower mental groups to the infantry, motor transport, or to supply. Surely we can make a cook out of him! As any of us know and recognize, if you've eaten in many military dining facilities, the quality of the food is a very significant factor in the morale of the force. It's important to have a cook who can read the menu and can put in the right amount of seasoning. It's also important to have a transportation man who can read road signs, who can reach his point of destination, and who can maintain his vehicle. Most important, and I think most often looked down upon, is the common ordinary "grunt," the infantryman. Think of being a squad leader. A common thought is that all he has to do is stand up and say "follow me" and he has done his job. He must do that, to be sure, but he also has to analyze his situation, understand the orders that are given to him, relay these orders articulately to his squad members, and coordinate supporting arms, perhaps while on the move. And, he has to do all this while somebody with an AK-47, about 150 meters away, is trying to kill him. Under this scenario, we tend to think that the smarter he is, perhaps the greater his survivability, and that of those he leads.

I would like to address one additional point made by Mr. Johnston, who suggested that perhaps technology is an offset to quality requirements. That has not been our experience. Rather, we sense that technology enhances weapons-system effectiveness, but it does not necessarily reduce the number of people that it takes to fix the systems. It may take fewer mechanics at the organizational maintenance activity of a fighter squadron to remove the engine on a new FA-18 and to unplug some of its components, but we tend to see the requirement for maintenance simply transferred back an echelon. So, we have not necessarily seen a reduction in the number of people required simply because we're getting higher technology.

I would say, since I am a recruiter, that at present we are recruiting about the highest quality marine in recent history. This year we averaged 92% high school graduates, 6% category IVs and about 61% in our categories I-IIIA. We are about where we want to be. I can tell you with optimism, looking at the next year, that the start pool we have for the next twelve months, representing over 50% of that twelve-month quota, is about 97% high school graduates and just under 1% category IVs. Therefore, we are aiming at the relative elimination of all but truly outstanding (on a whole-person basis) Category IVs as long as the market is there. We think that quality begets quality. We see young people who believe that it's okay to be in the military; patriotism is up. We believe that this better quality and attitude will, to a degree, perpetuate itself.

I would add that there's a direct correlation between the number of quality recruiters in the field and the number of quality recruits we get. I would add also, that in the few years of the AVF, the recruiting machinery of all the services has become a very fine-tuned, marketing and sales organization. We have some of our best marines on recruiting duty. We have training programs and machinery in place to bring in extraordinarily high-quality people. And we're doing it. We need to continue the support for that. We believe that with continued support, we can recruit quality marines in the numbers we need. As our former commandant used to say, "You make hay while the sun shines," and remember that "success in battle is not so much a function of how many show up, as who they are."

AUDIENCE

W. B. LaBerge: Could I supplement Jesse Orlansky's discussion? The unique characteristic of computer-based education is that it is transportable. An additional thing recent studies have shown is that retentivity is almost as important as the initial ability to learn. This means that when you get a force in the field, unless you can maintain currency of instruction, people's performance will fall off substantially. You now can bring computer-based instruction to the field, and you can also update the instruction as you need it. If the fielded system is a large one, imbedded system computers can train, and monitor daily or weekly, the performance of its operators and that makes a very substantial difference. This feature of transportability is very important. It goes far beyond just the fact that the computers do about as well at teaching as people do.

Question for Admiral Kidd: Dr. LaBerge spoke of contract incentives to cause contractors to pay attention to training. Before that will happen it will be necessary to first provide incentives for the procurement manager to be as interested in training as in engineering performance. I challenge the panel to name one military project manager who was promoted, or even specifically not promoted, because of the quality of the training program associated with his weapons system development. What can be done to make training program development as important to the PM as the hardware development?

Admiral Kidd: Threaten them with a fate worse than death, I guess. I tried for four-and-a-half years and failed. Until we can get the people pregnant with the proposition of providing that which they promised to provide with the requisite smarts, on time, and in adequate numbers, the hardware problem will persist. Up until the time I retired, the navy had not been successful—and I'll defer to my army and air force colleagues—in obliging the providers of personnel to write a contract with the civilian contractor guaranteeing the level of smarts that the Bureau of Personnel would be able to provide to the weapons system in question. Industry has told the services, ad nauseam, that if they only knew in good time they could front-end load with designs to protect against the vagaries of the stupid sailor. Well, I had a tummy full of being told by industry that it was the stupid sailors who were screwing up their great stuff, and on the other side of the coin, that it was the horrible equipment, poorly designed, that the stupid sailors couldn't find the "on" switch to. Whichever side of the equation is at fault, the nation must understand that whether stupid or brilliant, they are the only sailors we've got. We jolly well, as Dr. LaBerge undertook to point out, better design precautions into the front end. Would the air force or the army care to comment?

LaBerge: Could I just say that the army is trying a noble experiment to make these requirements stick. It's unclear whether it will succeed or not. The concept is being forwarded by the vice chief, a guy who most recently came from being the deputy for personnel where he had responsibility for all the personnel problems. Therefore, General Max Thurman knows the problems and now has the opportunity to fix them. Max is unmarried, works twenty-eight hours a day, and has taken on as a first priority this issue of making the equipment and the people get together.

Admiral Kidd: The appointment of General Thurman as vice chief is absolutely great news. Admiral Zeck, tried extremely hard to do that sort of thing for the navy and write guarantees to the material command. The air force similarly is doing the best it can, but we haven't been at this a very long time.

General Roberts: I think the point is well taken: We need to marry up the people and the hardware. The air force does have a unit at Edwards Air Force Base, where we test our new aircraft, for the express purpose of designing training programs and identifying the types and numbers of people needed to support that system. For example, the B-1 system program office has an air training command member assigned. We've had it for nine, ten, or eleven months. So I think there is a very definite effort underway to solve that particular problem.

Question for General DePuy: What are the relative effects of experience versus innate ability, such as measured by AFQT scores, in order to operate weapons systems? Or, what do we know about it?

General DePuy: Well not much. The SQTs are given after the men have been trained. To the extent that training is equivalent to experience, we have that data. We also have not taken into account in this very simpleminded approach such things as forgetting curves. We need to have a lot more data, as Admiral Kidd just mentioned, on training. There is a seven-year program underway to collect background and performance data for all the services. I urge all of you not to let that effort fall between the cracks. We should have done it fifteen years ago. It's the kind of thing that could very easily drop out under budget pressure because most of the top managers in the services, in OSD, and certainly in the Congress and on congressional staffs, probably don't feel the way we do about the importance of the matter. So you are going to have to fight to maintain a program to collect performance data, collectively and in each service. I urge you to do that. The answer to your specific question is that I don't have it and I don't know what the answers are.

Question: What does the future hold for people in the services in the way of manpower, personnel, and training? Are we conducting sufficient R&D in the manpower, personnel, and training areas and, more specifically, what's the ratio of hardware to human R&D knowledge?

Admiral Kidd: With us is Captain Paul R. Chatelier, the Military Assistant for Training and Personnel Technology in the Office of the Secretary of Defense, who counts the money. Paul, what's the answer to that question?

Chatelier: The ratio is very small. Frankly, I don't have the exact answer because we are still awaiting the funding figures from Congress. If we say 1% we're being generous.

Admiral Kidd: When the Defense Science Board addressed this question two summers ago, we were asked how much R&D money for hi-tech training and regular training could be used right now. The answer was, new money, right then, $2.4 billion. Paul, how much have you gotten in new money in the eighteen months that have elapsed since those profound recommendations were submitted to the secretary of defense?

Chatelier: Not counting inflation, it's probably going to range around 5% to 8% between 1983 and 1984. When you take inflation into account, its virtually a dribble. We're talking around 1% or 2% of $280 million, but some of these dollars are going to the new B-1 simulator. Therefore, it doesn't all show up for manpower and personnel training R&D. That is, much of the money doesn't figure into the technology base needs or what we're doing to increase our knowledge or capability in manpower and training R&D.

Question for General DePuy: To what extent are artificial intelligence and expert learning systems being brought to bear to improve human performance and reduce the demand for high-quality personnel?

General DePuy: When anybody asks me about artificial intelligence, I always think about the project which is the army's part of the joint-fusion program. It was always interesting to me that the army put E-6s on the analyst station and the air force put captains. Whether the army is that much smarter than the air force, of course I don't know. I suspect that nobody has the slightest idea of what the problem really is and what the performance of sergeants or captains might be in that environment. Yet, we are now designing systems in the total absence of any information about how people perform in connection with the closest thing we now have to artificial intelligence.

Question for Robert J. Murray: Why is the navy so slow in emphasizing manpower and training R&D given its large projected force structure increase?

Murray: I don't know the answer. I know that when I was the under secretary I did nothing to emphasize manpower and training R&D, so I share in the blame. Of course, this has had some emphasis for some time in the navy and with some results—shipboard manpower has been saved. But many problems remain, particularly in the shore and training establishment and in support units. My belief is that we need to spend more money on manpower and training R&D and that we would be well-advised to do so. We really need to do something on the shore side, and on the non-ships company side of the navy. We particularly need to take a very close look at the training and the training technologies that are now available.

Part IV

MANPOWER SUPPLY IN THE 1980s

Introduction

EDGAR A. CHAVARRIE

Although the military was able to meet its manpower demands adequately with volunteers during the first decade of the AVF, the question for the next decade is whether or not this policy can be maintained, presuming we desire to do so. Even precluding the event of war, numerous factors bear on the answer to this question. Among them are the shrinking size of the youth cohort, the desired size of the active force, the adequacy of the reserves, quality requirements, and the effects of an improved economy. Additionally there is the question of congressional willingness to continue to nurture the venture through its potentially traumatic teenage years and on into early adulthood.

In their comprehensive analysis of the active enlisted supply and short-range policy options, James R. Hosek, Richard L. Fernandez, and David W. Grissmer focus their projections on the entire enlisted force, stressing that the shift to a more senior force alleviates the need for large numbers of accessions. Arguing that this trend also alleviates the near-term demand for high-quality recruits, they express concern over how the services will manage a force composed of a large number of senior careerists and how the structure of personnel costs will be affected by a force requiring more dependents' related expenses, for example, but less spending on recruit training. Moreover, there is concern for maintaining an orderly force structure when the current crop of careerists reaches retirement age. Policies to dampen the boom and bust cycle of enlistments also have implications for reserve manning which currently is being adversely affected by declining prior-service accessions.

Addressing the issue of reserve and mobilization manpower in more depth, John R. Brinkerhoff and David W. Grissmer contend that the Gates Commission forecasts were off the mark on this issue. Both the size of reserve forces and the quality, given less than expected numbers of pretrained manpower, are at issue. It is argued, however, that the advent of the AVF has focused attention on the problem of the individual ready reserves (IRR) and that recent policies serve to move the reserves forward to becoming a more viable deterrent force.

Robert T. Hale's chapter addresses congressional attitudes toward the AVF in general, including reserve manpower. He expects increased emphasis on the reserves in a period when budget deficits and fluctuating public opinion toward the military foster the search for cost-effective alternatives to larger active forces. Additionally, he foresees a swing to a preference toward G.I. Bill benefits over bonuses, restrictions on pay raises, and a restructuring of the retirement system. Changes on the horizon, in his opinion, do not include a serious challenge to the premise of a volunteer force.

11 Active Enlisted Supply: Prospects and Policy Options

JAMES R. HOSEK
RICHARD L. FERNANDEZ
DAVID W. GRISSMER

INTRODUCTION

In 1978, on the eve of the sixth anniversary of the All-Volunteer Force, the Department of Defense study, *America's Volunteers*, summed up the prospects for the AVF in the years ahead:

> The major problems for the active force of the AVF lie in the prospective decline in the population of youths of recruiting age. The population declines 15% between 1980 and 1985 and about 25% by the early 1990s. Moreover, economic changes and other changes could compound these effects.[1]

Even as the report was being issued, the active services were experiencing recruiting shortfalls that by the end of FY1979 totaled 7% of the year's requirement. Enlistment supply studies suggested that the situation was not going to improve. Retention rates at the first and second reenlistment points were also falling, raising the possibility that career-force strength might overshadow recruiting as the major problem area for military personnel policy. At the same time, it was becoming apparent that scores on the Armed Services Vocational Aptitude Battery (ASVAB), the test administered to all applicants to determine their suitability for military service, had for several years been erroneously inflated.[2] These three events—recruiting shortfalls, plummeting retention rates, and the ASVAB scoring error—exacerbated fears that the services would fail to attract and retain enough high-aptitude individuals to meet the requirements of the modern military.

Fortunately, more recent events have sharply modified this pessimistic view. Retention rates have risen to new highs, and army recruiting, a notable problem area in the late 1970s, has improved dramatically. A few years ago predictions of a return to peacetime conscription by the mid-1980s were common. Many now believe that goals for military personnel strength and quality can be achieved, provided the nation maintains its commitment to keeping military compensation, broadly construed, competitive with civilian compensation.

FORCES AFFECTING SUPPLY IN THE 1980S

Forecasting enlistments and retention requires an understanding of the forces that will be operating to affect individual decisions in the future. (See Figure 11.1.) Four Factors seem particularly important through the end of the decade: the decline in youth population, the improvement in the economy, possible changes in the ratio of military to civilian pay, and a coming change in the age structure of civilian pay. After describing these factors, we combine them into scenarios for our forecasting.

Figure 11.1. Schematic of Forecasting Approach

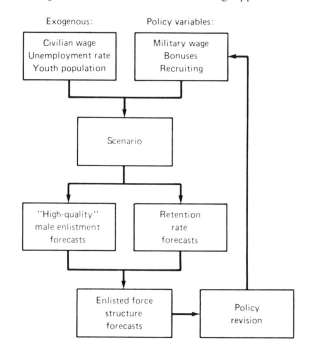

The Factors

Youth Population Decline. Throughout the 1970s the number of young people reaching enlistment age rose steadily; during the 1980s the trend reverses. The Census Bureau projects 12% fewer seventeen-to-twenty-one-year-old males in 1990 than there were in 1983. This should translate into a decline in enlistments, but as our forecasts suggest, the decline may be less than equally proportionate.

Improving Economy. The economic recovery is expected to continue over the next few years. Forecasts of the speed of recovery made as recently as the spring of 1983 have proved too pessimistic; the adjusted forecasts we utilize were made by the Congressional Budget Office (CBO) in August 1983. These cover the period 1983-1986. For 1987 to 1990 we have roughly interpolated between CBO's older optimistic and regular scenarios. Our unemployment series shows a persistent, gradual recovery, with unemployment falling from 9.7% in 1983 to 6.8% in 1988, and holding there through 1990. Given recent years of high unemployment, the 6.8% figure may seem too bullish, but as recently as 1977 the rate was under 6%, and it stood at 4.8% when the AVF began in 1973.

The future of the economy is, of course, very difficult to predict. Although the recovery may continue for several years, a new recession is certainly a possibility before the end of the decade. The declining unemployment rates we assume should make enlistment and retention goals harder to achieve, other things being equal, but a new rise in unemployment could reverse this trend.

Military/Civilian Pay Ratios. We specify two alternative pay series that should bracket the plausible range of variation in the military/civilian pay ratio. The first shows slower growth in military pay than in civilian, as occurred over the past two years and in the late 1970s—relative pay fell by 8% between 1976 and 1979.[3] Our series assumes a fall similar to that of the late 1970s, with military pay rising by about two percentage points less than civilian in each year from FY1985 through FY1987. Given the research evidence (and belief in Congress) that low pay contributed to the recruiting difficulties in the late 1970s, one might think that this pay scenario would not materialize. Yet the same could have been said in 1973 of the pay history of 1976-1980.

The second series specifies that the FY1985 military pay raise will match the average change in civilian pay, as will the raise in FY1987 and beyond. For FY1986, the budget cycle after the presidential election, we assume a "catch-up" raise, offsetting the relative pay declines brought about by the 4% raise in FY1983 and the delayed 4% raise in FY1984.[4]

Civilian Pay Structure. Although it is widely known that the youth population will decline steadily through the mid-1990s, it is less well understood that the changing youth cohort size should affect the structure of civilian pay. The large influx of young workers in the 1970s forced their wages to fall relative to the average wage of all workers. This trend will reverse during the 1980s and into the 1990s. As the proportion of youth in the labor market declines, their wages will tend to increase relative to the average wage. New entrants to the labor force will feel this effect first and most strongly. The wage increase will be smaller in size and later in coming for somewhat more experienced workers.

Recent Rand work has developed estimates of the effect of cohort size on wage.[5] Based on this work, Figure 11.2 shows what will happen to the wages of recent high school graduates relative to the average wage across all education and experience groups. The high school graduates are divided into three experience groups: two years or less, three to five years, and six to nine years. These three groups approximate the civilian wage trends relevant to the points of enlistment, first-term reenlistment, and second-term reenlistment. By extension, the figure also shows by how much military pay will fall behind civilian at these three points if across-the-board military pay increases match the rise in average civilian pay. For instance, the estimates indicate shortfalls in 1990 of about 5%, 3%, and less than 1%, for the three points respectively.

The Scenarios

Table 11.1 and Figure 11.2 summarize the historical and projected values of the youth population, the unemployment rate, and the military/civilian pay ratio. They define two scenarios, "low pay" and "high pay," based on the two alternative pay series. The youth population and unemployment rate series are common to the scenarios. The separate panels in Figure 11.2 for youth population, the unemployment rate, and the military/civilian wage ratio show that these variables were at or near a peak in FY1982-1983. Population and unemployment are expected to return to the range observed in the recent past, FY1977-1981, but the path of relative pay depends on the scenario. The figure also includes a panel showing the change in the civilian wage structure, as discussed above. In generating our forecasts we use these relative pay changes to adjust the military/civilian pay ratios shown here, creating separate pay series for the enlistment, first reenlistment, and second reenlistment points.

Table 11.1. Historical and Projected Paths of Factors Affecting Enlistments
and Retention in the 1980s

Fiscal Year	Male Youth Population[a]	Unemployment Rate (percent)[b]	Military/Civilian Pay Ratio[c]	
			Low[d]	High[e]
Historical				
1977	10,720	7.5	.95	
1978	10,826	6.4	.93	
1979	10,809	6.1	.90	
1980	10,758	7.1	.89	
1981	10,686	7.7	.90	
1982	10,524	9.4	.97	
Projected				
1983	10,229	10.9	.97	.97
1984	9,918	10.2	.93	.93
1985	9,602	9.2	.93	.95
1986	9,334	8.4	.92	1.00
1987	9,204	7.6	.90	1.00
1988	9,225	6.8	.90	1.00
1989	9,139	6.8	.90	1.00
1990	9,000	6.8	.90	1.00

[a] 17-to-21-year-old males, including armed forces overseas, in thousands.
[b] For total labor force.
[c] Index: October 1, 1981 = 1.00. Pay figures shown refer to mid-fiscal year.
[d] Assumes no FY1986 catch-up.
[e] Assumes FY1986 catch-up.

FORECASTS

This section presents enlistment and retention forecasts based on the two scenarios described in the previous section. Extending the traditional assessment method, we also trace the effects of these future levels and rates on the enlisted-personnel force structure through the end of the current decade. This new analysis makes it clear that the transition from compulsory service to a volunteer force—even now only half completed—is profoundly affecting the force structure, so much so that, notwithstanding the declining youth cohort size and recovering economy, the traditional concern with recruiting should diminish in the 1980s.

The forecasts derive from models of enlistments, retention, and force structure that were developed at Rand.[6]

Enlistments

The enlistment model relates the enlistment rate for "high quality" males to measures of the military/civilian pay ratio, the state of the economy, the numbers of recruiters, and indicators for important policy changes (such as the introduction of the Army College Fund). The model is estimated separately for each service using monthly data. For the current forecasts these data cover the years 1975 to 1981. The estimation methodology explicitly allows for the tendency of enlistment rates in different states, and different services, to move together.

The model assumes that the number of "high-quality" male recruits—high school graduates who score in the upper half of the AFQT—depends solely on the willingness of such individuals to enlist (their "supply" behavior) and not on the services' willingness to have them ("demand"). This assumption is a primary reason why studies of enlistment supply have focused on the

Figure 11.2. Recent and Forecast Paths of Key Variables

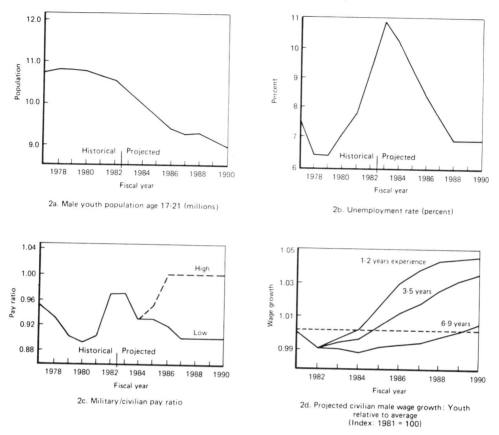

2a. Male youth population age 17-21 (millions)

2b. Unemployment rate (percent)

2c. Military/civilian pay ratio

2d. Projected civilian male wage growth: Youth
relative to average
(Index: 1981 = 100)

high-quality group. The army forecasts have been adjusted, however, to reflect the effects of a new system of recruiter incentives and recruiting quotas that was introduced during 1981. This change contributed to an unprecedented increase in army high-quality enlistments between FY1981 and FY1982. Recent analysis has confirmed the link between the army's changed recruiting policies and the subsequent enlistment gains, indicating that the gain is not likely to be short-lived.[7]

The principal assumptions behind the forecasts are that (1) no changes will be made in the number of recruiters fielded by each service, and (2) no new major enlistment incentives will be introduced. Because the forecasting model does not estimate the effects of advertising, we implicitly assume no change in advertising expenditures or effectiveness. Further, the underlying taste of young men with respect to the military, whether determined by patriotism or by other factors, is presumed to remain unchanged.

Figure 11.3 shows the projected levels of high-quality male enlistments under the two pay scenarios, both for DoD and for the army, as well as the actual levels since FY1977.[8] The solid lines indicate enlistments under the low pay scenario (continued decline in relative pay); the dashed lines show the higher enlistment levels of the high pay scenario (the relative pay cuts of FY1983 and FY1984 are restored in FY1986). Both sets of forecasts reflect the gradual erosion in relative pay (about 5% by 1990) that will result from the projected rise in the wages of young workers relative to the average civilian wage. Without this adjustment to the military/civilian pay ratio series shown in Table 11.1, the enlistment forecasts would be about 3% higher.

In examining the forecasts, the reader should be aware that the forecasting model we have used shows smaller estimates of the effects of pay and population changes than do some other models. The commonly used estimate that pay changes cause equiproportionate changes in high-quality enlistments, for example, would push the lower forecast lines down by about four percentage points in FY1988 and beyond, or about 5,000 fewer high-quality male enlistments for the DoD as a whole and 1,700 fewer for the army. Similarly, it is generally thought that a 1% decline in the youth population would, other things being equal, cause a 1% decline in high-quality enlistments. If this were true, it would move both of our forecast lines down by six to eight points in the later years. This common view, however, implies that recruiters have

Figure 11.3. Actual and Projected High-Quality Male Enlistments (thousands), DoD and Army

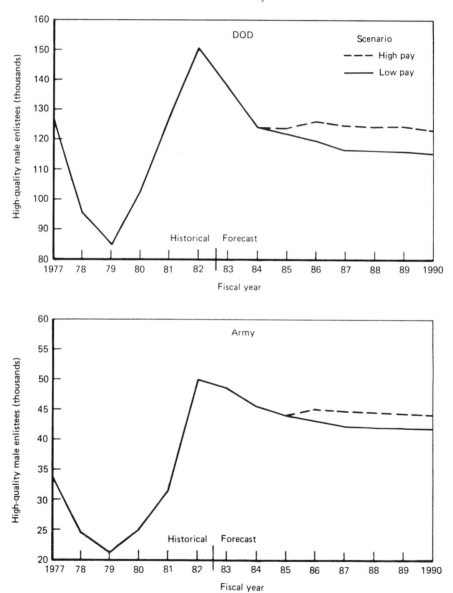

completely saturated the "market," when in fact even the army, the service with the largest number of field recruiters, has only one recruiter for every 300 male high school seniors. As a result, we do not accept the usual assumption about population effects, and instead have chosen to present forecasts based upon the smaller population effect estimated in our enlistment model. On both pay and population effects, however, we admit to some uncertainty about precise values. The reader may wish to imagine 95% confidence bands extending about twelve to fifteen percentage points on both sides of each forecast line—a little wider for the low pay scenario— and widening over time.

The forecasts show the same general pattern as has been predicted for some time, but the unexpected recruiting successes of the last few years have shifted the scale upward. The projected declines are considerable, but they should still leave the DoD, and especially the army, in a much better position than they were in the late 1970s. It does not appear, however, that even the high pay scenario can maintain current high-quality enlistment levels. Still higher military pay—at least another 10%—would be required to offset the effects of the declining youth population and the recovering economy.

Will the projected supply meet the services'"needs" for high-quality recruits? Total accession requirements depend on end strength objectives and retention rates, but requirements for quality are not so easily defined. Further, the measurement of "quality" is not the simple task implied by our use of the standard high-quality definition: "high school graduate above the 50th percentile." Thus, we cannot say whether the projected decline in high-quality enlistments indicates trouble for the services or whether the improvement over what was expected a few years ago means that the rest of this decade will be considered a succession of good recruiting years. As will be seen however, a focus on accession supply alone may give a misleading, overly pessimistic picture of the AVF's future. Past, present, and future retention rates, and their effects on the demand for new enlistees, deserve equal attention.

Retention Rates

Movements in retention rates,[9] especially the first-term retention rate, carry implications for the ability of the AVF to meet its career-manning requirements. The active-duty military relies on new recruits for nearly all of its manpower. Because little lateral entry occurs, a decline in retention rates can create a shortage of trained, experienced personnel. Such a shortage would have to be accommodated by modifying personnel assignments as well as the pace of military operations and maintenance. Reduced retention rates would also trigger an increase in accession requirements, which, while helping to maintain overall force strength, would not solve the immediate problems raised by the shortage. Anticipating a shortage, then, and acting to prevent it would obviously be preferable to seeing one materialize.

To forecast retention rates, we use models of first- and second-term retention behavior. The models, estimated separately for the DoD and for the army, relate occupation-specific retention rates to explanatory variables that include the military/civilian pay ratio, the unemployment rate, the presence and level of a reenlistment bonus, whether the bonus was lump sum or installment, the percent nonwhite, and the percent without a high school education. The data cover the period from mid-FY1976 to the end of FY1981. By setting the demographic variables at appropriate values, we produced forecasts of the retention rates for four subgroups of male enlisted personnel (whites and nonwhites by high school and non-high school). These rates later feed into a model used to project enlisted force structure.[10] Also, in obtaining the forecasts, we set the bonus variables, which are not a feature of the scenarios, at their average values for the period FY1977-FY1981.

To illustrate the historical and projected changes in first- and second-term retention rates, we focus on a single subgroup of personnel: white male high school graduates in their fourth year of service and within a year of the end of their first term of service. Figure 11.4 shows the DoD retention rates for this subgroup. The period from FY1977 to FY1982 depicts actual recent experience. The period from FY1983 through FY1990 displays forecast rates under the high- and low-pay scenarios. Historically, all of the retention rates fell from FY1977 to FY1979 and then recovered strongly. For instance, the first-term DoD retention rate goes from 24% (FY1977) to 22% (FY1979) to 38% (FY1982)—a remarkable increase.

Over the forecast period, FY1983-FY1990, we observe sizable declines under the low pay scenario. Improving employment conditions and declining relative pay reduce the first-term DoD retention rate from 32% in 1983 to 21% in 1990, a drop of one-third. The higher pay scenario, in contrast, shows a modest near-term rise followed by a decline to 33% in 1990.[11] In other words, the high pay scenario sustains the robust retention climate of 1983.

The story for second-term retention is much the same. The low pay scenario diminishes the second-term retention rate from a forecast value of 66% in 1983 to 53% in 1990. The high pay scenario increases the rate from 66% to 69% in 1986, after which the rate declines to 65% in 1990.

The army pattern (Figure 11.5) follows the DoD forecasts closely, although the first-term decline is a little more rapid. Under the low pay scenario, first-term retention falls from 41% in 1983 to 25% in 1990—from one in every 2.4 men remaining to one in every 4.0. The rate drops only to 35% in 1990, however, under the high pay scenario. The second-term retention rate falls from a forecast 66% in 1983 to 54% (low pay) or 64% (high pay) by 1990.

In sum, the high pay scenario works toward maintaining the current prosperity of the force in retaining first- and second-term personnel. The scenario suggests that their retention rates may actually increase in the near term. Contrasting with the higher-pay results, the low pay scenario produces retention rates so low as to raise serious concern about maintaining force strength in the mid-career years. The implications of the two scenarios for the personnel force structure are examined in the following section.

Personnel Force Structure

The retention forecasts, coupled with the delayed effects of rising retention rates during the past ten years, imply striking changes in the experience mix of the enlisted force. Changes in the experience mix of the force, while holding force size constant, mean changes in force costs, productivity, and force effectiveness. A more senior force, for example, would bring higher current compensation costs, greater future retirement benefit payments, and increased current costs of certain benefits such as medical and housing. It would also be likely to exhibit greater productivity and force effectiveness, as fewer personnel would be involved in initial skill-training activities and the average enlisted person would have more job experience. Determining the "optimal" experience mix, therefore, means striking the right balance between productivity and effectiveness on the one hand and costs on the other. We do not attempt to determine the proper balance, but report the prospective changes in the experience mix and some of their implications.

Before discussing our force-structure forecasts, we want to describe several important assumptions underlying the forecasts which will aid in their interpretation. Congress establishes an "end-strength" *ceiling* for each service, specifying a required strength level as of the last day of the fiscal year. We assume that these end-strength ceilings will stay constant at their FY1982 levels through FY1990[12] and that the services will be able to meet their end-strength objectives as they have in the past. The services adjust their end strengths by controlling the flows of accessions and losses throughout the year. In practice, adjusting the flow of accessions is much easier and offers greater flexibility for making large short-term adjustments, so accession management is

Figure 11.4. Actual and Projected Retention Rates for DoD,
White Male High School Graduates

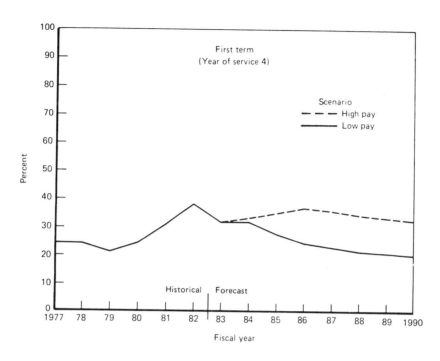

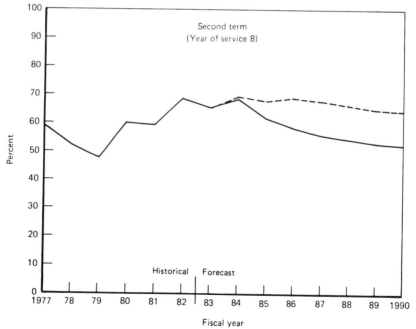

Figure 11.5. Actual and Projected Retention Rates for Army
White Male High School Graduates

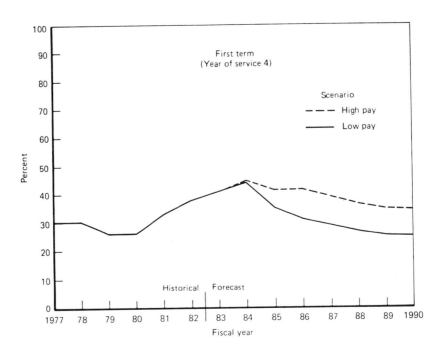

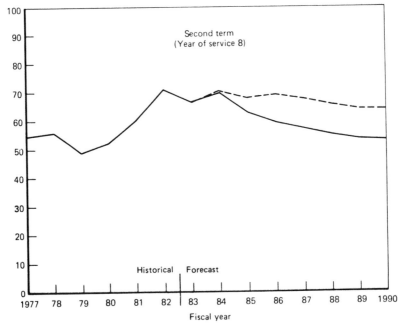

the most common short-term tool for meeting end-strength objectives. For this reason, and because of our interest in exploring the consequences of a continuation of current policies, we assume for our forecasts that annual accessions will be adjusted to levels sufficient to meet end-strength goals. Thus, we ignore short-term policy adjustments that could affect losses, such as changes in reenlistment eligibility standards, promotion rates, or "early out" policies.

Our assumption of an accession-managed end strength leads to predicted overall annual accession requirements, but does not specify the makeup of the accession groups. Assumptions are necessary as to the mix between prior service and nonprior service and the characteristics of the enlistees within each of these two groups. We assume annual levels of prior-service accessions and of nonprior-service female accessions equal to those in the services' current five-year plans.[13] For male nonprior-service accessions we assume that high-quality enlistments are given by the forecasts presented above. The remainder of the accession requirements is filled by a mix of lower-quality males determined by historical enlistment levels and by apparent service preferences.[14]

The above assumptions enable the force-structure forecasting model to predict the experience distribution of the force, the nonprior-service accession requirement, and the quality mix. We have produced forecasts for every year from FY1983 to FY1990. For the sake of brevity, we use only the FY1990 structure and compare it with the structure existing in FY1982, which was the last year for which complete data were available. We do not mean to imply that the structure in FY1982 should be preferred to any other; rather, it provides a timely and tangible basis for comparison.

We represent a personnel force structure by the percentages of active-duty personnel in four year-of-service categories: one to two years, three to five, six to nine, and ten or more. The first group consists of personnel largely occupied with basic and advanced training, or in their first duty assignments but not yet performing at journeyman level. The second and third groups correspond approximately to trained personnel in their first and second terms of service. The last group contains the senior careerists, individuals in their third terms and beyond, whose jobs might comprise supervisory and managerial functions as well as direct skill-related tasks. We divide the accession requirement that the structure implies into two portions: that filled by high-quality males and females (based on the enlistment forecasts and an assumed quality mix among females), and that filled from other sources. This gives a simple picture of the quality mix.

The forecasts (Table 11.2) show enlisted-force dynamics being dominated in the next seven years by a very dramatic increase in the size of the senior career force if current personnel policies continue. The number of DoD enlisted personnel with ten or more years of service will increase by 35% and 42% between FY1982 and FY1990 under the low and high pay scenarios, respectively. For the army the percentage growth in the senior career force is even larger; 59% under the low pay scenario and 69% under the high pay scenario.

The dramatic increase in senior career-force manning, if allowed to occur, will reduce FY1990 non-prior service accession requirements to levels well below those of the recent past (Table 11.3). This is true for both the DoD and the army and under both pay scenarios. The high pay scenario shows an FY1990 DoD requirement for nonprior service accessions 18% below the FY1982 level and 22% below the average level for FY1976-1982. Under the low pay scenario the drop would be 5% relative to FY1982 and 9% relative to FY1976-1982. Army data show slightly higher percentage declines. The forecast declines in requirements would keep accession quality comparable to that of the excellent recruiting year of FY1982 under both pay scenarios, notwithstanding the youth cohort decline and falling unemployment rates. A marked improvement would occur under the higher pay scenario.

These results raise a number of policy issues with respect to enlisted-force manning over the next seven years, as well as the question of how the current situation has evolved and attracted so

Table 11.2. Enlisted Experience Mix Comparisons, FY1982-1990 (In Thousands)

Year of Service	FY1982	Low Pay Scenario		High Pay Scenario	
		FY1990	% Change	FY1990	%Change
DoD					
1-2	578	528	-8.7	458	-20.8
3-5	534	436	-18.4	414	-22.5
6-9	267	274	+2.6	336	+25.8
10+	408	549	+34.6	580	+42.2
Total	1787	1787		1787	
Army					
1-2	233	191	-18.0	173	-25.8
3-5	204	171	-16.2	159	-22.1
6-9	109	108	-.9	124	+13.8
10+	129	205	+58.9	218	+69.0
Total	674	674		674	

Columns may not sum to totals because of rounding.

Table 11.3. Comparisons of First-Year Enlisted Personnel Required to Maintain End Strengths

	Historical		Projected FY1990	
	FY1976-1982 Average	FY1982	Low Pay Scenario	High Pay Scenario
DoD				
Personnel (thousands)	307	292	279	241
high quality (percent)	43.7	48.8	45.8	56.1
Army				
Personnel (thousands)	133	110	101	92
high quality (percent)	28.6	34.6	46.7	53.8

Accession requirements would be somewhat greater than the numbers shown here because of losses during the first year.

little notice. If accurate, the projections show that the AVF is definitely sustainable through 1990 under current force sizes and assumed pay conditions. Further, accession quality can be maintained under historical levels despite declines in the youth cohort and unemployment. This view of the AVF's future sharply contrasts with recent assessments of the AVF.[15] We conclude this section by examining the reasons for the disparity between our results and other assessments.

The major reason for the common misperception of the AVF's sustainability appears to be a preoccupation with accession supply rather than the match between supply and demand.[16] The focus of policy concern and analysis has been the projected decline in supply resulting from the coming decline in youth cohort sizes and, more recently, from the expected recovery of the civilian economy. The even larger potential decline in accession requirements, however, has been overlooked.

The enlisted force has quietly evolved a solution to the accession supply problem by retaining people at historically unprecedented rates, thus reducing the demand for new enlistees. This trade-off, substituting greater stocks of experienced personnel for the large flows of junior personnel through the first term that were characteristic of the draft years, has been taking place for a number of years. A good portion of the high retention can be attributed to four factors: the change to an all-volunteer force, recent increases in military/civilian compensation, the worsened national employment conditions, and increases in the coverage and level of reenlistment bonuses.

The change to an all-volunteer force is important because true volunteers can be expected to reenlist at a higher rate than draftees or draft-motivated volunteers. As a result, the retention experience since FY1977-1978, by which time virtually all of those reaching the first reenlistment point had entered after the draft ended, is better than it would have been under a pre-AVF type force. The actual increase in retention attributable to the AVF concept is difficult to quantify. However, we can gain a rough idea by examining the retention rate for enlisted personnel in the fourth year of service who are approaching their reenlistment decision point. (These refer to all personnel, not just the subgroup used for illustration above.) In FY1971-1972 the average rate was 13.0%; in FY1977-1978 it was 25.6%.[17] This near doubling in first-term retention created a "bow wave" of personnel moving toward the senior force. We are now seeing that wave penetrate the ten-plus year of service group.

Recent changes in military pay, unemployment, and reenlistment bonuses will also contribute to the development of a more senior force over the next seven years. Between FY1979 and FY1982 our military/civilian pay series grew from .90 to .97, and the unemployment rate rose from 6.1% to 9.4%. During the period FY1979 to FY1981 the proportion of first-term reenlistees covered by bonuses rose from 36 to 40%. At the second reenlistment point the coverage increase was even greater: from 22% to 42%. The average reenlistment bonus also rose, from $2,700 to $3,900 (in constant 1976 dollars) at the first reenlistment point and from $5,200 to $5,800 at the second reenlistment point. These changes helped boost retention rates to all-time highs. From 25.6% in FY1977-1978 the first-term retention rate had climbed to 38.6% in FY1981-1982. This increase was not due to the shift to an all-volunteer force, for since FY1977-1978 virtually everyone reaching the first-term reenlistment decision point has been a true volunteer.

In addition to the upsurge in retention rates, the level of accessions in the mid and late 1970s was high. Large numbers of new enlistees were required to maintain overall force strengths in the mid 1970s because the higher retention rates of the AVF had not yet fully manifested themselves. The decline in retention rates from FY1977 through FY1979 further fed the demand for accessions. This decline can in part be attributed to a fall in the military/civilian pay ratio and an improvement in national employment conditions (see Figure 11.2).

The high accessions levels of the mid and late 1970s have combined with the recent high retention rates to create a relatively large stock of personnel in their second and third terms of service. These second- and third-term personnel, present in our benchmark year (FY1982), constitute a major factor in the evolution toward a more senior force. The large stock of mid-career personnel in the 1982 enlisted force can be viewed as the product of the shift to an all-volunteer force, the rapidly rising retention rates of the last few years, and the large accession cohorts of the late 1970s. In addition, the stock of personnel nearing the end of their first terms, in conjunction with high current first-term renlistment rates, present further potential for senior force growth. Within this context, our force-structure projections demonstrate the likelihood of a movement toward a more senior force over the remainder of the decade. In the final section of this chapter we consider whether the shift to a more senior force is desirable, and how such a force can be managed. Consideration of such questions, however, requires an understanding of the policy options available for changing the force structure, the subject of the next section.

SELECTED POLICY OPTIONS

For reasons we discuss in the concluding section, policy actions may be taken in the future to reduce the growth or alter the composition of the senior force. Therefore, even though our forecasts indicate the potential to meet tomorrow's end-strength goals and accession requirements, it is valuable to consider policy options that can affect the quantity, quality, and skills of personnel recruited and retained. The options we consider include educational benefits, two-year enlistment terms, enlistment bonuses, recruiting resources, and reenlistment bonuses. These options can help insure that high-quality individuals continue to enter the force. They also aid in channeling personnel into hard-to-fill occupations and in preventing shortages of trained personnel. Other options, such as changes in promotion rates or reenlistment eligibility criteria, also deserve attention. They, too, will surely be used to shape the force. We do not discuss them because at present, considerably less is known about their quantitative effects on enlistments and retention.

Postservice Educational Benefits

The current basic program of postservice educational assistance in all four services is the Veterans Educational Assistance Program (VEAP). This program differs in two important respects from the GI Bill, which it replaced on January 1, 1977. First, VEAP requires the individual to make monthly contributions to his own benefit fund, which are later matched two-for-one by the government. Second, VEAP is less generous; the maximum government payment is $5,400, compared to the more than $13,000 available under the GI Bill to enlistees who entered the military before 1977. In the legislation establishing VEAP, however, the Congress authorized the secretary of defense to enhance the benefits offered to selected enlistees. This authority was exercised in the Multiple Option Recruiting Experiment of 1979, in which lump sum enhancements of up to $6,000, called "kickers," were offered to high-quality enlistees entering specified "critical skills." However, the results of this experiment with respect to the kickers were inconclusive.[18] The kickers were retained by the army in FY1980 and expanded in amount to a maximum of $12,000 as part of the FY1981 Educational Assistance Test Program (EATP). In that larger amount they form the major incentive in the current Army College Fund. Kickers are not currently offered by the other services.

The best evidence on the effectiveness of educational benefits as enlistment incentives comes from the FY1981 experience.[19] Among its results, the EATP showed that the large kickers of the Army College Fund produced a 9% increase in army high-quality accessions.[20] The magnitude of this gain was confirmed when the Army College Fund was extended nationwide in FY1982. A 9% response may not seem large, given estimates of up to 30% for the effect of ending the GI Bill,[21] but it must be remembered that the Army College Fund was being compared with a control program that already included smaller kickers.

The EATP results do not bear directly on the desirability of a more broadly-based program, such as the old GI Bill, or on whether the Army College Fund is a cost-effective means for maintaining or improving recruit quality. They do provide some guidance, however, on how the most cost-effective educational benefits program should be designed. First, it would retain the contribution requirement of VEAP. A noncontributory version of the basic program, tested in the EATP, did not raise enlistments appreciably. Although some observers claim that the contributory feature has made VEAP a failure by discouraging participation,[22] this feature appears to have done more to limit the cost of the program than to limit its effectiveness as an enlistment incentive. Second, the most generous benefits would be reserved for enlistees in selected hard-to-fill specialties. Such "skill targeting" further limits program costs and ensures that most of the program dollars spent go to those enlistees with the greatest commitment to pursuing further education. Finally, to be most effective an educational assistance program should be narrowly targeted on those specialties, and services, where its effects are most needed. When the list of specialties eligible for the Army College Fund kickers was broadened midway through the EATP, many recruits were drawn away from the combat arms specialties that comprised the initial list. A second test program, which equalized benefits across the four services, reduced army enlistments.

Estimates of the annual steady-state costs of broad-based programs range as high as $2 billion or more.[23] Consequently, the cost-limiting features described here may make the difference between a program that serves primarily as an aid to recruiting and one that should perhaps be viewed as an extensive federal grant to the higher education of military veterans. Another concern in the use of an educational benefit program as an enlistment incentive is its possible adverse effect on retention. Because these benefits are used primarily after the individual leaves the military, the introduction of a more generous program may reduce retention rates at the end of the first term. This will likely be true not only for those service members whose initial enlistments are directly attributable to the program, but also for others who, though they entered the military for other reasons, find the lure of a free or low-cost college education too great to resist. The latter phenomenon should be more pervasive in a broad-based program. At present, we have no way to estimate the adverse retention effects of VEAP educational benefits. Within the next few years such estimates will come from the retention decisions of enlistees who came in during the EATP period.

Other Enlistment Incentives

The two-year option. A two-year enlistment option was tested as part of the Multiple Option Recruiting Experiment of 1979. In general the option was limited to high-quality recruits, tied to certain specialties (primarily combat arms in the army), and offered in conjunction with educational benefit kickers of $2,000.[24] It was hoped that the option might appeal to college-bound youths who, though discouraged from enlisting by the three- or four-year commitments usually required, would find a shorter break in their educations more appealing. Two separate analyses of the two-year option test, however, found no appreciable effect of the option on the number of high-quality male enlistments in the army, the service with the most extensive test.[25] Smaller-scale navy and marine tests showed larger effects when the option was open to enlistees in all specialties, but these effects could not be estimated with any precision. Given the potential that shorter enlistment tours have for drawing recruits away from the standard tour lengths—a potential that seems to have been fully realized in the army—the two-year option does not appear to be a valuable tool for improving force manning.[26]

Enlistment bonuses. Enlistment bonuses have been used primarily as a tool for channeling quality recruits into hard-to-fill specialties and for eliciting additional man-years of service in those specialties. They require longer-than-normal enlistment tours and are limited to high school graduate enlistees scoring above the thirtieth percentile on the AFQT. The availability of enlistment bonuses has not, in general, been advertised. This situation has been changed, however, in the army's enlistment bonus test, begun in July 1982. For this test, Congress authorized bonuses to high-quality enlistees in selected specialties who choose the standard three-year tour. The test also includes higher bonuses for a four-year tour. As the test results become available over the course of the next year, we should learn whether skill-targeted enlistment bonuses can, like the kickers in the Army College Fund, yield an enlistment response that is larger than might be expected given the limited number of specialties covered.

Recruiting Resources

"Recruiting resources" consist of recruiters, recruiters' aides, advertising, and a variety of less-quantifiable factors such as funds available to recruiters for transporting potential recruits to testing centers, and support given to recruiters to help them identify the most likely candidates. Of these, the number of recruiters has received the most study. The effects of advertising were studied in a 1980 navy experiment and are now under study in an experiment covering all four services, but firm conclusions are not yet available.

Early studies indicated that adding 1% to the size of a service's recruiting force would increase high-quality male enlistments by perhaps ½%.[27] More recent estimates place the effect in the 0.7 to 0.8% range.[28] Based on these higher estimates, the projected 10% decline in high-quality male enlistments (high pay scenario) could be offset by a 13% increase in the number of recruiters DoD-wide—1,800 additional recruiters, with about 750 of those going to the army. Estimating the cost of additional recruiters is difficult, but it is probably in the vicinity of $40,000 per recruiter per year. This would make the cost of the 1,800 added recruiters in excess of $70 million annually. We caution, however, that the estimates of recruiter effects were based on data from the mid to late 1970s; as the youth population declines, the contribution of an additional recruiter may fall.

The army's recruiting successes in FY1982 and FY1983 demonstrate that gains in high-quality enlistments may be achieved *without* corresponding increases in the resources devoted to recruiting.[29] The army's improvement was obtained largely through a restructuring of its recruiter incentive system. The basic element of this restructuring was the introduction of the mission box. This gives each recruiter a specific quota for recruits, or "mission," by AFQT category, high school graduate/nongraduate, and sex. Previously, each recruiter had been expected to achieve a total quota, but there were only informal pressures on him to concentrate on high school graduates or to avoid low-AFQT individuals. The mission box gave the army recruiting command, for the first time, a mechanism for maximizing the proportion of its accession requirements taken from the most desirable categories, and the ability to do so even in the face of rapidly changing recruiting conditions.

Whether the other three services can make gains similar to the army's remains to be seen. The air force probably stands to gain least from a switch to more detailed quotas because its enlistment standards already exclude most low-scoring and nongraduate applicants. The navy also starts from a position of higher average quality in its recruits than did the army, but it has begun to examine whether it could gain from the introduction of a system like the army's mission box.

Reenlistment Bonuses

The selective reenlistment bonus (SRB) program offers reenlistment bonuses in selected skills in order to reduce manning shortages in those skills. Analysis indicates that such bonuses can increase the retention rates. Because they target particular skills, reenlistment bonuses are probably more cost effective for eliminating specific shortages than is an across-the-board increase in military pay. Reenlistment bonuses also offer greater flexibility, for they can readily be removed from a skill whereas a pay increase cannot be. Bonuses can help control transitory shortages, and the persistence of bonus payments in many skills indicates that they also play a role in alleviating long-term imbalances due to such factors as persistently differing civilian pay levels or the disamenities of particular military occupations. Reenlistment bonuses currently constitute under 2% of the military personnel appropriation (less than $1 billion of about $45 billion in FY1983).

Although bonus coverage and (real) bonus amounts rose from 1977 to 1980, and the jump in bonus coverage among second-term reenlistees from 1980 to 1981 was a phenomenal leap from 22% to 40%, the prospects seem to be for reenlistment bonus usage to return to the levels experienced in the late 1970s. Nonetheless, should shortages in critical skills grow rapidly, the DoD would presumably request additional SRB dollars.

In Table 11.4 we show estimates of the amount of increase in bonus amounts required to offset the effect of a 1% decline in relative pay (e.g., from 1.0 to 0.99) or a one percentage point drop in

Table 11.4. SRB Bonus Increases Required to Maintain
the Retention Rate (1983 Dollars)

Change	First-term	Second-term
One percent decrease in military/civilian pay ratio	$1,930	$2,010
One percentage point decrease in unemployment rate	$2,380	$6,970

the unemployment rate (e.g., 9% to 8%).[30] The indicated increases would be enough to hold the retention rate constant in a typical bonus skill. Without going into the details of the SRB system, we note that the changes indicated by the table are well within the range of routine operation except for the largest amount shown, which is not far outside the usual range.

Aggressive use of the existing SRB program could blunt the effects of declining pay and unemployment on retention in critical skills. Moreover, because SRBs are payable only to personnel who sign on for three or more years, they tend to lengthen the average term of commitment. This in turn would increase the number of man-years of service, improve the military's return on its training investment, and reduce accession requirements.

CONCLUSIONS

Five years ago it appeared that the future of the All-Volunteer Force could be summarized easily: through the 1980s the numbers of young men and women reaching enlistment age would be declining, raising serious doubts that the services could meet their accession requirements for skilled personnel. These requirements are expected to grow as the process of force modernization continues. More recently, this pessimism has waned, but fears remain that the recruiting successes of the early 1980s would not have been achieved without a prolonged, deep national recession. Adding to this concern, new research indicates a faster-than-average rise in the wages of young workers—five percentage points by 1990—because of the falling numbers of such workers available to civilian employers.

As the AVF heads into its second decade, it is time to recognize that the traditional method of assessing its success has been too limiting. The picture of the AVF's future painted by a single line tracing high-quality supply leaves equally important parts of the canvas blank. Our work draws attention to major trends within the entire enlisted force. Absent any major policy changes, the current decade will see a shift toward a more senior force, requiring fewer and fewer new enlistees. The projected decline in the supply of high-quality accessions creates less alarm, then, when accession demand is also forecast to decline. As in the past, it will be important to monitor accession quality. However, we believe it will be equally important to monitor the emerging trend in force structure. In addition, policymakers need to consider the costs and benefits of this trend. We raise such considerations after presenting several caveats to our analysis.

We think the general picture presented by our forecasts is correct, but three qualifications should be borne in mind. First, our forecasts of high accession quality depend in part on estimates of the effects on enlistment supply of youth population changes and of relative pay, that some may find implausibly low. Some researchers believe that the "baby bust" will have more telling effects, and military pay erosion more serious consequences than our forecasts show. Thus, despite the reduced accession demand that the future force structure will generate, concerns about recruit quality may not disappear. Second, our forecasts of career-force growth depend, to a certain extent, on assumptions about continuation rates for the individuals who have recently reenlisted in such large numbers. Individuals induced to stay for an additional term of service by generous reenlistment bonuses, and especially high unemployment, may reenlist at lower rates at the second and subsequent reenlistment points than we have predicted, at least over the next few years.[31] We should note, however, that our low pay scenario allows military compensation to decline to what is probably an unrealistically low level. Were pay somewhat higher, it would tend to offset the possibly optimistic retention projections.

Third, there are reasons to question whether the force-structure change we predict will be allowed to happen. "A continuation of current policies" has meant, for the purposes of our forecasts, that mid-career service members can expect the same opportunities for promotion to the senior enlisted grades as their predecessors. Grade table constraints, however, might force slower promotion or reduced promotion opportunities. Whether these changes would significantly reduce continuation rates, we cannot say. In addition, the ASVAB misnorming of the late 1970s has focused new concern on the quality of recent reenlistees. Pressures may arise to force out some of those mid-careerists whose test scores were inflated when they first entered the services. Such a policy might be ill-advised. An individual's promotion history would seem a better measure of his "quality" at the reenlistment point than his initial test scores, and low-scorers are promoted almost as rapidly as high-scorers.[32] But this has been urged, and if instituted, it would obviously reduce continuation rates below those we forecast.

The future may not follow our forecasts exactly, but the general nature of the coming force-structure evolution will very likely obtain if nothing major is done to change it. The movement toward a more senior force, however, raises some fundamental questions, among them: How is such a force to be managed? Is it sustainable? Is a more senior force desirable? If it is not desirable, what can be done to forestall it?

The principal management question arising from the evolving force structure is what is to be done with all these senior careerists. As previously noted, current grade limits seem likely both to slow promotion and to reduce promotion opportunities. Some relaxation of the present limits would therefore be necessary if morale (and perhaps retention) were not to suffer. Permitting an increase in the number of senior NCOs, however, would require a parallel change in the services' definitions of job responsibilities. Instead of the situation in the past where junior NCOs were filling the slots of E-6s and E-7s, in a more senior force many direct job-skill tasks would fall to individuals with ten, fifteen, or even twenty years of service.

A principal obstacle to the long-run sustainability of a more senior force is, paradoxically, the sharply-reduced accession requirements that current tendencies are forcing. The "bow wave" moving into the senior career force was generated, in part, by the large accession demands of the last ten years. Lowered accession requirements in the 1980s may help to maintain recruit quality, but they will likely generate a trough moving into the senior force in the next decade that will pose new management problems and lead once again to higher requirements. Avoiding such a boom and bust cycle will require dampening the current wave, perhaps tightening reenlistment standards across the board, and ensuring that reenlistment rates for the coming smaller cohorts are not allowed to fall too low simply because end strengths can be met with smaller numbers of second- and third-termers. In addition, minimum accession levels could be maintained to ensure that flows into the mid-career years are sufficient to support the new force structure. This might require relaxing both end strength and budget constraints. Another option would be to plan for a policy of lateral entry in the nineties, if needed.

On the question of the desirability of the evolving personnel force structure, we offer no judgements. Instead, we outline some of the considerations that should affect such judgements. First, the structure of personnel costs would change significantly. If end strengths are held constant, more money will be spent on basic pay, retirement benefits, and on in-service benefits such as medical, subsistence, schooling, and housing. Less will be spent on training and on supporting junior personnel through their largely unproductive first and second years. However, there may be more spent on retraining or cross-training senior personnel. Second, given constant end strengths the force should be much more productive and effective, particularly in areas where training and experience are more important than youth and vigor. This is, in effect, the benefit corresponding to the higher cost of the more senior force. Third, reduced flows through the first term may adversely affect selected reserve manning, and will raise concerns that the "citizen army" concept is being lost. On both points, we note that although the absolute numbers of recruits flowing into the services each year will fall, the percentages of successive youth cohorts serving in the military will actually rise, even under our high pay scenario (which leads to lower accession requirements than the low pay scenario). In addition, the trend in reserve accessions is now toward greater reliance on individuals without prior active service. Even so, the reserves can attempt to counter a decline in prior-service recruits by offering larger enlistment incentives. Finally, adaptation to the more senior force will require active management initiatives, restructing job tasks to conform to the availability of personnel at various experience levels.

If DoD policymakers believe action should be taken to modify the trend toward a more senior force, such action should be taken fairly soon. We have identified the presence of a relatively large stock of personnel with three to nine years of service. Many of these personnel will be making first or second reenlistment decisions in the next three years. It is at these reenlistment points, rather than later ones, that personnel management and compensation policies can be most readily tailored to trim the force and insure the retention of high-quality personnel. Also, because personnel shortages and overages vary from skill to skill, as does the quality of personnel, such policy changes should probably be skill-specific. Delaying actions to trim the force until the late 1980s will deny policymakers much of the leverage they could exercise today.

NOTES

1. Office of the Assistant Secretary of Defense (Manpower, Reserve Affairs, and Logistics), *America's Volunteers: A Report on the All-Volunteer Armed Forces* (Washington, DC: Government Printing Office, 1978) p. 183.
2. The extent of the ASVAB mis-scoring is shown in: Office of the Assistant Secretary of Defense (Manpower, Reserve Affairs, and Logistics), *Aptitude Testing of Recruits: A Report to the House Committee on Armed Services*, July 1980.
3. Our military/civilian pay variable employs the average hourly wage in manufacturing as the civilian wage series. This wage series does not always change from period to period by the same percentage as the wage index of professional, administrative, technical, and clerical (PATC) workers, which is used as the basis for adjusting the pay of federal civilian employees and for gauging the extent of adjustment required in military pay. The PATC index, however, has been criticized as being unrepresentative of military jobs (an alternative, the Employee Cost Index, was recently proposed but not accepted as a replacement for PATC). The average wage in manufacturing seemed to us to be at least as appropriate a measure of civilian pay as the PATC index, and possibly more so. We were, after all, interested in a wage series reflecting civilian earnings opportunities in jobs that were similar to those in the military. For those who would have preferred PATC we note that the two series have moved fairly close together, so that our forecasts would have been roughly the same had we used the PATC index instead.
4. We compute the size of this "catch-up" as the Congress probably would, comparing the 4% raises to the corresponding changes in the PATC index. This results in a larger raise than would be necessary, according to our civilian pay variable, to restore the pay ratio to its FY1982 level.
5. Hong W. Tan and Michael P. Ward, *Forecasting the Wages of Young Men: The Effects of Cohort Size* (Santa Monica, CA: Rand Corporation, forthcoming) R-3115-Army.
6. Robert F. Cotterman, *A Time Series of Cross Sections Model for Forecasting Enlistment Supply*, forthcoming. James R. Hosek and Christine E. Peterson, *Selective Reenlistment Bonuses and Retention Behavior (forthcoming) R-3199-MIL*. This research was sponsored by the Office of the Assistant Secretary of Defense (Manpower, Reserve Affairs, and Logistics; now Manpower,

Installations, and Logistics)—OASD(MIL). The forecasts do not necessarily reflect the position of OASD(MIL).

7. James Dertouzos, *Recruiter Incentives and Enlistment Supply* (Santa Monica, CA: Rand Corporation, forthcoming) R-3065-MIL.

8. At the time the enlistment projections were produced, enlistment data for FY1983 were not available. The projected levels for that year (shown in Figure 11.3) have proved to be too low. More recent projections from the same model, reestimated to include FY1983 data, show approximately the same levels of high-quality enlistments in FY1984 and beyond as those appearing in the figure.

9. As used here, a retention rate is the percentage of individuals completing a given term of service who continue into a subsequent term. Those retained include both reenlistees (additional commitment of two years or more) and extenders (additional commitment of less than two years).

10. In addition, the force-structure forecasting model requires information on the retention behavior of women. For this we simply employ an average of recent female retention rates.

11. The small initial rise in the forecast retention rates may appear puzzling. It occurs because the underlying retention-rate model allows for a lagged response to unemployment and the unemployment rate was rising in the early 1980s. This causes a positive effect on retention which dominates the negative effect from the declining relative wage.

12. Active duty enlisted strength stood at 1.78 million and army strength at 0.674 million in 1982. Although current plans call for increased end strengths for the navy and air force, Congress has recently deleted these active-force increases and instead directed reserve-force expansions. With current federal budget realities, constant force size seems a reasonable assumption, although the force-structure model can easily accommodate alternate force-size assumptions.

13. The assumed annual female accession level for FY1983-1990 is 41,000. This is approximately equal to the average level for FY1980-1982 and to current serice planning submission estimates for FY1984-1989. The assumed education and AFQT distribution for these women is similar to that of FY1977-1982. For prior-service accessions we use estimates made by the services in planning submissions. The average level of these over FY1983-1990 (24,000) is somewhat below recent experience (28,000 over FY1977-1982). We assume that prior-service accessions will be distributed by years of service as they were in FY1982.

14. The lower-quality male enlistment groups in the model are assigned maximum values based on the highest enlistment levels achieved between FY1976-1982, and each is given a recruiting priority. The priorities are such that high school graduates are always enlisted before nongraduates, and that within equivalent education groups higher-AFQT enlistees are chosen before lower.

15. The quote that opens this chapter sums up the DoD view of the future in 1978: major problems for the AVF in the 1980s as youth cohorts decline in size, possibly exacerbated by cyclical employment conditions. A summary of the perceived strengths and weaknesses of the AVF, and a prediction of a return to the draft in the 1980s due to a failing AVF, appears in James L. Lacy, "The Case for Conscription," in Brent Scowcroft, ed., *Military Service in the United States* (Englewood Cliffs, NJ: Prentice-Hall, 1982). Arguing even more strongly for a return to a draft are Andrew J. Goodpaster, Lloyd H. Elliott, and J. Allan Hovey, Jr., eds., *Toward a Consensus on Military Service: Report of the Atlantic Council's Working Group on Military Service* (Elmsford NY: Pergamon Press, 1983).

16. By "demand" we specifically mean the level of accessions needed to achieve force strength goals, given projected retention behavior. In other contexts, demand might refer to manning requirements built up from assessments of the number and skill mix of personnel needed to man fully capable units. The accession requirements implied by the latter approach will not necessarily equal the accession demand we refer to.

17. Other factors probably contributed to the increase in first-term retention. Retention may have been held down in FY1971-1972, for example, by the Vietnam conflict, or by service attempts to reduce their force sizes during the withdrawal from Vietnam. The retention increase cannot be attributed, however, to the large military pay raise in November 1971. This raise affected only the most junior personnel.

18. See Gus W. Haggstrom et al., *The Multiple Option Recruiting Experiment* (Santa Monica, CA: Rand Corporation, November 1981). R-2671-MRAL.

19. In addition to experiments, researchers have attempted to analyze the effects on high-quality accessions of dropping the GI Bill. Unfortunately, such analyses are hampered by the one-time nature of the change. Comparisons of pre- and post-G.I. Bill enlistment levels may confound the effects of the change with those of other forces operating at the same time. This problem was eliminated in the EATP. The test programs, of which the Army College Fund was one, were offered in limited areas of the country. In half of the country, potential enlistees were offered only the educational assistance program available nationwide during the preceeding year—the "control" program.

20. Principal test findings and some results from a survey of military applicants during the test period appear in J. Michael Polich, Richard L. Fernandez, and Bruce R. Orvis, *Enlistment Effects of Military Educational Benefits* (Santa Monica, CA: Rand Corporation, February 1982). N-1793-MRAL. Complete test results were given in Richard L. Fernandez, *Enlistment Effects and Policy Implications of the Educational Assistance Test Program* (Santa Monica, CA: Rand Corporation, September 1982). R-2935-MRAL.

21. See, for example, the Army results in Lawrence Goldberg, *Enlisted Supply: Past, Present, and Future* (Alexandria, VA: Center for Naval Analyses, September 1982). CNS-1168.

22. See, for example, a statement by Congressman Duncan Hunter in U.S. House of Representatives, *New Educational Assistance Program for the Military to Assist Recruiting*, HASC No. 97-45 (Washington, DC: Government Printing Office, 1982), p. 364.

23. See Congressional Budget Office, *Improving Military Educational Benefits: Effects on Costs, Recruiting, and Retention* Washington, D.C.; March 1982.

24. For a complete discussion of the test format and results, see Haggstrom et al., op. cit.

25. A small-scale test of the two-year option was continued into 1980. This was the baseline comparison period for the FY1981 EATP, so the analysis of that later experiment also yielded an estimate of the two-year option effect.

26. We are aware of the alternatives to the AVF proposing mandatory national service, one option of which would be a short tour in the military. Discussion of such alternatives is beyond the scope of this chapter.

27. See, for example, D. M. Huck and J. Allen, *Sustaining Volunteer Enlistments in the Decade Ahead: The Effect of Declining Population and Unemployment*, McLean, VA: General Research Corporation, September 1977.

28. See Goldberg, op. cit., and Cotterman, op. cit.

29. The conclusions drawn here are based on the work reported in Dertouzos, op. cit.

30. The example draws from Hosek and Peterson, op. cit.

31. Warner and Simon found that roughly one-half of those induced to reenlist by bonuses leave at the next expiration of term of service (John T. Warner and Bruce D. Simon, *An Empirical Analysis of Pay and Navy Enlisted Retention in the AVF: Preliminary Results*, Memorandum 79-1878 (Alexandria, VA: Center for Naval Analyses, December 1979). In unpublished simultations, Gotz and McCall estimated similar effects for officers. The retention model predicting these results is reported in Glenn A. Gotz and John J. McCall, *A Dynamic Retention Model for Air Force Officers* (Santa Monica; CA: Rand Corporation, December, 1984) R-3028-AF.

32. A telling analysis of enlistee "quality" as indicated by the persistent tendency of some individuals to be promoted faster than others, almost regardless of their AFQT scores and, to a lesser extent, of their education, is presented in Michael P. Ward and Hong W. Tan, *The Retention of High Quality Personnel in the U.S. Armed Forces* (Santa Monica, CA: Rand Corporation, February 1985). R-3117-MIL. Characteristics of the individual that do not appear in his personnel records, but that are presumably clear to his superiors, apparently carry more weight when his "quality" is evaluated within the military than do the traditional measures based on entry characteristics.

12 The Reserve Forces in An All-Volunteer Environment

JOHN R. BRINKERHOFF
DAVID W. GRISSMER

The Gates Commission staff was faced with a nearly impossible job in estimating the size of volunteer reserve forces sustainable under different levels of pay. This was due largely to the highly artificial manning environment for reserve forces created by both the Vietnam War and the draft. Another complicating factor was the highly decentralized personnel management system that could produce only sketchy estimates of key parameters like losses, reenlistments, and accessions. It was further complicated by the absence of research on effects of pay increases on reserve enlistment and retention and, more generally, by a lack of understanding of the moonlighting labor market (which economists had yet to address in a systematic way) and the sociology of voluntary service organizations.

Nonetheless, the commission stated that selected reserve forces of between 900,000 and 1,000,000 volunteers—strength levels which matched those in the 1960s—could be sustained with their recommended pay levels. Today, selected reserve strength is 982,000 with the potential, in the absence of strength caps imposed in FY1983, to grow even further. The fact that today's strength levels and Gates Commission predictions are similar hides both a precipitous decline in strength between FY1972 and FY1978 to 788,000, and a fortuitous combination of large but compensating errors in predictions made in the analysis of reserve volunteer accession, attrition, and retention levels by the commission.

The commission was mute on the subject of an individual ready reserve (IRR), a pool of pretrained manpower used to provide fillers during mobilization. This pool, which consisted primarily of active-force veterans with remaining time on their six-year service obligation, declined sharply with the end of the draft. The ongoing rebuilding of this important mobilization resource has meant utilizing other sources of trained personnel, possible extension of the six-year service obligation as well as testing of retainer type pay.

This chapter will review in separate sections the selected reserve and pretrained individual manpower. The first section will review the AVF experience for the selected reserve in the light of projections made by the Gates Commission and present future strength projections. Given today's high strength levels, it will then speculate on an important demand-side question, namely, the relative costs of active and reserve units. The second section reviews the strength trends for pretrained individual manpower and reviews the policy actions and future trends for this part of the military manpower problem.

Table 12.1. Selected Reserve Strength 1960-1983 (In Thousands)

Period	Years	Annual Fiscal Year End Strength DoD	Army Components
Pre-Vietnam	1960-1964	948 (average)	NA
Vietnam	1965-1969	953 (average)	NA
Declining Draft Calls	1970	987	670
	1971	978	665
	1972	925	623
AVF Years with Low Retention	1973	919	621
	1974	925	638
	1975	897	620
	1976	823	557
	1977	808	544
	1978	788	527
AVF Years with High Retention	1979	807	536
	1980	850	573
	1981	898	614
	1982	963	665
	1983[a]	982[a]	670[a]

[a] Strength caps imposed.

Table 12.2. Comparison of Active and Selected Reserve Personnel for FY1982 (Enlisted)

	DoD (%) Active	Reserve	Army (%) Active	Reserve
Education				
high school graduate	91.6	86.5	88.4	84.1
non-high school graduate	8.4	13.5	11.6	15.9
Mental Category				
Cat. I-II	35.3	38.2[a]	25.1	35.0[a]
Cat. III	45.5	51.7[a]	44.0	55.3[a]
Cat. IV-V	19.1	10.2[a]	30.9	9.7[a]
Minority Participation				
black	22.0	18.5	32.7	21.2
non-black	78.0	81.5	67.3	79.8
Female Participation				
female	9.1	9.7	9.6	9.8
male	90.9	90.3	90.4	90.2
Age				
average age	NA	29.6	NA	28.8

[a] Reserve AFQT data are not yet renormed for the years 1976-1979. The effect of renorming will be to shift more people into lower mental categories and narrow considerably the differences between active and reserve mental category distributions.

Table 12.3. Comparison of Characteristics of Nonprior-Service
Selected Reserve Accessions FY1971-FY1982 (Percentage)

	DoD	
	FY1971	FY1982
Education		
some college and		
college graduates	52.3	4.2
high school graduates—		
no college	39.9	72.7
non-high school	7.8	24.1
Mental Category		
I	17.3	3.0
II	41.0	23.2
III	34.8	59.9
IV	6.9	13.5
Sex		
male	99.5	82.5
female	.5	17.5
Race		
black	1.7	9.7
non-black	98.3	90.3

Table 12.4. Years of Combined Active and Reserve Service
of Selected Reserve Enlisted Personnel

Fiscal Year	Percentage		
	Under 6	6-10	10+
1976	51.4	31.3	11.3
1977	45.3	34.3	20.4
1978	41.6	35.2	24.2
1979	44.2	30.8	25.0
1980	45.6	27.4	27.1
1981	46.3	25.5	28.1
1982	45.8	25.1	29.1

CHARACTERISTICS OF THE SELECTED RESERVE IN THE ALL-VOLUNTEER ENVIRONMENT

Following a somewhat perilous transition period[1] (1972-1978), the strength of the all-volunteer selected reserve today stands at levels comparable to that of the draft years between 1960 and 1972 (see Table 12.1). The quality and demographic compositon of selected reserve personnel is roughly comparable to personnel in the active force (see Table 12.2), and, like the active force, today's reserve volunteers entering the force differ from their draft-motivated counterparts in having a lower educational achievement and mental category level, and having a higher percentage of minorities and women (see Table 12.3). However, the average reservist has more years of combined active and reserve experience[2] (see Table 12.4) since volunteers have brought lower overall turnover levels (Table 12.5) and a more efficient balance of more prior-service (PS) and less nonprior-service (NPS) manpower utilization[3] (see Table 12.6). Moreover, the recent strength trends of the last four years which saw reserve strength grow at a compound annual growth rate of 5% could, in the absence of strength caps imposed in FY1983, continue at a slightly lower rate of growth for the next few years without major changes in policy. Thus selected reserve manpower policy questions can turn from a preoccupation with supply-side questions to exploring demand-side questions. Chief among these questions is the proper trade-off between the size of the reserve and active force when both cost and capability criteria are evaluated.

Table 12.5. Losses to the Enlisted Selected Reserves (In Thousands)

Fiscal Year	DoD	% of End Strength	Army	% of End Strength
1976	244	34.5	196	40.2
1977	230	33.1	168	35.4
1978	219	32.5	161	35.2
1979	193	27.9	135	29.1
1980	183	25.0	120	24.1
1981	193	23.6	122	22.7
1982	192	23.2	131	22.7

Table 12.6. Accessions to the Selected Reserves (In Thousands)

Fiscal Year	DoD				Army			
	NPS	PS	Total	%PS	NPS	PS	Total	%PS
1970	179	84	263	31.9	149	28	176	15.9
1971	103	114	216	52.5	83	21	104	20.2
1972	95	150	245	61.1	62	54	117	46.2
1973	70	118	189	62.8	37	68	105	64.8
1974	46	180	226	79.6	36	115	152	75.7
1975	70	150	219	68.3	52	98	149	65.8
1976	74	146	220	66.2	57	100	157	63.7
1977	73	153	225	67.8	56	101	157	64.3
1978	70	131	201	65.1	53	88	142	62.0
1979	78	126	205	61.7	64	75	139	54.0
1980	94	128	222	57.8	76	80	157	51.0
1981	104	126	230	55.0	84	80	164	48.8
1982	106	138	244	56.6	86	84	171	49.1

REVIEW OF GATES COMMISSION ANALYSIS AND RECOMMENDATIONS FOR RESERVE FORCES

The Gates Commission and others studying the All-Volunteer Force (AVF) realized that reserve forces would take on an enhanced importance in an all-volunteer environment due to the smaller planned size of the active force[4] and the diminished capability, without an operating draft, to rapidly expand the active force during mobilization. This role was recognized, at least on paper, as part of the total-force policy enunciated in 1971. Evidence was available at the time of the Gates Commission to indicate that the reserve forces would probably be the weak link in the total-force strategy in an all-volunteer environment. To the credit of the Gates Commission analysts, much of this evidence was recognized.

The commission recognized a major problem in the reserve's heavy dependence on draft-motivated youth. Survey estimates made in 1968[5] showed that 75% of first-term reserve enlistees were draft-motivated, and, in fact, queues of individuals waited to enter the reserve rather than be drafted into the active force. These potential enlistees would disappear along with the draft. The commission saw a second problem in the scarcity of research on the responsiveness of reservists to pay increases and in the poor quality of the data to support force-sizing estimates. This research gap seemed critical since increased pay was the principal means in an AVF of controlling force size and quality and addressing specific skill shortages. The Gates Commission's confidence in maintaining an active force of 2 to 2.5 million by raising entry pay levels somewhat above the minimum wage and maintaining the career force pay at inflation-adjusted levels[6] flowed directly from studies showing that enlisting youth responded to increases in military wages and that reenlistees responded to an even greater extent. The active force elasticities[7] were estimated at 1.25 for enlistment and 2.8 for reenlistment.[8]

Similar estimates were needed for sound "reserve" transition planning to the AVF. However, unlike the active force, elasticities for reserve forces were not available from previous research. Not only were elasticities not available, but critical historical data on accessions, losses, and reenlistments were often sketchy. Perhaps most importantly from a planning viewpoint was that any manpower data collected would reflect the highly artificial reserve "recruiting" environment produced by the Vietnam War and the draft. The war brought large numbers of reserve NPS enlistments of high aptitude and educational achievement for whom reserve service was essentially a deferment from active duty service and probable Vietnam duty.[9] The war also brought larger active service sizes which created a large veteran pool from which the reserves could easily draw PS accessions. The queues of high-quality NPS accessions probably crowded out both PS accessions and lower-quality volunteer NPS accessions. Thus, enlistment data for both PS and volunteer NPS accessions, even if available, are probably demand-constrained and of marginal use for planning.

The simultaneous ending of the draft and the war meant recruiting in a moonlighting labor market characterized by low participation rates (only 6%-7% of male working Americans hold two jobs).[10] There was also great uncertainty in this market of the extent to which monetary incentives—the core strategy for the active force AVF—would work for reserves. In the absence of empirical estimates, commission staff made several assumptions concerning reserve pay elasticities for both enlistment and reenlistment. They assumed that responsiveness to pay increases at enlistment would be somewhat smaller in the reserve than in the active force because of differences in the primary and secondary labor market. They estimated an enlistment elasticity with an upper bound of 1.25 (the active force enlistment elasticity) and a lower bound of 0.8.

On the basis of a 1968 survey of reserve personnel, the commission calculated the following reenlistment pay elasticities: for draft-motivated first-term members with four to six years of service, 2.0; volunteer first-term members with four to six years of service, 0.8; and members with six to ten years of service, 0.3. These reenlistment elasticities were much lower than those estimated for the active force. The commission also found from the 1968 survey that, as might be expected, draft-motivated youth reenlisted at much lower rates than nondraft-motivated enlistees and higher retention would occur even without pay increases.

Anticipating a more favorable reenlistment rate in the AVF and the adoption of its recommended pay increase,[11] the Gates Commission predicted that a selected reserve force of between 900,000 and 1 million officers and enlisted personnel could be maintained. It also warned, however, that its estimates were inadequately based:

Analysis of the reserve problem, however, suffers seriously from a lack of data. Even though special care was taken to provide against error of estimation, the assessments of what is required to maintain an All-Volunteer Force are much more tenuous than for the active force. . . . Given the uncertainty which surrounds projections of Reserve enlistments and losses, further steps beyond the recommended pay increase may be necessary. Any further steps should await the results of experience with higher pay during the first few years.

Table 12.7. Selected Reserve Strength by Component,[a] FY1970-FY1982 (In Thousands)

Fiscal Year	Army Natl. Guard	Army Reserve	Naval Reserve	Marine Corps Reserve	Air Natl. Guard	Air Force Reserve	Armed Forces Total
1970	409	261	128	49	90	50	987
1971	402	263	130	47	86	50	978
1972	388	235	124	41	89	48	925
1973	386	235	126	38	90	44	919
1974	403	235	115	31	94	46	925
1975	395	225	98	32	95	51	896
1976	362	195	97	30	91	48	823
1977	355	189	90	31	92	50	808
1978	341	186	83	33	92	54	788
1979	346	190	88	33	93	54	807
1980	367	206	87	35	96	59	850
1981	389	225	88	37	98	62	898
1982	408	257	94	40	101	64	963
1983	415[b]	256[b]	102[b]	44[b]	102[b]	64[b]	982[b]

Source: Official Guard and Reserve Manpower Strengths and Statistics, September 30, 1982.

[a] Excludes Coast Guard reserve data.

[b] March 1983.

SELECTED RESERVE EXPERIENCE IN THE AVF

Selected reserve strength, which stood at 987,000 in 1970, dropped to 788,000 by 1978, and then rose to 982,000 by FY1983 (see Table 12.7). Understanding this dramatic reversal is critical to both assessing Gates Commission predictions and projecting future strength trends. There are four major points that should be considered at the outset when understanding the manning of selected reserve units in the AVF:

1. The experience was markedly different by component.
2. A strength decline followed by a renewal was implicit in the Gates Commission analysis and should have been expected.
3. The sociology of reserve units and the economics of reserve supply is significantly different from that of active units and active supply, so financial incentives tend to obtain somewhat different results.
4. Application of management attention, targeted financial incentives, recruiting resources, and command emphasis to reserve problems lagged by several years behind similar application to active force problems.

The Air National Guard and the Air Force Reserve have gained strength during the AVF years, increasing from 89,000 and 49,000 in FY1972 to 101,000 and 69,000 in FY1982. This was not surprising since these components rely mainly on PS personnel, not on draft-motivated NPS personnel. The pool of PS personnel had been swelled by the Vietnam War, and any transition problems associated with NPS personnel seemed to have been anticipated by AVF reserve planning unique to the air force.[12] The increase in force size in the air components seems largely determined by demand and only the threat of a declining veteran pool clouds the future.

The naval reserve was similarly mainly manned by PS personnel and end strength seems determined by demand rather than supply. The large decline from 128,000 to 83,000 from FY1970 to FY1978 resulted from policy guidance by Office of the Secretary of Defense (OSD) on naval reserve manpower requirements rather than supply constraints resulting from an AVF environment. Congressional reversal of naval requirement trends since 1978 has resulted in increases, and naval reserve strength has risen from 83,000 to 104,000 in FY1983. Again, the relatively small size of the naval reserve relative to the active navy and their dependence on PS personnel make strength, except for certain skills, primarily demand-driven.

The decline in the army and marine components between FY1970 and FY1978 seemed to be attributable to the end of the draft. Like the active army, these components depended heavily on junior-level, draft-motivated personnel. Between 1970 and 1978, the Army National Guard had fallen in strength from 409,000 to 341,000, the Army Reserve from 261,000 to 186,000 and the Marine Corps Reserve from 49,000 to 31,000. While some attribute the marine reserve decline to demand and budget conditions similar in nature to the naval reserve, the decline in the army components undoubtedly stems from supply conditions.

The decline in army component reserve strength during the early years of the AVF raised questions about the original Gates Commision assumptions. Since the assumed pay elasticities were based neither on behavioral data nor on a well-developed theory of reserve participation, it was natural to question their validity. Actual elasticities might be much lower than assumed, resulting in lower levels of accessions and reenlistments. Also, the expected increase in reenlistment rates associated with volunteers might be smaller than expected, or estimates of basic parameters such as base-level volunteer accessions, retention rates, or losses might have been in error. We will now look at accession, attrition, and retention experiences in the reserves and compare them to the Gates Commission analysis.

RESERVE RETENTION

The Gates Commission estimates of first-term reserve retention were less than one-half of actual realized rates (see Table 12.8). The low estimate was primarily due to inaccurate estimates of base retention rates for volunteers from survey data collected in 1968. Survey questions attempted to distinguish between volunteers and those draft-motivated, and then probed reenlistment intention. A likely explanation for the large discrepancies is that many individuals answering the surveys misclassified themselves as entering the reserves as volunteers rather than as being draft motivated. This would tend to bias the reenlistment rate downward. A second reason for misestimation was that pay elasticities at first term turned out to be wildly optimistic. However, since service pay raises were relatively small for careerists, this difference is of little

Table 12.8. Comparison of Gates Commission Retention
Parameters with Subsequent Experience

	Gates	Experience
Continuation % at sixth year:		
draft-motivated enlistee	6	21[b]
Continuation % at sixth year:		
volunteer	22[a]	49[b]
Continuation % at eighth year	50-58[c]	57[b]
Pay Elasticity		
First term: draft-motivated	2.0	
First term: volunteer	.8	.2[d]
Careerist: six to ten YOS	.3	

[a] Base reenlistment rate estimated from survey data for those declaring they were volunteers with an assumed 6% pay increase and elasticity of .9.
[b] Estimated from individual level data collected from army reservists and national guardsmen making first-term decisions at six years in FY1978 (see [15]).
[c] Base rate estimated from survey data for those declaring they were volunteers with an assumed 5% pay raise and elasticity of .4.
[d] Measured for a group roughly equally divided between three groups.

consequence. Whereas the Gates Commission had assumed elasticities of 2.0 for draft-motivated first termers, .8 for nondraft-motivated first termers and .3 for careerists with six to ten years of service, the results of an econometric model estimated with data collected during a reserve reenlistment experiment in 1978[13] imply an elasticity of .2[14] for a group nearly equally divided among the three groups. The results of a reenlistment bonus experiment[15] also support a relatively inelastic pay response among reservists at first term.

Estimates of career retention rates at eight and ten years of service made by commission analysts were much closer to the mark. For instance, the commission gave estimates of 49.5% for army reservists and 58.2% for national guardsmen with eight years of service. Estimates of retention of individuals completing seven and eight years of service in 1978 for both groups were 57%.

The reserve pay elasticity is also much lower than similar elasticities measured for civilian moonlighting. In 1973 Rostker and Shishko[16] developed a theory of moonlighting, or secondary labor market participation, to explain the behavior of air force reservists. This theory portrayed the decision to moonlight as a trade-off between additional leisure time and income. The theory identified several important economic variables in a civilian moonlighting decision, including primary job hourly wages, primary job hours, and secondary job hourly wages. Empirical estimation on civilian moonlighting decisions confirmed the direction and importance of these variables. Moonlighting was less frequent among those having primary jobs with high hourly wages and longer hours. The most important finding for reserve compensation policy was that a 10% increase in secondary wages would result in a 9% increase in the probability of moonlighting. If civilian moonlighting decisions and reserve participation decisions are analogous, then the reserve pay elasticities assumed by the Gates Commission would seem reasonable.

However, participation in the reserves has several features different from civilian moonlighting jobs which could make the secondary-wage moonlighting elasticity and military-reserve elasticity quite different. First, work hours are quite different for the typical moonlighting job and the reserve job. The amount of time that a reservist works averages only four hours per week, whereas the median for a civilian moonlighter is thirteen hours.[17] Since average hourly civilian moonlighting pay and reserve pay are roughly equal, annual income from reserve participation is much lower than that from typical moonlighting jobs. This may imply that taste plays a larger role in reserve decisions than civilian moonlighting decisions.

Second, reservists must legally commit themselves for up to six years of service, and they can be mobilized during periods of threat to the national security or, in the case of guardsmen, to assist in peacetime civil emergencies. This term of commitment creates certain opportunity costs for reservists not present in civilian moonlighting jobs.

Third, reservists receive health, education, life insurance, tax, and pension benefits. For certain reservists, these benefits—all of which are usually not present for civilian moonlighting jobs— substantially boost reserve income. Reservists can, for instance, qualify for a pension after twenty years of satisfactory service. Although the pension is payable at the age of sixty, calculations show that for reasonable assumptions as to real interest rates and pay growth, the equivalent of over 50% of each reservist's pay would have to be set aside were the reserve pension system funded on an actuarially sound basis.[18] These types of benefits are usually not available in civilian moonlighting jobs, and their presence would tend to lower responsiveness to direct changes in base pay.

Fourth, unlike most civilian moonlighting jobs, reserve-duty time and primary-job time can directly conflict. The work schedule for reservists calls for a two-week period of full-time work during annual training requiring absence from civilian work. While employers are legally bound to provide military leave, evidence suggests that the requirement for annual training often creates conflict between the reservist and employer. Also, reservists must have full-time military training to qualify for reserve entrance and certain types of promotion. On entry, reservists must undergo at least twelve weeks of full-time training, and special training is often required for advancement. Again, for reservists employed full time, training interrupts the primary job. Consequently, individual decisions to join the reserves cannot be considered independently of the type of primary job held and the attitude of the employer toward reserve participation.

Finally, the reserve job offers certain nonpecuniary rewards. The work itself often offers opportunities for training and the use of unique equipment. The social environment seems to create a sense of camaraderie and cohesion. These rewards may play an important role in reserve participation and lead to a model of participation much closer to that of a voluntary association than that of a secondary job. In this view, reserve participation primarily satisfies leisure or avocational needs, and the income potential is secondary. If these needs are the prime reason for participation, one would expect small pay elasticities. So, one explanation of the relatively weak response to increases to current compensation is that reserve participation decisions might be dominated by taste variables or nonmonetary rewards more associated with decisions to join voluntary groups (i.e., volunteer fire departments).[19] Another explanation is that the effects of reserve retirement benefits which require twenty years of participation might exert strong influence even for first-term decisions.

The higher-realized retention rates due to an AVF played a key role in the strength reversal during the AVF period. Predicted higher retention rates would not occur until FY1979, when the first-year volunteer cohorts with six-year terms would reach first-term retention decisions (see Table 12.9). The increase in retention is one reason selected-reserve strength trends were reversed in FY1979, and the higher volunteer level of retention would cumulatively add strength for several years. Since Gates Commission analysis was for equilibrium forces having higher retention over a long period of time, their prediction of strength levels implicitly assumed a transition period of lower strength. This transition period would last as long as draft-motivated youth were in the force (1978) and for a period of time while higher retention rates would cumulatively add to overall strength. Thus, comparison of recent 1983 strength levels to Gates Commission predictions is best.

Unfortunately, between FY1973 and FY1979, NPS accession cohorts were small and of questionable quality. Attrition rates among lower-quality army reserve accessions is particularly high (i.e., in the FY1975 cohort only one in five accessions finished their six-year term).[20] Thus, the smaller size of accession cohorts and high attrition tended to hold potential strength gains from higher retention rates down.

Table 12.9. First Term[a] Continuation Rates for Enlisted Selected Reservists (percentage)

Fiscal Year	Component						
	ARNG	USAR	USNR	USMCR	USAFR	ANG	DoD
1976	62.1	61.0	66.2	60.3	59.4	68.7	64.0
1977	63.9	61.4	53.4	64.9	64.9	74.8	65.0
1978	65.5	55.7	54.3	72.1	69.6	71.3	66.3
1979	74.5	66.2	60.0	74.3	77.2	80.4	72.6
1980	78.9	70.7	58.3	76.2	78.4	82.4	75.7
1981	78.9	70.6	60.2	74.1	76.7	80.4	75.5
1982	78.6	69.7	61.3	76.6	75.8	81.5	75.4

[a] Denominator is personnel in base year with less than six years of service.

RESERVE ACCESSIONS

The level of NPS reserve accessions fell dramatically between 1970 and 1976 from 149,000 to 36,000 (see Table 12.6). The pay raise given in FY1972 was not sufficient to prevent this drastic decline. In the absence of NPS personnel, the reserves increased PS recruiting, and were quite successful (see Table 12.6). Prior-service recruiting levels went from 28,000 in FY1970 to 115,000 in FY1974. Utilization of increased PS personnel saved training costs of between $5,000-$10,000 per individual incurred by NPS accessions. However, overall accession levels between 1973 and 1979 were insufficient to maintain desired strength.

It was not until the late 1970s that several actions were taken to boost NPS recruiting for the reserves. Enlistment bonus payments or educational tuition grants of $1500 were offered beginning in FY1979. Army reserve recruiting responsibility was given to the active army recruiting command. Additional recruiting and advertising resources were targeted and unit manning was given priority. Reservists themselves can be effective recruiters since they reside in their home community but need to be satisfied themselves before recruiting for their units. Several measures aimed at increased readiness and unit morale probably aided this process. These included additional full-time support personnel for administration and training and efforts at improved training and closer links to active units. These actions, together with higher unemployment and a more favorable environment toward military service boosted total reserve NPS enlistment totals to 104,000 and 106,000 in FY1981 and FY1982 respectively.

The Gates Commission predicted levels of NPS accessions for the army components of 83,000 for FY1977-1979 compared to actual levels of 55,500, 53,000 and 64,000 in FY1977-1979 respectively (see Table 12.6). A major reason for the overestimate is the assumed pay elasticity of .8 compared to current estimates of around .1 to .3.[21] There also appear to have been overestimates of the percentage of reservists in 1968 who were volunteer accessions as reported from survey data. It should however be pointed out that volunteer NPS accessions did reach levels of 80,000 and 86,400 in FY1981 and FY1982, respectively.

The level of long-term equilibrium PS accessions predicted by the Gates Commission for the army components was around 15,000. This number took into account the smaller size of the active force and the reduced level of losses from a volunteer active force. Levels of PS accessions from FY1977 to FY1982 have been between 75,000 and 101,000 (see Table 12.6). One reason the Gates Commission estimate was so low is that the historical data used to estimate these levels were demand-constrained. Given the ready availability of high quality NPS personnel, the reserves probably never accepted the level of PS personnel willing to join.

How is it that the commission's estimates on the overall strength levels sustainable under an AVF of 900,000 to 1,000,000 are fairly accurate, while each of the individual components (retention, NPS accessions, PS accessions, and pay elasticities) are inaccurate going into the calculation, often by factors of two to six. Fortunately the errors tended to be in compensating directions. Low PS accession levels were partially offset by high NPS accession levels and low first-term retention rates were offset by optimistic assumptions concerning attrition, i.e., more of a cohort would reach first term. In the end, the fact that elasticities were not estimated correctly was relatively unimportant and was largely overshadowed by misestimates of base enlistment, reenlistment, and attrition rates caused primarily by the lack of good data and the highly artificial reserve manpower environment due to the draft and war.

SELECTED RESERVE STRENGTH TRENDS

Selected reserve strength, which has grown at a compound annual rate of 5% since FY1978 has not yet reached AVF equilibrium levels. Since FY1981, there has been an increase in the accession levels of higher-quality volunteers and the entrance NPS cohort sizes have tended to be larger. As these cohorts move through the force, both the large size and the documented lower level of attrition of the higher-quality accessions will tend to maintain the growth trend in overall strength, which was initially fueled by higher first-term retention. If the size and quality of accession cohorts can be sustained at the FY1982 levels, strength growth would continue, in the absence of strength caps, at an annual rate of 4% over the next seven years. In reality, the current strength levels could be maintained even in the face of accession levels significantly below FY1981-1982 levels.

These strength projections for the selected reserve enlisted force were made using a set of assumptions which attempted to balance the recent favorable recruiting and retention experience of the last two years with the more unfavorable experience of FY1978-1980. Good estimates are not currently available which could attribute the change between these two periods to increases in unemployment, recruiting initiatives, increased pay and benefits, and more fundamental changes in attitudes toward military enlistment. Thus the permanence of the recent recruiting experience is uncertain.

The projections were made by assuming continuation rates by years of service would be equal to average levels over the last five years. Thus these continuation rates reflect both high and low levels of unemployment, and periods before and after several recruiting, pay, and benefit initiatives. Since satisfactory behavioral models do not exist for reserve accession levels, we have assumed four levels of accessions ranging from the FY1982 level (244,000) to 70% of the FY1982 level (171,000). The latter pessimistic level is well below average accession levels in the FY1973-1981 period (218,000) and even below the single worst recruiting year in 1973 (189,000). Thus this level leaves adequate room for declines due to unemployment and youth cohort and veteran pool decline. An additional assumption is that the mix of PS and NPS accessions will stay at the FY1982 level of 56.6% prior service. In FY1982 PS reserve accessions (138,000) were well below the historically high period of FY1974-1977 (157,000), while NPS accessions reached historically high levels (106,000). It is likely that this mix could change somewhat to more PS personnel over the period if NPS personnel decline. However, the projections are relatively insensitive to changes in this accession mix.

The results of the enlisted strength projections show that strength levels would grow by 5% between FY1982 and FY1990 even under the most pessimistic accession scenario (see Table 12.10), while a 37% growth would occur under the optimistic scenario of maintaining FY1982 accession levels.

Table 12.10. Projections of Selected Reserve Enlisted Strength (In Thousands)

Accession Levels	82 (Actual)	Fiscal Year							
		83	84	85	86	87	88	89	90
FY1982	827	892	946	990	1026	1058	1086	1111	1134
.9 FY1982	827	871	907	937	963	985	1007	1026	1044
.8 FY1982	827	848	868	884	899	913	927	941	955
.7 FY1982	827	826	829	832	836	841	848	856	865

The reasons for the somewhat surprising growth trends can be more easily seen if the projected force is displayed by experience level (see Table 12.11). The dominant factor behind force growth in each scenario is a sharp increase in reservists with greater than ten years of active and research experience. Under the pessimistic scenario this group increased by 49%, while under the optimistic scenario the increase is 75%. This rapid growth in the senior group is attributable to at least three factors.

The first is the predicted higher retention rates during the AVF era. The doubling of first-term retention rates created a "bow wave" of additional personnel moving toward the senior career force. Since this effect occurred around FY1978 for personnel with six years of service who were making first-term reenlistment decisions, this "bow wave" will move into the senior group beginning in 1982 and beyond creating very large groups of senior careerists. It is thus a legacy of the AVF decision.

Table 12.11. Comparison of Experience Mix of Enlisted Selected Reservists (In Thousands)

Years of Service	1982 (Actual)	Projections			
		1990 .7 FY1982	1990 .8 FY1982	1990 .9 FY1982	1990 FY1982
0-5	379	297	340	382	424
6-10	208	209	236	263	290
10+	240	358	379	399	420
Total	827	865	955	1044	1134

The second factor leading to increased senior reservists is the very high percentage of PS personnel taken in during the poor NPS recruiting years of FY1972-1977. Prior-service personnel start with more years of experience (typically three or four) and this bulge in PS personnel helps to boost senior careerist strength in the early projection years.

The third factor is the increased retention due to reenlistment bonus payments initiated in 1978. These reenlistment bonus payments were given only if reservists chose three- or six-year terms of reenlistment. An evaluation of these experimentally designed bonus payments[22] showed that long-term retention increased by 25% due to the bonus. This long-term retention increase occurred primarily due to the presence of longer terms of service. Since this program is continuing it has boosted first term retention from FY1978 until present, creating yet higher levels of enlisted personnel heading for the senior career force.

The growth in the senior career force does not come at the expense of the less experienced groups for the two more optimistic scenarios. However, for the two more pessimistic scenarios the size of the 0-5 years of service (YOS) group declines. This decline reflects the fact that NPS accessions levels are not high enough to sustain the size of this group. Although strength could be maintained even if accession levels drop to 70% of FY1982 levels, this level of decline would probably leave a force with an unbalanced experience mix. It would leave little flexibility to cut back on the swelling career force in order to leave room for more junior personnel.

Whether the FY1982 level of accessions can continue to be recruited depends on the explanation for the increase between FY1974 and FY1983. Possible explanations for this increase range from changes in unemployment to changes in the recruiting procedures (including increased resources, management attention, shifting the responsibility for recruiting to the active army recruiting command, and initiation of enlistment bonus and educational grant programs in FY1979). Forecasting reserve accession levels is beset with a great deal of uncertainty until ongoing research is able to sort out the various factors affecting enlistments and make some determination regarding their possible magnitude and direction of effect. Still, using data and research that are at best extremely sketchy, we can establish some reasonable bounds for enlistment levels over the next five years.

It is certain that over the next seven years, the pools from which both the NPS and PS reservists are drawn will decline. First, the number of seventeen through twenty-one year-olds will decline between FY1983-FY1980 by 12%. Second, separations from the active force will continue to decline due to smaller force sizes and increased retention (see Table 12.12).

As the economy recovers, the unemployment rate will decline. The relationship between unemployment and accessions to the reserves is difficult to characterize in an unambiguous fashion because there appear to be countervailing effects. Among the NPS pool, the reserve job tends to be particularly attractive for the unemployed (recall that the reserve job offers full-time employment during the initial active-duty training) and for those civilians with a propensity to moonlight. A decrease in unemployment reduces the size of the unemployed pool; in addition, it offers increased job opportunities, both full-time and part-time, thus reducing NPS accession

Table 12.12. Active Duty Enlisted Separations (In Thousands)

Fiscal Year	Army	Navy	Marine Corps	Air Force	DoD
1971	492	168	93	137	890
1972	469	140	69	122	800
1973	226	143	52	131	546
1974	204	118	56	119	497
1975	209	121	54	100	484
1976	193	115	62	96	466
1977	175	109	47	84	415
1978	146	88	43	71	348
1979	156	92	48	83	378
1980	154	95	43	82	373
1981	132	96	42	74	344

levels. There is an additional factor that tends to reinforce this effect. In times of high unemployment, the active force tends to select higher-quality recruits. The "overflow," as it were, consisting of persons with a marked taste for the military, tends to be a rich recruiting ground for the reserves. During periods of declining unemployment, the active force draws down the eligible pool with a strong taste for military service, thus coming into direct competition with the reserves.

The effect of declining unemployment is more difficult to predict for PS personnel. On the one hand, we have much the same effect described above: increased civilian opportunities would reduce the attractiveness of the reserves and reduce enlistments. Research has shown that the propensity for reserve service depends on primary wage levels and primary job hours, both of which tend to increase as unemployment declines. On the other hand, it has been well-documented that the pool of active-force veterans increases as unemployment declines because of lower retention in the active force. These individuals are prime candidates for reserve enlistment, although there is some evidence to suggest that there are frequently long delays between active force separation and reserve enlistment. Perhaps the best way of characterizing the effect of unemployment on reserve accessions is to talk in terms of the short-run and the long-run. In the short-run, declining unemployment will cause reserve accessions to decline. In the long-run, this effect may be counteracted to some unknown degree by the increase in PS accessions due to the increased eligible pool.

Measurements of the effects of unemployment have tended to vary considerably. Nonprior-service elasticities range from .2 to .8, and PS elasticities range from .2 to .5.[23] With reduction in unemployment from 10.8 to 8.0, declines in accession of 6% to 10% might be expected.

The reserves initiated enlistment bonus payments or educational incentives of $1,500 in FY1979. The incentive program was limited to certain units and skills based on deployment time and manpower shortages. For a typical enlistee over a six-year term the amount would add roughly 15% to 20% to discounted base-pay levels. On the basis of coverage and current estimates of elasticities, the programs probably have added 5% or less to enlistment totals.

The effects of added recruiting resources for reserve forces and changes in organization and recruiting emphasis are harder to estimate. This is due partly to the different ways each component organizes and performs the recruiting function, and partly because reservists themselves can make effective recruiters in their home community. The national guard components have their own recruiting organizations in each state, and the service reserve components can recruit through the active recruiting commands of their own organizations. Reserve recruiting can thus be affected by active recruiting goals and priorities. Both the presence of reservists themselves in the home community as potential recruiters and the joint active/reserve recruiting organization make it difficult to estimate at any time the resources being devoted to reserve recruiting. However, it is probably the case that a major cause of the increase in NPS recruiting levels from 46,000 in FY1974 to 106,000 in FY1982 has been the development of an effective recruiting organization which includes reservists themselves, added resources to recruiting and advertising, and assignment of a higher priority to reserve recruiting.

The portion of added accessions due to recruiting, enlistment incentives, and changes in attitudes toward military service should remain, while those due to unemployment and effects due to the decline in the youth cohort or veteran pool will tend to change enlistment levels. For the purposes of the projections, we have assumed that enlistment levels could remain as high as FY1982 levels and decline to 70% of that level. These estimates would seem to bound possible declines in the next several years.

Of course, the optimistic strength projections raise issues concerning the desirable experience mix for the reserves. A more senior force will cost more money but will offer higher levels of individual productivity. It will mean higher budgetary costs for present compensation and future retirement. For many types of units the substitution process of more senior people for more junior people may not be efficient. The larger number of senior reservists will also mean markedly reduced promotion opportunities, which should have a moderating influence on career-force growth. If it appears desirable to moderate this career-force growth, it will not be easily done. Retention rates after ten years of service are fairly insensitive to current compensation and promotion control, or direct bars to reenlistment may be necessary. This, of course, would raise issues of equity and difficult choices among personnel with similar records. Severance pay would be another alternative for encouraging separation. However, before these issues need to be faced, a more important issue of reserve-force size needs to be decided. The growth in career force opens the alternative to have larger reserve-force sizes. Essentially, the expanded career force would already be in place and accession levels could be raised to achieve a balanced expansion. This long-term decision needs resolution before manpower policies addressed toward experience mix issues can be implemented.

RESERVE/ACTIVE COSTS

The potential for growth in the selected-reserve force and the rapid shift to a more senior force raises many issues which will dominate reserve manpower policy discussions over the next seven years. These issues are the appropriate size of selected reserve forces, the most efficient experience mix, and the appropriate level of pay and benefits. While these questions are certainly not new, the results of the projections place them in a somewhat different perspective.

The current budget deficits, together with the future obligations connected with the force modernization program, are forcing a review of the appropriate levels of reserve and active forces. One area of suggested saving is to increase the size of reserve forces, while maintaining the size of active forces. While the above projections suggest that reserve force growth is feasible, the questions of how much saving is achieved by this substitution and the impact on readiness remain. We will not address the tougher question of readiness here, but will offer some preliminary thoughts on the question of savings.

Savings estimates resulting from placing military units in the reserve rather than the active forces are made generally from studies which compare current peacetime costs for existing similar units in the active and reserve forces. These estimates generally show that the saving achieved is a strong function of the type of unit and required readiness or activity level. Units where the capital/labor mix is high and where readiness demands high activity levels (more typical of air force and navy flight units) show savings of roughly 25% to 33% for reserve units, whereas more labor-intensive units (typical of army infantry units) show savings of as much as 70%. The savings flow directly from reduced personnel costs of reserve units and somewhat lower activity levels is perhaps attributed either to the low activity required to sustain skills of more experienced reserve personnel or to lower readiness levels. Part of the savings also arises because reserve forces depend partially on prior-service personnel and have reduced initial training costs. The fact that these savings are not higher surprises some people who focus on the ratio of annual hours for reservists who typically are paid for around 300 annual hours while active personnel are paid for 2,100. Overlooked in this simple comparison are several factors which tend to narrow considerably the cost differences.

First is the fact that labor costs for capital-intensive units can be less than half of annual operation and management (O&M) costs. The nonlabor costs for similar activity levels of active and reserve units tend to be similar, thus making cost savings in this category depend on slightly lower activity levels of reserve units. Second, the simple comparisons overlook the large number of full-time civilian and military personnel associated with reserve units who are needed to service and maintain equipment and perform administrative and training functions. In the selected reserve air components, full-time technicians make up about 17% of personnel, while in army components the ratio is about 4%. More full-time personnel are needed where activity levels are high and capital equipment accounts for a large part of unit costs. Third, selected reservists tend to have higher average pay levels from their greater experience and the hourly rate of pay for drills is twice hourly pay for active personnel. Average hourly wages for reservists are thus higher than for active personnel. These factors tend to narrow the reserve/active costs differences made from simple perceptions of reservists as part-time and actives as full-time.

However, there are additional complications in making reserve/active cost comparisons which could significantly affect even the more detailed unit comparisons made on the basis of peacetime O&M cost. These estimates leave out two important factors associated with reserve/active substitutions: the effect of different active- and reserve-force levels on overall pay levels and the costs of new military construction. Changing the size of either active- or reserve-force levels will exert upward or downward pressure on long-term pay levels. Increasing the force size means higher accession levels and retention rates which are adjustments typically made through pay or bonus levels. It is more difficult to predict when and how these pay changes would be made due to the congressional decision process than it is to estimate the magnitude. However the size of these adjustments, since they could affect overall pay levels, needs to be included in the reserve/active calculus.

Small changes in the size of existing forces probably would not entail large construction costs since the tendency would be to collocate new units with existing units and utilize the existing capital base. However larger changes in force sizes would entail new construction such as armories, airfields, training and equipment storage facilities. These costs would probably tend to be higher in the reserve forces since their geographical spread tends to lead to lower utilization and the need for more facilities. However, the extent to which existing facilities can be more intensively utilized is not known.

Initial work on active/reserve costing suggests that substitution leads to savings, although somewhat less than commonly perceived, and that additional factors need to be included to improve estimates. Underlying these savings is the question of the extent to which substitution is possible without sacrificing readiness. Reserve forces currently are a large portion of total forces, and it is not clear that large-scale substitution is possible wihout reducing readiness. It also appears to be the case that equivalent readiness in active and reserve units can be most easily maintained where saving differences are smallest. Thus, more savings are generated in army units than air units, but more uncertainty currently exists in achieving equivalent active/reserve readiness in army units than for air units.

MOBILIZATION MANPOWER IN THE AVF ENVIRONMENT

Mobilization manpower is needed to bring active and reserve units to full wartime strength, provide replacements for losses, and assure that the essential nonunit manpower accounts are sufficient so that unit strengths are not reduced because of travel, illness, and training. Since the active and reserve force structures are undermanned in peacetime to save money, it is essential that a large number of personnel be available immediately upon mobilization to fill the units to their intended wartime strengths. It is necessary also to set up the replacement stream so that combat and other losses are replaced promptly without undue loss of unit combat effectiveness. Many of the people needed to meet these demands have to be trained in advance so that they can meet the time-urgent schedules for the mobilization and deployment of the units. Some of the people intended for later use primarily as replacements can be trained after the mobilization starts. So those are two general classes of mobilization manpower: pretrained individuals and post trained individuals.

Post trained individuals are provided by the selective service system to the Department of Defense. Under the current law, young men from nineteen to twenty-one years will be drafted and sent to basic combat training and initial skill training for at least the three months mandated by law. After that initial training period, they are available for assignment to units as fillers or replacements. The posttrained manpower system is in pretty good shape now, although it did not fare well in the early years of the AVF, despite the Gates Commission admonition to assure that an effective standby draft was in being.

Pretrained individuals, however, were overlooked by the Gates Commission and by almost everyone else until the late 1970s. Starting in 1978 intensive actions were taken to assure an adequate supply of pretrained individual manpower, and these efforts have been successful to an extent. However, problems persist, and this area must be rated as one of the still weak areas of the AVF.

One major reason why the problem was overlooked in the early AVF years is that all of the services had on hand in 1973 large numbers of personnel assigned to their IRR pools. These large numbers created a false sense of security. Little attention or money was devoted to the management and training of these people. For the most part, they were simply ignored. The word "pool" indicated the feeling about this group: that they were a vast resource from which the services could fish to get the skills they needed when they needed them.

This sense of security evaporated in the mid-1970s when the IRR pools dried up. The new methods of computing wartime manpower requirements which were emerging in this same time frame gave some substance to the need for fillers and replacements upon mobilization. The new and large requirements were firmed up at the same time that the supply was shrinking, and it became obvious that the services could not support a full mobilization because they did not have enough pretrained individual manpower to meet their own stated demands. Initially there was a lot of confusion about the extent to which a draft could substitute for pretrained individuals. However it soon became clear that even the fastest draft could not meet demands for entry level skills in the first three or four months and for more advanced skills in the first six to eight months. At this point serious attention finally was paid to the pretrained individual manpower problem.

Actions to Provide Pretrained Individual Manpower

Recognition that this was a pretrained individual manpower problem was essential to taking appropriate corrective action. As long as the problem was an "IRR shortfall," emphasis was placed only on efforts to increase the number of people in the IRR itself. The IRR-shortfall approach led inevitably to proposals for various forms of a peacetime draft for the IRR alone, for the reserve components, and even a draft for the active component to provide people for the

IRR. None of these proposals for a peacetime draft, however, was feasible in the AVF climate and other solutions had to be found if the problem were to be solved.

The phrase "pretrained individual manpower," and the concept for which it stands, allowed a partial solution to this problem. It will provide a complete solution in time if followed to the logical conclusion.

The concept of pretrained individual manpower expanded the solution space to include sources other than the IRR. This converted a supply problem to a management problem. The critical step in the solution of this problem was to get people to understand that there are sufficient personnel with prior military training in the United States to meet the demands of a full mobilization. The real problem is that not all of these pretrained individuals are available conveniently in the event of a mobilization. Table 12.13 shows the total universe of pretrained individual manpower arranged in order of availability.

Table 12.13. Pretrained Individual Manpower Sources

Source	Availability
Active Component Individuals	Partial Mobilization
Individual Mobilization Augmentees	Partial Mobilization
Retired Regular Personnel	Partial or Full Mobilization
Individual Ready Reservists	Full Mobilization
Standby Reservists	Total Mobilization
Retired Reservists	Total Mobilization
Veterans w/o Obligation	Not Available

Once this understanding was achieved, there were two obvious things that had to be done. The first was to get as many assets from each of the potential sources as possible. The second was to apply intensive management to these personnel sources to provide a satisfactory degree of assurance that the right people would get to the right jobs at the right time. Actions that have been taken are as follows:

1. Policies have been adopted which would make significant numbers of active component personnel in the individuals accounts available as fillers and initial replacements immediately after mobilization. These policies include cessation or curtailment of schools for certain skills, cancellation of leave or delay en route, and acceleration of training courses.

2. The Individual Mobilization Augmentation (IMA) program has been extended from the air force, where it had been very successful, to all of the other services. The advantage of this program is that it can supply a highly skilled person to a wartime augmentation job with minimum delay. IMAs are trained on specific jobs as well as specific skills, and they provide a highly reliable method of assuring immediate augmentation, although with relatively high peacetime training costs. The IMAs were all placed into the selected reserve so they would be available if desired as part of the 100,000 man call-up in a partial mobilization prior to a declaration of national emergency or full mobilization.

3. Management of IRR personnel has been improved. The services realized that it was not good to have just a vast pool of trained people if they could not be used promptly when needed. One valuable program has been preassignment. Under this program, some IRR personnel are assigned in advance to the units or stations to which they will report upon M-Day. This saves time in the event and provides the preassigned IRR personnel with some morale-enhancing identification with a wartime job. Another program has been increased refresher training in peacetime for IRR personnel. This has been very successful with officers, but less so with enlisted personnel. These and other programs to improve the management of the IRR have served to

improve the training, readiness, and responsiveness of IRR personnel for active duty in a mobilization. However, this action has been implemented halfheartedly, and much more needs to be done.

4. The standby reserve has been recognized as a valuable source of trained personnel. An inventory of this source revealed that it did contain significant numbers of personnel with valuable skills. The services have included the standby reserve in their mobilization assignment procedures and are able now to make effective use of this source.

5. Retired personnel have been included in mobilization planning. Because of the early retirement age of most officers and enlisted personnel, there are a substantial number of retirees who are still vigorous and possess skills and experience of value in a war. Retired personnel would be recalled to replace younger personnel, who in turn would be assigned to the fighting forces. Once this possibility was pointed out, the services adopted the idea enthusiastically and created programs for recalling retired personnel for mobilization. These programs are very inexpensive, costing little more than some minor record-keeping, but they add several thousand people to the numbers available promptly upon mobilization. The law allows recall of retired regular personnel rather easily, and these have been brought into the mobilization system first. Actions are underway to incorporate the large number of retired reservists who also could be used. This action has been a very satisfactory one.

6. The effort to make use of veterans without military obligation, on the other hand, was a resounding failure. The idea was quite simple. The current military service obligation incurred upon enlistment is six years. Personnel with an obligation were already in the selected reserve or IRR. It was discovered that there were large numbers of people with prior military service who had completed their obligation. Three ways to obtain the services of these veterans in a mobilization were considered:

a. The most effective method was to recall these people involuntarily in time of war (draft them, in effect) to meet the shortages which remained after all of the other sources of supply had been used. This method proved to be infeasible politically. The major policymakers in the executive branch and the Congress rejected the idea of making people who had served already go into combat again, particularly before people who had never served. Thus, a solution which appeared rational proved to be unworkable because of human considerations. It should be noted, however, that many officials who professed publicly to detest the idea of using veterans admitted privately that they would need and want the veterans in a "real" war.

b. The next approach was to create an "emergency reserve" which veterans could volunteer to join in peacetime, understanding they would be recalled in the event of mobilization. This method would be less reliable than a draft but did not require any coercion. The emergency reserve would receive no peacetime pay or training but would receive refresher training immediately when mobilized. Preliminary surveys showed that there were sufficient veterans willing to do this to warrant going ahead with the program, but by this time the whole idea of using veterans, even volunteers, was considered to be political poison.

c. The least reliable approach was simply to give priority to veterans (called "prior-service accessions" for this purpose) during the volunteering phase at the outbreak of war or declaration of mobilization. The Department of Defense intends to accept volunteers for service at the same time that the wartime draft is being established to deliver draftees. It is more efficient in the initial days of a mobilization to accept a PS volunteer requiring only two to three weeks of refresher training before becoming a useful asset, than to accept an NPS volunteer requiring twelve weeks of training just to reach an entry level skill. This concept gained a degree of acceptance but never seemed to become entrenched firmly in manpower mobilization planning.

Despite these successful actions, there remains a shortage of pretrained individual manpower for a full mobilization. Each service has a shortage; the army has the most severe problem. Not only does the army need more pretrained individuals, it has particular need for pretrained individuals with combat skills.

THE OUTLOOK FOR PRETRAINED INDIVIDUAL MANPOWER

While the problem of providing sufficient pretrained individual manpower has not been solved, there is no reason to attribute that failure entirely to the AVF. The problem also was not solved in the draft years, when there were large numbers of people but no appreciation for the problem and insufficient management of existing pretrained individual resources. The lower IRR strengths caused by the advent of the AVF forced the DoD to pay attention to this problem and take actions that alleviated the problem to a great extent but which did not provide for a complete solution.

The current situation is that the DoD has done about all that it can to use sources of pretrained individual manpower other than veterans and the IRR. The complete solution to the problem requires more actions to be taken in these two areas.

Veterans

The Department of Defense presently has no plans or programs to make effective use of veterans (prior-service personnel) in the early days of a mobilization, either voluntarily or involuntarily. These plans and programs would have to be improvised at the outset of the mobilization because it is evident that the veterans would be used to prevent military collapse from lack of replacements.

Some plans to make use of the veterans should be accomplished now, perhaps on a contingency basis. The idea of accepting, even encouraging pretrained personnel to volunteer for wartime duty at the start of a mobilization should be reconsidered. Such an approach would be well in keeping with the AVF concept. It makes good sense also to consider recruiting some of these veterans in peacetime to join the IRR or a special reserve component established just for them. The army is studying the possible use of veterans, and that is an encouraging sign.

The IRR

The IRR will have to be increased in strength and managed better to provide assurance that the combat skills needed by the army and marines, and the technical skills needed by the other services upon mobilization, are going to be available. While the other sources of pretrained individual manpower are valuable and necessary, the IRR is the best source in terms of availability and trainability. However, IRR strength is not sufficient, and its enlisted members are not participating sufficiently in training. Table 12.14 shows IRR strength during the AVF years.

IRR strength dropped dramatically with the advent of the AVF and its strength, when it reached its low point in FY1978, was less than 30% of strength in FY1973. Today, despite great efforts, IRR strength remains well below pre-AVF levels for every service. Even more disturbing is that the strength continues to decline for the navy, marines, and air force.

There are three ways to increase IRR strength: extend the military service obligation, provide financial incentives, and institute appropriate personnel policies. The least expensive and most reliable way to increase IRR strength is to increase the length and coverage of the military service obligation (MSO). This, of course, is a form of involuntary service.

Table 12.14. Individual Ready Reserve Strength (In Thousands)

Fiscal Year	Army	Navy	Marine Corps	Air Force	DoD
1972	1060	215	138	157	1571
1973	759	217	116	137	1229
1974	540	179	90	121	931
1975	363	122	58	87	631
1976	240	106	54	83	485
1977	160	106	45	63	375
1978	178	93	40	46	356
1979	206	86	59	44	396
1980	212	97	57	46	413
1981	224	99	52	44	419
1982	230	78	45	43	396

Each person joining a military service incurs an obligation to serve for a fixed period of time, currently six years. The person may serve this six-year period in any combination of active and reserve duty. During the draft era, the six-year MSO created the large strengths in the IRR. Draftees typically served two years or less on active duty, then finished up their MSO by serving four years in the IRR. (A few went to the selected reserve.) The large IRR of the pre-AVF years consisted primarily of these obligors. The AVF changed that. As initial active duty enlistments increased to three years and more people reenlisted for the active component, fewer people ended up in the IRR and strength dropped.

It was recognized that increasing the MSO to eight or even ten years for new members would provide a larger IRR. However, the additional strengths would not pay off for six years, assuming present members were kept on the six-year MSO. Moreover, the services were concerned that a longer MSO would reduce active component NPS accessions. Obtaining approval for a longer MSO appeared to be a lengthy project, so immediate attention was given to closing loopholes in the existing MSO law. The 1973 MSO had a lot of loopholes: women were excepted, voluntary transfers to the standby reserve were permitted, and other minor exceptions were permitted. When these loopholes were closed, there was a surge in IRR strength which helped, but failed to provide sufficient IRR strength. In the meantime actions to increase the MSO continued, and an eight-year MSO measure passed in the Congress in 1983. The new law gives the secretary of defense the authority to extend the MSO up to eight years for new military personnel. When this is done, IRR strength will increase substantially in about six years.

Financial incentives to induce people to serve in the IRR consisted of an enlistment bonus and a continuation bonus. The enlistment bonus was for NPS persons who would receive initial training and serve their entire six years in the IRR. This direct enlistment program was not supported with great enthusiasm by the army, and it did not prove to be an outstanding success with the prospective enlistees either. The value of an IRR person who had never served in an active or reserve unit was considered to be marginal at best. The continuation bonus was more effective. This was an inducement to get people leaving active duty or selected reserve duty without any remaining obligation to join the IRR for three more years. In effect, this is an IRR reenlistment bonus. The program was poorly supported with funds and authority expired. It is scheduled to start up again in FY1984. There is every reason to believe that financial incentives which have proven effective for the active component and for the selected reserve will be just as effective for the IRR. However, the services have not given this program the interest, analysis, or funds that the other programs had. If the services want a larger IRR in the six-year period before the MSO increase pays off, the effective use of financial incentives needs to be considered seriously.

Appropriate personnel policies will help increase IRR strength. Some of the policies still in effect in the services, particularly in the field, originated in the pre-AVF era. At that time, when strength was large, the philosophy was to make it easy to get out of the IRR. Training participation standards were set high, and personnel who did not meet these standards were discharged. As recently as November 1983, people with required skills were being discharged routinely by personnel centers without regard for mobilization requirements. While many of these vestigial policies have been changed, it would be a good idea still to review IRR personnel management policies to assure that they are consistent with an era of shortage. That is, the policies should make it easy to get into the IRR and hard to get out.

Training Participation

Another important action that can be taken to improve the IRR is to increase training participation. Since strength is insufficient, it is absolutely essential that each IRR member is ready and willing to report when ordered to active duty for a mobilization. The way to do this is to provide effective and interesting training, which is not easy. While it is hard to persuade young people to participate faithfully and enthusiastically in reserve-unit training one weekend a month, it is much more difficult to get individual reservists to train at all.

IRR training is primarily a problem with junior officers and lower-ranking enlisted personnel. Senior officers and the NCOs are willing to participate in training because the pay is fairly good, and the senior people have more attachment to and understanding of their services. Most of the IRR, however, consists of junior officers and low-ranking enlisted personnel who really do not want to interrupt their civilian lives to perform military training, particularly if that training is poor. There is anecdotal evidence that some IRR training is indeed poor. IRR personnel assigned to train with active-component units have sometimes been used for work details. Individual IRR members sometimes arrive for training to find that their active-component hosts are unprepared and unwilling to take the time to provide good training. Finding school quotas for IRR personnel remains a problem. While there certainly is some good training for IRR personnel, it is likely that overall it is not as good as it could or should be. Three things that could be done to improve IRR training are as follows:

1. Adopt new forms of IRR training which are convenient and attractive to the IRR members. A major concern for IRR members is conflict with civilian employment; training could be conducted on weekends to minimize this problem. Training time could be split up into small doses instead of requiring two weeks at a time. Weekend symposiums have been both effective and popular when they are well-organized, fast paced, and professional. More school quotas, more courses designed for IRR personnel, and more special offerings at training centers would improve IRR training and increase participation. The United States today is full of adult education courses, seminars, and conferences. There is no reason why some of these methods cannot be applied to IRR training.
2. Improve IRR training by putting more money and more people into it. IRR training has very low priority in the budget. However, if the mobilization manpower requirement is valid and a trained IRR is needed to meet the requirement, the money would be well spent.
3. Put high level command emphasis on IRR training. The DoD can perform magnificently when it tries. The military services are expert at providing good training, when they try. If the DoD and the services decide to have outstanding training for the IRR, it will happen.

Impact of the Pretrained Individual Manpower Problem on the AVF

While the problem of insufficient pretrained individual manpower to support a full mobilization is not entirely a result of the AVF, it may well be the Achilles' heel of the AVF. The persistence of the shortage of pretrained individual manpower is recognized as a serious problem among those who are responsible for planning for mobilization and deployment. There have been attempts in Congress and elsewhere to institute some form of peacetime conscription to solve the pretrained individual manpower problem, including an IRR draft. Pressure for these kinds of measures will grow if the problem cannot be solved in the AVF context.

It would be ironic if the mobilization manpower problem, not entirely caused by the advent of the AVF, were to bring about its demise.

Reporting Policy

There is a long-standing controversy about how many of the reservists actually would report when ordered to active duty upon mobilization. The real answer will not be known until the mobilization, but it is essential to estimate the show rate to provide enough extra people to take care of the "no-shows." In effect, the DoD needs to know how much overbooking to do so that the required numbers will be present. An old study had used show rates of 95% for the selected reserve, 70% for the IRR, and 50% for the standby reserve. These show rates were derived very loosely from a few previous mobilizations. It is certain that they are invalid. Nevertheless, they were used as sacred numbers for many years and may still be engraved in stone.

The approach adopted by the DoD to provide a better fix to this problem was to emphasize management actions to improve the likelihood that an individual reservist or retiree would report for duty. The idea was than an individual's propensity to report for duty could be increased by putting that individual into a group, reducing his fear of the unknown, and increasing his own confidence. Personnel in organized units tend to report because they want to stay with their group, but individual reservists not in units do not have that particular support mechanism, and so other management actions are necessary. This led to the adoption of more intensive and personalized management of IRR personnel, more IRR training, and preassignment of various types. It also led to actions to keep track of the reserve personnel more closely and eliminate in advance those who could not or would not be available in time of need.

Guard and reserve units have no credibility if they have personnel who are too old, too fat, or too ill to serve effectively in wartime. It is common sense to screen the personnel of these units periodically to assure that all personnel can serve if ordered to active duty in a mobilization. It also makes sense to remove from the units in advance those personnel who will not be able to report with their units because of their civilian jobs. A person can be in only one place at one time. A reservist who also is a critical defense worker or an important federal official cannot remain in that civilian job and also report to active duty. A choice must be made, and it must be made in advance. Once the mobilization starts, it is too late for members with job conflicts to attempt to get out of the reserve obligations. To allow this would be to upset the mobilization process, which already will be confusing and difficult because of shortages caused by legitimate absences. The necessary policy, which has been adopted by the DoD, is that there will be no delays, deferments, or exemptions once the order to mobilize is issued and that all ready reservists will report when ordered. Transferring personnel out of the ready reserve must be accomplished prior to mobilization and will stop upon mobilization. While this policy will not assure that everyone does report, it does assure that everyone is supposed to report.

To be successful, this hard-line policy must have the overt support of high officials because any visible flouting of the screening policy will cause it to lose credibility and be enforced laxly among the rank and file. Unfortunately, there appears to be poor support for this policy among some high ranking officials, and the show rate of the reserves in a mobilization is bound to be lower as a result than it otherwise would have been.

SUMMARY

The unsolved problem of pretrained individual manpower has been characterized as the greatest failure of the AVF. While this is an accurate statement, it is not a complete diagnosis. There also was a problem with pretrained individual manpower during the draft years. While there were large numbers of people in the IRR then, they were not managed, trained, or available for immediate service, and it is unlikely that a rapid full mobilization could have been supported. The reduced strengths brought about by the end of the short-term, active-duty periods have required the DoD to pay attention to the IRR, bring other sources of pretrained individuals into a state of availability, and devote some attention and money to the problem. In that sense, the advent of the AVF has contributed positively to solving the problem. It appears also that actions already taken and underway will provide a satisfactory solution in the future, provided that some plans are made for the use of veterans as an interim measure, the IRR improves in strength and training, and that a hard-line reporting policy is maintained.

NOTES

1. There is a common misperception as to when both active and reserve forces can be considered to be "all volunteer." The transition period to an all-volunteer equilibrium force occurs only when the first volunteer cohorts in FY1973 reach retirement—a thirty year process. Thus, in one sense it is too early to evaluate the AVF. Practically speaking the major effects of having volunteer cohorts—higher retention rates at first term—are felt in the first ten to twelve years as the number of mid-careerists swells and accession requirements decline. The effects of these phenomena are still taking place in the active and reserve forces.
2. This point is harder to document since distribution of reservists by year of service is not available for draft years. However, the distribution for FY1976 and FY1977 in Table 12.4 reflects draft level turnover somewhat since there was still a significant percentage of draft-motivated youth in the force who had entered before the draft ended in FY1972.
3. As long as the draft was supplying the reservists with almost unlimited NPS accessions of high quality, there was little incentive to utilize larger numbers of already trained PS personnel. The heavy use of NPS personnel is shown in Table 12.6 for FY1970 and FY1971.
4. The current active force of 2.1 million members is the smallest since 1949.
5. *The Report of the President's Commission on an All-Volunteer Force,* Chapter 9 (Washington, DC: Government Printing Office, 1970).
6. Ibid.
7. An elasticity is the ratio of the percentage increase in enlistments to the percentage increase in compensation. An elasticity of 1.25 indicates that a pay raise of 10% would increase enlistments by 12.5%.
8. Alan E. Fecther, "Impact of Pay and Draft Policy on Army Enlistment Behavior," and Gary R. Nelson, "Economic Analysis of First-Term Reenlistments in the Army," in vol. 1 *Studies Prepared for the President's Commission on an All-Volunteer Armed Force* (Washington, DC: Government Printing Office, November 1970).
9. Even though educational level and aptitude were high, the military effectiveness of units filled with personnel who enlisted to avoid active military service and Vietnam duty might be questioned.
10. Selected reservists are primarily moonlighters. Over 90% hold a primary job in addition to their reserve job. Multiple job holding rates have been fairly constant over the period 1956-1971, see "Multiple Jobholding in 1970 and 1971," Special Labor Force Report 139 (Washington, DC: U.S. Department of Labor, 1972).
11. The commission did not actually recommend separate reserve compensation initiatives. Rather, reserve pay increases followed from their recommended pay increases for the active force because

reserve and active pay levels are linked. Raises in active-duty base pay result in equal percentage increases in reserve pay.

12. The air force initiated a series of studies of reserve personnel in the early 1970s which developed the theory of the moonlighting labor market and developed estimates of volunteer accessions. See: Bernard Rostker; *The Personnel Structure and Posture of the Air National Guard and Air Force Reserve*, R-1049-PR, Air Reserve Forces Personnel Study, vol. 1; April 1973; Bernard Rostker and Robert Shisko, *The Air Reserve Forces and the Economics of Secondary Labor Market Participation*, R-1254-PR, Air Reserve Personnel Study, vol. 2, August 1973; Bernard Rostker, *Total Force*, R-1430-PR, Air Reserve Personnel Study, vol. 3, October 1974 (Santa Monica, CA: Rand Corporation).

13. John P. White, assistant secretary of defense (Manpower, Reserve Affairs and Logistics) requested funds from Congress in FY1977 to test several reserve pay and benefit initiatives. The first reserve pay incentive authorized by Congress was a reenlistment bonus. This test provided the opportunity to test several hypotheses underlying the Gates Commission analysis of reserve retention rates.

14. Burke K. Burright, David W. Grissmer, and Zahava D. Doering, *A Model of Reenlistment Decisions of Army National Guardsmen* (Santa Monica, CA: Rand Corporation, October 1982). R-2866-MRAL.

15. David W. Grissmer, Zahava D. Doering, and Jane Sachar, *The Design, Administration, and Evaluation of the 1978 Selected Reserve Reenlistment Bonus Test* (Santa Monica, CA: Rand Corporation, July 1982). R-2865-MRAL.

16. Bernard Rostker and Robert Shisko, "The Economics of Multiple Job Holding," *American Economic Review*, vol. 66, no. 3, June 1976, adapted from their Air Reserve Personnel Study, vol. 2, *The Air Reserve Forces and the Economics of Secondary Labor Market Participation* (Santa Monica, CA: Rand Corporation, August 1973). R-1254-PR.

17. *Multiple Jobholders in May 1978*, Special Labor Force Report 221. Reprinted from *Monthly Labor Review*, vol. 102, no. 2, pp. 59-61. (Washington, DC: U.S. Department of Labor, Bureau of Labor Statistics, February 1979).

18. Richard V.L. Cooper, "Accrual Accounting for Reserve Retirement" (unpublished research) (Santa Monica, CA: Rand Corporation, January 1978).

19. It is interesting to note that measurements of the effects of primary civilian job wage and working hours on reserve reenlistment produced highly statistically significant effects with expected signs, but the elasticities (.21 for wages and .26 for hours) were much smaller than measures for civilian moonlighters. See Burke K. Burright, David W. Grissmer, and Zahava D. Doering, *A Model of Reenlistment Decisions of Army National Guardsmen* (Santa Monica, CA: Rand Corporation, October 1982). R-2866-MRAL.

20. See David W. Grissmer and S.N. Kirby, *Attrition During Training in the Army Reserve and National Guard* (Santa Monica, CA: Rand Corporation, August 1984). N-2866-RA.

21. Current measures are more consistent with small elasticities although they generally have very weak or no statistical significance, or occasionally wrong signs. See: Robert Kelly, "The Supply of Volunteers to the Selected Reserve," mimeographed (United States Military Academy, West Point, NY: Department of Social Sciences, May 1979); William McNaught, *Projecting Future Accessions to the Selected Reserve Components*, (Santa Monica, CA: Rand Corporation, August 1980) N-1563-MRAL; and William McNaught *The Supply of Enlistees to the Selected Reserves*, (Santa Monica, CA: Rand Corporation, July 1981). N-1562-MRAL.

22. See David W. Grissmer and John R. Hiller, *Followup of Participants in the 1978 Selected Reserve Reenlistment Bonus Test* (Santa Monica, CA: Rand Corporation, February 1983). N-1880-MRAL.

23. See McNaught, *Projecting Future Accesions* and *Supply of Enlistees*.

13 Congressional Perspectives on Defense Manpower Issues

ROBERT F. HALE*

The U.S. Constitution provides the Congress with preeminent powers regarding the military. The Congress has the power to raise and support armies, provide and maintain a navy, and make rules for the government and regulation of land and naval forces (Article I, Section 8). In carrying out these duties, the Congress has understandably devoted much attention to the dollars and policies that govern defense manpower. As has often been said, the ultimate capability of an armed force depends critically on the ability and dedication of its people.

Key congressional decisions about manpower and other defense issues usually get made in its committees and are determined in part by the roles and political inclinations of these committees. Thus, this chapter discusses the roles of the congressional committees that most influence defense decisions and the broad factors influencing these committees and Congress as they excerise authority over defense. Prominent among these factors is a concern over the size of the federal deficit and a recognition of changed public attitudes toward the defense portion of the budget. With this as a background, a discussion of congressional perspectives and likely future actions on six key manpower issues follows.

HOW CONGRESS EXERCISES ITS AUTHORITY: ROLES OF KEY COMMITTEES

Six congressional committees influence defense most heavily. Many of their activities go on concurrently, but it helps clarify the process to discuss the roles of the six committees in the order of their actions during a normal legislative year.

---

*This paper reflects the opinions of the author and not necessarily those of the Congressional Budget Office or any members or employee of the Congress and was current as of mid-1983.

Budget Committees

Created in 1974, the House and Senate Budget Committees are the newest committees that influence defense issues. They are also generally the first to act each year. In the spring, the budget committees are required to recommend a target for total federal revenue and targets for federal spending in nineteen broad budget functions (the four largest are income security, national defense, health, and interest on the federal debt). The Congress ultimately approves these targets in the form of the First Concurrent Resolution on the Budget. The resolution, which does not require the president's signature, provides guidance for the remainder of the congressional budget debate.

Given their task of setting targets for taxes and all federal spending, the budget committees concentrate on aggregate tax and spending policies. Both eschew "line-item" decisions in defense or other budget areas. Nonetheless, their recommendations on aggregates can influence the line-item debates. For example, this spring the budget committees recommended less of an increase in defense budget authority for 1984 than the administration had requested.[1] The Congress ultimately took their recommendation and approved about 5% "real" growth—that is, growth after adjustment for inflation in defense budget authority rather than the 10% requested by the administration. This slowdown required a reduction in 1984 of about $12 billion in budget authority in the administration's national defense budget and has already prompted the Congress to make a wide range of changes, including a number in defense manpower.

While the budget committees concentrate on broad spending targets, they do sometimes influence specific defense decisions. For example, this year the budget committees rejected the administration's call for a pay freeze, allowing instead a 4% pay raise. While this action did not have the force of law, it probably influenced eventual adoption of the 4% figure. The budget committees may also comment on detailed issues in ways that do not affect law but suggest areas of committee interest. In its most recent report, for example, the House Budget Committee called for a thorough review of military retirement programs in light of the need for budget restraint.[2]

The budget committees also supervise an important procedure known as reconciliation. Under reconciliation, the Congress instructs its committees to make legislative changes to bring the costs of programs into conformity with spending limits in the congressional budget resolution. In recent years, the administration and the Congress have used this procedure to enact a package of spending reductions that might have been difficult to achieve through pieces of legislation. To date, reconciliation has focused on nondefense entitlements but defense spending could be more heavily involved in future reconciliation actions.

The budget committees, then, help provide guidance to the other congressional committees on overall spending plans. The authorizing and appropriating committees must propose the detailed changes to implement those plans.

Authorizing Committees

The two defense authorizing committees, the House and Senate Armed Services Committees, propose legislation setting national defense policies. Once approved by the Congress and signed by the president, the manpower portions of that legislation specify the maximum number of personnel that can be on active duty at year's end, set pay levels, and establish many other personnel policies. Authorizing committees are also charged with oversight of the defense establishment, including manpower. Each of the armed services committees has a subcommittee devoted to manpower issues. Most detailed decisions are made by these subcommittees, though key decisions are debated and sometimes changed by the full committee.

According to one student of the Congress, the authorizing committees have historically seen themselves as advocates of their program areas.[3] They have also concentrated more on legislation than on the budget.[4] However, in recent years with defense budget issues of paramount importance, the authorizing committees have paid much attention to reducing defense spending in order to insure that they retained some control over key defense decisions. This has muddied the distinction between the authorizing and appropriations committees.

Appropriations Committees

The House and Senate Appropriations Committees are the last to act in a normal legislative year. The legislation recommended by these committees, once approved by the Congress and signed by the president, makes budget authority available in various appropriations categories. For manpower, these categories consist primarily of military personnel appropriations and reserve personnel appropriations for each military service. The committees may also place detailed restrictions on budget authority, sometimes requiring reports or the achievement of certain milestones before budget authority is made available.

The appropriations committees are bound to some extent by the actions of the Congress in the budget resolution and the authoriztion legislation. In recent years, the first concurrent resolution targets for defense—while not legally binding—have been the maximum amount that the political process would allow. The authorization bill also sets limits, since the appropriations committee generally cannot make available budget authority for weapons, personnel, or other items not authorized in the authorization legislation. However, the appropriations committees can make less available than these ceilings provide, and they often do. Last year, for example, the appropriations committees cut defense budget authority substantially more than required in the congressional budget resolution. Moreover, under Section 302b of the Congressional Budget and Impoundment Control Act which set up the budget committees and the budget process, the appropriations committees have the power to allocate total federal budget authority to their various subcommittees without regard to the budget resolution totals. The committees have sometimes used this power to hold defense budget authority below the ceilings imposed by the budget resolution and authorizing legislation.

Many of these actions are consistent with the classical analysis of the appropriations committees. That analysis pictures the House Appropriations Committee as the guardian of the public purse, striving to reduce administration budget requests in defense and other areas while still providing adequate funding for key programs. In previous years, the Senate Appropriations Committee often acted as a "court of appeals" for reductions imposed by the House. Both committees, but particularly the House Committee, were highly powerful.[5]

In the 1970s, some argue that numerous factors, including the new congressional budget process and a reform movement that weakened the ability of appropriations committee members to withstand spending demands, reduced the power of the committees. The roles of the House and Senate committees may also have become blurred; last year, for example, the Senate committee acted before the House.[6]

Nonetheless, many of the "classical" attributes remain. Appropriations are key committees that have important influence over defense spending. They are typically less inclined toward increasing defense spending than are the armed services committees.

Concerns over Committee Roles and Procedures

Review by six different committees produces a substantial work load and is a time-consuming process. Concern has been expressed, most recently by the secretary of defense, over the timeliness of congressional action. Secretary Weinberger noted that, during eight of the last ten years, the Congress has not completed final action on the defense appropriation by the beginning of the fiscal year. (Indeed, the Congress has been late by an average of ninety-seven days during those eight years.) The secretary of defense also criticized the organization restrictions imposed by the Congress, such as the vote to create an independent testing and evaluation unit.[7]

Numerous solutions to these problems have been recommended. The secretary of defense recommended a two-year defense budget, as have others, and also urged the Congress to strive for timeliness.[8] Senator Sam Nunn, now the ranking minority member of the Senate Armed Services Committee, recommended combining the budget and appropriations committees into one and leaving all defense decisions, except those about aggregate resources, to the armed services committees.[9]

Because of the varying inclinations of the committees, such changes could have important effects on defense issues, including manpower issues. Also some action may eventually be taken to streamline the congressional budget-making process. However, major changes seem unlikely in the near future. Organizational changes are inherently difficult because they involve shifts in power. They will be all the more difficult during a period when the Congress must make many hard decisions on the substance of the budget.

FACTORS INFLUENCING CONGRESSIONAL USE OF AUTHORITY

Regardless of their historical inclinations toward defense, committees and the Congress as a whole are influenced by current trends. For the next few years, the Congress seems likely to accept the need for some increases in defense spending in order to keep pace with, and hopefully restrain, Soviet military actions. But many factors, especially concern over the composition of federal spending and the size of the deficit, also point toward a Congress willing to reduce the annual rate of growth of defense spending below the high levels recommended in the administration's latest budget. Such reductions will certainly influence defense manpower decisions.

Concerns over Federal Spending

Differences in Composition. The Congress and the administration generally agree on a desirable level for total federal spending. In its most recent budget resolution, the Congress agreed that total federal spending in 1986 should be no more than $989 billion.[10] The administration called for total spending of $991 billion, an almost identical amount. The Congress and the administration differed, however, in the allocation of their spending to national needs. In 1986 the Congress would spend about $269 billion, or 29.9% of its total on national defense; the administration would allocate $321 billion, or 32.4% of its total to defense. This variance implies substantially different paths for the defense budget over the next three years. In 1984-1986, the congressional budget resolution assumes annual real growth of 5% a year in defense budget authority; the administration's January 1983 budget proposed annual real growth averaging 8.8% a year over the same period. Obviously, since they end up at the same total, the Congress also plans on faster growth in nondefense spending than does the administration.

Frequently, the Congress and the administration compromise such differences by doing a little more of both. The large federal deficit will, however, make such a compromise difficult in the next few years and may require cuts in the total spending below those contemplated to date.

Large Deficits Likely. Even under the assumptions of the latest congressional budget resolution, federal deficits would be substantial. The latest estimates by the Congressional Budget Office put those deficits at as much as $192 billion in 1984, declining to $146 billion in

1986, as the economy gradually recovers. Measured as a percentage of a growing gross national product (GNP), deficits decline from 5.4% in 1984 to 3.5% by 1986 (see Figure 13.1), but these deficits will still be high by historical standards. Over the last ten years, deficits averaged about 2% of GNP and between 1973 and 1982, never ran above 4%.

Moreover, the congressional budget resolution assumes reductions in spending and increases in taxes that may well not be enacted. As was noted above, the administration puts more emphasis on reductions in nondefense spending; the Congress emphasizes defense reductions and tax increases. If this disagreement means no changes are made in current policies, deficits would remain about $200 billion a year through 1986, declining as the economy grows but remaining at about 4.8% of GNP in 1986 (see Figure 13.1).

Figure 13.1. Federal Deficit as a Percentage of GNP

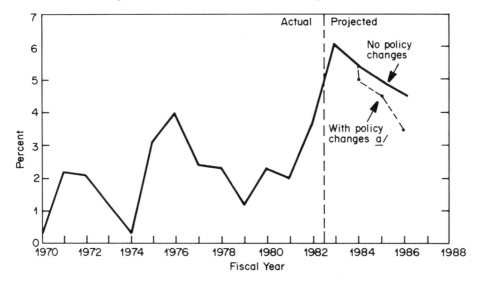

a Assumes changes called for in the First Concurrent Resolution for FY1984, excluding the reserve fund.

Effects of Large Deficits. Large deficits that are not caused by high unemployment mean that the government will be borrowing heavily at a time when private businesses and consumers are also trying to borrow money. If the Federal Reserve reacts to this heavy demand for credit by allowing only moderate growth in the money supply, then interest rates may increase above their already high levels. Private borrowing could then be "crowded out" by these higher rates, leading to less capital spending by business and a reduction in productivity and living standards. If, instead, the Federal Reserve allows large increases in the money supply to keep interest rates down, then inflation could be rekindled.

Unfortunately, historical data provide an ambiguous picture about the effects of deficits as large as those the United States faces. Thus economists differ in their assessment of the risk, but it seems clear that the Congress is concerned about them.[11] In its 1983 report on the first resolution, for example, the House Budget Committee said that a "credible deficit reduction plan is absolutely essential" if the economy is to improve.[12] The Senate Budget Committee expressed similar convictions. Indeed, the great concern over the deficit has produced what Allen Schick termed a "fiscalization" of the debate on policy issues.[13] Issues get debated almost solely in terms of their effects on dollars, without great regard for effects on programs.

Implications for Defense Spending. Reductions in overall defense outlays will not by themselves solve more than a small part of the deficit problem. Even if there was no real growth in defense budget authority in 1984 and beyond, defense outlays by 1986 would be lower by about $56 billion.[14] Moreover, all else in the economy being equal, reductions in defense spending will reduce federal revenues and so will not produce a dollar-for-dollar reduction in the size of the federal deficit.

While reductions in defense spending alone cannot solve the deficit, such reductions will probably have to be part of the solution. In 1983, about 70% of federal outlays consisted of defense, social security, health care, and interest on the debt. Excluding any one would make it all the harder to change any of the others yet spending certainly cannot be substantially reduced if 70% of the budget is left untouched. Without some reductions in spending, it will be politically much more difficult to raise taxes, another policy change that will probably have to be part of any large reduction in the deficit.

Other Factors Also Favor Slower Growth of Defense Spending

Concern over the size of the federal deficit and the allocation of federal spending, while key, is not the only factor suggesting that the Congress will slow growth in defense spending. Public approval for increased defense spending has declined markedly in recent years. In January 1981, as President Reagan took office, the *New York Times*/CBS poll showed that 61% of the U.S. public favored higher defense spending and only 7% favored a decrease. By January 1983, only 11% favored higher defense spending and 48% favored a decrease. The 1983 destruction of the Korean airliner by the Soviets may temporarily reverse this trend, but it seems unlikely that the large percentage favoring higher defense spending will be reachieved quickly unless, of course, there is a major international crisis.

Pattern and Size of the Administration's Requests. The pattern and size of the administration's requested increases in defense also suggests reductions. The United States has increased defense budget authority in real terms for the five years (1979-1984). The administration proposes to continue real increases through at least 1988, a string of nine or more consecutive years. However, since World War II, the longest previous period of consecutive increases was four years (1948-1952). Thus, if history is a guide, nine or more years of consecutive increases is unlikely.

The size of the increases also suggests substantial congressional cuts. For FY1984 and 1985, the administration's January 1983 budget requested real increases in defense budget authority of 10% and 11%, respectively; these come on top of real increases averaging 10% a year over the years 1981-1983. Over the last ten years, there is only a slight correlation (not statistically significant) between large increases and large cuts by the Congress ($r = 0.34$).[15] Excluding the one year in those ten (1981) when the Congress added to the defense budget, there was a modest correlation ($r = 0.52$, significant at $a = 0.1$).[16] Thus, history suggests that large proposed increases make congressional reductions in defense spending modestly more likely.

Trends in Membership on Defense Committees. Trends in committee membership may also influence congressional action. Defense committee members are more conservative than are all members of Congress, at least as measured by most commonly used voting ratings (see Table 13.1). Between 1972 and 1982, there was a shift toward many more members with liberal ratings on some committees, particularly the Defense Subcommittee of the House Appropriations Committee. Moreover, in 1983 several more liberal members joined or assumed leadership roles on the armed services committee. Senator Edward Kennedy joined the Senate Armed Services

Table 13.1. Trends in Ratings of Defense Committee

	Average ADA Rating ("liberal" rating)[a]			Average ACA Rating ("conservative" rating)[b]		
	All	Republicans	Democrats	All	Republicans	Democrats
Senate Armed Services						
1972	27	16	35	58	68	50
1982	35	17	56	66	79	49
Senate Appropriations (Defense Subcommittee)						
1972	33	17	45	52	71	36
1982	37	21	56	53	62	43
House Armed Services						
1972	23	6	34	65	83	53
1982	26	13	36	61	77	49
House Appropriations (Defense Subcommittee)						
1972	21	5	35	62	72	55
1982	33	21	39	54	71	44
Total Senate						
1972	38	24	50	45	62	30
1982	45	25	68	53	66	37
Total House						
1972	36	16	51	50	70	36
1982	43	19	62	49	75	27

[a] The Americans for Democratic Action (ADA) annually rates members of Congress based on their votes on about twenty issues selected by ADA, including key defense and foreign policy issues. Higher ratings suggest more "liberal" tendencies.
[b] The Americans for Constitutional Action (ACA) annually rates members of Congress based on their votes on about twenty issues selected by ACA, including defense and foreign policy issues. Higher ratings suggest more "conservative" tendencies.

Committee, and Congressmen Les Aspin and Ron Dellums became subcommittee chairmen on the House Armed Services Committee. These trends may make it more likely that defense committees will accept pressure to scale back defense spending.

Implications for Defense Manpower

It seems likely, then, that concern over federal spending and other trends will cause the Congress to scale back the administration's proposed defense increases. The long-range plan adopted this year by the Congress bears this out. Under that plan, defense budget authority would be reduced by $33 billion or 10% in 1985. This would be a very large reduction by historical standards. Over the past ten years, the House has cut the administration's proposed defense budget by an average of 3.4% per year, and the Senate by 3.2%. Overall congressional action has resulted in an average cut of 3.4% (see Table 13.2).[17]

Historically, reductions in the military personnel appropriation have been the smallest of any major appropriation, averaging only 1.1% a year over the last ten years.[18] Nonetheless, a sharp reduction in the growth of overall spending will probably cause the Congress to review manpower spending plans carefully and make some reductions. Manpower cuts may be much more likely because they produce quick reductions in outlays, and hence in the deficit, whereas reductions in procurement do not result in large outlay savings for several years until new weapons are actually manufactured.

Broad trends like concern over federal spending are, of course, only one of the many and varied influences on congressional attitudes toward defense manpower issues. The remainder of this chapter combines these broad trends with other relevant factors to indicate congressional perspectives and likely actions on six key manpower issues.

Table 13.2. Average Congressional Reductions of Administration Requests for Defense Appropriations, 1974-1983 (In percentages)[a]

Appropriation	Percent Reduction[b]		
	House	Senate	Congress
Total Defense[c]	3.4	3.2	3.4
Military Personnel	1.5	1.4	1.1[d]
Operation and Maintenance	2.7	3.0	2.8
Procurement	5.5	5.4	6.0
Research, Development, Test, and Evaluation	6.4	4.5	5.2
Military Construction and Family Housing	10.3	5.6	7.4

[a] Figures are based on presidential requests in the January budget (or the revised version submitted at the beginning of a new administration) compared to final action (appropriation bills through 1982, continuing resolution in 1983). Figures exclude any supplemental appropriations.

[b] The Congress cut the total defense budget in nine of the years 1974-1983 and added in one year. Percentages in this table reflect the net effects of the one addition and the subtractions. The average of the absolute values of the changes are: House, 3.8%; Senate, 4.0%; Congress, 4.1%.

[c] "Total defense" includes all appropriations in the defense appropriations act. Military construction, which has its own bill, is excluded.

[d] This percentage excludes action on the pay supplemental. Including reductions in the pay supplemental increased this reduction to 1.7%. Data on House and Senate action on the pay supplemental were not readily available.

CONGRESSIONAL PERSPECTIVES ON KEY MANPOWER ISSUES

Prospects for the All-Volunteer Force

With few exceptions, the Congress has not debated changes to the All-Volunteer Force (AVF) during the last two years. The obvious reason is recruiting success. In 1982 the army, which this chapter emphasizes since it faces the most serious recruiting challenge, met its numerical goals for enlisted recruits. At the same time, 85% of all its male enlisted recruits without prior military experience held high school diplomas. This greatly exceeded the legally-required minimum of 65% as well as typical draft-era averages of 65 to 70%. Moreover, in 1982 only about 19% of all army recruits scored in the lowest acceptable group (category IV) on the entrance examination given to all new recruits. This was below the 20% minimum required by law and approximated draft-era results.

Critics assert that high unemployment propelled army recruiting to these extraordinary levels, which is partly true. Other policy changes also aided recruiting, and some of these should survive even as the economy recovers. The army has improved its recruiting practices, placing explicit emphasis, for example, on attracting those with high school diplomas. More accurate knowledge of recruiting problems spurred some of these improvements; for example, because of errors in the norming of the recruit test, the army in the late 1970s thought it was experiencing much better recruiting than it was.[19] In addition, the administration and the Congress increased military wages and bonuses in recent years and improved educational benefits available under the Army College Fund. Finally, improvements in the attitudes of youth toward the military may have aided recruiting.[20]

In light of these trends, the Congressional Budget Office forecasts that the army will be able to meet its numerical needs for recruits for the next few years and still stay well within the limits on recruit quality established by current law.[21] This forecast takes account of gradual improvements in the economy that will make recruiting harder. The forecast also assumes a decline in the number of young males, the army's prime recruiting pool. Between now and 1985, the number of young males will decline by 6%; it will decline another 8% between 1985 and 1991.

Policy changes could, of course, alter the favorable outlook for the AVF. A large increase in the size of the army, say 100,000 or more additional troops, would make recruiting much more difficult. Today's army is about 80,000 smaller than it was during any year between 1951 and 1971. Some, like former Army Chief of Staff General Edward Meyer, have argued that in the long run the army will need larger forces to meet potential military commitments in NATO, the Persian Gulf, and elsewhere.[22] Recruiting goals, such as the percentages of recruits holding high school diplomas and scoring well on entrance examinations, could also be increased above the minimum level now required by law. The army could argue for more high school graduates and recruits with higher test scores because new and more sophisticated weapons demand them. Such increases would also help answer a frequent criticism of the AVF since they would tend to make the army more representative in racial terms; on average, blacks do not score as well as whites on recruit entrance examinations.

For the next few years, however, these policy changes seem unlikely. They have not been recommended by the administration. In this era of intense fiscal restraint, the Congress will probably not push for such increases, particularly in active-duty military strength. If anything, the Congress will require smaller increases in active-duty strengths and more use of reserves.

Pressures to hold down federal spending do not seem likely to alter the favorable outlook for the AVF. Ending the AVF and returning to conscription would save substantial amounts of money only if recruit pay were cut. Even then, savings would probably amount to about $1 billion to $2 billion a year, which is less than 1% of today's defense budget.[23] Given the intrusions on private lives imposed by conscription, it seems unlikely that the AVF will fall victim to spending restraints.

The only event likely to topple the AVF in the next few years would be a war with substantial numbers of casualties. Indeed, three out of the four times that the United States reinstituted conscription were in periods just before or during a war. Only in 1948 did the United States reinstitute conscription during peacetime.

This rosy outlook for the AVF has silenced but not ended the concern among some in the Congress about the desirability of the volunteer military. Earlier this year, Senator Ernest Hollings, one of the Democratic candidates for the 1984 presidential nomination, underscored that concern by introducing legislation to return to conscription.[24] Senator Hollings restated the misgivings of many AVF critics: the AVF is manned by the poor, the black, and the disadvantaged; recruit quality is a problem, evidenced by low reading skills; the AVF has "civilianized" the military; its current success is due to high unemployment and a last fillip from the baby boom. Senator Hollings is the only member of the Congress who has spoken out recently against the AVF. In earlier years, some form of compulsory service was supported by key members including Senator Sam Nunn (ranking minority member of the Senate Armed Services Committee), Senator John Stennis (ranking minority member of the Senate Approrpriations Committee), and Congressman Sam Stratton (senior member of the House Armed Services Committee).[25] Moreover, the Congress as a whole has been comfortable with the draft in the past. From 1951 to 1967, there were five congressional votes to extend the draft. No more than five members of the Senate or forty-four members of the House ever opposed extending conscription.

Public support for the AVF also seems lukewarm. A 1982 poll by the National Option Research Center did show that 59% of all American adults thought that relying on volunteers to man the military had worked out fairly well or very well. But 35% thought the AVF had not worked well. Moreover, 42% favored a return to a military draft.[26] A 1979 Gallup poll also found that 45% of all adult Americans favored a return to the draft (though only 25% of those age eighteen to twenty-four supported conscription).

A comparison of U.S. demographics and force size reinforces the likelihood of continued debate over the AVF. Most of our NATO allies that rely on conscription, including West Germany and France, conscript 50% or more of their young males (see Table 13.3). Great Britian,

Table 13.3. Percentages of Eligible Males Required to Man Military Forces in NATO Countries[a]

Country	Type	Percent Required
France	Conscript[b]	near 100
Norway	Conscript	97
Netherlands	Conscript	64
Portugal	Conscript	60
West Germany	Conscript	50
Denmark	Conscript	34
United States	Volunteer	17-26[c]
Britain	Volunteer	8-11[d]
Canada	Volunteer	N/A

Source: Except for the United States, all figures come from North Atlantic Assembly, *Manpower Issues for NATO* (Brussels, Belgium, 1983). See note [c] for origin of U.S. figures.

[a] The North Atlantic Assembly publication is not precise about the meaning of "eligible." Usually it appears that the percentages refer to male recruits entering active duty as a percentage of all physically and mentally qualified youth who, for those countries with conscription, do not receive status as conscientious objectors.

[b] France requires almost 100% of its young males to serve in a national service program.

[c] U.S. figures show the total number of male enlisted recruits without prior military service who entered military forces in 1981 as a percentage of the eligible population of U.S. males. The lower percent shows recruits entering active duty only; the larger one includes those entering the reserves. Eligibles were estimated as the total population of males less 10% for those mentally fit (category V) and another 15% for those not physically qualified.

[d] Percentage growing from eight to eleven over this decade due to demographic shifts.

with a volunteer system, can meet its military needs if only about 10% of its young males volunteer. In the 1980s, the United States will probably need about 20 to 25% of its young males to man its military forces, depending on decisions about force sizes and other manpower policies. This puts the United States in an uncomfortable middle ground. Needs are sufficient so that an AVF, particularly one with large forces, will be difficult to maintain. However, needs are small enough so that conscription for the military alone would be quite selective, and hence might be viewed as unfair; conscripting all might be viewed as fair but would greatly exceed military requirements for personnel and would substantially add to costs.

For the next few years, congressional debate over the AVF will be largely silenced by recruiting success, but some in the Congress remain concerned about the desirability of the AVF. Thus the great debate will recur quickly if recruiting falters in the later 1980s. Moreover, though the debate is temporarily silenced, continuing concern about the desirability of the AVF will color congressional discussion of other military manpower issues, such as strength and pay levels.

Active Duty Strength Levels

Between 1980 and 1983, the Congress approved increases in active-duty end strengths of about 77,000. The administration seems likely to continue asking for increases. In its January 1983 budget, the administration proposed increases of about 180,000 in active-duty strengths between 1983 and 1988. Most of the total would be in the air force (91,000) and navy (46,500); army strength would increase more modestly (34,400), and Marine Corps strength even less (8,700). In the future, however, there could be pressure for more substantial increases, particularly in the size of the army. The former chief of staff of the army has indicated that three to five more army divisions (the United States now has sixteen) will eventually be needed to carry out the army's missions in NATO and the Rapid Deployment Forces.[27]

The Congress has generally accepted the administration's proposals for changes in the size of the military. Over the past five years (FY1979-1983), the authorizing committees changed the administration's proposals by an average of about 20%.[28] But the results for FY1984 differ. For

1984, the administration proposed an increase in active-duty strength of 37,000. The authorizing committees approved an increase of only 8,500, a reduction of about 75%. Every service lost a substantial part of its increase, though the navy and Marine Corps lost the least.

The concerns over defense spending discussed above played some role in this cut. In today's dollars, the addition of 180,000 personnel would, by the time all were in the active forces, add $4 to $5 billion a year to costs. In their reports on the authorization bills, both the legislative committees noted the need to hold down strength increases in order to restrain costs. The House Armed Services Committee report also noted that, as the economy improves, the larger strengths could make AVF recruiting more difficult.[29]

The key reason for holding down increases in active-duty strength levels is the congressional belief that reserves could accomplish some of the missions the administration plans for added active-duty personnel. The committees used strong language to emphasize their support for more reserves. The House/Senate conferees concluded, for example, that they were "fully prepared to deny further active-duty personnel strength increases" if the services do not investigate more use of reserves.[30] While the navy got more than the other services of its proposed 1984 increase in active forces, the conferees emphasized that the navy should also examine the use of reserves. The legislative committees even provided illustrative examples such as more use of round-out battalions in active army divisions, transferring additional continental air defense roles to the Air National Guard, even changes in deployment patterns of active navy ships to facilitate use of reserves.

This strong congressional stance reflects conviction that the services could use more reserves at less cost. It also reflects long-standing congressional advocacy of reserve forces. As an example, the legislative committees authorize a maximum on active-duty personnel but place a minimum on reserve strengths. In 1983, the Congress also authorized an assistant secretary of defense for reserve affairs that the administration did not want.

Some of the enthusiasm for use of more reserves could diminish as more facts become available. Greater use of the reserves would probably not save enough to offset substantially the added cost of buying new weapons.[31] Also, it would be difficult to make use of large numbers of added reserves in the navy and air force because of those services' peacetime operating commitments and the need to maintain complex equipment. The army could use a higher percentage of reserves in peacetime than the navy or air force, but it already has a larger reserve percentage than the other services. Moreover, attracting large numbers of high-quality recruits into the army reserve components may be difficult as the economy recovers.

There may also be better ways to hold down the growth of active-duty manpower. For example, the size of the navy's shore establishment is driven in part by the need to avoid extended sea duty, which drives people out of the service. The navy could, however, increase the amount of its sea pay and induce people to volunteer for more time at sea. As the navy adds personnel to man its new ships, this would reduce the need for proportional increases in its shore establishment. A recent study suggested that, even after including the extra costs of added sea pay, this approach would save money and hold down the size of active-duty strength increases.[32]

Whatever the means, the Congress has indicated strong support for limiting the growth of active-duty forces, which makes large increases unlikely. This should help hold down manpower costs, an advantage in this "fiscalized" period. Holding down active-duty force increases will also avoid undue pressure on AVF recruiting as the economy recovers and, by easing recruiting and retention needs, should minimize pressure for large military pay raises.

Military Pay and Bonuses

Over the last ten years, the Congress has generally accepted the administration's recommended military pay raises. In the two years when the Congress disagreed, it provided a larger increase. In 1981 the administration proposed a 9.1% increase but the Congress provided an 11.7% increase in basic pay plus increases in many allowances. For 1984, the administration proposed no pay raise for military or civilian personnel (then altered to a 3.5% increase); the Congress provided a 4% raise.

Military pay raises fell behind those in the private sector in the 1970s and 1980s and then recovered much of that loss in 1981 and 1982. Between 1972 and 1980, military pay fell behind increases in hourly earnings of private-sector workers by 12%.[33] By 1982, it was back within about 2%. The pressures on the administration and the Congress explain this pattern. In the mid-1970s, there was pressure to hold down defense spending, and recruiting and retention success was thought to be sufficient to allow lower raises. By 1980, the services clearly had failed to attract and retain enough personnel of adequate quality. Thus the Congress took the lead in granting a large pay raise in 1981; the administration recommended and the Congress approved another major increase in 1982.

This pattern of declines followed by catch-up increases may well repeat itself. In FY1983, the military pay raise was held to 4% while hourly earnings of private-sector workers increased by about 6%. The pay raise for FY1984 will be 4%, but private forecasts suggest an increase in private-sector wages of about 5%. As in the mid-1970s, the desire to hold down spending is creating pressure for low raises; reducing pay raises is especially attractive because it immediately cuts outlays, and hence the federal deficit, whereas cuts in weapons programs do not substantially affect the deficit for several years. At the same time, extraordinary success in recruiting and retention allows pay raises to be kept low. If recruiting and retention falter, however, the Congress seems likely to grant the military substantial "catch-up" raises despite their costs. The availability of widely-accepted measures of recruiting and retention makes it easy to dramatize the need for large pay raises during periods of manning problems; clear measures are not so readily available for some weapons or R&D programs. Moreover, the Congress seems well aware that limitations on pay raises contributed to the problems of the AVF in the late 1970s and 1980s.[34] Most lawmakers are not likely to risk re-igniting the debate over the AVF by holding down increases if manning problems recur.

The Congress has required "targeting" of raises toward senior personnel in several recent years, to the relative detriment of recruiting. Pay raises for 1982 ranged from 10% for junior enlisted personnel to as much as 17% for some senior enlisted personnel; for 1984 the Congress gave no raise to E-1 personnel with fewer than four months service, while all others will receive 4%. Pressure for targeting stems largely from the Senate. During the debate over the 1982 raise, some senators argued that targeting would help retention by making career service more prestigious and financially attractive. They also argued that lower raises would not hurt recruiting because small increases in entry-level pay, in their judgment, were not a factor in a young person's decision to enter the military. No senator argued explicitly that recruit pay should be held down in anticipation of a return to conscription. Indeed, one stated explicitly that targeting was not intended to be "anti-AVF."[35]

The pressure for targeting may well continue in future years if recruiting results are good. But, especially given the House's preference for across-the-board pay raises, targeting toward senior personnel seems unlikely to survive if this action threatens the AVF.

While pay raises may catch up if recruiting falters, cash enlistment bonuses may fare less well. During the debate over 1982 pay levels, the Congress, especially the Senate, expressed concern that the administration wanted authority to pay enlistment bonuses of as much as $10,000 to some recruits. Senators of both parties argued that such large cash bonuses should not be given to unskilled recruits. They also expressed concern about recovering payments from recruits who quit early.[36] The Congress ultimately set the maximum enlistment bonus level at $8,000 and limited the amount that could be paid as a lump sum.

The Congress does receive information emphasizing a well-accepted analytic result: enlistment bonuses can meet selective recruit shortages more cheaply than across-the-board pay raises.[37] The Congress should also be aware that only a small fraction, about 3%, of the first-term military pay bill goes for enlistment bonuses. But congressional misgivings suggest that, if the AVF gets in serious recruiting trouble, rescue in the form of large increases in cash enlistment bonuses may be difficult to achieve.

Improving Educational Benefits: The GI Bill Debate

Instead of increasing cash bonuses, the Congress seems disposed to improve military educational benefits. In recent years, it has enacted major improvements in these benefits. The resulting program permits service members to contribute up to $2,700 toward their education; if they do, the government matches contributions on a two-for-one basis. In addition, those entering some hard-to-fill specialties can receive extra payments or "kickers." Thus, after contributing $2,700, some recruits who serve three or more years can receive $20,100 toward their education.

Despite these recent improvements, numerous "GI Bills" have been introduced in the Congress over the last several years. Most would terminate the existing program. In its place, almost all would install a program requiring no contribution and making benefits available to all military members who complete at least two years of honorable military service. Some proposals would also make extra benefits or "kickers" available to recruits entering hard-to-fill specialties. Still others would include special provisions to offset adverse effects on retention that would arise if members left in large numbers to use their benefits.

Analytic studies raise concerns about those proposals. To begin with, there are no current recruiting problems. Moreover, even if problems occurred in future years, expanded educational benefits would be an expensive way to meet them. The Congressional Budget Office estimated, for example, that some broad-based programs, or those that make substantial benefits available to all personnel, could cost as much as $200,000 for every extra high-quality recruit they attracted compared to costs of $22,000 to $35,000 using other recruiting incentives.[38] Costs would be high because all who enlist would get benefits, not just added recruits. Moreover, educational benefits might hurt retention as people left to get their benefits, thus cutting down on net recruiting improvements. Nor would high costs be the only problem. A Rand study of the 1981 test of educational benefits ordered by the Congress concluded that because many GI Bill proposals would terminate a plan that favors the army and substitute one that does not, they could actually weaken recruiting in the service with the greatest potential problems.[39] At least some members of the Congress recognize these arguments; recent Senate floor debate on a GI Bill proposal brought out each of them.[40]

Nor do analytic concerns seem the most formidable obstacles to enactment of a new GI Bill. Most proposals would add substantially to costs during a period of great fiscal restraint. The Congressional Budget Office estimates that some broad-based plans could eventually add more than $1 billion a year to costs (in today's dollars); most bills introduced recently are less generous but would still eventually increase costs by hundreds of millions of dollars a year. Moreover, these bills increase spending in a way that troubles many in the Congress. They create entitlements, binding obligations available to all who qualify, which, once passed, cannot be controlled through the annual appropriations process. Finally, improved educational benefits are opposed by the administration and in the Senate by the chairmen of the key Veterans' Affairs and Armed Services Committees.

Despite these factors, improved educational benefits enjoy remarkable support in the Congress. In 1982 the House Veterans' Affairs Committee and the House Armed Services Committee (HASC) reported a GI Bill favorably. (This HASC version of the bill, while broad-based, had considerable targeting of benefits designed to hold down total costs and cost per added recruit.) In 1983 the Veterans' Affairs Committee again reported a GI Bill that the House Armed Services Committee may take up during this session in Congress. On the Senate side, no committees have reported such legislation. But a number of senators introduced an amendment on the Senate floor to reinstate a broad-based GI Bill. The only vote on the amendment occurred on a procedural motion, but forty-six senators appeared to support it.

Why this support, even in the face of seemingly major political obstacles? Many members of the Congress may agree with GI Bill supporters who argue that, despite the lack of current recruiting problems, the AVF needs an expanded GI Bill as insurance against future problems. "Fixing the roof before it leaks" is the term supporters have repeatedly used. Then, too, education has always been viewed favorably by the Congress, and older GI Bills are seen as highly successful government education programs. Indeed, many members of the Congress probably went to school under older versions of the GI Bill; about 50% of all current House members and almost 70% of the Senate served on active duty and so could have been eligible. Despite the administration's formal opposition, the GI Bill is not without extensive high-level support. Many senior military leaders and civilian experts support it; President Reagan supported it in calendar year 1980 when he was a candidate. Finally, expanding educational benefits may appeal to many congressional instincts, including a desire to support U.S. troops and veterans as well as educational institutions.

Even with this remarkable support, enactment of a GI Bill during a period of extraordinary recruiting success seems unlikely. But if recruiting should falter, the Congress would almost certainly include expanded educational benefits in any package of improved pay and benefits. Those who share the concerns raised by studies of educational benefits might do well to concentrate their efforts on targeting added benefits toward recruits in hard-to-fill skills rather than opposing any change.

Revising Military Retirement

The Congress may also review retirement, another important military benefit, but most changes are likely to be reductions. The Congress has made a number of revisions in retirement benefits in recent years. Some have been increases, including improvement in the so-called "Catch-62" provisions and a more generous program for survivors of military retirees. Others have been reductions. In calendar year 1976 the Congress eliminated the "one-percent kicker" that caused military retirement benefits to increase at more than the rate of inflation. In 1981 the Congress decided that retirement pay would be based on average pay during the three years when pay was highest, rather than pay on the day of retirement, but limited the change to those who entered the military after enactment of the legislation. Also in 1981, the Congress allowed cost-of-living allowance (COLA) increases only once a year rather than semiannually. For 1983 to 1985, the Congress decided that COLA increases for retirees under age sixty-two would be based on half the normal amount.[41] In recent years, the Congress has also delayed the COLA increases.

Some of these changes have or will cut costs. Had the one-percent "kicker" been left in effect, military retirement costs in 1983 would have been higher by almost $2.5 billion. Basing retirement pay on average pay during the three highest years will eventually reduce retirement costs by 5 to 10% if pay raises average 5% a year. This would save $1 billion a year or more in today's dollars, but large savings will not occur until well into the next century. The half-COLA provision will also eventually have important effects on costs if it is left in effect.

None of the changes, however, has permanently altered the structure of the military retirement system. Pressure to do so will continue in the Congress. Pressure stems in part from concern about the generosity of all federal pension systems. The administration has fueled this concern by recommending a major reduction in civil service retirement benefits. The recent reports of task forces of the President's Private Sector Survey on Cost Control also suggested that military pensions should be less generous.[42] And some in Congress share the concern. Groups in the House Budget and Armed Services Committees recently held hearings and indicated that they expected changes in military retirement.[43]

Nor is there any lack of analyses recommending changes in the military retirement system. Since 1969, no fewer than seven major studies, including four by the Department of Defense itself, have recommended changing the system.[44] Increasing incentives for longer careers was one theme common to all these studies. Each made proposals that would reduce benefits for those who leave after just twenty years of service and so would provide less incentive to leave immediately. Increasing incentives to stay past the first term of service was another theme. Every study recommended providing some nondisability benefits to those who leave with more than about ten but fewer than twenty years of service. Today they receive nothing, and so retirement plays little role in reenlistment decisions that occur after the first few years of service.

Most of the proposals by these study groups would cut the costs of the system, which may prompt congressional attention. In 1984, military retirement cost about $16.8 billion. Changes like the half-COLA provisions, or others recommended by numerous studies, would eventually save several billion dollars a year in today's dollars. But these large savings would generally not be realized in the federal budget, and hence would not affect the deficit until the end of this century or later. This is because of "grandfathering" provisions designed to protect benefits already earned.

Starting in 1985, however, the full amount of eventual savings will appear *immediately* in the defense budget, which may stimulate debate in the administration and the Congress.[45] Under legislation passed in 1983, the 1985 version of the defense function of the federal budget will no longer show actual military retirement outlays but instead will show the "accrual" costs of military retirement. Accrual costs equal the amount that has to be set aside each year to fund fully the eventual costs of today's retirement benefits. Thus accrual costs will immediately reflect any change in those benefits.[46] Making the half-COLA provision permanent, for example, would reduce the 1985 defense budget by almost $3 billion if inflation continues at 4% a year.

In addiiton to highlighting the long-run effects of retirement changes, accrual accounting could involve military retirement in the congressional reconciliation procedures. Under reconciliation, the Congress instructs its committees to make legislative changes to bring the costs of programs into conformity with spending limits in the congressional budget resolution. Future reconciliation instructions could require that the armed services committees reduce the military retirement entitlement by a substantial amount, which could only be accomplished by altering its structure.

One other factor favors renewed debate over military retirement, at least in the House. This year Congressman Les Aspin became chairman of the Subcommittee on Military Personnel and Compensation of the House Armed Services Committee. He is also a member of the House Budget Committee. Mr. Aspin is a recognized expert on defense manpower issues and a long-standing critic of the military retirement system. His subcommittee has already begun holding hearings on the desirability of changes to the current system.

These pressures insure that the Congress, and particularly the House, will debate military retirement over the next year or so. But debate does not guarantee change. The administration has not yet recommended altering the system; without such a recommendation the Congress would find it especially difficult to act in this emotional and analytically complex area. The administration could make a recommendation based on the report of the Department of Defense's Fifth Quadrennial Review of Military Compensation. The results of this review will be subject to close scrutiny by the military services and a proposal by the administration would not be enough to guarantee change. Previous administrations made two comprehensive legislative proposals to revise the military retirement system in the 1970s, but the Congress did not act.

Even if the administration and the Congress cannot agree on a broad reform of military retirement, budget and other pressures could still lead to continued, piecemeal changes. Periodic extensions of the half-COLA provisions, which offer immediate budget savings and also increase incentives for longer military careers, constitute one likely action.

Civilian Personnel: The Neglected Issue

The problems of civilian defense workers, while outside the scope of this chapter, deserve some attention. Civilian personnel are the neglected factor in the defense manpower equation. Defense's one million civilian workers will consume about one-quarter of the defense manpower budget in 1984, but few conferences discuss their prospects. The secretary of defense's most recent annual report on defense matters devoted three pages to civilian personnel compared to twenty-three pages to military manpower issues. In their most recent reports, the two authorizing committees together devoted about fourteen pages to civilians versus nintey-five to the military.

Yet civilian manpower problems could develop. Demand for highly trained civilian personnel will grow as the services field more sophisticated weapons. Skilled federal civilians must help fix them. At the same time, federal wage increases have regularly been held down to save money. The administration argues that the lower raises granted to date have made up for generous federal fringe benefits, but the administration also proposes large reductions in the biggest fringe benefit, civil service retirement. On top of this, recent presidential candidates have regularly campaigned on platforms blaming many of the government's ills on federal civilian workers which is an attitude that does not contribute to good labor-management relations.

Not all signs are negative. There are currently no serious civilian manning problems. Even as the economy recovers, problems may be slow to develop; the civilian work force is generally older and more stable than the active-duty military work force. Moreover, declining blue-collar industries may provide a new source of skilled manpower for the federal government. Contracting out federal civilian jobs to the private sector could also ease federal civilian manpower problems, though opposition in the Congress, particularly in the House, may limit contracting out.

If civilian manning problems do occur, large across-the-board raises are probably not the efficient solution. Problems would likely be most serious for skilled federal workers. Bonuses, special pays, or faster promotions aimed at those skilled workers would solve the problems at least cost.

But will we know if and when problems occur? We do not now have the careful measures of recruit quality for civilians analogous to those being scrutinized by the military. Nor, despite some efforts by the Department of Defense, do we yet have careful studies of civilian retention.

Analysts and policymakers might do well to pay attention to defense's civilian work force, lest it gradually develop the kinds of problems that plagued military manpower in the late 1970s and 1980s.

SUMMARY AND CONCLUSION

The Congress has the ultimate power to set defense manpower policies. But no single influence or perspective dominates congressional attitudes. The desire to reduce the rate of growth in defense spending will play a role. So too will public attitudes toward conscription, domestic political support for the reserves, congressional distaste for giving large cash bonuses to new recruits, and many other factors.

Despite this diversity of influences, some likely actions emerge from a review of congressional perspectives on key defense manpower issues:

- For the next few years, the Congress seems unlikely to seriously debate, let alone enact a return to conscription. Recruiting success insures continuation of an all-volunteer military. Nonetheless, there remains considerable willingness in the Congress to reconsider the AVF should recruiting falter.
- The Congress seems likely to restrict the growth of active-duty manpower, both to save money and to force substitution of reserve for active-duty personnel.
- As long as levels of recruiting and retention remain high, military pay raises may well be held down to save money. They may also be targeted toward more senior personnel, but the Congress seems likely to grant catch-up raises if military manning problems recur.
- The Congress has reservations about large, cash enlistment bonuses. Indeed, if recruiting problems recur, the Congress seems more likely to enact improvements in educational benefits.
- Military retirement will be a continuing subject of congressional debate for the next few years. Absent enactment of a comprehensive reform, the prospect for continued piecemeal changes—such as extensions of the half-COLA provisions—seems good.

Some view the process the Congress will use to arrive at decisions on these issues as expensive and wasteful. Indeed, the wide diversity of opinion and attitude in the Congress toward manpower and other defense issues does provoke a wide-ranging and time-consuming debate.

Yet the debate has important advantages. It insures that all sources of opinion on defense issues, from the public and outside experts as well as from the administration, receive a hearing and an opportunity to influence policy. Congressional diversity also causes a broader debate within the administration. Since most major points of view can claim some support on Capitol Hill, each must be considered. The most recent examples of the effects of congressional debate, such as the administration's apparent willingness to be more forthcoming on arms control in response to public concern voiced through the Congress, do not involve defense manpower. If the country ever seriously considers a return to conscription, the Congress will insure a far-reaching debate.

Diverse perspectives and far-reaching debate do require that administration spokesmen defend their policies repeatedly in many forums. Some streamlining of the process may be in order, but extensive debate helps build the consensus necessary to maintain a large peacetime military in a democratic state whose citizens embrace widely varying views about national defense. Thus its widely varying perspectives on manpower and other defense issues may be the Congress' greatest asset.

NOTES

1. Except where noted, all years refer to fiscal years.
2. U.S. Congress, House Committee on Budget, *Report on the First Concurrent Resolution on the Budget for Fiscal Year 1984*, 98:1, March 21, 1983, p. 84.
3. Allen Schick, *Reconciliation and the Congressional Budget Process* (Washington, D.C.: American Enterprise Institute, 1981), p. 41.

4. Lance T. LeLoup, *The Fiscal Congress* (Westport, Ct.: Greenwood Press, 1980), p. 115.

5. Ibid., pp.120-121.

6. Allen Schick, *Congress and Money* (Washington, D.C.: Urban Institute Press, 1980), p. 427-442.

7. Caspar W. Weinberger, Statement before Senate Armed Services Committee on Review of DoD Structure and Decision-Making, July 28, 1983, pp. 10-11.

8. Ibid.

9. Richard Holloran, "Weinberger and Senate Arms Panel Politely Trade Charges Over Budget." *New York Times*, 29 July, 1983, p. A8.

10. Estimates in this section come from the Congressional Budget Office, *The Economic and Budget Outlook: An Update*, August 1983, pp. 58-62, 78, and 84-103. Except where noted, deficit estimates in this section are based on the CBO "baseline," which is put together at the beginning of each calendar year to provide a basis for congressional debate. The baseline assumes that national defense spending equals spending in the latest congressional plan. This plan called for less defense spending than was requested by the administration in its January 1983 budget. Under the administration's budget, defense outlays in 1986 would be higher by about $13 billion than they are under the baseline. The deficit could also be higher.

11. For a more complete discussion of the effects of deficits, see Congressional Budget Office, *Economic and Budget Outlook*, pp. 62-69.

12. House Budget Committee, *Report on the First Concurrent Resolution*, p. 19.

13. Schick, *Reconciliation*, p. 35.

14. Congressional Budget Office, *Reducing the Deficit: Spending and Revenue Options*, February 1983, p. 34. Reductions are relative to the administration request. Relative to the CBO baseline (see note 10), reductions would equal about $40 billion under no real growth and $10 billion under 5% growth. Outlay estimates assume that reductions in budget authority are distributed evenly across all nonpay accounts.

15. Earlier research found no correlation during 1960-1970. See Arnold Kanter, "Congress and the Defense Budget: 1960-1970," *American Political Science Review*, Vol. LXVI, March 1972, p. 135.

16. The correlation covered the years 1974-1983 (excepting 1981 in the second case). Correlation is between percentage reductions imposed by the Congress in defense budget authority in function 051 (excluding military construction) and the nominal increase proposed by the president. Congressional reductions are based on comparison of levels in the president's January budget (or the revised budget, submitted at the beginning of an administration) and final congressional action; reductions ignore all supplementals. Percentage increases proposed by the president are based on numbers in the president's budget for the budget year (including revisions during a change in administration) and the preceding year.

17. Congressional reductions in the total defense budget over the last ten years are only slightly larger than those since 1950, which averaged 2.6% a year. The administration itself, particularly the Office of Management and Budget, may impose larger reductions on initial defense requests. LeLoup suggests this finding, based on data for the Department of Agriculture; data for the Department of Defense were not presented. See Lance LeLoup, *Budgetary Politics* (Brunswick, OH: King's Court Communications, 1977), pp. 78-81.

18. The relatively small personnel cuts in Table 13.2 do not fully reflect the effects of congressional action. Some changes would not result in any first-year budget savings but could eventually result in large reductions. Examples include elimination of the "one-percent" kicker in retirement and the switch to "high-3" as a basis for calculating retirement pay.

19. The Department of Defense, *The Annual Report to Congress, Fiscal Year 1980* (Washington, D.C.: Government Printing Office, 1980,) p.281 reported that, in 1978, 11% of all army recruits were scoring in category IV. When the misnorming of the entrance test was corrected, it was learned that almost 39% were found to be in category IV.

20. Periodic surveys done for the Department of Defense indicate that between the fall of 1979 and the fall of 1982, positive propensity of high school seniors to enlist in any service increased from 17.9% to 25.7%. Some or all of this increase, however, could be due to higher unemployment.

21. Statement of Robert F. Hale, Congressional Budget Office, before Subcommittee on Defense of the Committee on Appropriations, U.S. House of Representatives, April 21, 1983, Table 1.

22. Richard Holloran, "Army Chief Reports a 'Renaissance'," *New York Times*, 15 October, 1982, p. 24. William Kaufmann also argues that a larger army, and larger versions of the other services, may be needed as a hedge against contingencies like a NATO war that are low in probability but high in prospective danger. See William K. Kaufmann, "U.S. Defense Needs in the 1980s," in Brent Scowcroft, ed., *Military Service in the United States*, (Englewood Cliffs, NJ: Prentice-Hall, 1982), p. 36.

23. Congressional Budget Office, *Reducing the Federal Deficit: Strategies and Options* (February 1982), p. 49. The study finds that savings of $1.1 billion a year would occur if special pay raises given during the transition to an AVF were eliminated. Savings could be somewhat higher if other amenities that could be associated with the AVF—such as improved barracks—were gradually eliminated. Savings could be lower if enactment of a generous GI Bill accompanied conscription.

24. Statement of Senator Ernest Hollings, *Congressional Record*, July 28, 1983, p. S11077-11079.

25. Interview with Senator Sam Nunn in the *Wall Street Journal*, 19 August, 1981, p. 8; statement of Senator John Stennis, *Congressional Record*, April 21, 1980, pp. S8403-8404; testimony of Representative Sam Stratton before the Subcommittee on Personnel of the House Committee on Armed Services, March 4, 1980.

26. James A. Davis, Jennifer Lanby, and Paul B. Sheatsley, *Americans View the Military: Public Opinion in 1982*, Report No. 131 (Chicago: National Opinion Research Center, University of Chicago, April 1983), pp. 19, 23.

27. See note 22.

28. There are sometimes further changes during the appropriations process, but they are generally smaller.

29. U.S. House of Representatives, *Report of the Committee on Armed Services on the Department of Defense Authorization Act for Fiscal Year 1984* (Report No. 98-107), 98:1, pp. 17, 184; U.S. Senate, *Report of the Committee on Armed Services on the Omnibus Defense Authorization Act for Fiscal Year 1984* (Report No. 98-174), 98:1, p. 188.

30. *Conference Report on Department of Defense Authorization Act for Fiscal Year 1984* Report No. 98-231, 98:1, p. 219.

31. The Congressional Budget Office found that substituting 22,000 reserve personnel for active-duty personnel in various services could eventually save as much as $540 millon a year in 1984 dollars in personnel and other operating costs. (Congressional Budget Office, *Substituting Reserve/Guard Units for Active-Duty Units to Reduce Costs: Five Examples*, June 1983). Thus this approach would offset growth of only one-quarter % in the total defense budget.

32. Congressional Budget Office, *Manpower for a 600-Ship Navy: Costs and Alternative Approaches* (August 1983), pp. 30-34.

33. The private-sector measure used here is average gross hourly earnings of total private, nonagriculture workers. (Hourly earnings were not available for fiscal years; increases were assumed roughly applicable to fiscal years.) Other indices, such as the index of professional, administrative, technical, and clerical workers used to recommend increases for some federal civilian workers, would show similar results.

34. See, for example, U.S. House of Representatives, Report 98-107, p. 209.

35. *Congressional Record*, September 10, 1981, pp. S9380-9390, S9458-9468.

36. U.S. Senate, *Hearings before the Committee on Armed Services on the Department of Defense Authorization for Appropriations for Fiscal Year 1981*, 97:1, February and March 1981, pp. 3188-3190, 3281.

37. See, for example, statement of Robert F. Hale before the Subcommittee on Defense of the Committee on Appropriations, U.S. House of Representatives, pp. 5-6.

38. Congressional Budget Office, *Improving Military Educational Benefits: Effects on Costs, Recruiting, and Retention* (March 1982), p. 50.

39. Richard L. Fernandez, *Enlistment Effects and Policy Implications of the Educational Assistance Test Program* (Santa Monica, CA: Rand Corporation, September 1982), p. vii.

40. *Congressional Record*, July 13, 1983, pp. S9838-9840.

41. The Congress specified the raises (3.3%, 3.6%, and 3.3% in 1983, 1984, and 1985, respectively) based on CPI projections in 1983. Because of reduced inflation, the half-COLA provisions are likely to have only a small effect on retirement costs during these three years.

42. President's Private Sector Survey on Cost Control, *Task Force Report on the Office of the Secretary of Defense*, July 13, 1983, p. 213.

43. *Military Retirement Systems*, hearing before the Task Force on Entitlements, Uncontrollables, and Indexing of the Committee on the Budget, U.S. House of Representatives, 98:1, July 20, 1983, p. 2; see also report of a hearing in "Aspin Prods Defense for Retirement Plan," *Navy Times*, September 26, 1983, p. 1.

44. The seven include: the First Quadrennial Review of Military Compensation (a DoD study in 1969); a study of the uniformed services (retirement and survivor benefits programs by the Interagency Committee, 1971); a report to the Secretary of Defense by the DoD Retirement Study Group (a DoD study in 1972); report of the Defense Manpower Commission (1976); the Third Quadrennial Review of Military Compensation (a DoD study in 1976); the report of the President's Commission on Military

Compensation (1978); and a study that led to the Uniformed Services Retirement Benefits Act (a DoD study in 1979).

45. Accrual accounting may also permit a better debate on grandfathering. Without accrual accounting, any substantial grandfathering of benefits already earned made it appear that there were no savings. With accrual accounting, savings will be obvious even if there is grandfathering.

46. Congressional Budget Office, *Accrual Accounting for Military Retirement: Alternative Approaches* (July 1983).

COMMENTARY

DISCUSSANTS

David S. C. Chu*

First, I'd like to congratulate the authors involved for making significant contributions to the literature of defense manpower.

Robert Hale has been courageous in offering specific predictions. (Perhaps at the twenty-year conference we could reconvene to see if he was correct!) More important, he has reminded us of the significance of the Congress in formulating military manpower policy. Too often in the executive branch we believe that our job is finished when a military service or the secretary of defense has made a decision and that it's just a formality to send it to the Hill. Bob reminds us that the job has then only begun, and that our proposal may be subject to very substantial changes. This process is a good one—and a healthy one—for the country as a whole.

John Brinkerhoff and David Grissmer have done a great service in providing some facts about the reserve situation, at least on the supply side. This is an area in which, at least to my observation, there is often a great deal of emotion but very few facts. We deal with reserve issues too frequently on the basis of casual empiricism. Their presentation is a step in the right direction. It indicates how far we have to go: if we look carefully at the footnotes to other references in their study, most of the authors' names are the same!

---

*The views, opinions and conclusions are solely those of the author and do not reflect any endorsement or approval by the Department of Defense or any other person of the U.S. government.

Third, I think James Hosek, Richard Fernandez and David Grissmer have done a valuable service in pulling together in one place some very insightful and thoughtful new work at Rand on manpower supply methodology. Their forecast sets a high analytic standard for the Department of Defense. (That's probably appropriate, since we're paying them to set that standard!) I would urge them to expand the scope of their presentation, since if you are not familar with some of the specific studies on which their conclusions rest, it may be a little difficult to follow their arguments and to understand the various relationships that are driving the conclusions they reach.

Let me comment on what I see as the four main issues raised by these previous chapters and offer my own views on them.

A first issue is our vision of the future. Taken together, there is an attempt to do what Robert Hale did very explicitly: forecast where we're headed, trying to answer the question, "What will the future be like?"

Simplistically put, the AVF has passed through three phases. There was an early phase of moderate success with some difficulties. Then there was a middle phase when things were quite disappointing, and a more recent phase with a very, very strong record. The forecasts in these presentations predict something more like the early phase of the AVF than either the middle or last phases. In addition, if you look carefully at the qualifications offered by the authors (Hale put probabilities on his predictions), the risk tends to be on the down side.

Hosek, Fernandez and Grissmer warn us that youth wages may rise, and that relative to all wages in the economy, an increase is not likely to be picked up by the broad indicators we use.

Hale warns us that the Congress is likely to be sparing about pay increases, at least until hard evidence of a problem arises. The difficulty with that approach is that it then takes a couple of years to correct the problem. (Parenthetically, I take issue with Hale's view as to the motivation behind congressional attitudes. I don't think it has much to do with the deficit. Thus, even after the deficit problem is solved we will still see the Congress reluctant to push big increases in defense. I think it has much more to do with the composition of the federal budget; the opportunity cost, at least as the Congress sees it, of defense expenditures versus other kinds of things that the federal government might do with its money.)

There is also the trend in unemployment. Unemployment is clearly going down, perhaps quite sharply, in the immediate future. Hosek, Fernandez and Grissmer warn us that in periods of high unemployment people sign up for long periods of time. What they don't address is whether the converse is true in periods of low unemployment or, worse, whether that leads us to a "one-horse shay" situation. That is to say, we coast along, riding on this cushion of people who signed up earlier in more difficult periods, and then we suddenly find ourselves in difficulty, quite rapidly, when all these conditions take effect simultaneously.

I also worry a little about what we might do if faced with the changes in force composition that Hosek, Fernandez and Grissmer indicate could happen. They point to a more senior force made up of a lot more people with ten or more years of service. Whether or not that will happen will depend on both supply and demand considerations. Would that kind of seniority be acceptable? It would run the department right up against the grade limits that we use, and it could create difficulties with the way we manage and promote people. For a variety of reasons (including concerns about the quality of cohorts now moving through the force from the period of difficulty in the late 1970s), it may be decided not to keep everybody who might otherwise stay under those predictions.

As Robert Hale has pointed out, retirement changes could affect these forecasts adversely. Of course, given the Hosek, Fernandez and Grissmer results, perhaps we need not worry quite so much about retaining people with many years of service. If a package were passed that gave people with just a few years of service important incentives to stay maybe 10 more years, then the changes might actually be mildly helpful, but they could easily go the other way quite dramatically.

The second issue, the reserves, is highlighted by Brinkerhoff and Grissmer. I think we need to work not only on the supply situation, as they have done, but also on what the economists call the demand side or, "requirements." How do we really want to use reserve forces? What kind of roles can they play in our force structure? Under what circumstances would the American public permit the reserves to be mobilized? Under what circumstances would it permit large ground combat reserve formations to be commited to action? (Consider what happens when casualties come from one small region of the United States, as has happened when everyone was recruited from the same place.) I believe that we need a lot more experimentation with new ways of using reserves.

The third issue touched on very briefly by Robert Hale, is the role of civilians. I do think that is an important issue, and I would urge that its purview be expanded beyond just the civilians we hire directly. We hire a lot of civilians indirectly and the most obvious vehicle is contracting out. I think that is likewise an important area for research.

Finally, there's an implicit issue in all presentations concerning the role of analysis. The implicit assumption is that analysis matters, and I think it does. However, I do think we have to be modest about how much it matters. Hale's presentation, as far as the Congress is concerned, is a lesson in that regard. Hosek, Fernandez and Grissmer comment on the same point regarding educational benefits. Analysis has demonstrated again and again that broad-based benefits do not produce the results that are advertised, yet, they remain a very popular idea. I think this is a good lesson in how much analysis can do for us. Similarly, I think we have to be modest about how much analysis can tell us about how our various institutions work. Hosek, Fernandez and Grissmer point that out in their review of how well the army did in the last few years. Leadership and institutional change, made by one commanding officer, produced results that were way beyond the range of any of the predictions of the models.

I think we also have to be persistent in the application of analysis. It is not enough to do a study one time, to prove a point once, if the point is controversial and runs counter to deeply held intuitive feelings. Then, I think, repeated study is worthwhile, notwithstanding the laudable efforts made to eliminate "duplicative" studies. As a practical political matter, the study has to be done again and again in order to make sure everybody really does understand and accept the point, that no mistake has been made and that no conclusion is reached with just one piece of evidence. That, of course, for those of us who are analysts, is a very happy conclusion, because it will keep the demand for analysts high in the future!

Richard V.L. Cooper

First, at least to many of you, my views are reasonably well known. Second, I think what we have shown over the last ten years is that we can sustain a military force without a draft. I think the future is likely to focus much more on whether there are some other kinds of trends, political, social or otherwise, which would take us back possibly to conscription. Rather than discuss the "whys" and "wherefores" of the volunteer force, what I would like to do is reflect on the research process, the analysis, and its impact. In this regard, I believe that, in fact, research has played a rather substantial role in shaping manpower policy over the last dozen years.

This is not so much due to the results of any particular study because those are often subject to a great deal of debate, discussion, and the like, but rather because research has formulated a basic set of facts. People would argue ten years ago that education benefits might have a major impact on enlistment supply, yet most research suggests otherwise. I think it has revealed facts that policy planners can use on a regular ongoing basis in evaluating the supply process. In fact, I know of few other areas where applied research has had such an impact on the policy process.

I think this is a credit to two types of people, namely the policymakers who have been willing to utilize available results, thus opening themselves to the usefulness of the research; and also to the researchers who have tried to tune themselves to the very real world problems that the policymakers face. If you look at much of the manpower research, it's not overly theoretical; it continues theory with applied work. I think it has been fairly successful, and certainly in my mind, more successful than in many other policy areas.

As I look at the status of today's manpower research policy, I am both heartened and discouraged. On the one hand, I think we have accomplished a great deal. I still remember a meeting, I think it was in 1974, where we were talking about variable reenlistment bonuses. We all sat around the room and literally voted on different occupational skills to determine which skill would get what bonus. That meeting stands out very vividly in my mind and I think we've come a long way since then.

I think these presentations reflect that process. Hosek, Fernandez and Grissmer present a much more sophisticated approach for looking at active-force manning than we had even as recently as five years ago. I think their presentation enables us to gauge some of the changes in manpower manning that would occur under different kinds of scenarios and under different kinds of policies. Brinkerhoff and Grissmer's findings show us really how far we've come in the reserve area. When the Gates Commission put forth its recommendations on the reserves, the ignorance of that area was overwhelming. I see our understanding about the reserves now approximately where we were with the active forces in the early 1970s. It's got a long way to go, but I think we've come a long way. Hale presents a really excellent overall view of the congressional process.

At the same time, I must admit to a sense of frustration. We seem to be looking at the same issues with many of the same tools, through much the same eyes. We're more refined now, to be sure, but I still see us arguing primarily about pay elasticities, unemployment elasticities, and the like. These are important issues, but I think we need to do more.

I knew it was time to leave Rand when I started to have the same ideas I had had four years earlier and thought they were new ideas. I think much the same could be said for the manpower research community as a whole. We've gone through the process; now it's time for us to really break out of the mold that we have been in. Clearly, we are taking steps in that direction as these presentations indicate. What the Defense Manpower Data Center has done in obtaining some very basic kinds of information and what's been done in the survey area at DMDC both illustrate the progress. But there's a lot more we need to do.

I see three areas in particular where we need to do a better job. We've got to do a better job in crosscutting policy problems. It's no longer sufficient to look at problems such as supply and retention separately. We must look at them as part of the larger problem of manning the force. Again, I think that Hosek, Fernandez and Grissmer make an important step forward in that process. However, they do not go far enough when you realize the differences in force structures in terms of the seniority mix, for example, that their findings demonstrate. These could have rather dramatic impact on how we man not only the active forces, but the reserve forces. We've got to begin looking at the really tough problems, such as reserves, attrition, personnel management, and maybe most important of all, requirements.

I feel that we have made remarkably little progress in understanding military manpower requirements. What drives them? What's important? What's not important? Which of these force structures make a difference and why? Finally, I think we need to do a better job of integrating the different disciplinary approaches. I believe it will be well worth the effort. I think that DoD has received enormous returns for the investments that it's made. However, the problems of the next decade seem to be far more subtle. As a result, they are much less easy to recognize and solve. It's time we move toward a new manpower policy research agenda, one that tries to attack these crosscutting areas and one that really sets a much broader foundation.

John P. White

I think we can all endorse what Robert Hale said about supporting the GI Bill. After all, most of the money will go for education for the next generation of econometricians!

I started in this business in 1968 as an analyst. I'm glad I'm not trying to make a living at it today. The papers, and the people in particular, have gotten a lot better. While we're here talking about how good it is, and there's a certain amount of nostalgia, good analysis if correct, still does take a long time. I'm reminded of the two old veterans sitting around the old soldiers' home. One turns to the other and says, "Remember that saltpeter they gave us in France in 1918? Well, it's beginning to work." Well, I think it's finally beginning to work, and I think that's good. What we have here, basically, is an issue which has matured.

The country at large settled the issue many years ago. Because it's such a fundamental issue, the country should and will be asked regularly to rethink it and settle it again. In the short run, it's largely been settled. The defense system has delivered, as was predicted it could, partly because of the analytical skills involved, partly because of the people in the Pentagon, and partly because of the leadership of several administrations. Most of all, the defense system has delivered because of the military services and their particular competence in doing things once they set about the chore of getting them done in a professional way.

I think most of the success with the All-Volunteer Force has to do with the recruiting commands, the leadership, and the people in the military services. This is a mature issue, and we ought to move on to other policy debates. We must, however, never give up the issue. We ought to continue, as David Chu has said, to revisit, restudy, reanalyze, and improve upon what it is we know. But this is an issue that, in terms of priority, ought to move down on the list. It is something that, at least in this current context, has been largely solved.

However, the problem, and the apparent success of the AVF, as viewed in this book, is measured in terms which people find comfortable and measurable. That is, we have tended to measure the success in terms of variables which we understand, not necessarily the appropriate definition of the larger problem, nor the appropriate measure of success. Therefore, I would urge us to shift to some other issues. Some of these issues do not lend themselves as readily to analysis, but today they should be much nearer the top of the list. I will very quickly describe them and not make a particular argument about any one of them.

The first issue is the quality of life. I run a computer software company, and the success of our company is vitally dependent upon having high-quality software engineers. I am convinced that there are four things that make for our success in terms of attracting, retaining, and getting high output out of very skilled people. First is the challenge of the work. Second is the environment in which they do work. Third is ownership in the company, and fourth, a very last fourth, is pay.

The next thing that I would worry about, as has been mentioned previously and as David Chu alluded to, is force-structure management. We may end up with a force structure which is not appropriate to the mission simply because of success in other arenas, such as recruiting or retention. I believe this happened to us during the draft era, and it could happen again although the bulge will come at a different place on the chart than it did in those days.

Third, I would urge that a good deal more attention should be given to civilian pay reform which is a long neglected and very important subject. Fourth, as mentioned by Robert Hale in his excellent presentation, is military retirement. Again my concerns with retirement are partly with cost but, more importantly, with the allocation of resources, and with what I consider distortions in the structure of the force. Management policies as they are conducted under the aegis of the retirement system, and what that retirement system means in terms of the behavior of the career force are also important issues. My final issue, and in my judgment the most important issue, is the reserve. While compensation is critically important, also of importance are the overall equipping and manning of the reserves, the structure and management of the reserves, and the ready reserve mix.

In summary, I would plead with all the contributors that you shift most of your energy to problems that are yet unsolved and are equally important. They will be even more important when the AVF unfortunately may have to end. That day will come if we have to go to full mobilization.

Bernard D. Rostker

Before I start my review, I would like to express my appreciation to Dr. Lawrence J. Korb and his staff and the conference organizers at the Naval Academy for hosting this historic gathering. They have brought together most of the important players in the creation and management of the All-Volunteer Force (AVF). Although it is a pleasure to see so many old friends again and to reflect on the past, the true importance of this conference is on the future. The AVF is the active policy of the Department of Defense. It is an unforgiving policy that requires continual adjustment over a wide range of management actions such as recruiter goaling and assignments, the size and mix of advertising budgets, and screening tools and enlistment criteria, as well as traditional compensation policy.

The presentations here are both impressive in their technical application of advanced econometric techniques and disappointing in their lack of appreciation of the full range of management challenges presented by the AVF. Ten years ago, the Gates Commission described the AVF problem in terms of finding a compensation policy, commensurate with projected unemployment rates, that would provide the Department of Defense with enough nonprior-service enlistments to staff a projected force level. (In economists' terms, the problem was to estimate a supply curve and then to move along that curve until the supply of new personnel was equal to the projected demand.) The skill with which we can now estimate supply curves and carry out the analytic challenge laid down by the Gates Commission is far greater than that exhibited in the studies of ten and fifteen years ago. Unfortunately, however, the problem today is more than just estimating supply curves. Overall compensation policy is important, but the issues have matured and cannot be specified simply in terms of the traditional economics of supply or retention. The larger question is, "How should the Department manage its personnel resources?"

The various aspects of personnel management are broader than the list of variables traditionally examined by econometric studies that focus on compensation and unemployment. (In economists' terms again, the broader problem is to find feasible policies that will permit decision makers to determine a cost-effective mix of pecuniary and nonpecuniary policies, i.e., movement along a supply curve versus shifts to higher supply curves.) For example, Hosek, Fernandez and Grissmer in a technically outstanding presentation, emphasize the traditional disclaimer that noneconomic factors are difficult to quantify so their importance is more difficult to assess, much less change through policy. I would submit that from the vantage point of a senior personnel manager in one of the services, it is the noneconomic variables that are dealt with every day, and that there is hardly anything more difficult to change than the compensation policy of the Department of Defense.

In their discussion of the historically assumed unitary elasticity between population changes and the supply of nonprior-service personnel, Hosek, Fernandez and Grissmer illustrate the importance of noneconomic factors and the significant opportunities for effectively managing military personnel under the AVF without changing the compensation system. In effect, they acknowledge that recent increases in army enlistments cannot be explained by changes in unemployment and compensation. Rather, they note that new research has confirmed a recent link between the army's changed recruiting policies and the subsequent accession gains. I suggest that the potential for such increases existed all along, that the recruiting policies have been largely neglected by the policy research community and recorded after the fact instead of suggested as an important policy option, and that they could have made a substantial impact on the AVF over the last decade.

The need to develop the full range of options for managing personnel is clearest in the area of retention. It is here that our research strategies have been the weakest. Most retention research is based on models that analyze relative pay, unemployment, enlistment bonuses, and demographics. I know from my experience in the navy, however, that there is a broader range of policies that have a profound impact on attrition and retention. I recall a trip to Norfolk early in my tour in the navy secretariat. We had a significant attrition problem, and I wanted to talk to some of the young men and women who were leaving before the end of their first term of service. My escort officer asked, "Why do you want to talk to them? They are bad apples, and we are throwing them out." I replied, "Those are exactly the people we have to keep in the navy if we are to reduce attrition. We have to listen to what they are saying." I can assure you that what they were saying had little to do with relative wages and unemployment. Moreover, what they were saying was directly related to factors that were fully within the control of the Department of Defense.

One subject that has recently received much attention is the reserves. (See Hale's excellent presentation.) However, this subject should be viewed as an AVF issue in only a very limited sense. It is first and foremost a force-mix question, i.e., the desired mix of active and reserve forces in the total force. Some would argue that active-duty strength and accession requirements can be reduced if more of our military posture is shifted to the reserves, but it is very unwise and dangerous to decide the proper posture of our military forces on the basis of reducing the requirement for active-duty accessions. Once a desired active/reserve mix is decided upon, however, it is legitimate to ask how best to manage the force. Brinkerhoff and Grissmer, in their excellent review of the past ten years of reserve force personnel under the AVF, argue that there are few supply problems that would impair the ability of the Department of Defense to substantially expand the size of reserve forces and the number of nonprior-service enlistees recruited each year. I do not share their optimism. Their conclusion aside, they clearly point out that the analytic work necessary to support such a finding has not been done. Futhermore, in FY 1983 the Army National Guard failed to meet its goal for nonprior-service accessions, and, the FY 1984 goal is half again greater than actual accessions in FY 1983.

I would be remiss if I did not end my comments with at least one observation about the selective service system and its role in the overall AVF system. As the Gates Commission asserted, a strong standby selective service is a necessary component of the All-Volunteer Force. I am not concerned about the ability of the selective service system to respond during a major mobilization emergency, because I know great strides have been made so that today the selective service system is the strongest of our mobilization organizations. What I am concerned about, however, are the particular policies that selective services would follow if called upon to reinstitute conscription in an emergency. Such policies as the age-cohort-order-of-call reflect the experience of the late 1960s and early 1970s during the Vietnam War; they may not be appropriate for the type of mobilization that is the current force of selective service planning. A year and a half ago, a report by the Atlantic Council raised this issue in the context of unfinished AVF business.[1] I would like to raise it again, and emphasize that it should be addressed as we continue our prospective view of the AVF.

NOTES

1. See the Atlantic Council's Working Group on Military Service Recommendation #9 in Andrew J. Goodpaster et al.: *Toward a Consensus on Military Service* (Elmsford, N.Y.: Pergamon Press, 1982), p.302.

AUDIENCE

Question for John R. Brinkerhoff (from Gen. Paul Phillips): You didn't have time to finish your comments. What was it you hoped to add?

Brinkerhoff: A final but important thought: it is this group (present at this conference) here that is going to determine to a great extent the future of manpower policy for the United States. It is distressing that this group pays little attention to the reserve components or to the mobilization manpower problem, which is not the same thing as the reserve component. Mobilization manpower comes from the total force, including the active individuals, retired people, the reserves, and people not even in the military services today. Mobilization manpower is a total-force personnel problem, yet I'm distressed that the personnel managers and manpower policymakers treat this problem as a reserve problem and leave it to a small group of people who ignore them.

What I would like to advocate today is that we do some total force analysis. With due respect to my colleagues, they have analyzed, very brilliantly, the 1,700,000 active enlisted personnel, but they have left out another million reservists. I think that's the worst thing you could do as far as analysis. What would the difference be as far as our retention rate goals and in our preferred profiles if we included *all* of our enlisted members? Would it make a difference? Why can't we stockpile senior people in the IRR with some sort of incentives and retainer pay as a deliberate policy if it makes more rational use of our people? Why can't we have a single, unified retirement system where a person can "cross the line"? Why can't we realize that we can have a closed system, if we want it, where once a person enlists we've got him until he or she dies? If we have the right policies, we can put them in various states of readiness. All I'm saying basically is, why can't we analyze the whole thing instead of doing it piecemeal?

Question for Bernard D. Rostker (from Charles Groover): You spoke of concern about our inability to employ any significant fraction of our active force without a substantial reserve call-up. I would like to comment on the proposition that it is in the nation's best interest to have our active and reserve forces highly integrated so that we cannot make a large commitment of forces without a comparatively large call-up of the reserve forces. It seems to me that this would provide insurance against the kind of situation we had in Vietnam where President Johnson was able to expand that conflict substantially without calling a significant part of the reserves.

Rostker: I think that is very dangerous. Our business should be to provide a military force that can respond to the national command authority. I do not think that we should use force structure issues to place political blocks in the path of our leaders. I would rather let the president and the Congress have as much flexibility as possible and let the political process deal with questions of appropriate checks and balances in the use of military force.

I would like to make one more point on the issue of active/reserve integration. I believe that a case can be made that the very nature of the reserves, namely the limitations placed on reservists by their part-time commitment, is such that even if called to active duty many missions may not be adequately performed. I have two specific concerns. First, without a major call-up of the reserves, important elements will be missing, and second, even with a call-up of the reserves the proficiency of our forces may not be as high as required.

Question for John R. Brinkerhoff: How well do we evaluate the IRR? Do we know where those 400,000 people are?

Brinkerhoff: Well I think that whether we know where they are or not is a direct function of the amount of money each service puts into finding out. The army put in the most, and the air force and navy put in very little. I suggest that the individual naval reservists are the navy's people, and if the navy wants to know where they are, the navy should start finding them and doing a good job. That's part of the whole problem with the IRR. My view of why the navy, air force, Marine Corps, and army IRRs are declining in strength is that the services are not really trying. People are leaking out of this system after eight years and nobody even asks them at the separation center if they would be willing to go into the IRR. There are a lot of reasons for that, but I don't think we have time to get into them.

Question for Bernard D. Rostker: It appears that not only do we have to hold our high quality accessions but there are projections that if we bring in high technology, we'll need a great increase in high-quality people. My question is, if we can't get it all through the AVF, what help would the draft be?

Rostker: You can do almost anything you want with the draft. The problem is one of perception and fairness. Under a conscription system that equates randomness with fairness, the answer is that selective conscription would most likely be considered as unfair. Let me make one related point: I think one of the missed opportunities is to use new training technologies to reduce the need for high-skill and highly trained individuals. If there is one area in the manpower, personnel, and training system that has been neglected, and is going to become much more critical in the next ten years, it is the area of training. There are training technologies that can be used to counter the technological revolution, but we are extremely slow in developing and fielding them.

Follow-up comment: Some people feel that a draft will solve all the quality problems. You're suggesting that training may be a solution.

Rostker: That's correct.

Comment (from Maj. Gen. Mohr): First of all I'd like to point out that the urgency of the requirement of the reserve component is illustrated by the fact that a third of our force is in the reserve components. In the army, we have half of our combat units, two-thirds of our support units, and two-thirds of our medical units in the reserve components. You might ask, how well do they perform? This is for the most part dictated by the availability of equipment and manpower, both of which are generally under strength. However, where they are up to strength, they perform well. I have in my briefcase a letter from General Rogers, Supreme Commander, Europe, which points out that the reserve perform extraordinarily well in Europe. I have many letters from commanders of active components praising highly the reserve forces for their ability to perform. This is no miracle because all of them are active-force trained, and carry with them not only that training but the civilian experience they've had.

I'd like to now address one final issue without making a long speech, and that's the individual ready reserve. In this regard, the AVF is a total failure. It has not met the needs of our mobilization base in supplying the manpower that is required for our rapid mobilization before selective service can fill the gap. What is going to fill the gap? John Brinkerhoff addressed it briefly; I'd like to hear him address it a little further because the gap makes it clear that we really don't have our hands on a source for these people. The AVF pulls the rug right out from under the availability of that manpower. We have not replaced it since the AVF took over. It was not a consideration of the Gates Commission and has really not come under consideration at this conference. I think this is a major criticism of this conference.

Question (from Admiral Finneran): I'm an interested civilian observer and retired admiral. I have two things to offer. I am disappointed that the analysis format has not advanced as far as I would expect it to. One particular topic is public esteem. It has been measured, maybe not very well, and I recognize it's very difficult to measure, but there's been a marked change. Allegedly we're at a high point of public esteem for military service. I'm not sure many of us know if that is attributable to institutional change along the lines Bernard Rostker suggested or other events. Nevertheless, I would like to see it measured and added to our data bank. Of even greater importance is the question of readiness, or the capability to perform missions. It was lightly touched on in a couple of presentations, but it's largely an untouched area. We are still talking about providing manpower to do something, but from an analytical viewpoint, I'm not sure what it is we're doing. We deal in marginal numbers, we deal with skills, we deal with skill differentiation by AFQT or various other variables (educational achievement or educational potential) but have nothing to say about performance on the job. There is a great deal of work that needs to be done on that. I'm amazed that there hasn't been a greater effort made to integrate various data bases into manpower analysis that ought to be available from the services, the Joint Chiefs of Staff, and the material commands.

James R. Hosek: Just briefly, even though persistent efforts have been made to achieve such an integration, they've been frustrated. Apparently the services are not anxious to divulge information concerning the performance of specific units. Another facet has to do with the difficulty of deciding how to measure performance. Basically, I'm very much in favor of the point of view you've stated. Rand has tried to get research going on this and so has MRAL, but it has been an extremely difficult nut to crack. Maybe it's a topic that will emerge for the remainder of the decade.

Follow-up comment (from Admiral Finneran): My concern is not so much for the broad data being made available to you, but the potential is there to abuse or misnorming the analysis by not being allowed to perform the sensitivity analysis. For example, in your particular analysis you suggested relatively large possible errors for the pay factor between now and 1990 for particular segments of the force. If you increase the sensitivity of that by having a mission-readiness input, you may find there is a dramatic difference. I have no idea. You may find the cost increment associated with less investment is much more sensitive.

John P. White: I want to make one comment because I agree with everything you've said. I think part of the problem is not so much to raise the issue and criticize people doing the analyses which we have now become so familiar with. Those people are doing far better analyses than when I was involved in it and are trained with a particular set of tools to address a particular subproblem and they're doing that very well. The point that you've made that I think is very important is that another set of information and considerations have to be included. I suggest that the solution to getting that information before the policymakers is not to exhort and criticize people doing these kinds of studies but rather to search for other ways of finding professional, analytical researchers and advisers to address that set of issues in the same way.

Question (from Bernard Udis): I was intrigued yesterday by Admiral Kidd's suggestion that IQ or mental categories are not fixed forever and that there is a use for people in the lower category. I was wondering if anyone on the panel would care to comment on that, particularly in light of the fact that category IVs were mistakenly taken into the army and are still there. They may be available to see whether or not the admiral's belief is valid.

Hosek: There are certainly a whole set of studies that can be done based on the example of General DePuy's presentation where he related SQT to performance with a particular weapons system. I think that's an area yet to be explored. Some of the work that has been done, including the particular study I have in mind, has related an individual's first-term performance as measured by his speed of promotion and level attained during the first term to variables available at time of entry such as AFQT and education. This research has attempted to measure a quality index of the individual, and the index shows the importance of what I'll call an unobserved factor, probably having to do with the individual's leadership potential, motivation, willingness to work, attitude toward his job and ability to get along with his companions. The unobserved factor emerges as the major weight in the quality index that is estimated. Far and away the least weight is attached to AFQT, somewhat more weight to education (that is, high school/non-high school graduates). But primarily, for the specific set of skills examined, the majority of the weight went to this factor that is unobserved at the time of entry. This finding does not mean that AFQT is a poor entry screen because it's designed, in part, to predict training performance and performance in such tasks as the Skill Qualification Test that measures the performance of a specific set of tasks in an MOS. It does mean, however, that a lot of revealed information occurs during the first term and may, to some extent, be summarized in the promotion process. Other kinds of measures could be used in this particular methodology but haven't been. The upshot of this is that when we consider first-term reenlistment, it probably would be a better idea to base reenlistment eligibility decisions more on the basis of revealed performance during the first term than on entry-level screens such as AFQT and education. There's still a lot remaining to be done in this field.

Question (from John Blair): A potential fly in the ointment that seems to have come out of this conference is the long-term availability of high-quality recruits. I'm wondering whether any of the analysis here might have underestimated the potential for exactly those kinds of people in the post baby-boom/baby-bust period. If the number of available people goes down 10 or 15%, the number available to the military is going to go down substantially more than that. Not only are the competitors in industry going to need higher and higher quality people, but the universities are not going to voluntarily close up shop and go home. Professors don't like reductions in force any more than anybody else, particularly since they have few useful skills. As a result, I'm really suggesting that models that look at wage elasticity are really ignoring the fact that universities are going to go after the same kind of people you most want in terms of effectiveness, that is high-quality high school diploma graduates. They are going to go after them in a much higher proportion than they have in the past. So, I think the pool available to the military will be quite a lot different than we are predicting. Would somebody like to comment on that?

Hosek: The models that have been discussed on active enlisted supply are simplistic in terms of the few variables that are described to the audience, but underlying them are a variety of studies, one of which has to do with microdata. These studies are not used in this specific forecasting model, but they help give us additional insights into the behavior of individuals. Basically, I agree with your point; more needs to be learned about the decisions of individuals to choose whether to go to school, work, or enter the service. Gary Nelson's presentation pointed out that it may not be a sequential choice whereby they consider school first and then, if not school, work or the service. Research going on now tries to estimate a model that allows for what is called selectivity of individuals between school and nonschool, and for those who choose not to go to school what their enlistment decision-making behavior will be, and for those who choose to go to school, what their subsequent enlistment decision-making behavior will be. It turns out that from microdata, we're finding that among higher-income individuals, particularly in the upper quartile of the income distribution in the country, there is a declining tendency to enlist in the service. For a broad range of income classes, however, it does not decline; it is constant. Individuals with higher AFQT scores in the population at large are far more likely to want to go to college. However, once you look at the population of individuals who are not in school, but have become nonstudents for the time being, there is very little relationship, in fact no statistical relationship that I recall, between AFQT level and the decision to enlist. Those people may be interested in coming into the service for one of two reasons. One is to obtain further training which they may see as the services as providing as a substitute to school. The second is to provide financing for education which they would obtain after their service career. A large fraction of nonstudents are quite interested in getting more education. Another survey has shown that these individuals are quite happy to consider educational benefits or other incentives, such as bonuses, as a way of helping pay for their education after service. Basically, you've come onto a good subject. What I'm saying is that work is underway to try to consider different market segments and to study the decision-making process that leads an individual to go to college immediately after high school, or to delay the decision and go to junior college, be a part-time student, or enlist. In closing, enlistment incentives are going to be designed to try to anticipate some of the factors that you put your finger on.

Follow-up comment (from John Blair): This is very interesting and important. Depending on when you state the end of the baby-boom was (some people think it was 1961) those people graduated from universities in 1983. We have not yet begun to see universities fight. I think universities are starting to gear up for the battle, and I think what you've seen in the past may not yet be very relevant to the kind of recruiting environment that is coming down the line.

Brinkerhoff: I'd like to make one comment on that. It's true that the decision by high-quality youth to go to college probably precludes them from enlisting in an active component, but it does not preclude them from enlisting in a reserve component which, after all, is a part-time job. If receipt of school aid is linked to national service, and that is very possible, the forces of higher education and the national security may find themselves in an alliance.

Question: Richard Cooper was piling dirt on the question of education as an enlistment incentive for the active force, but there is a heatbeat of life in the data presented by Hosek, Fernandez and Grissmer. Broad-based educational benefits perhaps are precluded by cost but the question I have is as follows: Couldn't we make coming first into the active forces then later going to college and entering a reserve unit simultaneously be a tandem process as a continued targeted postservice educational benefit that would be given to the kinds of high-quality people that we need?

Robert F. Hale: It seems to me we're doing that in the area where we need the help. We have a highly targeted educational benefits program right now for the army, and the law would certainly allow it to be expanded to the other services. If you want to expand it, it's a matter of deciding how to pay for it and which services should use it.

Richard V.L. Cooper: First of all, I did not say that educational benefits do not work. What I did say is that they are not a panacea and that broad-brush "GI Bill" type programs are not very cost-effective. Target programs like this current program may have a great deal of payoff as do other kinds of highly targeted programs.

David W. Grissmer: Let me make two comments concerning the reserve forces. One is that there is a distribution problem and one solution to that problem is targeted programs such as educational benefits and bonuses that directly affect units that are short. I want to make a second point which is that all the projections which I showed you are for the selected reserve units as a whole. Ordinarily, since the army comprises about two-thirds of the reserve force, you would think that those trends automatically transferred down to the army. It's not necessarily true because there is a wide disparity among the air and naval units and the army units. Some of the trends I showed are not so optimisitic for the army component. I think the kinds of educational programs we're talking about are one of the things we need to use to solve both the strength and the distribution problems for the army.

Question for Robert Hale (from Stanley A. Horwitz): Do you think events such as in Grenada and elsewhere change attitudes in Congress?

Hale: Assuming that we will withdraw from Grenada and that we will not greatly expand our role in the Middle East, I doubt these military operations will change attitudes toward the AVF. My sense also is that the "half life" of these events, especially something like Grenada, is short in the Congress. Therefore, I wouldn't expect it to have much of an effect six to twelve months from now. If, however, we extend our role in Lebanon in a way that continues casualties but doesn't seem to be reaching any goal, I could see it having a negative effect; that is, there would be even more unwillingness to increase defense spending. I should close with one caveat, however; wise men do not forecast the Congress!

Part V

ALTERNATIVE MANPOWER PROCUREMENT POLICIES

Introduction

William K. Brehm

The final chapters address the alternatives (the volunteer force, the draft, and national service) for meeting future military manpower requirements. Building on the earlier chapters, a general consensus was reached that the AVF will continue to meet manpower requirements during peacetime as long as the American public is willing to pay the price. However, the cost will not be cheap, and the debate is far from over.

In chapter 14, General Thurman's optimistic outlook for continuation of a voluntary recruitment policy is based upon a dynamic, flexible management style that will allow the Defense Department to quickly and adequately address problems when they arise, especially in the army which historically has had the major manning problems. The author argues that manpower policymakers have learned from prior mistakes and successes and now possess the managerial expertise to use policy options to meet the quantity and quality needs of the future. Implicit is the presumption that the Congress and the American people will continue to support paying military wages comparable to the civilian sector.

In chapter 15, John G. Kester adds several insights to the conscription-volunteer debate. Citing recent standings in NATO competition, imbalanced racial mix, periodic underfunding, class-bred discrimination, and other factors, he argues that the AVF has not worked and will not "work" in the future. In support of the conscription alternative, Kester stresses that it is not only the most effective means of meeting objectives but the only fair approach. A conscripted force would meet surge mobilization demand, reaffirm our seriousness of purpose to our allies, and have a salutory educative effect on society.

Chapter 16, by Richard J. Danzig, provides both a description of national service options and a balanced discussion of the strengths and weaknesses of the national service alternative to military recruiting. Mr. Danzig describes four national service options, each having features not typically discussed in the existing literature. The author asserts that most national service options are too costly and inefficient. For now, these alternatives may best be considered interesting concepts and not practical manpower alternatives for the next decade.

14 Sustaining the All-Volunteer Force 1983-1992: The Second Decade

MAXWELL R. THURMAN*

INTRODUCTION

The All-Volunteer Force is an institution well suited to the purpose it must serve; that is the defense of our vital national interests in an increasingly interdependent and complex world. We have met many challenges in the last decade and have shaped a military force that is adaptable to the environment of the 1980s. Our army draws its strength from the American public, is guided and supported by the Congress, and is led by dedicated men and women who are responsive to changing times.

The United States' need for a large standing army has spanned only two generations of American soldiers. Before World War II, two oceans, friendly neighbors, and the pace of warfare itself allowed us to mobilize at a leisurely pace and to lay down our arms once they had accomplished the intended purpose.

The United States found in the late 1940s that its most fundamental interests (national survival, freedom as a way of life, and continued prosperity) were directly challenged. The technology and speed of warfare had all but erased the geographical advantages we had previously enjoyed. Further, the extreme differences between the social and political beliefs of the United States and the Soviet Union, coupled with active propagation of the latter's ideology through force, raised the ante in crisis spots throughout the world.

These differences, coupled with Soviet expansion in Europe and adventures elsewhere, convinced the American people of the need for military vigilance. The draft remained a part of American life, and military strategy became a continuous topic of debate in Congress and the press as well as in the Pentagon.

---

*The views expressed are those of the author and not necessarily those of the U.S. Army.

The evolution of strategies following World War II, which were containment, massive retaliation, and coalition warfare amongst others, required a large standing army (large, that is, when compared to previous postwar eras). A strong strategic nuclear force, the triad, was the focus of national strategy for decades and was our nation's principal deterrent. Land forces played a complementary role. As nuclear parity was reached in the late 1970s, increasing emphasis was given to strengthening conventional forces. A large standing army is now essential as a deterrent and offers decision makers viable options to the use of nuclear weapons.

The draft accommodated this evolution. We had a system which supported our need for manpower regardless of the demand. We kept the payroll low and went more than a decade without a structural pay increase for American servicemen and women. Because the draft affected so few people, and because the American public supported a strong defense, the draft remained effective, up to the Vietnam War era. Even so, draft deferments and exclusions became so numerous that representativeness eroded. Questions of equity, and later the unpopularity of the Vietnam War itself, focused the frustrations of the American people on the draft. Opposition to the draft, as a symbol of a war the American people no longer supported, was the most significant environmental factor for military manpower since World War II. It was a symbol of a war they no longer supported. It became a political liability and was stopped in 1973. There was a national concensus in support of the All-Volunteer Force. Concurrently, the trauma and perhaps fears went further. Questions of the utility of military force itself led the public, through its Congress, to restrict the president's ability to use that force by passage of the War Powers Resolution in 1973. These were watershed years for our nation's defense. The temperament of national support for defense had changed and so had the threat. It had become more awesome.

MANNING THE FORCE

Our armed forces are drawn from society at large and will be returned to that society. At present only 13% of those who enter the army will stay until retirement and 87% return to the communities of America. Among enlisted soldiers, only 6% reach retirement. Consequently, the military services reflect American values at home and abroad. This is particularly important overseas, where the American soldier may be the only visible manifestation of our national culture and character. It is our belief that the army inculcates in its soldiers a sense of purpose, loyalty, discipline, dedication, and work ethic, for these are our values. Principled young men and women, carrying army values and ethics back to their civilian pursuits, have made, and will continue to make, a strong America, supportive of its defense structure. We should be proud as a nation and as an army that young Americans come to us, not for a career, but to do their part as the next generation of adult citizens.

As army leaders, we strive to assure societal support by setting goals which allow our population to take pride in the army as an institution. These goals, which Secretary Marsh and Chief of Staff, General Wickham, have set for the army, are: an army of excellence in how it is manned, in how it is organized to fight and win, in how it plans to meet the challenges of mobilization, in how it programs for research, development and procurement, and in how it leads and cares for its soldiers and families.

These goals serve another purpose as well. They foster the support of the American people by showing clearly that we are always seeking improvement in the way we perform our principal mission and in the way we manage the nation's resources entrusted to us—recognizing always that our most valued resource is their sons and daughters.

I would submit that today's volunteers are representative of the spirit of America. They are free young men and women who willingly serve their country. They are from the same stock that built this nation and made it great.

The success of the all-volunteer army has not come easily. To understand its success and to predict its future, one must look to the factors that have made it work. These factors are reflected in the army's history. We have often spoken of the volunteer army since its inception, but I submit that since 1973 there have been four distinct all-volunteer armies. Each reflected the sensitivity of recruiting and retention in the total army (active, National Guard, and reserves) to the combined effects of pay, unemployment, educational benefits, and recruiting resources.

THE FIRST ALL-VOLUNTEER ARMY

The first volunteer army began with high uncertainty in 1973 and ended in 1976. In 1972, Congress gave our young, first-term soldiers pay comparability with a 61.2% pay raise (unheard of in the history of the United States Army) and adequate recruiting resources were initially provided. Unemployment was rising, as was the population from which we recruited; both helped us. The Vietnam era GI Bill retained its power to attract high-quality recruits, despite the increasing influence of federal aid for higher education to individuals not in the military. (Figure 14.1)

Figure 14.1. The First All-Volunteer Army, Environmental Conditions

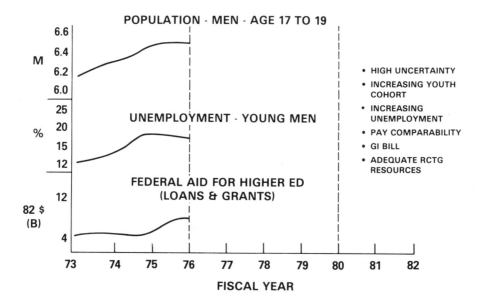

But things were going wrong on two planes that were not readily apparent to society or the army. First, there were the physical things that touched us daily. Second were the factors that affected our spirit.

In the first category, the initial surge to pay comparability had two effects. First, the nation was left with the impression that the military was suitably paid. That impression would lead to a degree of neglect which would (coupled with inflation) later severely reduce the soldier's buying power. (Figure 14.2) Second, the initial large pay increases for privates caused pay compression causing privates to earn nearly as much as their sergeants. This factor would soon contribute, along with eroding pay comparability, to lower retention of mid-level, high-quality NCOs.

Figure 14.2. The First All-Volunteer Army, Incentives and Recruiting Resources

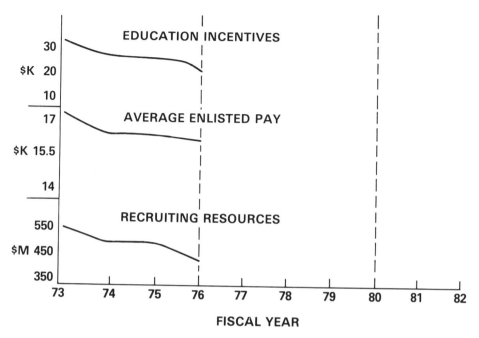

Recruiting resources as a whole were thought to be at least adequate, if not excessive, and thus became targets for cost-cutting. Recruiting is not a simple task. Knowledge of the needs and aspirations of the nation's youth is essential. Advertising must be carefully based upon sound research; in the early days it was not. When the army began using paid broadcast advertising in the early 1970s, we did not understand the market properly. Improvement took research, time, and dollars. The recruiting force itself required maturation, and we had precious little time to learn. Finally, education incentives dropped precipitously at the end of the first volunteer army era with the loss of the GI Bill in 1976.

Our spirits were sapped in four ways. Quality of leadership began to erode in 1974 as uncertainties about the future drove out high-quality NCOs and officers. The influence of the Vietnam War had left the services demoralized and equipped with outdated systems which could not draw smart, technologically oriented soldiers. The absence of a draft and tailored incentives weakened the reserve components. They could not attract nor retain high-quality soldiers in the quantities needed. Initial efforts to improve quality of life were unsophisticated and largely cosmetic attempts to improve barracks life, such as installing beer vending machines. They added little to the spirit of soldiering. Some efforts were successful; however, as a whole, they gave the impression that the military was becoming soft and permissive.

THE SECOND ALL-VOLUNTEER ARMY

The army's first all-volunteer force ended, and the second began in 1976. The end of the Vietnam era GI Bill signaled a downturn that was to last four years. With the GI Bill went smart high school graduates who gave us the quality needed to perform the army's mission and to sustain the strong backbone of the NCO corps.

Pay comparability lapsed, the nation's economy expanded, federal education assistance in the private sector and employment rose, making recruitment of high-quality soldiers increasingly difficult. (See Figures 14.3 and 14.4) It is no small wonder that missed recruiting objectives were the norm in FY1977 through FY1979, and the mental category I, II and IIIa content (which measures the upper-half youngsters in America) of the army shrank from 49% in FY1973 to 26% in FY1980.

Figure 14.3. The Second All-Volunteer Army, Environmental Conditions

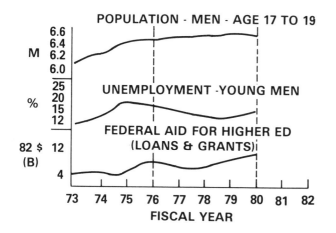

Figure 14.4. The Second All-Volunteer Army, Incentives and Recruiting Resources (1982 Dollars)

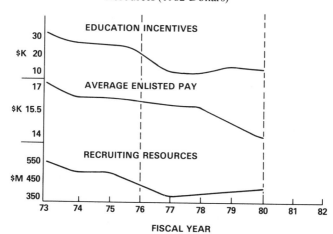

Importantly, high-quality NCOs and officers were now leaving the army in increasing numbers. The high-quality NCO is even more sensitive to pay comparability and unemployment than his less-talented fellow sergeant, as Figure 14.5 suggests. Evidence clearly shows that high-scoring NCOs leave first, and low-scoring soldiers stay irrespective of pay or other incentives.

Figure 14.5. Reenlistment Trends by Test Score Category
(Secondary and Subsequent Reenlistments)

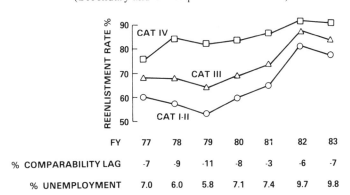

FY	77	78	79	80	81	82	83
% COMPARABILITY LAG	-7	-9	-11	-8	-3	-6	-7
% UNEMPLOYMENT	7.0	6.0	5.8	7.1	7.4	9.7	9.8

THE THIRD ALL-VOLUNTEER ARMY

From the depths of the FY1977-FY1979 period, there was no way to go but up. The third volunteer army began in 1980. We had seen that lapsed pay comparability cost us quality new recruits and continued to drive mid-career NCOs out. It was time to regain comparability. (Figure 14.6) Thanks to two caring Senators, Nunn of Georgia and Warner of Virginia, the 11.1% pay increase in 1981 and the 14.3% pay raise in 1982 gave a big boost towards that goal. Retention increased across the board, but most noticeably among the best of our soldiers.

We saw that education incentives drew smart, college-bound or college-capable soldiers. The end of the GI Bill had heralded a dramatic drop in our quality content. It was time to improve the Veterans Educational Assistance Program (VEAP), the GI Bill's successor. It had not worked in its minimal, contributory form. However, with the addition of the VEAP "kicker" during 1979, the corner was turned. We validated a test of increased education incentives in 1981 in 18% of the country and began the Army College Fund countrywide in 1982 (Figure 14.7).

Research conducted by the U.S. Army Research Institute for the Behavorial and Social Sciences (ARI) found that the most important reason for enlisting for upper mental category soldiers during FY1982 was money for a college education. As shown in Figure 14.8, unemployment was a significant, but not the most important factor for our success in recruiting quality. In fact, the economists' estimates of unemployment elasticities vary from less than one to about two. The changes in quality and quantity of recruits during this period can in no way be attributed solely or largely to unemployment.

We saw that our recruiters were struggling, unaided by knowledge of the marketplace and by the influence of advertising. It was time to learn more about the people who we wanted to serve in the army. We used academia to help us focus on smart, college-bound youth. We assigned recruiters missions by education level and test category. Our recruiters rose to the occasion. They knew their mission, and it was not to fill quotas. It was to recruit high-quality soldiers.

Additionally, we realized that we had underestimated the importance of quality of life (QOL) issues and also, the programs were underfunded. We saw the soldiers' families so neglected that our NCOs were taking the only option truly open to them which was leaving the service. It was time to make up for years of neglect. We increased spending to support QOL construction (both military and nonappropriated fund) from $11.5 million in 1979 to $52 million in 1983.

We saw that the public's image of the military had deteriorated following the initial flush of success at the beginning of the All-Volunteer Force. It was time to raise the image of the army. To raise the image, we had to raise the army . . . and we did.

Figure 14.6. The Third All-Volunteer Army

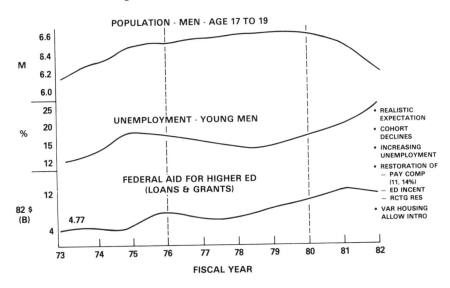

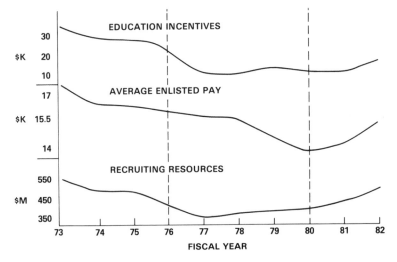

Figure 14.7. The Turnaround

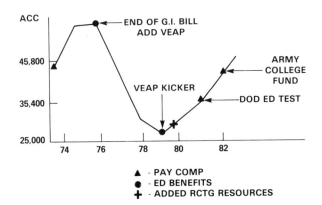

Figure 14.8. Reasons for Enlisting (Male High School Degree Graduates)

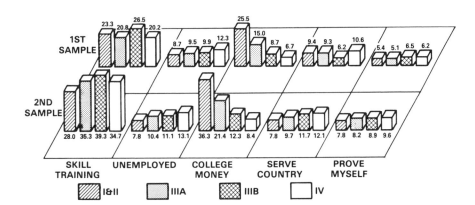

THE FOURTH ALL-VOLUNTEER ARMY

The fourth all-volunteer army began in 1983 with the downturn in pay comparability and marketing review. To date the impact has been slight. Its end will be determined by congressional action and by personnel policies. But with the full support of the Congress and the American people, it will continue through the next decade.

There are pitfalls before us, however. The tangibles, such as pay, benefits, recruiting resources, and QOL facilities and manning are all under pressure. The intangibles are apt to follow. Recruiting and retention resources are being whittled away.

The Vietnam era GI Bill terminates in 1989 for those 295,000 eligible soldiers still on active duty. Enlisted and officer alike, those eligible to retire and those not yet fully committed to a twenty or more-than-twenty year career, have noted this. In 1985 and 1986, we will begin to lose soldiers who value the chance for further education more than military careers. With uncertainty about pay and retirement complicating the future, these soldiers have difficult decisions to make. Many high-quality soldiers may not reenlist. As Figure 14.5 depicts, the smartest leave first and in greater numbers. Our reenlistments of category I and II career soldiers dropped from 82% to 79% in FY1983. The call of the private sector, where I must stress, these people can also make a superb contribution to the nation, is being heard. If they go, the leadership necessary to keep a quality force viable goes with them.

In 1983 we enjoyed a surplus of applicants, thanks to recent problems with the economy and to our success in convincing the public that the military is a good place to serve for a few years or for a career. This success brings calls for reduction of our recruiting resources. Reducing them today would be disastrous. We only have to consider the relationship of quality enlistees to resources to see that the mistakes of the late 1970s cannot be repeated.

Stewardship of all resources is also critical. If we cannot keep quality in the force and use it properly, the nation will not long sustain a high regard for the military. If that regard decreases, defense of the legitimate yet expensive needs of an all-volunteer force will become impossible. The hue and cry will be for a simpler era. The need for resources to support a good all-volunteer force will be overlooked; the problems of a draft will have been forgotten; the lower budget cost will be remembered.

FACTORS THAT HAVE MADE THE ALL-VOLUNTEER ARMY WORK

As we look back on the first decade of the All-Volunteer Force, I feel that we have learned how to make it work. We have found the levers to pull. We have determined the influences of bonuses and education incentives. We have seen the power of effective advertising. We have seen the importance of providing a challenge to our soldiers. We have learned that recruiting must be scientifically, professionally, and morally sound. Market research and sound advertising contribute. Recruiters must be selected, trained, and given full support to ensure they can accomplish the tasks assigned to them. In short, we have a better understanding of the supply of available youth, the recruiting environment, and the use of recruiting resources.

We have also learned more about people. We cannot consider people to be a free resource; the supply is not unlimited. We have seen that the pool of young men from which we draw most recruits is declining, and that we must compete with the civilian economy for both quality and quantity.

We have learned how the propensities of individuals to serve in the military and to choose one service over the others affects us. The air force and the navy have traditionally been far more popular among American youth than the army and the marine corps. The air force and navy project an image of technology and are more popular among high-quality, college-bound youth. Too many see hardship and deprivation as a way of life as a ground soldier, without recognizing that high technology as well as hardship exists in each service.

Ohio State University has tracked the propensity of youth for military service for a decade. Their results, shown in Figure 14.9, reflect the factors I have described, showing the rapid decline in the mid-1970s in the propensity to serve, how the army turned the trend around in 1979, and improved it in 1980. As plates B and C show, the army is now second in propensity but remains third among the high-scoring (mental category I-IIIa) youngsters of America. Thus, our work to sustain the all-volunteer army is cut out for us. Only 27% of the seventeen- to nineteen-year-old male high school graduates have a propensity to serve (plate A) at latest count, and we must seek ways to attract them to our army and to our way of life. There are techniques to do so. Each requires resources.

The economics of the all-volunteer force are constantly debated. The Gates Commission correctly concluded that an all-volunteer force would be expensive and that the costs would be highly visible elements of the nation's budget. It noted that pay comparability was essential to filling army ranks with first-term soldiers. Yet, it paid less notice to the needs of careerists and to the increasing demands for quality. Evidence is explicit that the smarter, more educated young men and women respond to personal and economic incentives. Such is the nature of competition for talent and an advantage of being bright. The Gates Commission was dead right in the most important respect that in eliminating the "conscription tax" the nation had a large bill to pay. The nation has not always done so, and we have learned a lesson. In the mid-1970s we learned that when we were unable to pay competitive salaries, we lost the heart of our NCO corps and, with it, the mid-level troop/technical leadership we needed. We also learned that our stewardship of recruiting and retention resources must be superior and our defense of needs clear and convincing.

Few people agree completely on the proper allocation and distribution of resources to meet the needs of our armed forces. The All-Volunteer Force has been seriously affected by the fundamental disagreement of domestic versus defense spending. Nowhere has the debate been hotter than in Congress, where it should be. The evolution of our all-volunteer force can be traced by the resources that Congress has given us and in the use we have made of them as shown in Figure 14.10. The quality of the enlistee tracks with the expenditure of recruiting resources. We must understand this relationship throughout the next decade and so must the Congress. An interesting aspect of these data is the lag in the response of applicants to resource application, particularly advertising.

Figure 14.9. Propensities

A

17-19 YEAR OLD MALE HSDG AND SENIORS

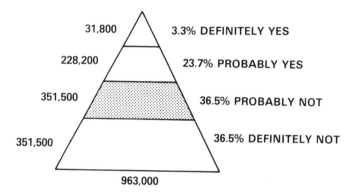

31,800	3.3% DEFINITELY YES
228,200	23.7% PROBABLY YES
351,500	36.5% PROBABLY NOT
351,500	36.5% DEFINITELY NOT
963,000	

SOURCE: YOUTH ATTITUDE TRACKING STUDY FALL 1982

B

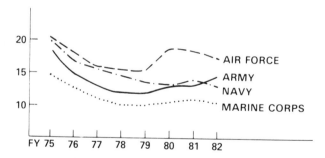

GROSS PROPENSITY

AIR FORCE
ARMY
NAVY
MARINE CORPS

FY 75 76 77 78 79 80 81 82

SOURCE: 1982 YOUTH ATTITUDE TRACKING STUDY (YATS)

C

QUALITY PROPENSITY
(PERCENT)

	ARMY	NAVY	AIR FORCE	MARINE CORPS	COAST GD & RESERVES
I-IIIA	14.7	24.6	43.3	11.0	6.4
IIIB-V	23.8	14.0	40.3	13.0	8.9

SOURCE: NAT LONGTDL SURVEY (DOL/DOD)

Figure 14.10. Quality Versus Recruiting Resources

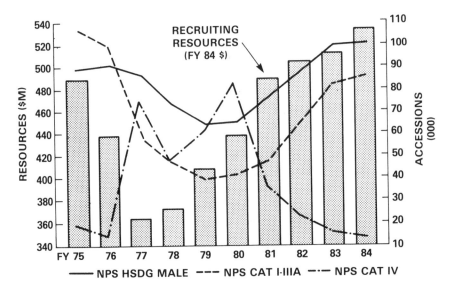

THE SECOND DECADE OF THE ALL-VOLUNTEER FORCE

The second decade of the All-Volunteer Force will certainly test the country's will. The uncertainties of how to make it work, and even if it could work, are gone. The sensititivities of environmental factors, human behavior, and the power of incentives are understood. The levers to pull are marked. The question is, will we pull them?

The size of the force and the cost to man it are affected by the availability of physically, mentally, and educationally qualified people. Since 1973 the number of seventeen- to nineteen-year-old males has decreased by 3.2% (Figure 14.11). This trend will continue and will not turn up again until 1993. Although the total population of eligible males decreases by 9.4% between 1978 and 1987, the number of minorities, including Hispanics, will increase. Thus, as we look to the future, we must be mindful of both numbers of highly qualified individuals available to serve, and the cultural implications of the population from which the All-Volunteer Force must be sustained. The force must be maintained by quality soldiers drawn from the nation's pool of high school graduates. Therefore, it is of great importance to the nation's defense that all young men and women in the United States are assured the advantages afforded by good elementary and high school educations. We who are leaders bear an unusually great responsibility to restore scholarship to our public and private schools. Education has been a torch lighting our national path far too long to see it dim. Furthermore, it is a torch each concerned American must carry.

A clear picture of the competition for high school youth is reflected in Figure 14.12, which shows that the services must take one of four high school graduates on an annual basis or 18% of a four-year cohort. The army must take one in ten in today's environment. With demographics the way they are, the competition from industry and the other services will become even more intense throughout the next decade.

This competition for these high school graduates has been keen since the inception of the volunteer army. Industry seeks smart young men and women for the same reasons we do. They perform better. Similarly, the youth of America seek challenges. Many choose higher education as a means to self-improvement. Our national education programs of grants and loans (Figure 14.13) have served the nation well. Yet, this national generosity has not been matched with a

Figure 14.11. The Shrinking Market:
Projected Population of 17-21-Year-Old Males (in millions)

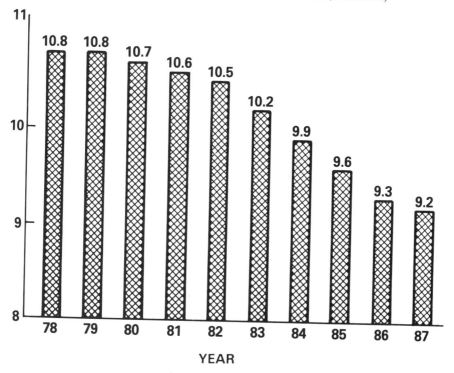

Figure 14.12. Supply and Demand—The Numbers

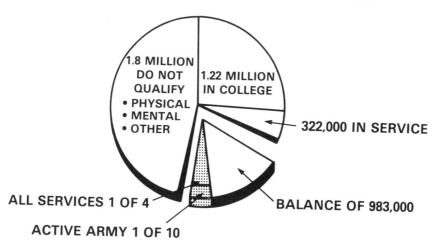

SOURCE: DEPT. OF LABOR, 1981

Figure 14.13. Nonmilitary Education Assistance (In Billions of Dollars)

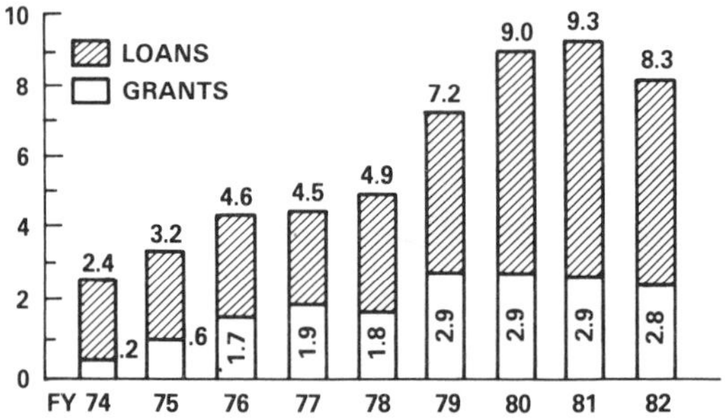

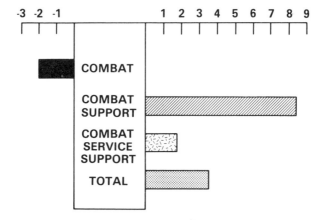

SOURCE: US DEPT OF EDUCATION, OFFICE OF STUDENT FINANCIAL
ASSISTANCE, OSFA PROGRAM BOOK, JULY 1981.

concomitant service obligation. Thus, the very people we must reach are attracted by other
federal incentives. In my opinion, this is a bankrupt national manpower strategy and should be
remedied.

Technology will continue its advance. From a personnel perspective, increased technology is a
double-edged sword. It is perceived by American youth as a drawing card for recruitment. On the
other hand, technology, and the sophistication it brings, demands smarter soldiers.

We have seen, and will continue to see, a not-so-subtle shift in demand for skills, as Figure
14.14 indicates, from combat arms to higher technology support positions. In sum, technology
drives our need for quality and at the same time it complicates our recruiting. We can offer
modern equipment to attract bright soldiers, but we absolutely must succeed in getting them.
Again, we are looking for the same bright young individuals that industry needs and as a rule
industry is willing to pay more, making our job tougher.

Figure 14.14. Enlisted Increases by Functional Area (Percent)

THE DECADE AHEAD: COMPOSITION AND COSTS

The evidence is now conclusive that each military service needs high-quality enlistees. They
perform better, are better disciplined, and in the final analysis, cost less. The ARI tracked and
analyzed the performance of soldiers entering the army during FY1976 through FY1978 on such

measures as first-term attrition and performance on the Skill Qualification Test (SQT). Findings, as shown in Figure 14.15, underscore the importance of prior education as a predictor of both "staying power" and aptitude.

The sophisticated systems each service has in its inventory, the doctrine now developed to meet the diverse threats we face, and the relatively small force we can afford to field demand no less than the most capable servicemen and women America can provide. The questions is, however, when the cost of high-quality manpower becomes perceived as excessive, will the nation revert to a simplistic economic model which suggests that all men and women enjoy

Figure 14.15. Education as a Predictor

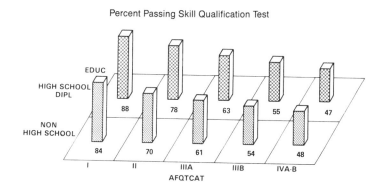

Percent Passing Skill Qualification Test

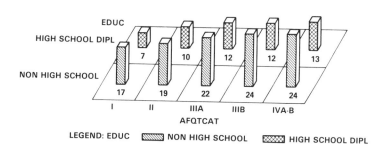

Percent Early Attrition

comparable abilities? Will we revert to the less expensive notion that all we need are numbers, not quality? These are vitally important questions to which America must provide answers. We must insist on quality and provide resources to achieve it. We must not sacrifice our national defense nor ask our soldiers to bear the burden of this defense without a total commitment to their excellence.

We have examined the probable demand for nonprior-service enlistees in the decade ahead. Requirements for accessions will rise by about 10% during the next decade as the armed forces expand. However, the army's growth in accessions is much less than that of other services, as shown in Figure 14.16, even though the army's need for accessions exceeds that of any service. Concurrently, there is a growing need within the army for mental category I-IIIa high school graduates during the next decade.

Figure 14.16. Nonprior-Service Requirements

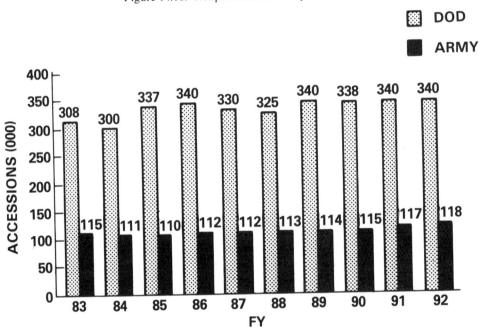

Therefore the competition for high school youth will become much more intense as other service accessions expand. Both the navy and air force have a much higher appeal to mental category I-IIIa high school graduates than does the army because of their perceived use of higher technology. In addition, projections of an expanding, high technology, service-based economy will increase competition for high-scoring youth nationwide. The army must meet this competition if we are to meet our enlistment goals.

We must prepare to deal with these conditions. To do so, the Office of Manpower and Economic Analysis, established at the United States Military Academy last year, has developed predictive models to tell us what is needed to recruit and sustain the force. The "Fagan" model, developed at West Point, by Lt. Col. Thomas Fagan and others, measures the impact of educational level, test score category, unemployment rates, racial and marital status, gross national product, sex, and family size on a recruit's enlistment propensity and once in service, on his or her stay rates by MOS. It is a tool with which we can describe azimuths to chart our course. The course looks expensive, but in the long run it may in fact be cheaper than the alternative which saves "up front" by abandoning efforts to attract high quality.

Analyses conducted by the Training and Doctrine Command (TRADOC) and reported by General DuPuy indicated that the army of the next decade must have as a minimum a high school diploma graduate (HSDG) content of 85% and a mental category content I-IIIa of 65%, while not exceeding the 20% mental category IV. Similarly, we will need a career force whose composition is at least 50% mental category I-IIIa, with a category IV content not to exceed 15%. This distribution will put sufficient higher-quality soldiers at the controls of the more sophisticated equipment the army must field to meet the projected threat. Table 14.1 compares these mental category goals with the mental category distribution of American youth and today's army.

Table 14.1. Army Mental Category Goals versus Current Reality (%)

Mental Category	Army Goal	American Youth	Army Current
I-IIIa	65	49	41
IIIb	20	19	25
IV	15	27	34
V	None	4	None

The distribution required by the army, coupled with the 1992 projected enlisted end strength of 685,000 (of whom some 65,000 to 70,000 will be women), requires that our 1992 distribution of males look like this:

	1990-1992	Current
HS Graduate MC I-IIIa	310,000	188,000
HS Graduate MC IIIb	124,000	101,000
HS Graduate MC IV	93,000	148,000
Non-HS Graduate MC I-IIIa	93,000	51,000
Non-HS Graduate MC IIIb & IV	None	73,000

At the moment, we are short 125,000-educated, upper mental category soldiers, and have too many (125,000) poorly educated, low-scoring soldiers. This imbalance is unsatisfactory, but it is not impossible to correct. Our objective must be to grow the proper mix over the decade by recruiting and then retaining quality in the proportion needed.

The "Fagan" model, mentioned above, has also projected the proper mix of test score categories in our year groups. (See Table 14.2) A discrete distribution by year groups, 5, 10, and 15 illustrates both the problem and the solution:

Table 14.2. Year Group Requirements by Mental Category

	Years of Service					
	5		10		15	
	A	B	A	B	A	B
HS MC I-IIIa	16,668	9,733	7,738	7,541	5,627	4,418
HS MC IIIb	6,682	5,491	3,487	4,056	2,686	1,554
HS MC IV	5,028	14,624	2,664	2,111	2,106	1,646
Non-HS MC I-IIIa	5,127	2,358	2,266	1,412	1,647	1,124
Other		5,300		1,600		1,500

A = Required

B = Current

These data reveal clearly that our current year of service 5 cohort (column 5B) is too small to feed year of service 10 (column 10A) in the higher test score/educational levels given current retention behavior. This problem results from the misnorming of the ASVAB 1976—1980 and the concurrent lower mental category intake during this period. The data also show an excessive number of mental category IV soldiers in both the high school and non-high school categories. Our objective must be to increase our high school degree graduate mental category I-IIIa intake, which we are doing. Then we can pull through sufficient high-scoring soldiers into the 5-year cohort and subsequently into the 10-year cohort. At that point, expected stay rates, in an era of rough pay comparability, will sustain the outyear needs.

To recruit this high-quality force, our annual recruiting requirements will be:

Male	HS graduate, mental category I-IIIa	64,890
	HS graduate, mental category IIIb	22,780
	HS graduate, mental category IV	16,470
	Non-HS graduate, mental category I-IIIa	22,250
Female	HS Graduates	13,935

The total of about 140,000 is not significantly different from the "recruiting vector" (as labor economists are wont to say) that we enlisted in FY1983. Essentially, with 10,000 more educated, high-scoring soldiers, we'd be there. We stress, therefore, that this is not a "pie-in-the-sky" program. It is clearly achievable in today's environment. It is achievable through incentives and an equitable compensation system.

The structure of the compensation system for the enlisted force is inequitable and insufficient to meet the requirements for the next decade. Indeed, the compensation for the army we have, let alone the army we need, is too low. Figure 14.17 suggests basic military compensation (BMC) (the heavy black line) for our youngest soldiers is about right, tracking as it does with the pay of the fiftieth percentile civilian high school graduate. Note that the base pay or the sum total of "take-home" pay for the young soldier living in barracks lags even in these early years. But a greater concern is the BMC lag that starts in the 22 through 24 year age group: we stop paying our

Figure 14.17. Average Lifetime Earnings

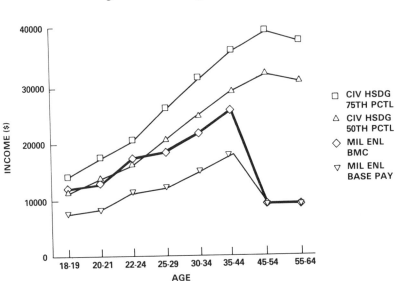

junior enlisted people comparably right about the same time we're asking the best of them to make their career decision. The graph also demonstrates they will never catch up, even to those high school graduates at the fiftieth percentile of ability, unless they land a $20,000-a-year job when they retire. This gap is large when we compare our NCOs to the average civilian high school graduates. Comparison to the seventy-fifth percentile is worse, especially when we talk of retaining the best people. Let's compare winners to winners, because we want our soldiers to be winners. They have to be winners!

Closing either gap would be expensive; perhaps $1 to $2 billion a year for the army, depending on which gap you close. Let's use $1.5 billion a year for a targeted raise; this would go a long way towards retaining the high-quality career force we desire. It would certainly put us into the range where we could take care of specific skill shortfalls with judiciously applied bonuses in the approximate amount we now receive.

As noted previously, we also need to attract 10,000 more high-quality youngsters into the army each year. Research at West Point and Rand suggests that the youth market is segmented; half aspire to go to work and half want to go to college. Enlistment bonuses help enlist those who go to work, and the Army College Fund helps enlist those who go to college. Most of our high-quality youngsters have come from the half who go to work. This is true of all services. This is also the half of the market which is most affected by employment conditions and the economy. Roughly, at the October 1983 level of 9.3% unemployment, a 1% decline in the unemployment rate (e.g., from 9.3 to 8.3) produces a 10% decline in high-quality accessions. This could be overcome by a 10% increase in the enlistment bonus, but the system (Congress- OSD-Army) is not quite flexible enough to deal in a timely manner with changes like this. Our budget process has a two-year lag. However, my view is that we should look more to the untapped half of the market: the college-bound group or that group that goes to college and wants a break or hiatus, for two or three years. A recent national survey of high school seniors conducted by Col. Dennis Benchoff at the Army War College suggests that an educational offer of $26,400 could yield great benefit. The Congressional Budget Office estimates the additional cost of educational incentives at roughly $104 million per year through 1990. These are budget costs, but as with most educational subsidies, we know that society's net benefit is positive.

The final cost is a transitional one. If we could create a "steady state" force today, the costs we have cited are all that would be required. However, to get from where we are to where we want to be, we need to "pull through" almost all of the high-quality soldiers we have. Recall that, as Table 14.2 indicates, in the current fifth year of service, we have only 9,700 high-scoring soldiers. Historically, 44% of them would stay until the tenth year of service. To meet our goals in 1988, however, we have to retain 80% of the high-quality soldiers in their fifth year of service. The annual retention rate that compounds to 80% over five years is 96%. Figure 14.18 illustrates this logic and points to a temporary need for some large special reenlistment bonuses.

Virtually all retention models suggest that the high-quality youngsters respond more readily to bonuses. Economists say that their behavior is more "elastic." The structural pay increase would go a long way toward pulling them through. Bonuses in the neighborhood of $13,500 should be targeted specifically to the mental category I-IIIa high school graduates in the year of service five cohort over the next five years, with a total price tag of $104 million. The special bonus would be $13,500 for the first year and decline to zero at the end of five years as our quality-rich accession cohorts begin reaching five years of service.

We would like to give you some idea of our best estimate of what the army would recommend if the economy improves. The Congressional Budget Office's six year "high-growth" path looks like this (we have assumed structural factors would hold unemployment around 6% in 1990-1992.):

Figure 14.18. Growing Quality Cohorts

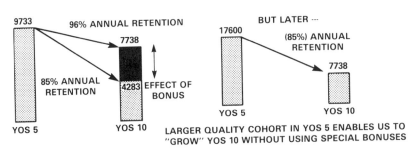

	1983	1984	1985	1986	1987	1988	1990	1992
Unemployment Rate	9.7	8.5	7.7	7.0	6.4	6.0	6.0	6.0

We used the high-growth path because the economy's recent performance indicates that we are on that path. As overall unemployment improves, youth unemployment should also improve. To the extent that unemployment affects recruiting, we may lose some high-quality potential entrants who will choose the civilian economy over military service. In the segmented labor market, we could overcome this shortfall in three ways: higher bonuses, a more generous Army College Fund, or a return to the GI Bill.

If we tried to overcome the entire shortfall with bonuses, we would request the following additional spending for each bonus recipient (each drop in unemployment causes a need for an additional bonus increment):

	1984	1985	1986	1987	1988	1990	1992
Additional Bonus ($)	2100	1600	1800	1800	1400	0	0
Cumulative Bonus ($)	2100	3700	5500	7300	8700	8700	8700
total Cost($millions)	75.6	133.2	198	262.2	313.2	313.2	313.2

The preceding data assume 36,000 bonus recipients which is roughly 10,000 more than the 26,000 who received bonuses in 1982 and 1983. On the other hand, we could attempt to overcome the entire shortfall with a more generous Army College Fund. Our offer would be much like the GI Bill plan proposed by Charles C. Moskos, Jr. but without his "two-tiered" pay system. The Moskos GI Bill gives $3,000 tuition assistance each year for four years and $300 per month living expenses. The total price tag of $26,400 is deferred for three to seven years. Costs also depend on the usage rates: 40% with the GI Bill and much lower with VEAP or ultra-VEAP. The Army War College study and ARI research mentioned previously suggest that high-quality youngsters are very interested in educational benefits. The modified Moskos proposal, according to the Congressional Budget Office, costs:

	1984	1985	1986	1987	1988	1990*	1992*
Total Costs ($ millions)	103.2	103.2	103.9	103.9	102.6	103.0	103.0

(*extrapolated)

If you gave me a choice of the three alternatives in an improving economy, I would reinstate the GI Bill. The GI Bill still has awesome symbolic value. I do not believe that there are any "economic" costs at all to a nation which rewards its youth for service to the country, and indeed there are great benefits. My second choice would be to increase the offer in the Army College Fund. For me, bonus increases rank last.

In summary, the focus of the All-Volunteer Force as it enters its second decade must lie in two primary areas:

1. Recruiting a high-quality force which will provide high-quality reenlistees in the outyears; and
2. Retaining as many high-quality soldiers as possible from the current force.

Both of these objectives will require resources not currently available. Army leaders must be ready to justify and defend short-term increases in resources in light of the long-term cost benefits which will result from our quest for an army of excellence. But in the final analysis, the success of the All-Volunteer Force in the second decade rests upon support from the spirit of the American people and the allocation of resources from their representatives. "Be all you can be."

15 The Reasons to Draft

JOHN G. KESTER

I was asked to provide some thoughts on conscription as an alternative to this country's ten-year-old All-Volunteer Force. Over those ten years the AVF has seen more ink spilled than blood, and I shall try not to add unduly to the verbal hemorrhage. But I do want to present a few reasons why I believe the draft would serve our country better.

You may or may not condemn as extreme the views of my two panel colleagues. We all recognize that how the country raises military manpower is an issue about which thoughtful people can differ. Indeed, this particular controversy has been characterized by more sincerity and reason on all sides than is sometimes the case in our public debate. Perhaps that is because all of us here have the detachment that comes from being too old to be drafted. In keeping with that spirit of candor, I shall try to give at least a tip of the hat in passing to some arguments for other viewpoints, though no doubt less convincingly than Max Thurman, Richard Danzig, and others whose attachment to competing views is warmer than is mine.

Although advocates of the draft are not politically aggressive at the moment, there is some reassurance for those of us who favor it when one looks at where the leading supporters of the AVF fit on the political spectrum. Anything that John Kenneth Galbraith and Milton Friedman agree upon can't be all good.

On this issue the customary party divisions do not provide an adequate road map. On one extreme are the libertarian conservatives like former Nixon advisors Dr. Martin Anderson and Dr. Milton Friedman, who look askance at governmental compulsion of any kind and believe that the economic market should determine virtually all public issues. Surprisingly, the other big bloc of AVF enthusiasts is way across on the other side, the left wing of the Democratic party, who tend to see good intentions as a substitute for military strength, the United States as a threat to world peace, military service as an employment program, and who in their egalitarianism are uncomfortable with suggestions that the services of one recruit might be more valuable than another's.[1] For many of them the AVF is the only instance in which they are willing to allow social policy to be set by the market.

For supporters, the draft has attracted conservatives like William F. Buckley, Jr.,[2] Dwight D. Eisenhower, who supported both "modern Republicanism" and universal military training,[3] and, of all people, Richard Nixon, who ended the draft but lately says he wishes it were back.[4] Among Democrats and others, conscription's advocates are traditionalists, southerners, neoconservatives, the American Legion, those who mistrust the Soviets, a few in the labor movement, and a good many office holders whose heart is in the right place but who find this an uncomfortable time to come out of the closet.[5]

I do not mean to suggest that the AVF has no support in the middle; indeed, it has always appealed to some pragmatists and still does, on the basis of short-term expediency. But it is the draft that finds its greatest appeal in the center, among the moderates of both parties. The AVF always has being the favorite of the extremes. Perhaps it is not surprising that it should dominate in a decade where bipartisanship in national security policy unfortunately has vanished, and the center often is difficult to find.

I had started to say that I shall try to define the case for conscription precisely and dispassionately, with no appeal except to numbers and icy logic. We might as well recognize that subjective considerations figure in here also, and that we are better off to try to articulate and evaluate them than to pretend they have no role. Since the issue of raising an army touches fundamental concerns about the reciprocal duties of man and the state, it is a controversial topic and is likely to remain so.[6]

It is reported that Earl Warren, when he was chief justice, used to peer down over the bench and ask counsel, "Yes, but is it fair?" That, of course, is not always the basis on which justices should interpret the law. However, it is exactly a basis, among others, on which major legislative decisions of public policy should be made. There are occasions when the public interest is not served simply by letting individuals act in free markets. It is on that criterion of fairness, as well as some others more directly affecting our defense and more quantifiable, that I believe the current system of recruiting for the armed forces is a public policy that has failed.

THE NATURE OF THE ISSUE

The central question usually asked concerning our present military manpower policy is, is the All-Volunteer Force working? And will it continue to do so?

That, it seems to me, is the wrong question. What works depends on what you are satisfied with. Military manpower policy is not an end in itself. It exists first to serve our foreign policy and our national security interests; and secondarily, it should as much as possible reflect the domestic consensus of what is desirable social policy. It is particularly difficult to agree on what constitutes success in a peacetime force, because a peacetime force doesn't fight. For example, not long ago virtually identical data were looked at by a Reagan administration task force and by the Atlantic Council's Working Group on Military Service headed by Gen. Andrew J. Goodpaster. The administration group concluded that the AVF was a near-perfect marvel;[7] the Atlantic Council found worrisome deficiencies and said that if things did not promptly improve, the draft should be resumed.[8]

To ask whether the present method of assigning citizens to the armed forces "works" implies that there are some hard, objective criteria which we can measure against. Some would assert that indeed there are such criteria, and that these call for simply a certain number of recruits of a certain level of military aptitude perhaps within a certain budgetary cost, though some AVF proponents will always say that the existence of any manning problem simply demonstrates that the AVF is being shortchanged and not enough pay is being offered to recruits. Probably with such measures of quality and quantity in mind, the secretary of defense asssured last year, for instance, that the volunteer force "is working extraordinarily well" and that this proves that "the ideas guiding the Gates Commission were sound."[9]

I would disagree—because I believe that the criteria to look at are vastly broader and more complex than that. I can imagine a volunteer force that meets today's accession requirements at the skill levels currently set, without breaking the budget, but nevertheless still does not "work." That, indeed, is what we are stuck with today. It does not "work" because first, we now tend to cut the customer to fit the cloth, and second, because how we raise armies is a central question, a gut issue, of what kind of country we are; by reasonable standards of political wisdom and social justice, the All-Volunteer Force falls flat on its face.

Its failings are in two clusters:

- **From the national security aspect**, the AVF tends endemically to be too small for our international commitments; its competence in good economic times tends not to be as great as this country can and should muster. Most importantly, it is inflexible and cannot mobilize in time of crisis.
- **From the standpoint of national policy**, it saps the sense of duty, and it is not fair.

There is no reason to apologize for measuring the AVF by such broader tests of policy because considerations of politics and policy are what caused it. Oliver Wendell Holmes, Jr., in an insight that was then revolutionary, announced a century ago that the life of the law has not been logic but experience.[10] The same applies to the volunteer force, which is not in place because a few people reasoned that it would raise the best armies at the lowest cost. The volunteer force is one more legacy of the Vietnam War. It was invented by politicians, rationalized by economists, and is today sustained by a shortsighted political leadership in both political parties which cares more about who wins an election two or four years from now than about whether we have elections twenty years from now.

When I first came to the Pentagon as a junior officer in 1965, it was understood that the selective service system then in operation was unfair because it was granting too many openended deferments and effectively exempting the children of the middle class. By 1970, after I joined the amry's manpower office, it had become clear that the draft was becoming politically impossible precisely because in the meantime it had been reformed, culminating in the abolition in 1970 of most deferments, and now like a runaway steamroller it was chasing the sons of businessmen, editors, college presidents, and even federal judges.[11]

That was when the All-Volunteer Force really began. If its intellectual father was indeed Martin Anderson, its out-of-wedlock grandfather was Burke Marshall, chairman of a presidential commission whose 1967 report on selective service set in motion the reform of selective service that made the draft, coupled with the Vietnam War, political poison.[12] Richard Nixon recognized this when in October 1968, with Hubert Humphrey moving up towards a photo finish, he announced that if elected he would end the draft.[13] Because in close elections every little bit matters, it may plausibly be argued that by that stroke as much as any other Nixon won the 1968 election. The continued appeal to the left of ending conscription was later confirmed when Jimmy Carter embraced the same policy, even as accessions dropped and standards for recruitment plummeted.

By my reading of the AVF's history, the role of Nixon, responding to pressures of election and the Vietnam War, was all-important; that of the 1970 Gates Commission was really not significant at all. We should recall that President Nixon never asked the members of the Gates Commission whether the All-Volunteer Force was a good idea. Their charter, he directed, was "to develop a comprehensive plan for eliminating conscription."[14] The commissioners, dominated by Dr. Milton Friedman, went about that task with optimism and enthusiasm, and volunteered their own endorsement of the new policy. With all respect to some able people who worked on its staff, the Gates Commission turned in, dressed in the language of economics, one of the most fanciful public documents of our time.

All that, you may say, is just politics, not manpower analysis, to which I would reply: exactly. The deepest issues of the All-Volunteer Force remain political, by which I mean the kinds of issues that are debated and resolved in our political system. I have been struck by how much of the writing on this subject, much of it very good, has been by economists. A paradox of our time is that economists have had a larger role in sustaining our current military manpower program than they ever have been allowed in writing or administering our tax laws. Seldom have they been able to relish so fascinating an experiment in applied economic theory.

I have great respect for economists. I believe that our country could profit from more, not less, economic analysis in its decision making. The marketplace operates with a good deal of reason underlying it, albeit short-term reason, and when government wants to interfere with the free market, probably it has an obligation to explain why.

Nevertheless, economists would, I hope, concede that like anyone else's, their peculiar insight is imperfect and limited. One limitation is that the world is too complicated to embrace within any economical model. Another is that data are ambiguous and imperfect and that any computations, however sophisticated and elegant, are no better than the assumptions on which they rest, or, as the irreverent computer people say, "garbage in, garbage out." Finally, there is a tendency for some economists to ignore, even to sneer at, behavior patterns, policy preferences, and external influences that cannot be measured in economic models. To forget such limitations can lead to bad public policy. One example, perhaps, is Pentagon program analysis for the Vietnam War, which proved quantitatively month after month that we were always winning (and indeed, by some criteria, we were). Economic analysis probably could prove that this country would be better off if we contracted to have our naval ships and major defense weapons manufactured in Korea, Taiwan, and Japan. What makes sense in narrow economic terms sometimes is not consistent with overall national security.

Economics is a spin-off from what two hundred years ago was called "political economy," an activity of armchair theorists that no doubt was insufficiently quantitative. Sometimes nonquantifiable considerations, such as fairness, are among the most important. While free markets may produce the best short-term economic results, there is no reason to expect them to produce the best results when noneconomic factors are valued, nor should anyone claim they necessarily do. Economists are good at forcing politicians to acknowledge exactly what they are doing. Economists offer a unique insight that identifies the economic cost of social and political choices. They cannot tell which social and political choices are wisest.[15]

Raising armies is one of the half-dozen issues of public policy that not only affects our security in the world, but also determines who we are as a country. It should be approached not just as a problem of economics, however illuminating economic analysis may be, but also as a dilemma requiring the insights of history, political science, military science, sociology, psychology, law, and, yes, political and moral philosophy. Just as war is too important a matter to be left to generals, so military manpower issues are too far-ranging to be treated as the technical domain of econometricians. The issue is one not just of price, but of principle.

So the AVF is celebrating, if that be the word, its fifteenth, not its tenth, anniversary. It was conceived in a political campaign, politics was its midwife, and it exists today not because it is the right way to raise military manpower, but only because of a political consensus that can, and I believe ought to, change.

Why should it change? The proposition in simplest terms is this: The United States cannot indefinitely maintain its position in a very perilous world as a country which cannot mobilize manpower quickly in a major nonnuclear military crisis and in which, with respect to the danger and inconvenience of military service, the middle class does not pay its dues. The AVF has a great deal else wrong with it too, but those inherent failings are uppermost.

The balance of this chapter reviews, first, some of the shortcomings of the All-Volunteer Force; second, some advantages of conscription; and third, some disadvantages of conscription, because there certainly are some. It concludes with a few slams at the "national service" idea, the only proposal I have heard of for raising armies that is worse than the AVF, and unconstitutional besides.

PROBLEMS WITH THE AVF

I start with the proposition that there are no perfect solutions to questions of social policy or of national security policy, for that matter. What is involved are trade-offs; we have to give up some of X to get more of Y and less of Z. With some straining we may be able to agree on the same basic facts, though even that often is not easy. The amount of one good we ought to sacrifice in return for more of another is usually a matter of perference and judgment. Sometimes that judgment alters with experience because, except for the human condition itself, most problems are the result of earlier solutions. "To govern," as the French are fond of saying, "is to choose."[16]

The question that AVF proponents must answer is why, in a matter this important, should social policy be set by economics? Why should this country's military posture depend so heavily on a marketplace shaped by the transitory collective calculations of teenagers about their own short-term economic interests? If AVF proponents do not assert that raw economics should set the policy, then they must persuade that the AVF method is at least as fair as the alternatives.

The volunteer force may be "working" to the satisfaction of some, but certainly it is not yielding the results its proponents in 1970 claimed it would, and the differences are important. Yet, paradoxically, it is working exactly as any dispassionate economist (or psychologist, for that matter) would have predicted. Economists teach that increased economic incentives attract more supply at the margin. Not surprisingly, the AVF has purchased for the enlisted force the economically marginal man.

History records that it was not until January 9, 1970, eight months after the Gates Commission first met and only a month before its printed report went on sale, that the commission took time to hear from the then secretary of the army. It was not a comfortable session. He urged caution, pointing out that assumptions of supply elasticity were guesswork, and that "the elasticity for combat and non-combat positions within the Army will surely be different." He worried that the cost of higher pay would eat into the military budget, reducing overall capability. He argued that "while we can run the Army with a mix of people, we cannot have a force in which all are of a level just sufficient to meet the enlistment standard." He predicted problems in manning the reserves. He warned that "a volunteer Army will be to some extent an Army of the poor. . . .Yet perhaps some unpleasant tasks in society should be borne by all, or at least by a fair share from all economic groups." He reminded that the issue "involves both cost estimates and value judgments as to the ordering of priorities for our Government and our society."[17] Over dinner he was debated heatedly by Milton Friedman and the commission's executive director, William H. Meckling. The other commissioners had little to say.

The Gates Commission did make several important predictions, and it was wrong about every one of them. It assured that "the mental, physical, and moral standards for enlistment will ensure that neither [AVF] force recruits an undue proportion from minority groups or the poor."[18] Yet that is exactly what has happened. The AVF created an enlisted army* of the economically disadvantaged, with large numbers of blacks and of very poor whites. In order to fill the ranks, the army, until about three years ago, was enlisting practically anyone it could get (many of whom are now reenlisting). The composition has broadened a bit recently because of educational incentives. The phenomenon is not tied to race; for several years white recruits have come in with educational credentials on average below those of the blacks, heretofore regarded as the most disadvantaged. These are, as Charles C. Moskos, Jr. has pointed out, most often whites from a sociologically identifiable backwater not connected with the mainstream of American society.[19]

The Gates Commission confidently predicted that "the racial composition of the armed forces cannot be fundamentally changed by ending the draft." It said that if the AVF were enacted, blacks on active duty would not exceed 14.9%, 18.8% for the army, and that "even extreme assumptions would not change the figures drastically."[20] The figure as of March 1983 was 19.6% for the Department of Defense, 27.1% counting all minorities. The army had 29.1% blacks, comprising 32.8% of the enlisted force, plus an additional 8% other minorities.

The commission predicted that the added budget cost (after credit for income taxes paid) for recruiting volunteers for a force at the $2.5 million level would be only $2.1 billion annually for 1971 dollars. For a force of 2,000,000, the increment would be only $1.5 billion.[21] Manpower costs as a portion of the defense budget undeniably have risen; exactly how much of that rise can legitimately be blamed on the AVF is a topic for endless controversy. There is no budget line-item called "AVF." But to recruit and pay volunteers for today's force of 2.1 million, the incremental cost, even after discounting inflation, probably is several times what the Gates Commission predicted. And clearly for a force increased to 2.5 million, the added pay necessary to attract those extra nearly half-million volunteers would be astronomical. In short, the commission's cost predictions were wrong.

The commission also assumed that an effective standby draft system would be in place, which it is not.[22] The commission did not even attempt to predict how long it would take to produce the first soldiers through such a system in an emergency. It did not explain how any system not operating on a day-to-day basis could be brought out of mothballs and at once start efficiently drafting America's youth.

The commission believed that "using the most conservative evaluation,"[23] there would be no difficulty filling the reserve components. In the event, the reserves have become a disaster area.

These are not minor flaws of analysis. These are central errors on issues that go to the heart of knowing what to expect if conscription were abolished. They stand, incidentally, in sharp contrast with the conclusions of the Marshall Commission Report three years earlier (in which member Thomas S. Gates concurred) that "an exclusively voluntary system would be expensive;" that it "could easily, it is feared, become a mercenary force unrepresentative of the nation;" that it "would preclude the ability to meet changing demands;" and most importantly that without selective service, it "would permit no flexibility for crisis."[24] Every one of those predictions has proved correct.

In detail, the deficiencies of the AVF are these:

---

*References here will often single out the army; it historically has been the service with the greatest recruiting problem, and historically and predictably, a draft means a draft for the army. Statistics compiled DoD-wide mask the AVF's real problems, which are mostly in the army. When the DoD statistics register a sneeze, the army generally has pneumonia.

Fighting War. It is perplexing to try to understand how we adopted a system to man our armed forces which even its proponents admit will do us no good if we get into any serious conflict. Inflexibility, the inability to mobilize, is from the national security planner's view the cardinal failing of the volunteer force. The AVF is not a reliable source of added manpower in any kind of pinch; as the chairman of the Joint Chiefs of Staff, General John W. Vessey, Jr., concedes, "In time of war, we know we will need compulsory military service."[25] The army's Chief of Staff, General John A. Wickham, Jr., acknowledges the same thing.[26] Nor can the AVF even come up easily with more volunteers if planners decide on small increases in force structure. The response of AVF advocates for ten years has been, "Not to worry—we'll use the reserves and then in a few months Selective Service will be in place."

But how? Does anyone really believe that with the halfhearted and unenforced registration system we have today, with registrants not even classified, without the machinery of ongoing local draft boards, we could induct and train troops quickly enough to make a difference in a major conflict? Current plans pretend that the Selective Service and examining machinery will spring into being and produce 100,000 recruits in thirty days.[27] Even in World War II, with the induction system already in place and operating, it took seven months to get the first draftees on the field. No doubt other components besides manpower would be difficult to mobilize quickly as well. But, for a war in Europe, current plans say we need substantial reinforcements from the draft or the reserves sixty days after attack. And does anyone really think it would be a simple matter to call up the reserves, something that has scarcely ever been done in our history?

Nobody, not even economists, expects that money will attract many recruits to enlist when they are confident that if they do, in a few weeks they will be shot at. Most teenagers, being rational and selfish economic men, will decide that that is an ideal time to stay home. Does it really make sense to have adopted a system that performs inversely to how badly it is needed? Can we continue forever to pretend that a workable selective service system can be put into place in a time of national stress and confusion, within a matter of days?

The absence of any quick-expansion capability suggests that, at the very least, a volunteer force should be somewhat larger in peacetime than a force sustained by selective service. Yet the opposite is the case. The volunteer force is smaller, and so has less margin of safety, than the pre-Vietnam draft-era armed forces it replaced. And Soviet military capability is greater now than it was in 1970, while the Soviet's willingness to use or threaten to use military force, directly or through proxies, has grown also.

The ability to mobilize, of course, is less important if one assumes that we never really will have to mobilize and that there will be no more Koreas (even in Korea), no substantial forces ever tied down in the Middle East or Central America, and that any superpower conflict will quickly escalate to a nuclear spasm, anyway. Such thinking may turn out to be correct. Correct or not, it certainly is a congenial rationalization for dismissing some failures of the volunteer force. But if such assumptions are accepted as the basis for planning forces, then by limiting flexibility and options, they tend also to become self-fulfilling. Paradoxically, this country's strategic planning hopes against hope that even nuclear systems can be fitted to a doctrine that would provide options short of universal conflagration. Constraints imposed, even self-imposed, on the ability to mobilize manpower tend over time to become unquestioned and to work their way as axioms into strategic doctrine. Thus through manpower policy can the country's options to protect its legitimate interests and defend itself become narrowed, and the world consequently more dangerous.

One's attitude towards mobilization risks is likely to be different, depending on whether one views the military manpower needs of the country as uniquely important or as just another governmental program. The draft historically is associated with national peril. As one draft advocate put it, "those who oppose the draft, at bottom, simply refuse to believe that we are in danger."[28]

Deterring War. Most would agree that the single most important mission of our armed forces is to deter nuclear war. Also essential is that they be able effectively to protect this country's interests with military force when ordered to do so. This implies conventional forces of a generous size and capability. It also recognizes that usually the Soviets respect only countervailing military strength. To the extent that obtaining military personnel through a volunteer system limits the quantity or quality of the armed forces, and thereby diminishes the military strength of this country. it is not good.

Certainly it is true that no one can prove exactly how large our armed forces need to be;[29] most attempts to derive such a number are discouraging, because they conclude that the forces we have are far too small already for the missions assigned and the contingencies envisioned. Most informed observers consider that the active-duty strength of the armed forces could not prudently get much lower without significantly diminishing U.S. security. Yet the tendency of volunteer mercenary forces is to shrink, reflecting cost and recruiting difficulties (see Table 15.1).

The armed forces as a whole are about 25% smaller today than they were before the abandonment of the draft (excluding the Vietnam years). Periodic suggestions by the services that they could use more men to meet the country's commitments are routinely brushed aside; although the current administration deserves credit for a small increase, no one really expects much movement on the upside any more.[30]

Expansion is expensive. The Gates Commission assumed, with no evidence, that the elasticity of supply of enlisted men was approximately constant over a wide range of sizes of peacetime armies. In other words, if it took additional pay of $1 more to enlist the fiftieth recruit, it would take additional pay of only $1 to add to the 150,000th as well. But, experience and even economics suggest that the increase in incentives has to go up steeply as the amount of increasingly reluctant people, with more competing job offers and less military inclination, are recruited. That drives the cost of larger forces up exponentially—not to speak of the waste involved in paying, as we do, the eager first recruit the same amount as the reluctant 150,000th.

The size of the armed forces has dwindled below what was considered the minimum prudent level ten years ago and looks likely to go even smaller (partly because of the high cost of manpower even at current pay rates, partly because of competition for funds to pay for expensive new weapons and equipment). In 1970, when I worked in the Department of the Army, 800,000 to 850,000 was considered the lowest prudent post-Vietnam size. The active army today is about 780,000, the smallest in thirty-three years,[31] and probably headed down. Some may argue that manpower now is used somewhat more efficiently and that soldiers now have more capable weapons. That may be so to a limited extent, but in part increased efficiency is simply wishful thinking, and adversaries have better weapons, too. Great gains in productivity to come from more efficient use of military manpower are at best speculative. The basic fact remains that a smaller army is a smaller army.

Table 15.1. Size of Army and Department of Defense Active Duty Military Personnel (FY end strength in thousands)

	Army	DoD
1964	972	2,687
1968	1,570	3,547
1974	782	2,161
1984	783	2,165

This is at a time when our country's commitments around the world have, if anything, increased.[32] This is at a time when, if we are cautious, we will be very careful to maintain adequate and ready conventional forces to reduce the likelihood of confrontations at the nuclear level. The Congress debates increasing defense expenditures annually by 3% or 5% or 7%, yet no substantial increases in force numbers are contemplated. Each successively smaller force level is duly rationalized. But in reality our forces are sized in part to acknowledge the enormous cost of manpower expansion and to fit where the supply and demand curves meet.

If the forces shrink some more, do not expect an announcement from the Pentagon that because of high first-term pay, we simply can't afford all the recruits we need. More likely there will be press releases praising new achievements in leanness, efficiency, and professionalism, and also noting that it is time for our allies to do more. There may be some more of the customary flim-flam that active units are not really being cut, they are just being moved into the reserves where pieces of eight (and soon to be more)[33] out of the sixteen active army divisions, plus much of the support the active army needs to fight, now theoretically reside. Economists will note with satisfaction that military labor is being priced at its true cost, and that it is up to the taxpayers to decide whether to spend more. Military planners will be less detached.

As for the reserves, even most supporters of the volunteer force concede that even by economists' measures, not to mention military planners', it has not worked. The draft always was the spur for the reserves. Our current military planning imagines that the reserves, which now are supposed to supply most of the army's logistical backup, are more likely to be used than ever. But they are difficult to fill (though lately units are at strength), their level of training is poor, and their mix of critical skills is out of balance.[34] The number of individual fillers, who would be crucial in mobilization, has dwindled in quantity, and probably in quality and training as well (some are persons discharged from the active army for unsatisfactory performance), far below what used to be considered the bare minimum[35] (see Table 5.12). A volunteer force, over time, is a shrinking force. Its insigne might well be, not the helmet of Mars, but the bed of Procrustes.

Quality. Discussions of the AVF seldom say much about war or fighting. Yet the first purpose of military manpower procurement, of course, is to raise armed forces that can carry out the military orders of the duly constituted political leadership. Creating and maintaining such forces require recruits with qualities that permit them to be disciplined, motivated, and trained to perform necessary military functions proficiently.

A good deal of comment appeared in the press in the late 1970s (less since the recession hit) about low intelligence and about discipline problems among enlisted personnel. Such reports were duly denied by various official pronouncements.[36] Our army's recent habit (lately improved) of placing last in NATO tank gunnery competitions, for instance, raised the question

Table 15.2. Size of Army Reserve Components
FY End Strength (In Thousands)

Army Selected Reserve	
1964	651
1974	621
1984	694
Army Individual Ready Reserve	
1964	461
1973	759
1978	177
1984	225

whether it really makes sense to entrust a $2.6 million tank to an enlisted man who cannot do simple arithmetic and is deficient in reading. The word-of-mouth data are mixed, but these propositions merit consideration:

1. The average level of intelligence of enlisted recruits dropped for several years to less than it was in the last peacetime draft years; for a while it was markedly so. Perhaps just as important, as William K. Brehm has pointed out, the curve even today is flatter, so the number of soldiers with education and intelligence much above average is smaller. For example, the portion of the enlisted force with some college experience has dropped from nearly 30% (in an era of college deferments) to near zero[37] (see Table 15.3).

2. Intelligence is a useful attribute both for running an army and for fighting. What evidence we have suggests that recruits with higher aptitudes do a better job, and we should not be embarrassed to say so.[38] The introduction of more sophisticated weapons, though some are simpler to operate, does not lessen the need to be able to perform better than the enemy. (At the same time, if AVF recruits serve longer terms, then turnover is reduced and unit cohesion perhaps is increased.) In hardware, this country is betting that weapons of more clever design can permit us to deter the Soviets with smaller numbers. Does not the same reasoning apply in manpower, where, because our forces are much smaller, they perhaps must themselves be more clever to survive?

3. The AVF has caused the armed forces to reexamine, and then usually lower, their qualifications for many skills. This has not been an entirely good thing. It lowers average competency. The lower the average capability of a squad, the more risk for all, particularly if key members become casualties. Easy standards also tend to work against notions of competition and excellence, of winners and losers, yet aggressive competition is at the heart of the military ethic and function. True, a military organization can lower its standards and still put up a fight of some sort. But war is not a sporting contest. Hitler had the *Volkssturm* in 1945, composed of old men and boys, and infantry battalions of *Luftwaffe* ground crews who had no planes. Some of these fought bravely, but most without much effect.

Table 15.3. Active Army Enlisted Nonprior-Service Recruit Quality Distribution as Measured by Mental Groupings and Educational Level (Fiscal Year Percentages)[1]

| | Pre-War Draft | | War Peak | Post-War Draft | | PMVF | | | | | | | |
	(1960) 60	(1964) 64	(1969) 69	(1972) 72	73[2]	74	75	76	77	78	79	80	81
Mental Categories													
I & II (highest)	32	34	35	33	32	31	35	31	21	21	17	14	24
IIIA (just above avg.)	20	22	18	23	24	21	23	22	15	16	13	12	16
Subtotal (above avg.)	52	56	53	56	56	52	58	53	36	37	30	26	40
IIIB (just below avg.)	31	25	20	26	27	30	31	36	24	23	24	22	29
IV (lowest accepted)	17	19	27	18	17	18	10	11	41	39	46	52	31
Educational Attainment													
College Degree	5	5	6	4	3	1	2	2	1	2	1	1	1
Some College	26	15	19	11	11	4	5	3	5	4	3	2	3
High-School Diploma	36	50	45	46	48	45	51	54	53	68	60	51	76
Subtotal (At least HSDG)	67	70	70	61	62	50	58	59	59	74	64	54	80
Nongraduate	33	30	30	39	38	50	42	41	41	26	36	46	20
Total NPS Accessions (000)	185	268	455	187	215	182	185	180	168	124	129	158	118
At least High-School Diploma Accessions (000)	124	187	319	114	133	91	107	106	100	91	83	86	95

Source: William K. Brehm, "Peacetime Voluntary Options," in Andrew J. Goodpaster et al., *Toward a Consensus on Military Service* (Elmsford: Pergamon Press, 1982), p. 170.

[1]Numbers may not add to 100 percent due to rounding. U.S. Army data, current as of December, 1981.
[2]Year of transition to the Peacetime Military Volunteer Force.

4. The need for more members able to maintain and repair sophisticated military equipment will increase sharply in the next decade, and may be even more critical than the need for trained operators.[39]

5. The competence of our military forces in peacetime can decline substantially without anyone noticing, or being sure.[40]

Because this is a tenth anniversary, we ought to be looking at performance at least over those ten years and not just at the current moment. The AVF has had a tendency (so that skill categories could be filled) to lower skill requirements and standards unless someone could somehow "prove" that higher standards were necessary. The disastrous period was in the late 1970s, when an unfavorable recruiting environment existed, combined with unwillingness on the part of some political leaders to recognize that recruits vary in military aptitude, and that it matters. The focus even afterwards has tended to shift from finding the best recruits for a job, to filling jobs with those who meet only minimum standards.

One result has been to reduce flexibility, and probably combat effectiveness. If war is characterized by anything, it is by everything going wrong, by plans falling apart, by fear and confusion and improvisation. A retired general who could speak of combat first-hand once pointed out to me that the soldier who with maximum effort may become minimally competent as, say, a loader, may be unable to cope on the battlefield if the man beside him is killed and he has to aim or fire the gun himself, or even take over a leadership position. Yet that kind of flexibility, as much as learning one's programmed job, is what survival or victory may depend on. Winners tend to be those who can adapt quickly to the unexpected. Moreover, while a unit may fight competently with a few slow thinkers in the group, it is less likely to do so if they all are that way.[41] Recently a study was published trying to determine why in World War II the German Army, man for man, fought half again as effectively as the American.[42] One datum is that every German soldier was expected not just to know his own job, but to be able quickly to step into another.[43]

Part of the difficulty on this point, I think, is that military commanders and systems analysts analyze conflict completely differently from each other. The systems analyst, tending, like the economist, to focus at the margin, looks for the minimum input that will give the desired edge. The commander, by contrast, looks for decisive, overwhelming force, knowing that the most desirable victories are not evenly matched battles that rage back and forth for days and days, but rather those where one side is so superior that the other simply surrenders or is quickly overcome. The successful securing of Grenada illustrates the point. The military leader expects large errors in plans and calculations, and he would rather have too much force available than too little. In the manpower area, he is likely to conclude that the United States is safer with a *very* good army than with a *pretty* good army.

There was a good deal of handwringing four or five years ago about the intelligence and military aptitude of enlisted recruits, particularily in the army. In 1979 the army not only failed to meet its recruiting objectives, but 42% of its recruits were in the lowest enlisted mental category, and 50% of recruits had never finished high school.[44] The army's current problem is that the same groups, if they manage to get through training (the attrition rate is very high, about 30%, 40% in the combat arms, compared to 10% in the years of the peacetime draft), tend to want to stay. Half of army reenlistees in FY1982 were in the lowest acceptable mental group.

The army's difficulty has eased off now and the credentials of its 1983 recruits are very good; the services, temporarily at least, are enlisting more high school graduates (an indicator not so much of intelligence as of diligence and obedience, which also are important), and the newspapers now carry reports by senior officers that things have never been better. The army lately has pursued an intelligent and productive policy of using bonsuses and college education incentives, rather than pure pay, to attract recruits of higher aptitude and motivation, and it has quietly put limits on how many lower-mental-category persons it will enlist.[45] So far, things are going much better than four years ago. The army chief of staff says that current soldiers are the best ever and the draft isn't necessary.[46]

But what will happen as the country pulls out of the current serious economic recession and as the number of available eighteen-year-olds drops in the next ten years by 22%?[47] (Army accession requirements are projected to be less, also, because of high reenlistments, but the Office of the Secretary of Defense has predicted that manpower requirements will increase).[48]

To judge whether the army's improvement is permanent, we can ask, how has the army been able to do this? Partly by better management, but mainly by the combination of three factors, only one of which the army can control even partially. The first has been the worst economic recession since the 1930s. The second has been congressional support: a major pay raise two years ago, and for the army, special pay incentives (combat arms bonuses and the army's college scholarship program) that for the first time have given the army a competitive advantage. Finally, by congressional mandate, enacted over Department of Defense resistance,[49] the army raised its standards by applying test-score and education quotas. The army also, in the past two years, has consciously targeted its recruiting efforts on middle-class neighborhoods rather than inner cities and Appalachia.

What the army's recent experience perhaps shows is that in a sick economy, with sufficient resources and nonneutral management, it is possible to obtain sufficient recruits of acceptable quality.[50] But what happens if the current conditions change? The economy has improved. The Congress is whimsical and inconstant in its support of defense; steady pay raises, and certainly special incentives for army enlistees, cannot be counted on year after year. And the army itself ought not to expect that politicians always will give it a free hand to target its recruitment efforts or set its own enlistment standards; the Office of the Secretary of Defense has resisted even these efforts, and it is likely that the attitude of political leadership will fluctutate over time, especially when, inevitably, lowering quality is recognized as a handy substitute for raising pay. If the proponents of the AVF expect that the politicians will always give it whatever financial support it needs, they expect to enjoy more support than any other group in society ever has consistently received.

AVF supporters may argue that it was not given a fair chance in the 1970s because of low pay, and that all it needs is constant pay raises. In effect, they seem to be saying that the AVF almost by definition can never fail of itself; if it cannot attract enough of the right recruits, the problem always will be lack of political support and underfunding (which some may even darkly call sabotage).[51] But experience as well as academic analysis[52] confirm that the Congress will always tend to underfund the military, including military pay, because of the relative ineffectiveness of defense concerns (and others which relate to general rather than particular interests) in our political system. Of course it is healthy up to a point, and often beneficial in personnel planning, that the services cannot treat recruits as totally free goods. But anyone who has worked within range of the secretary of defense's manpower office knows that over the years, in both Republican and Democratic administrations, it has been particularly concerned to fill the recruiting quotas; and that office, often over the objections of the services, has pushed to lower enlistment standards, to lower skill qualifications, and also to lower the number of recruits who are discharged for failure to perform. Whether such a permanent policy is usually a good thing or a bad one (I would say it is bad), there is not much doubt that it is a bureaucratic reality brought on by the volunteer force, and it will be felt again as the external recruiting climate changes.[53]

Social and Racial Distortion. The AVF is not remotely representative of the United States. Even less so is the army. Even less than that are the combat units of the army (see Table 15.4).

Black accessions in FY1983 were about 23% of army recruits without prior service (21% of males, 28% of females). The reenlistment rate for blacks is about 150% that for whites, so that

Table 15.4. Minorities as Percentage of Army Enlisted Force
(August 1983)

	Blacks	All Racial Minorities
1964	10.9	—
1974	19.0	—
1983	31.5	39.7
By Grade		
E-1	24.4	30.8
E-2	26.4	30.8
E-3	29.3	37.0
E-4	38.1	47.0
E-5	38.8	47.9
E-6	29.1	37.0
E-7	23.9	30.3
E-8	28.6	34.7
E-9	24.7	31.0

currently half of first-termers who reenlist are black, leading towards a far disproportionately black NCO corps. Although blacks are only about 13% of the U.S. population, they are 23% of army recruits, and 32% of the current army enlisted force; the figure the Gates Commission assumed would never exceed 18.8%. Current data also mask the growing share in the enlisted force of nonblack minorities, some number of whom do not communicate well in English. The figures on Hispanic soldiers are not accurate or readily available, but it is clear that nonblack minorities now form at least 8% of the army enlisted force. This means that over 40% of that force now are members of minorities.

A recent comment on racial composition by an administration task force is that it "does not look on this as a problem" and that "the fact that many blacks volunteer is a tribute to their patriotism."[54] (It is odd to have motivations in this particular instance officially explained as patriotic when the volunteer work force works on an incentive system that is avowedly economic).

It is quite beside the point to observe that the armed forces have provided more opportunity to minority group members than does much of civilian society. That is commendable, but for society to have its dirtiest fighting done by some of its least privileged members is not. It is also beside the point to recognize the loyalty of black soldiers and say they would always fight as ordered, even in Africa or Detroit; no one has any reason to doubt it for the forseeable future, though perhaps if mercenary forces developed ethnic or regional qualities over decades, that might ultimately affect deployability. What cannot be gainsaid about the current army, even if every enlisted man were as disadvantaged but tough a tiger as Sergeant York (who, we might remember, was a draftee), is that it is an army of the poor—white and black and Hispanic—paid to defend the comfortable, mostly white.

Must the army be an exact mirror of society? Of course not. Nor would it be exactly a mirror under the draft, for the nondrafted volunteer portion of accessions still would come disproportionately from the less advantaged. The question however is, should we effectively allow major social and economic groups to exclude themselves from military service, and how much distortion can we bear? There is no doubt that the problem is caused by the AVF. The representativeness of today's army is nothing like that of 1964, the last prewar draft year. The AVF is an official ratification of the reluctance of many citizens to do their part. And the reasons this country has adopted that policy is that the political leadership of both parties is timid and fears that the middle class, which still calls the shots in this country, likes things as they are.

However accurate that perception, one of the duties of leaders, as Churchill showed, is not just to ratify current public opinion, but to shape it and to lead.

Constraint and Deployability. As a corollary of the AVF's nonrepresentative composition, every president now must be aware that if he deploys U. S. troops to combat, the first casualties will be outrageously, disproportionately black. If our Second Infantry Division in North Korea has to fight, its casualties will come from a troop strength 41.1% black with another 5.9% other minorities. If the First Cavalry deploys to Europe, its casualties will be from a unit 38.2% black. If the Eighty-second Airborne, which is part of our Rapid Deployment Force, goes to fight, 26% of the body bags coming back will have black corpses inside them, 7.8% other minorities. The army's 197th Infantry Brigade, another rapid deployment unit, is 51.8% black.[55] Worse, the replacements going into the line would similarly be far more disproportionately black. The army is indeed a great vehicle for equal opportunity; but that is equal opportunity with a vengeance.

Even during Vietnam, rumor quickly exaggerated the far smaller black imbalance in early casualties from the army's volunteer units (an imbalance which disappeared as the draft took over).[56] Some may argue that it is good to have our public officials constrained by fears of political outcry, so that they will use troops only *in extremis*; the answer to that is that we have invented a curious political system indeed, if constraints on presidential decision making are planned to come not from constitutional processes, but through the back door from racial imbalances in military manpower.

Fairness. Quite apart from the effect on minorities, there is a basic question of social fairness which the AVF simply assumes away. The issue is whether service in the armed forces (which no doubt is a positive experience for many people, but which also represents inconvenience and an enhanced risk of sudden death) should be distributed among citizens purely on economic incentives. In other words, should people be forced into the army by a lottery or because they need the money? How is the volunteer force different analytically from the Civil War draft's option of paying $300 to buy a substitute? Conscription may appear existentially unfair on an individual basis; but the AVF effectively is class-based discrimination.

Economists of Dr. Friedman's persuasion finesse this issue first by defining coercion so that it does not include economic coercion. "Economic coercion" to them would indeed, I suppose, be an oxymoron; when someone enters the army because there are not better economic alternatives, the economist calls this a "volunteer" because, to borrow the title of Milton and Rose Friedman's often valuable book, he was "Free to Choose."[57] Secondly, an economist might argue, it is unfortunate that some people have opportunities so limited that they want to enlist, but their situation is not improved by filling spaces in the army with other people who do not even want to be there. Yet for reasons like those underlying child labor laws, or the recent outrage about a company inviting volunteers to sell their kidneys, there are some limits society chooses to put on people's bargaining away their lives. There simply has to be some sharing of risk in a just community. It is not enough to have a system like that derided a century ago by Anatole France, who observed that the law in its even-handed majesty forbids rich and poor alike to steal, to beg bread, and to sleep under bridges.[58]

Community. It is a bit ironic that at a time when many are complaining that the armed forces have become too "managerial," to the neglect of old-fashioned leadership, we persist in a recruitment system whose message very distinctly is that wearing the uniform is just another job. Charles C. Moskos, Jr. again has been one of the first to identify the phenomenon.[59] The volunteer force, for instance, proceeds on the economist's assumption that payments in cash are worth more than payments in kind. (Payments in cash also have the virtue of being much easier for economists to measure and analyze.) Yet there is every reason to believe that service personnel value housing, PXs, commissaries, medical care and the sense of belonging and privilege that these entail, far in excess of what the economists say they cost. The army's recent education incentives are a notable and successful bucking of the trend. Paternalism is a legitimate part of military life, as is a sense of community.

Nevertheless, the pressure of the AVF managers persistently has been to reduce fringe benefits and increase cash. The country's method of recruitment ought to recognize that military service is something qualitatively different from any other calling, just as marriage has never been treated as an ordinary contract. Military manpower procurement is not just a special case of labor relations. Military service not only involves at times high danger; it is the only job around where the boss may order an employee to sacrifice his own life, and the employee has to go do it. The question is not just who serves, but who dies. Also unlike other occupations, military service is directly essential to preserving the state and society which is, essentially, everybody else. The volunteer force tends to imply that all at stake is dollars, and that a difference in kind does not exist.

Total reliance on pay also has had some other undesirable side effects. Enlisted men formerly were distinctly underpaid; now, however, first-termers probably are paid too much. It's not that they walk from the paymaster's table to a crap game, it's that they go out and acquire wives and babies who tend to follow them around. Of army first-termers, 31% are married. Partly it is the money, and partly the social background of our atypical army. Since the end of the draft, the number of married E-4s has climbed, and now is 44%.[60] As applied to an E-2 private soldier or an E-4, there was some sense to the sergeant's old growl that "If the Army wanted you to have a wife, they would have issued you one." Family life may have stabilizing qualities, but when one considers personnel management, it may not be appropriate for the first-term recruit. Camp followers are a headache for commanders and a very real mobilization and readiness problem.[61] The volunteer force makes it worse (see Table 15.5).

Even as a matter of pure economics, perhaps first-term pay should be lower. Politically mandated minimum wages and union bargaining power have raised the cost of unskilled or semi-skilled labor far above its true market value.[62] Many teenagers consequently are unemployed. Why should eighteen-year-olds not be paid something closer to what their services are really worth? It might also be inquired why, if we do not plan to pay soldiers at market rates in the event of war (when we know the market price would go sky high), we nevertheless would feel compelled to do so in peacetime, when the differential is much less.

Table 15.5. Percentage Married in the Army, 1983

	Married to Military Spouse	Married to Civilian Spouse	Total Married
Male E-4s	3.0	40.6	43.6
Female E-4s	26.5	16.9	43.4

Enlisted Married by Grade:
(June 1983)

E-1	14
E-2	18
E-3	24
E-4	44
E-5	76
E-6	86
E-7	90
E-8	92
E-9	94

Cost. The volunteer force is expensive and contributed to the secular tendency of the services to try to get along with fewer and fewer men. However, one must concede that a volunteer force costs more than a drafted one only to the extent that in the drafted one, draftees are paid less than their market value. Also, if tours of duty are shorter in a conscripted force, added training costs will drive up total costs as well and perhaps will be offset by lower attrition.

I would not argue that cost is the principal failing of the volunteer force; reduced capability when recruiting goes sour, inability to mobilize, and social unfairness are. If one assumes that recruits are paid at the marginal market rate, then a conscript force at any particular size could even cost more. However, as noted, recruits perhaps should be paid less than it takes to induce them to volunteer for a 2,100,000-member force. And cost really begins to bind, however, if one contemplates what it would take to buy volunteers for a force of 2,500,000.

The Gates Commission predicted that an active-duty force of 2.5 million could be sustained at an incremental pay cost of $2.1 billion. Because of the various jiggerings and increases in military pay that have occurred since then, including an enormous 25% pay increase in 1981, current recruit pay is at least adequate. For first-termers, it may well be too high in light of needs of mobilization, readiness, and the military mission.

It is clear, however, that the current 2.1 million force could not be raised to 2.5 million without vast and expensive pay increases. Whether acknowledged or not, the limited ability to recruit within the pay scales set by Congress has now become a constraint on force-structure planning. It is bad enough that we pay our auto workers so much that they cannot compete with Toyotas. There is more to worry about if we make the incremental budget cost of recruits so high that we cannot add enough of them to deter our adversaries.

It also is important to distinguish economic cost from budget cost. Budget cost is what in the real world of congressional appropriations affects overall military capability. For all the arguments about whether we should have 3% or 5% or 10% annual increases in the DoD budget, the budget fluctuates within a rather small range. Increases in budgeted manpower costs are not automatic add-ons to the total; instead, generally the DoD budget simply has to eat them, and they are paid for by cutting other defense programs. (Even the Joint Chiefs of Staff, who remember their own constituencies, never resist pay increases even if these inevitably mean a smaller force.)[63] The practical effect of the AVF, therefore (even if economists are pleased at the way it reveals the true cost of labor) is that manpower costs absorb a larger portion of a roughly fixed defense budget, and this country's overall defense capability is to that extent reduced. This also means, if we ignore the plight of the draftee, that the cost per unit of defense capability for the average taxpayer is less under the draft than under the budget-swallowing AVF.

Women. A related aspect concerns women in the military. Women saved the AVF in its darkest days; and conversely, the AVF has provided an additional rationale for the military's using more women.[64] Women have made the difference between success and failure in meeting overall recruiting figures. They now constitute nearly 10%[65] of the active military force, and currently are 12.5% of army nonprior-service accessions. "For the first time in world history, a nation has fielded an army composed significantly of women."[66] (Other countries that called on women during struggles for survival later restricted them to a narrow set of non-combat jobs [as in Israel], or gave up the practice [as in the U.S.S.R.]).[67] In October, 1983 the secretary of defense's manpower office announced that the army has acquiesced, contrary to its previous intention, to adding 5,000 more women and to opening more occupational categories to them (see Table 15.6).[68]

Policy on women in the military is too complex a matter for extended treatment in this chapter. It is an uncharted course on which our armed forces have embarked with little history or

Table 15.6. Women in Active Army*

1964	11,718
1974	30,716
1983	75,000

* In the World War II era, women in the army increased from 939 in 1940 to a high of 153,644 in 1945, organized in the Women's Army Corps and Army Nurse Corps, representing 3.2% of the active force. From 1945 to 1968, women never exceeded 1.5% of the active army force. Office of the Deputy Chief of Staff for Personnel, *Women in the Army Policy Review* (1982), pp. 1-2, 1-3.

experience to guide them. What makes it pertinent here is that, quite apart from the political support for opening opportunities for women, or the actual needs and desires of the services, the volunteer force has provided an independent pressure in this area,[69] all of it on the side of radical change; a change that some observers resent irrationally, but others sincerely question because of women recruits' higher first-term attrition, physical limitations, complications of pregnancy, and possible effects on morale and readiness.[70]

This is one example of how rigidity and limits of manpower acquisition under the AVF point military planners toward decisions they might otherwise reject. Whatever the merits of free markets, neither global policy nor the sexual composition of our forces should be hostage to our military recruitment method. Such issues should be addressed on their own merits and not under the external pressures created by the volunteer force.

The Future. The external environment enjoyed by the AVF in the past two years has been extraordinary. With the economy catatonic, with enormous pay raises, with temporarily low accession requirements, and with the current generous pool of eighteen-year-olds, recruiting youngsters has been like selling iced Coca-Cola on a hot day in the Sahara. The sales job by the end of the decade may more resemble the old challenge of selling iceboxes to eskimos with the number of eskimos depleted. It surely is a delusion to think that recruits will be bought in the late 1980s at current prices, even at low current force levels.

The future outlook for recruiting is much less rosy than the past.[71] The economy, we hope, will continue upwards. And the number of eighteen-year-olds, with the baby boom now exhausted, is heading sharply down. No crystal ball is required to discover the figures; the potential recruits are already born and counted (see Tables 15.7 and 15.8).

What this means is that, later in the decade, at current force levels (and even with lower projected accession requirements), the armed services will have to recruit one of every three eligible males. And the most able of those males, of course, will be sought even more avidly by the civilian sector. The prediction of some respectable analysts is that in less than a decade because of these realities the All-Volunteer Force "will fall flat on its face."[72]

Some of the bliss about the current enlistments figures recalls the story about the man who was falling from the roof of a forty-story building. Someone leaned out a tenth story window as he went by and asked him how he felt. "So far," the man replied, "I feel fine."

THE ADVANTAGES OF CONSCRIPTION

A sounder way to raise military manpower is a selective draft of mentally and physically qualified young male Americans.

First, there is an obligation to define what I mean by conscription. I do not mean by that a system that prohibits volunteers, as was in effect for the latter part of World War II. By conscription I mean a male-only selective service with very few exemptions and few deferments except for ROTC and some critical training like medicine. Registrants would be examined and classified and drafted for active duty of, say, fifteen months, some perhaps less, with a

Table 15.7. Projected NPS Enlisted Accessions by Service and
Component, Male and Female (In thousands)

	Active	Reserve Components	Total
Army	120-150	80-100	200-250
Navy	80-85	2-3	80-85
Air Force	65-70	8-12	75-80
Marine Corps	40-45	8-9	45-50
Total Force	305-350	98-124	400-470
Average	325	105	430

Source: Charles C. Moskos, Jr.

subsequent reserve obligation of several years. Draft calls would be as required to make up the shortfall of qualified volunteers. Pay of draftees would be lower than the level necessary to attract the same number of volunteers and might be set lower than the pay of persons who enlist for longer terms of service or who have valuable skills. The system should be structured by intelligence standards, by nature of recruiting, by length of term of obligated service, perhaps by also drafting for reserve duty so that a substantial number of the eligibles would be called. The proportion called upon should be sufficiently large that being drafted could be seen as performing a common service and not the moral equivalent of being struck by lightning.

Conscription, some have pointed out, has been the exception rather than the rule in our history. History, however, cannot answer what our policy ought to be right now. Moreover, the observation is a bit misleading. We have had conscription for three out of four years since 1940. And military service for able-bodied men was the norm before the Revolution; all originally were part of the militia, and varying from state to state, such service continued well into the nineteenth century, though usually not formally enforced.[73] The issue in our early history was whether to

Table 15.8. Percent of Males Required for 410,000 NPS Male Accessions Annually*

Year	Males Age 19 (thousands)	All Eligible Males	Eligible Males Excluding College Males**	Population***
1983	2,086	19.7	29.3	43.8
1984	1,994	20.6	30.7	45.9
1985	1,889	21.7	32.4	48.3
1986	1,836	22.3	33.3	49.8
1987	1,797	22.8	36.1	53.9
1988	1,819	22.5	33.7	50.2
1989	1,864	22.0	33.7	49.0
1990	1,910	21.5	32.1	47.8
1991	1,750	23.4	35.0	52.2
1992	1,656	24.8	37.0	55.2
1993	1,622	25.3	37.8	56.3

Source: Charles C. Moskos, Jr.

* Assumptions of Annual NPS Entrants:
  1. enlisted active force   325,000
  2. enlisted reserve force   45,000
  3. enlisted Guard force   60,000
  4. enlisted total force   430,000
  5. commissioned officers   30,000
  6. total entrants   460,000
  7. minus female entrants   50,000
  8. total male entrants   410,000

** Two-thirds considered eligible on physical, mental, and moral grounds.
*** One-third of cohort considered college population.

have standing armies of regulars; no one questioned the citizen's duty to serve. The consistent teaching of our history has been that when we needed big armies and military service was necessary to the country's security, in the Civil War, both World Wars, and the Cold War, the able-bodied would be called upon. It is the AVF, even its more candid supporters admit, that is "daring and unprecedented."[74] If there is no great need for armed forces at the present time, then the case for conscription is so much the less. I believe, however, that the threats of nuclear war and of Soviet expansionism make our having strong and capable armed forces, able to defend without resort to nuclear weapons, more essential than ever.

Here is a list of the reasons why I believe conscription is the sounder social policy. Afterwards I shall attempt to sketch, with what candor I can muster, its disadvantages, of which there certainly are some, as there are with all social policies. To some extent the advantages of conscription are the reciprocals of the problems with the All-Volunteer Force.

Equity. The draft is fairer. The middle class and the most fortunate individuals in society should not be able to shirk the state's most fundamental claim. Libertarian thinkers, who see the state as almost unjustified, will reach a different conclusion. So will those of the political left who deny the need for or legitimacy of strong armed forces. But in a society as devoted as this one seems to be to egalitarianism (often too devoted) it is totally anomalous to send the poor whites and the blacks to fight for the senior class at Exeter or even the freshman class at the University of Maryland. Because there still will be many volunteers, a draft will not make the military exactly representative of society, nor should it. What it will do is make the armed forces more representative, and stop allowing large segments of society to opt out of a basic civic responsibility.

Military Experience. Although no one often mentions it, broadening military experience has an educational effect on society. It also keeps the military from becoming a world foreign to the bulk of the citizenry, who in the next few years will have to make some significant decisions touching on military policy. For instance, a generation ago (reflecting World War II) nearly all the members of Congress were veterans. Recently it was down to 45% in the House of Representatives, still 69% in the Senate.[75] Can the military long remain a part of the fabric of society if the experience is limited to fewer and fewer, and to so few of the influential? Can the people of this country vote intelligently on issues of national security when their sole acquaintance with the military comes from reruns of "M*A*S*H" and "Hogan's Heroes"?[76] What are the consequences, already beginning to appear, of having a generation of decision makers who avoided the draft?

Allies. The draft will reaffirm our seriousness of purpose. The abolition of conscription sent a message, as George Wallace used to say. The message, for many of our citizens, is that national security is not much of a concern, except for worry of a nuclear exchange. For our allies, the administration is saying that this is once again a country of bellicose talk but timid actions. If we want to be taken more seriously, Helmut Schmidt has frequently observed,[77] why don't we draft our young men the way the Germans do? And the French. And the Dutch. And the Belgians. And the Norwegians. And our other Continental NATO Allies. And, for armed forces more than twice the size of ours, the Soviet Union. What do the Europeans know that we don't?

We do not have to play monkey-see, monkey-do with a policy this important. But there is no doubt that for our allies, whether we draft is one gauge of our seriousness and commitment. The impression of many Europeans is that we are a country that hopes to find its security in weapons and machines while the most able citizens sit on the sidelines. That is not the indicium of "will" that Richard Nixon, who now wants the draft back, said this country needs.[78]

Mobilization. No one, not even the optimists of the Gates Commission, has claimed that the volunteer force would work in time of war or national emergency. Having the draft in place and functioning guarantees that it would be able to work reasonably quickly. It also, of course, would provide adequate reserves to provide a cushion in a mobilization transition.

Reserves. The draft will fill the reserves and also create a pool of trained manpower. The volunteer force has failed, by practically anyone's measure, to provide adequate reserve forces even though we say we are relying on the reserves now more than ever, given the shrunken size of the active force. Conscription could replenish the store of trained manpower and fill the reserves, both with various options for longer reserve service coupled with shorter active duty and with reserve commitments on draftees. The readiness and manning of the reserves, of course, also reduces the strain of possible mobilization.

Officer Corps. Not much ever is written about it, but the draft once had a significant and beneficial effect on the composition of the officer corps. To avoid the draft, because they preferred to serve as officers, many young men entered commissioning programs and enriched both the services and their own experience. Now officer programs are mostly limited to the service academies and ROTC scholarships, hitting only those who, without draft pressure and under the inducement of money, are willing to commit four years or more of their future. That has narrowed both the base on which the officer corps draw and the experience of the millions of young men who now never think to enter it.

The "Draft-Induced." The draft as an excuse for military service of course affects the enlisted force as well. One reality of the draft era which would be difficult to quantify is that besides those who enlisted to get it over with or to choose a skill, another number of young men really did not mind being drafted, or enlisting ostensibly to avoid it; but they might not want to admit that to their friends. Some additional number, who came in to the service expecting to hate every minute, found it not so bad, and sometimes even stayed. Peer pressure counts for something among adolescents, and it takes some nerve to enlist when there is no need to and only the poor kids do it. The volunteer force fails to reach the young man who, with the excuse the possibility of being drafted would offer, would have signed up. It writes off that pre-1973 group who might be termed the "draft encouraged."

Cost. The incremental budgetary cost of having a volunteer force is almost impossible to measure but almost certainly is far higher than was predicted by the Gates Commission. If pay rates of recruits stayed constant at present levels, however, the budget cost of a conscripted force would stay about the same; indeed, if recruit pay stayed high enough to satisfy the market, no one would actually be drafted at all. True, recruiting costs would be less, and the draft would induce some additional volunteering, but if conscripts served shorter terms, more of them would have to be trained and overall costs would rise, offset to some degree by reduced attrition because of a higher average ability level of persons joining. And some of the cost of moving more people through the system is investment, to the extent they go into the reserves. But budget cost is not the big selling point for advocates of the draft.

It would be possible and probably should be part of the draft plan, to adopt a lower rate of pay for conscripted recruits than for volunteers and to require (as the army no longer always does) a longer period of service for reenlistees. It would also be possible, by skipping annual raises for a while, to let the pay of first-term recruits drift down to a lower level, reflecting a judgement that they ought not have families. This simultaneously could avoid "pay compressions"—or the belief that sergeants and petty officers ought to enjoy a greater advantage over privates and seamen than is now the case. (The higher cost of buying recruits is likely to lead to even more pay compression in the 1980s.) Lower pay, of course, implies an even greater tax on the time of the drafted eighteen-year-old, and from that point of view a greater personal unfairness, unless the differential is at least partially made up later in the form of, say, substantial post-service educational benefits. Low pay, however, was never the principal complaint of the reluctant conscript.

Overall, the budget cost of a conscripted army can perhaps be somewhat less if pay of conscripts goes back to relatively low levels which probably is sound military policy, but raises questions of overall fairness to those who are called to serve.

THE DISADVANTAGES OF CONSCRIPTION

Conscription will not, of course, end all problems. It carries a few of its own.

Universality. The most glaring weakness in selective conscription is its uneven impact. It may be fair in some sense to be one of a few drafted in a cleanly run lottery; in a more cosmic sense, to many people, it is not fair at all. "Why me?" is going to be a tough question, and it gets tougher the smaller the number taken from the pool of eligibles.

There are ways to ameliorate it, however, short of the universal military training that President Eisenhower recommended. Just as standards and requirements can be jiggered to make the volunteer army's needs fit what is available, so there are ways to plan to take a reasonable portion of the eligible pool. It would not hurt the services to raise the intelligence standards once in a while, for example (as the army lately has effectively done). I assume that a draft that takes many (though not all) of the eligibles in peacetime is sufficiently universal to satisfy fairness, though obviously some may disagree about what is the critical mass.

First, nature is going to help and has already helped, in fact. By 1992 the number of eighteen-year-olds will be down by 22%. Unless the armed forces shrink further, to meet accessions then it will be necessary to enlist more than one out of every three eligibles.

Second, there is nothing magic about a two-year obligated period of service. Shorter terms mean greater training costs, but they also provide more trained men for the mobilization base. The Germans for years have drafted three-quarters of all their eligible young men for a fifteen-month term of service. We could soundly do the same.[79] We might also draft for the reserves.

Third, with the draft in place, we might want to reconsider whether with all this country's commitments, and knowing that conventional forces raise the threshold of nuclear war, we really want an army of only 783,000, a navy of only 572,000, marines of 197,000, and an air force of only 613,000. More enlisted people would have to be paid for, but force structures could be planned without the additional worry of being able to come up with qualified recruits.

Fourth, standards could perhaps be raised somewhat, to a level commensurate with the sophistication of the weapons and equipment with which enlisted personnel today are entrusted.

With demographics not vastly different, this country prior to the Vietnam War drafted about 150,000 men a year for an army force of 974,000, resulting in a first-term enlisted force that was about one-half draftees. It would not take great contortions to do that again.

The crucial issue in making a draft work, assuming honest administration, is how far one can fall short of universal male military training without losing the public's sense that this is a service one can and should be expected normally to perform, or without stirring a public sense that an imposition of this magnitude (months of inconvenience and possibly risk of death) should not be assigned only to a few by, in effect, a dice roll. I do not know how many eligibles would have to be taken to satisfy that criterion, but I suspect that it is in a range somewhere between one-third and two-thirds. To take that many in peacetime, a rapid turnover of recruits may be required; that may make military service less onerous and provide a better trained body of manpower to call on in an emergency, but it also means more people to train and so tends to raise costs. That part of the price, in my opinion, probably is worth it.

Women. This draft excludes women, even though they can perform in many military specialties, particularly in a peacetime environment. To the extent women are spared being drafted, they are better off than men; on the other hand, society has long concluded, with ample reason, that there is a basis in some areas to treat women differently from men. Important to the military, women on average have less upper body strength than men, and at the ages they enlist they have a unique tendency to become pregnant. Currently about one out of six first-term enlisted women in the army is pregnant at any given moment.

Therefore, to adopt the language of economists, when it comes to military service, women are not perfect substitutes for men. They have higher first-term turnover (and therefore higher cost), they are smaller and not as strong, they miss more time from duty for medical reasons (though less for drug abuse, alcohol abuse, and disciplinary reasons), they get pregnant and have babies. Fewer data support other widely held views: that the reactions of men and women to each other alter the manner in which military units operate; that women overall are less aggressive than men; that the presence of women may affect the performance of men in a combat situation; and that one of the hallmarks of a civilized society is that as long as there are able-bodied men, it does not send its women to fight.[80] It is doubtful that without greatly changing their nature, and possibly their fighting qualities, the services could absorb much more than the sixfold increase in women to which they have adjusted during the past ten years.[81]

The duties of many soliders, sailors, and airmen may be not greatly different from private-sector jobs. But they become very unlike the private sector when the shooting starts and someone is actively trying to kill the employee. We know enough about Soviet military doctrine, for example, to know that rear areas, headquarters, and communications organizations would be prime targets. Moreover, for an army in combat, its rear echelons are also its reserves.[82] In a wartime environment, there are only so many military jobs that women can fill, unless they are to be put in frequent risk of life and limb, which is something our society so far has properly considered to be barbaric. Historically, war has been fought by groups of men, not by men and women together. Even if women were confined to the rear areas (and even if we could be sure there would be any rear areas), the effect would be to keep male soldiers constantly in the front lines.

There seems ample basis to conclude that, as in the past, it is reasonable not to conscript women. The unfairness, if that be what it is, of being unable to choose one's sex, is simply too fundamental a human problem to try to work out in military manpower legislation. And there is no serious doubt that as our jurisprudence currently stands, and is likely to remain, limiting conscription to men is clearly constitutional.[83] But controversy on this policy can confidently be predicted.

Conscientious and Other Objectors. Perhaps the biggest sleeper in planning conscription, as William K. Brehm has noted,[84] is the devilish problem of those who, for religious or other beliefs, are opposed to service. Without anyone noticing too carefully, the courts during the last years of the draft broadened conscientious-objector status far beyond the original concept of a few sectarian objectors to war to include atheists and anyone else who could talk glibly enough to establish a deeply felt revulsion to violence, or at least certain kinds of violence. The rulings had little practical impact then because they came as draft calls already were winding down.

Conscientious objection is one thing in a society where opinion-shapers agree on the need to defend the country and on the nobility of military service; it could turn out to be quite another in the current environment, where invoking conscience to avoid military service may not seem odd or disgraceful at all. Conscientious objection has not been declared a constitutional right; draft legislation should be carefully written to define the exemption, if there is to be one, narrowly and with as much precision as the evenhandness requirements of the Constitution allow. It should also ensure that service as a conscientious objector is again made sufficiently burdensome and onerous (as it was in World War II, but not after) that it is not an easy and attractive alternative to serving in the armed forces.

Enforcement. To work, and to be fair, conscription will have to be enforced firmly and with real legal sanctions. The halfhearted enforcement of the registration law, which has been trivialized by association with the U.S. Postal Service, would not be enough. That would require a major effort by assistant U.S. attorneys, who find such cases boring and many of whom have little sympathy with the military themselves. The services would have to deal with a certain number of recruits who wanted to get out, people who now can simply be discharged; the penalties for indiscipline and malingering would have to be adequate. For the draft to work, resistance would have to carry unpleasant consequences and not be socially acceptable. The draft would also have to deal with courts and judges that have come to expect all human activity to be litigated, that have imposed stricter and stricter procedural red tape on everything the government does, and that will be much less likely than the judges of a generation ago to give officials the benefit of the doubt when national security is invoked.[85]

A Tax. The economist's argument against the draft, indeed the only economic argument against the draft, is that it pays unwilling recruits less than their true opportunity costs, and thus gives the government an incentive to substitute excessive amounts of manpower for other defense inputs, or to provide an excessive amount of defense.[86] That is a valid economic objection, relating to the misallocation of resources and reduction of total economic output of the society. Any other objections that economists make to the draft, however, are based on their political or philosophical preferences and should be respected as such but treated as nonexpert opinion.

The draft, in economic terms, is undoubtedly a tax, and it is a tax that does not hit everyone and is not incurred by virtue of anything the taxee does. That still does not prove it is bad policy. There is, after all, only a limited group in society (basically, able-bodied young men of a certain intelligence) who can meet society's need for military service. (They are also, as a group, one of the luckier ones in terms of future opportunities.) It might be appropriate to tax others more and specifically reward those whose time is conscripted. But there also is a tradition of young warrior service. In all, to say the draft is an imposition on the draftee only points out the obvious. The question is whether for noneconomic reasons we ought to levy it. All defense expenditures, after all, if viewed narrowly enough look like economic waste.

Political Decision Making. Whichever way one raises armies can involve some constraints on foreign policy planners. Earlier the vast racial imbalance in the army's combat units was mentioned and how this might induce reluctance to order them to combat. Reserve call-ups, like President Kennedy's in the Berlin crisis of 1961, are not popular either, and seldom have been attempted. Selective service, of course, carries inhibitions of its own. It was not until draft calls began hitting the sons of the middle class that opposition to the Vietnam War became really widespread. Some may think that is good. The former army chief of staff, General Edward C. Meyer, said that the army should not be committed unless the American public is behind it, anyway—a remark that takes inadequate account of the fluctuations in popularity of a particular conflict.[87] But conscript armies, at least in our country's experience, do not seem to be suited for long wars, even at low levels of intensity, such as Korea and Vietnam. Even wars of that level, however, involve such an expansion of the forces that they could not be fought without using the draft anyway. Policymakers would prefer to have all the flexibility the constitutional process allows without the added political inhibitions that have to be reckoned with from either a draft or a reserve call-up. They would argue that the public in such matters tends to be shortsighted about its own long-term interest. The hard fact is, however, than an AVF can be used only to start fighting a war, not to finish it.

Political Feasibility. Sometimes it is suggested that conscription as an alternative should be ignored because right now it just isn't popular enough politically. Many people, particularly the more privileged, indeed are comfortable with the status quo (and so, surveys show, are many in the black community and others who emphasize the employment opportunities of military service). Conscription seldom has been popular, however; in 1941 the Congress continued it by a margin of a single vote. Yet compliance with the current, basically unenforced, registration requirement is claimed to be over 90%. And the campus uprisings that were predicted when the current generation of students was required to certify their draft registration as a condition of federal aid have not materialized.

The electorate today probably understands the imperatives of national security better than do some elected representatives or their Washington staffs. In any event, the task of political leadership is not simply to read public opinion polls, but also, occasionally, and particularly where national security is at stake, to lead. Conferences like this one can also play a part.

ALTERNATIVES TO CONSCRIPTION

There are four alternatives to the type of conscription proposed here that are worth mentioning. Two of them, the AVF and drafting women along with men, have already been mentioned. For a moment let me touch on the other two. One is an idea with positive possibilities and the other is absolutely terrible.

Educational Benefits

The positive alternative, if conscription is not to be reinstituted, is a decreased emphasis on pay and a greatly increased level of noncash benefits, particularly the kind of benefits that attract the kind of recruits the services want. Those recruits, the kind who do not cause disciplinary problems, the kind with ambition, the kind with aptitude for technological skills, are attracted in particular by educational benefits. Today 70% of the enlisted skills in the air force are technical, 60% in the navy, even 40% in our army, which is itself on the verge of deploying a new generation of equipment.[88] The army's unique "super-VEAP" college fund program, which for the first time gives it a competitive edge over the other services, has already yielded encouraging results. Charles C. Moskos, Jr., who for years has advocated such educational incentives, appears from the limited data to have had a good idea again.[89]

A broadened program of educational incentives could go at least part of the way toward controlling recruit quality when the economy recovers. It also can ameliorate somewhat the economic imbalance in the force, though obviously such benefits will appeal more to the poor, albeit the ambitious poor and lower middle class.

For a program of educational benefits to make a dent, however, it would have to offer benefits that are big like the post-World War II G.I. Bill that paid tuition at whatever level, with expenses and cash besides. It would have to be well-advertised. And just as importantly, the government would have to stop competing with itself. In recent years, the federal government, wearing its social welfare hat, has started shoveling billions of dollars to college students. Some is in grants, some in loans which the government too often has shown a disgraceful reluctance to try to collect. If a young man can get just as much education money, or nearly as much, without serving his country as he would by serving a tour in the military, which do you think he will choose? The attractiveness of an educational incentive will depend not just on the absolute dollars available, but on the selective attractiveness of the deal the army or navy is offering compared to what is available for nothing elsewhere.[90] Also, such a benefit program probably would not be closed to women, and if it worked might attract females in greater proportion than the services desired.

If conscription cannot be instituted now, I would warmly endorse the Moskos idea, or some version of it, as the best way to improve the current anxiety and the impending trouble.

National Service

Finally, I would not want you to think that I am happy about the compulsion that is a part of a draft. It is tolerable, as the Supreme Court recognized in 1918,[91] only when the military need of the country is very great. Yet, at the other extreme from the AVF admirers are those who say that military conscription is not enough. They seem to be saying that if one vitamin pill makes you feel better, then swallowing the whole bottle is bound to make you feel great.

Put positively, the advocates of this view correctly observe that there is a fairness flaw inherent in both selective service and the AVF, because neither takes everybody. If we have to draft some people for military service, they say, why not draft everybody to do everything under the sun? The less bold trim it down a bit to propose that draftees should all have the option, if they don't like to be in the military, to go do something else for the government or perhaps something else that the government approves.

One suspects that some Democrats, rejecting the caste nature of the AVF, nevertheless do not want to acknowledge that defense has any superior claims, and so are driven clear to this other extreme of forced labor. But it is appalling to note the loose and easy assumption of some writers in recent years that the government has the power to conscript people not just for defense of the country but for anything it wants.

"National service" is the generic designation of this collection of nostrums. It is a notion so alien to everything this country stands for, and beyond that it is so impractical, that I believe anyone who presents it for serious consideration faces a heavy burden of proof. In short outline, here are the most glaring things wrong with the national service idea:

1. *It is flagrantly illegal.* We have a constitution in this country, and its Thirteenth Amendment forbids involuntary servitude. The Constitution also restricts governmental takings without due process; and it empowers the Congress to raise and support armies and provide for a navy, but most certainly not to raise the populace generally for whatever purpose the legislators think might serve the general welfare. Recognizing that lawyers can write briefs for either side and clever judges can find ways to rationalize practically anything, nevertheless to sustain forced national service, either directly or under the threat of military induction, would be a vast departure from constitutional interpretation as it has existed and exists today.[92]

2. *It is impractical.* The federal government in this country does not have useful jobs for millions of eighteen-year-olds to fill.[93] National service proposals usually become vague when one inquires what all these people would be doing and who would watch them. There are nostalgic references to the good works of the paramilitary Civilian Conservation Corps (CCC) in the 1930s, to the plight of the elderly, and something about cleaning up the national parks or the South Bronx. But the exact nature of the activity being proposed for the country's teenage population is still baffling.

3. *It is costly.* Labor, which the armed services call manpower, is extremely expensive in this country. Presumably servants in national service would have to be paid, perhaps fed and clothed

also. Where would those extra billions of dollars for such a giant expansion of the public sector come from?

4. *It is unenforceable.* Conscription has been enforced by the threat of prison and by the general public condemnation, at least until the early 1970s, of draft-dodgers. After induction, recruits become subject to the Uniform Code of Military Justice, which means they live under military discipline whether they like it or not, and can be put in the stockade for disobeying lawful orders. They work in groups of a size and in locations designed to assure close supervision. But would anyone know if a conscripted national servant loafed, worked half a day, or walked off the job? Even if someone learned of it, how would that civilian be punished? Perhaps thousands could be conscripted to become assistant U.S. attorneys to prosecute the others.

5. *It would not be supported politically.* Teenagers are capable of discerning that some social needs are more fundamental than others, and teenagers today are not those of the 1960s. For every one who would see national service as fairer, there might be another like the young man who said to me, "Being drafted into the army is one thing. Being drafted to work in the welfare office for a bunch of liberals who want you to work for them for nothing is something else."

6. *It demeans the military.* To imply that other activities are as much a service to society as risking or sacrificing one's life for its very preservation puts too low a value on what soldiers, sailors, marines and airmen do. It suggests that one may be a practicing objector to military service with no stigma and with no conscience, only self-interest and personal preference.

7. *It is alien.* The day the Congress proposes national service is the day to reread the collected works of Milton Friedman and join the Libertarian Party. The unarticulated assumption in national service is that working in forced labor battalions on government-ordered projects is useful, while working at ordinary jobs in the private sector is not, or is less so. That is bad economics and even worse political theory. Our country stands for just the opposite. The state does have a claim on its citizens' lives, but only to defend the country. The only government project that justifies taking over its citizens' lives is defense, which might extend in wartime to conscription for essential war production, but dire necessity is what sets the limit.

CONCLUSION

I go back to my original point: the issue is not one of economics. In relative peacetime, and especially in a sick economy, anyone with ready funds and elastic standards and force levels can make an all-volunteer force "work" so that the slots someone says we need filled are filled. This is not difficult at all if you are willing to cut quality; pay a great deal of money to marginally able eighteen-year-olds; trim requirement figures even though the size of the active-duty force gradually declines to levels formerly thought dangerous; ignore the reserves, which theoretically are now responsible for missions given up by the shrunken active force; if you don't care who serves; if you don't care who dies; if you never have to mobilize quickly; and if the force never has to fight in a serious war. If enough of these considerations can be put aside, it is not likely that an economist would ever have to pronounce the volunteer force a failure. But whether or not it is a total failure, it is at best, it seems to me, an undesirable policy.

Some would put the proposition even more sharply. They would affirm that the citizen has not only rights but obligations to society which a healthy society will not hesitate to enforce.[94] They would talk about the Romans:

> The minds of men were gradually reduced to the same level, the fire of genius was extinguished, and even the military spirit evaporated. . . . Their personal valour remained, but they no longer possessed the public courage which is nourished by the love of independence, the sense of national honour, the presence of danger, and the habit of command. They received laws and governors from the will of their sovereign, and trusted for their defense to a mercenary army.[95]

Some would say that there are words to describe a society that tries to have security without risking the young men it values the most. One of those words is "decadent." Having an all-volunteer force in a time of peril is unworthy of us as a nation.

I realize that I have talked more of politics, fairness, and political philosophy than is customary at such conferences. That is because I think that, however limited my own perceptions of such considerations, these are precisely the concerns that the debate ought to be about. Even assuming that the AVF is sufficient in numbers and quality to be an effective military force—and there is, as noted, reason for serious doubt about that over the long term—and recognizing that it is a hopeless system for raising troops in time of emergency or war, the issue is one of social policy and morality and what citizens owe for the benefits they receive in the most widely civilized state that the world has ever seen. At that other academy up on the Hudson, and I am sure no less so here, there is reverence for "duty, honor, country." If our citizens' duty has no part in our planning, can a country of honor long remain?

We enact our tax laws to reflect some concept of equity and not just to raise money. We distribute public benefits by formulas that tell something about what kind of a people we are and where our aspirations lie. In our most serious public decision, which is how the country shall be preserved from foreign military domination, and who shall be the ones to serve and possibly die for the good of the whole people, we ought to give no less attention to fairness, to service, and to what kind of a people we ought to be.

NOTES

1. For discussion of some attitudes toward national security policy that tend to ally business-oriented Republicans and left-wing Democrats, see Norman Podhoretz, *The Present Danger* (New York: Simon and Schuster, 1980), pp. 67-75.
2. William F. Buckley, Jr., "Some Punishment," *Washington Post*, 16 September 1983, p. A15.
3. Dwight D. Eisenhower, "This Country *Needs* Universal Military Training," *Reader's Digest*, September, 1966, p. 49. See "Report of the National Commission on Selective Service," *In Pursuit of Equity: Who Serves When Not All Serve?* (Washington, DC: Government Printing Office, 1967), at n15 (hereinafter cited as "Marshall Commission Report").
4. Richard Nixon, *The Real War* (New York: Warner Books, 1980), p. 201.
5. See Edwin M. Yoder, Jr., "The Administration's Draft-Dodging," *Washington Post*, 1 June 1982, p. A17.
6. Cf. George F. Will, *Statecraft as Soulcraft* (New York: Simon and Schuster, 1983), p. 31.
7. *Military Manpower Task Force: A Report to the President on the Status and Prospects of the All-Volunteer Force* (Washington, DC: Government Printing Office, November 1982), pp. 1-1-1-6.
8. The Atlantic Council of the United States, Policy Papers, *Toward a Consensus on Military Service: Report of the Atlantic Council's Working Group on Military Services* (Washington, DC: Atlantic Council, June 1982), pp. 50-59. See also James L. Lacy, "The Case for Conscription," in Brent Scowcroft, ed., *Military Service in the United States* (Englewood Cliffs, NJ: Prentice-Hall, 1982), p. 195.
9. Caspar W. Weinberger, "Foreword," in Martin Anderson with Barbara Honegger, eds., *The Military Draft* (Stanford, CA: Hoover Institution Press, 1982), p. xiv. See also Caspar W. Weinberger, "Letter," *Philadelphia Inquirer, 31 August 1983*.
10. Oliver Wendell Holmes, Jr., *The Common Law* (Boston: Little, Brown & Co., 1881), p. 1.
11. For a chronology of the important policy changes that preceded the ending of the draft calls, see William K. Brehm, "Peacetime Voluntary Options," in Andrew J. Goodpaster et al., eds., *Toward a Consensus on Military Service* (Elmsford, NY: Pergamon Press, 1982), p. 154; Curtis W. Tarr, *By the Numbers* (Washington, DC: National Defense University Press, 1981), p. 45.
12. Marshall Commission Report.
13. This is not to say that the decision to inject the draft as a campaign issue, though politically helpful, was based only on political expediency. Nixon earlier had said he favored an eventual end of selective service. See Robert B. Semple, Jr., "Nixon Backs Eventual End of Draft," *New York Times*, 18 November 1967, p. 2. His Secretary of Defense, Melvin R. Laird, did not personally favor the idea and

had supported universal national service, although after the decision he loyally supported the AVF. See Melvin R. Laird, *People, Not Hardware* (Washington, DC: American Enterprise Institute, 1980), p. 2.

14. "Statement by the President Announcing the Creation of the Commission," March 27, 1969, reprinted in *Report of the President's Commission on an All-Volunteer Armed Force* (Washington, DC: Government Printing Office, 1970), p. vii (hereinafter cited as "Gates Report").

15. See generally Dwight R. Lee, "The All-Volunteer Army and Its Troubles: Where Economics Went Wrong," *Journal of Contemporary Studies*, 21 (1982).

16. Gaston de Levis, *Maximes Politiques*.

17. Stanley R. Resor to Thomas Gates, January 10, 1970, pp. 2, 4, 7, 8.

18. Gates Report, p. 142.

19. Charles C. Moskos, Jr., "Social Considerations of the All-Volunteer Force," in Brent Scowcroft, ed., *Military Service in the United States* (Englewood Cliffs, NJ: Prentice-Hall, 1982), pp. 132-133.

20. Gates Report, pp. 142, 143, 15-16.

21. Ibid, p. 8.

22. Ibid, pp. 10, 119-124.

23. Ibid, p. 117.

24. Marshall Commission Report, p. 12.

25. Ed Anderson, "General: Draft a Must in War," *New Orleans Times-Picayune*, 17 August 1983, p. 13. However, the former executive director of the Gates Commission staff has subsequently written that "conscription . . . comes down to pure, unadulterated physical coercion, which I object to on freedom grounds. . . . So I think that even in wartime conscription is probably a bad idea." William H. Meckling, "The Draft Is an Unfair Tax on Unlucky Young Men," *Fortune*, 14 July 1980, p. 169.

26. Eugene V. Tigher, Jr., "We Must Look to Wars of the Future," *Defense Systems Review*, October 1983, p. 7.

27. See Robert Pirie, *A Conversation with Robert Pirie: The Manpower Problems of the 1980's* (Washington, DC: American Enterprise Institute, 1981), p. 15; Laird, *People, Not Hardware*, p. 6. See also Keneth J. Coffey, *Manpower for Military Mobilization* (Washington, DC: American Enterprise Institute, 1977), p. 29.

28. Michael Levin, "Reluctant Heroes," *Policy Review*, Fall 1983, p. 97. See also Maxwell D. Taylor, "Volunteer Army: Long Enough," *Washington Post*, 16 June 1981, p. A19; Henry Mohr, "Major War May Be Disaster for All-Volunteer Military," *St. Louis Globe Democrat*, 26 November 1983.

29. *A Conversation with Robert Pirie*, pp. 6-7.

30. Laird, *People, Not Hardware*, p. 13.

31. See comments of Army Chief of Staff General John A. Wickham, Jr., in Tighe, "Wars of the Future," and in Drew Middleton, "General Says Army Plan Paid off in Grenada," *New York Times*, 16 November 1983, p. 6.

32. See Drew Middleton, "New Moves Stir Pentagon Manpower Fears," *New York Times*, 22 September 1983, p. 27.

33. See Secretary of Defense, *Annual Report to the Congress, Fiscal Year 1984* (Washington: Government Printing Office 1983), pp. 122, 124.

34. Currently the army's IRR is about 100,000 below prescribed strength, lacking particularly in young soldiers with combat arms skills. See generally Robert B. Pirie, Jr., "The All-Volunteer Force Today: Mobilization Manpower," in Goodpaster et al., *Towards a Consensus*, p. 127; E.C. Meyer, *A Conversation with General E. C. Meyer: The Army of the Future* (Washington, DC: American Enterprise Institute, 1981), p. 11.

35. Recent legislation authorized the secretary of defense to extend IRR commitments from six years to eight years; this will add to the IRR but also will increase its members' average age and time since active duty.

36. See examples collected in Charles C. Moskos, Jr., "Making the All-Volunteer Force Work: A National Service Approach," *Foreign Affairs*, 60, (1981): p. 20; Richard Halloran, "Doubts Persist on Quantity and Quality of Enlistees," *New York Times*, 29 September 1980, p. 7.

37. Brehm, "Peacetime Voluntary Options," pp. 154-155.

38. See, e.g., David J. Amor et al., *Recruit Aptitudes and Army Job Performance* (Santa Monica, CA: Rand Corporation, 1982); Fred Hiatt, "The Army Recruiting Dilemma: More Educated Join: But More Dullards Stay" Washington Post, 15 May, 1983. Tarr; *By The Numbers*, pp. 131-132.

39. Pirie, *A Conversation*, p. 8.

40. Lee, "The All-Volunteer Army," p. 27.

41. See Harold Brown, *Thinking About National Security* (Boulder, CO: Westview Press, 1983), p. 251. See also, Robert R. Palmer, "The Procurement of Enlisted Personnel: The Problem of Quality," in

Robert R. Palmer et al., eds., *The U.S. Army in World War II; The Army Ground Forces; The Procurement and Training of Ground Combat Troops* (Washington, DC: Office of the Chief of Military History, Department of the Army, 1948).

42. Martin van Creveld, *Fighting Power* (Westport, CT: Greenwood Press, 1982), p. 6.
43. See, e.g., van Creveld, *Fighting Power*, pp. 35-36; John Keegan, *Six Armies in Normandy* (New York: Viking Press, 1982), pp. 211, 243.
44. Tom Philpott, "Tice Sees Tough Times Ahead," *Army Times*, 15 August 1983, p. 22. See generally Melvin R. Laird, "People, Not Hardware: The Highest Defense Priority," in William J. Taylor et al., eds., *Defense Manpower Planning*, Elmsford, NY: Pergamon Press, 1981), p. 61.
45. See Don Hirst, "Education Lures Recruits, Study Shows," *Army Times*, 1 August 1983, p. 4. Beginning in FY1982, the Congress also became involved, mandating for the army a maximum of 25% accessions of the lowest acceptable mental group (category IV) and a maximum of 35% non-high school graduates.
46. "Draft Not Needed, Army Chief says," *Washington Post*, 9 August 1983, p. 7.
47. Males turning eighteen number 2,086,000 in 1983; 1,864,000 in 1989; 1,622,000 in 1993. See Table 15.8.
48. See "Korb Says Services Fail to Show Loyalty to SecDef," *Army Times, 29 August 1983, p. 3.*
49. See *A Conversation with Robert Pirie*, p. 11. The Congress directed that beginning with FY1982, the army could recruit no more than 25% in the lowest enlistable mental category, and no more than 35% who lacked high school diplomas. Although it is not a good idea in principle to have such variables as enlistment standards rigidly fixed by law, the Department of Defense's unwillingness to maintain adequate standards in the face of low enlistments made the congressional reaction understandable as well as beneficial.
50. Pamela S. Leven, "AF Chief Hails Boost in Quality of Forces," *Seattle Post-Intelligencer*, 26 August 1983, p. A6.
51. See Meckling, "The Draft Is an Unfair Tax: If they want a better force, they can always get it simply by raising the pay."
52. Lee, "The All-Volunteer Army," pp. 30-31.
53. See Brown, *Thinking About National Security*, p. 251.
54. *Military Manpower Task Force Report*, p. 1-2.
55. Martin Binkin and Mark J. Eitelberg with Alvin J. Schennider and Marvin M. Smith, *Blacks and the Military* (Washington, DC: The Brookings Institution, 1982), p. 181.
56. Over the entire Vietnam War, the number of blacks killed in action was 13.1% of the total. See Binkin and Eitelberg, *Ibid.* p. 77.
57. Milton Friedman and Rose Friedman, *Free to Choose* (New York: Avon Books, 1979).
58. Cournos, *Modern Plutarch*, p. 27.
59. See Charles C. Moskos and John H. Faris, "Beyond the Marketplace: National Service and the AVF," Goodpaster et. al., *Toward a Consensus*, pp. 132-141.
60. Moskos, "Social Considerations of the All-Volunteer Force," 34. In 1983, 40.6% of army male E-4s were married to civilian spouse, 3% to a military spouse. Of army female E-4s, 16.9% were married to a civilian spouse, and 26.5% had husbands in the military.
61. It was not long ago that an enlisted man needed his commanding officer's permission to marry. Today 85% of the army's single parents are men. They constitute 3% of the enlisted force.
62. See Peter F. Drucker, "Where Union Flexibility's Now a Must," *Wall Street Journal*, 23 September 1983, p. 30.
63. See Richard Halloran, "Military Leaders Would Rather Cut Arms, Not Salaries," *New York Times*, 14 January 1983, p. 1.
64. See *A Conversation With Robert Pirie*, pp. 23-24.
65. In March, 1983 women were 9.2% of the active force.
66. Levin, "Reluctant Heroes," p. 95.
67. Brown, *Thinking About National Security*, pp. 252-253; Martin Binkin and Shirley J. Bach, *Women and the Military* (Washington, DC: The Brookings Institution, 1977) pp. 9, 13, 123-125, 131-134.
68. Pete Earley, "Army Urges Rise in Jobs for Women," *Washington Post*, 18 October 1983, p. A3; Walter Andrews, "Army Eases Restrictions on Jobs for Women After 'Better Analysis,'" *Washington Times*, 21 October 1983, p. 1. Some observers attributed the most recent change to pressure from feminist groups, rather than recruiting concerns. See Charles W. Corddry, "13 Army Jobs Reopened to Women," *Baltimore Sun*, 21 October 1983, p. 13. Others, agreeing that the Army's policy change came "thanks in part to Defense Secretary Caspar Weinberger's own growing suspicion that the Army was retreating too far," have dismissed as "empty prissiness to keep women . . . out of range even of stray rounds." "Army's Strategy for Women a Winner," *Atlanta Constitution*, 19 October, 1983, p. 20.

69. See Tarr, *By the Numbers*, p. 148.

70. See generally Office of the Deputy Chief of Staff of Personnel, *Women in the Army Policy Review* (Washington, DC: Department of the Army, 1982). Those who support having an even higher proportion of the armed forces female acknowledge that to that end the Army "eased physical strength tests that were more arbitrary than germane." *Atlanta Constitution*, 19 October, 1983.

71. See Philpott, "Tice Sees Tough Times Ahead," *Army Times*, 15 August 1983.

72. Pamela Fine, "Volunteer Army To Fall on Its Face, Colonel Says," *Atlanta Constitution*, 28 October 1983, p. 11; see also Richard Reeves, "The Coming Draft and the Prospect of War," *Baltimore Sun*, 31 October 1983, p. 11.

73. See Militia Act of 1795, Act of February 28, 1795, c. 36, 1 Stat. 424.

74. *A Conversation with Robert Pirie*, p. 10.

75. Based on data in *Congressional Directory*, 1983-84 (Washington, DC: Government Printing Office, 1983).

76. As Robert Pirie points out, the concern is at least as much one of society becoming isolated from the military as of the military becoming isolated from society. See *Conversation*, p. 12.

77. See Hobart Rowen, "Schmidt's (Reluctant) Choice: Reagan," *Washington Post*, 1 September 1983, p. A23, "The 'Draft Debate' Is Over," *Washington Post*, 6 June 1980.

78. Nixon, *The Real War* p. 201.

79. The German Army pays draftees at approximately one-third the level of two-year volunteers.

80. Binkin and Bach, *Women and the Military*, pp. 88-89.

81. From 1.5% in 1977 to 9.2% in 1983.

82. See U.S. Department of the Army, Office of the Deputy Chief of Staff for Personnel, *Women in the Army Policy Review* (Washington, DC: Department of the Army, 1982).

83. See *United States v. Fallon*, 407 F.2d 621 (7th Cir.), *cert. denied*, 395 U.S. 908 (1969).

84. Brehm, *Toward a Consensus*, pp. 164-165; see also Tarr, *By the Numbers*, p. 154.

85. For an account of some of the enforcement problems in the waning days of Selective Service, Tarr *By the Numbers*, pp. 57-61, 145-148, 153-154.

86. See Richard A. Posner, *Economic Analysis of Law* 2d ed. (Boston: Little, Brown & Co., 1977), p. 364.

87. Richard Halloran, "U.S. Army Chief Opposes Sending Combat Forces to Aid El Salvador," *New York Times*, 10 June, p. A1; see also Drew Middleton, "U.S. Generals Are Leery of Latin Intervention," *New York Times*, 21 June 1983, p. A9.

88. Philpott, "Tice Sees Tough Times Ahead," *Army Times*, 5 August 1983.

89. See Moskos and Fairs, "Beyond the Marketplace," pp.141-146; Moskos, *Foreign Affairs* 60 (1981): 17.

90. See *A Conversation with Robert Pirie*, pp. 13-14.

91. *Selective Draft Law Cases*, 245 U.S. 366 (1918).

92. See *Butler v. Perry*, 240 U.S. 328 (1916) (upholding, referring to historical antecedents, requirement of work on public roads).

93. Approximately 4,000,000 persons in the United States currently turn eighteen each year. By 1990 the figure will be about 3,300,000. If two-thirds qualify for service, that leaves over 2,000,000 to place each year, surely an impossible task.

94. Will, *Statecraft as Soulcraft*, pp. 137-138; See also William C. Westmoreland, "U.S. Military Readiness Requires the Draft," *Wall Street Journal*, 26 May 1981, p. 32; Donald Kagan, "Military Services: A Moral Obligation," *New York Times*, 4 December 1983, p. E21.

95. Edward Gibbon, *The Decline and Fall of the Roman Empire*, vol. I (1776) (New York: Modern Library ed.), pp. 50-51.

16 National Service as a Deus Ex Machina in the AVF-Draft Debate*

RICHARD DANZIG

INTRODUCTION

In this chapter I make three arguments. In a first section, I explain why I believe that the debate about the desirability of a draft as compared with an all-volunteer force often offers little more than sound and fury. In its prescriptive aspects (I have no quarrel with descriptive analysis or even with predictive efforts), the AVF-draft debate is as remarkable for its limited utility as for its intensity and duration. In the end this dialogue signifies nothing because its resolution will depend on pragmatic variables not likely to be significantly affected by philosophy, ideology, or even politics. Worse still, the effort expended on debating a draft overshadows other issues that I think are more important and would profit from more discussion.

In a second section I seek to show why ideas of national service are appealing in this context. I take these ideas to include a variety of plans that would require or induce young people to devote some time to public service as a normal part of the process of coming of age in America. These ideas introduce a new dimension into a time-worn discussion; they offer the appearance of circumventing difficulties that afflict both the draft and the AVF positions; and not least significantly they provide an ideological choice that is independent of the particulars of the military manpower situation at any given moment. Preferences for a draft or an all-volunteer force are second-order considerations. A philosophic preference for one or the other will not prevail unless pragmatic considerations (the size of our military forces, the unemployment rate, etc.) conspire in that direction. National service is a different and bigger thing. If desired it will

*This chapter draws on a larger study of national service that Peter Szanton and I prepared for publication in 1986 under a grant from the Ford Foundation. I have benefitted from an analysis of the military effects of national service that was prepared for the Ford project by Gary R. Nelson, Robert F. Hale, and Joel Slackman. The views expressed here, however, are exclusively my own.

come to pass whatever the particulars of manpower supply and demand. In this respect, it is a veritable deus ex machina. It would come from outside of existing manpower scenarios and would put an end to them.

In the last section of this chapter I hope to show, however, that though national service is a deus ex machina, for those concerned with military manpower problems it cannot be more than that. It may descend from Capitol Hill, but is is not something that could be justified by military needs, sustained by military budgets, or achieved by military advocacy. Further, because the pace and form of national service plans, if they come at all, will come as a result of factors other than military requirements, it is likely that in the near future such plans will not affect the military. In the longer term, a form of national service that would be attractive to the military can be imagined, but by then the military rationale for such a system is likely to be lessened.

THE AVF/DRAFT DEBATE

I have three reasons for thinking that arguments about the desirability of a draft as compared with a volunteer force are mainly sound and fury signifying nothing. First, they set up a false dichotomy. Second, they typically debate in philosophic and ideologic terms an argument that I believe will be, and should be, resolved by largely unarguable pragmatic considerations. Third, neither side in the debate addresses the substantial manpower problems that plague our military establishment.

The volunteer-draft debate pivots around a false dichotomy because the vast majority of informed observers recognize that neither system is defensible in its pure form. Our volunteer force relies, and should rely, on the expectation of conscripted manpower in the event of a major war. Conversely, during all four periods of conscription that have occurred in the United States,[1] volunteering has been permitted, indeed even encouraged. Though a pure draft (with even volunteering for induction forbidden) has been occasionally urged, few would advocate such a position and even fewer would wager on the political likelihood of this view being adopted. I think the view that has always prevailed on this point is quite right. It would be ill-conceived to reject a qualified and willing volunteer in favor of coercing an unwilling, but otherwise identical, individual into serving.

What this means, however, in operational terms is simple. Just as one can't run a volunteer army without enough volunteers (and thus would have to draft if requirements went up in wartime, and volunteering went down), so one can't run a significant draft when there are adequate numbers of volunteers. One might believe that a draft would commendably reinvigorate our young people's sense of citizenship and national obligation;[2] one might believe that it would make the military a disciplined calling[3] instead of merely an economically motivated occupation;[4] one might believe that it would change the ethnic,[5] or the educational, or the class composition of the military. But just as long as we continue to receive and to accept a sufficient number of qualified volunteers, a draft is unworkable.

By this view America's transition from the draft to the volunteer force is best viewed not as a dramatic innovation, but rather as a natural response to the growth in numbers of each cohort of eighteen-year-olds, along with general stability in numbers of new recruits required by the military. As Richard V. L. Cooper put the matter in 1977:

Except for the period of the Vietnam conflict, between 1966 and 1970, the number of annual accessions into the military required to man the active duty forces has remained roughly constant since the late 1950's (in fact, it has actually declined modestly). However, beginning in 1954, the number of young men turning 19 increased every year, and dramatically so starting about 1961.

If we exclude those not legally eligible to serve for mental, medical or other reasons, we find that roughly 85 percent of those eligible to serve in 1954 could have been expected to actually serve. The proportion required to serve had fallen to 50 percent in 1964 (38 percent of the total population), and by fiscal 1980 it is estimated that the population required to serve will be only 20 percent.[6]

It is striking that just as the development of an excess of supply of manpower as against demand coincided in the United States with a movement to a volunteer force, so it is that the statistics of supply and demand among our Western allies correspond precisely with their conscription decisions (see Table 16.1).

How would the advocates of a draft move from an AVF system to a conscription system in the face of an adequate supply of qualified volunteers? There are several possible answers. They might keep pay, or at least recruit pay, below the minimum wage so as to deter volunteering. But this seems extraordinarily unfair: Why tax recruits as well as draft them? It would be reckless: What happens to recruit quality during the transition period while the AVF is made to fail? And it is apparently politically infeasible: there is a strong constituency in Congress, and since the pay raises of the early 1970s, in the military and in the public at large, for paying military recruits in the range of the minimum wage. In my view a draft cannot (and should not) be achieved by depressing pay.

As an alternative method to reach a draft one could raise the entry standards. But such a step would be hard to defend and hard to administer. The military already rejects 25% of the population and the army is required by law to accept no more than 35% of its male recruits without a high school diploma, and no more than 20% of its new accessions from those who score beneath the thirtieth percentile on military aptitude exams.[10]

Standards that are higher than this would reject many who the military indisputably can use for the bulk of its essentially blue-collar jobs. Moreover, a draft that claimed to reject, say, the bottom 40% of the population of eighteen-year-old males probably would be widely perceived as inequitable and would generate great pressures to underachieve on entrance tests.

Another tack would be to expand our armed forces so that even though the supply may not be depressed, it will nonetheless be swamped by increases in demand. But this is to put the cart before the horse. A manpower system should meet military needs; military needs should not be created to justify manpower theories. Moreover, though occasionally ambitious plans for manpower are suggested, the military often, and the Congress even more frequently, postpones or negates these plans in favor of dollar investments elsewhere. Though growth on the order of 180,000 personnel is projected in the FY1984 five-year plan,[11] plans for growth of that magnitude, even if achieved, would not warrant a return to the draft.

The main hope of the draft proponents is not that a draft would arise from something they would do, but rather that it may occur in the normal course in the later 1980s as a result of adverse demographic trends and an improving economy. These two phenomena have already been the subject of much discussion and I will therefore not dwell on them. I note, however, that

Table 16.1. Percentage of Eligible Males Required to
Man Military Forces in NATO Countries[7]

Country	Type	Percent Required
France[8]	Conscript	100
Norway	Conscript	97
Netherlands	Conscript	64
Portugal	Conscript	60
West Germany	Conscript	50
Denmark	Conscript	34
United States[9]	Volunteer	20-25
Canada	Volunteer	12
Britain	Volunteer	8

reliance on these events is suggestive of the irrelevance of the AVF-draft debate. Draft proponents are not pressing a policy alternative for today's world. They are expressing a policy preference, and indicating that they hope and expect that the world will change enough to make their views relevent. In this sense at present they are stronger on predictions than on prescriptions. To continue the stage metaphor with which I began, they are doing no more than waiting for Godot.

Meanwhile there are very real problems that afflict our manpower system. Within the manpower field too much is said in panels at conferences, at congressional hearings, and in papers and in books about the AVF as against the draft. Too little is said about what size our military ought to be, about the reserve-active mix, about our inadequate training systems, about the too costly turbulence in our assignment systems, and about the distortive effects of our promotion and compensation systems. These are not unknown topics, but they are, in my view, underdiscussed topics, while the issue of volunteers versus conscripts is an overdiscussed topic. Moreover, in no respect (except perhaps marginally in regard to the reserves) does a decision about the draft significantly affect these issues.

THE APPEAL OF NATIONAL SERVICE

National service is naturally appealing in this context. In the first place, though its roots can be traced to the 1910 William James essay, "A Moral Equivalent of War," national service is a relatively new approach to an enduring problem. If the draft-AVF debate is both long running and sterile, it is not surprising that many people seek a third position, and that many of these are interested in national service. Moreover, national service profits by the fact that it means many different things to many different people. Since World War II we have lived with the draft for a quarter of a century, and with a volunteer system for more than a decade. The limitations of both are well known and plausible variations within their moulds are familiar. National service, however, encompasses almost as many ideas, most of them described in only general terms, as it has proponents. It is not so much an idea as an ideal. If politics generally produces strange bedfellows it is particularly prone to do so under a blanket as broad as that provided by the ideal of national service.

The uncertainty about what national service is, and of how it might mesh with other manpower options, is manifested by the fact that both proponents and opponents of the AVF have been attracted to the concept as a means of reaching their diverse ends. To proponents of conscription, national service is attractive because it offers a means of circumventing three fundamental difficulties that would otherwise afflict a draft. The first arises from the already noted supply and demand factors that make any peacetime U.S. military draft too small to take more than a fraction of the eligible male population. (The problem is compounded if women are included.) It seems very likely that the resulting draft, one that would impose a burden on only a small fraction of the cohort, would encourage resentment in those who were called and would undermine that sense of nearly universal public obligation and shared experience that draft advocates associate with the World War II and Korean War experiences, and seek now to reestablish.

Second, so long as a draft is random and volunteers are accepted, the middle and upper classes are likely to be dramatically under represented in the enlisted force. If, for example, 200,000 male volunteers are accepted and 100,000 male draftees are inducted, then the volunteers are not likely to include much more of the middle and upper classes than they do now, and in a perfectly representative draft only 30,000 of the 100,000 draftees would be from the top 30% of the population.[12] It is highly debatable whether this increment in the quality or representativeness of junior enlisted men serving two years would have a substantial positive effect on the over 2,000,000-member American military. It is even harder to argue that it is better to obtain these high-quality people by the relatively cumbersome mechanism of a draft (with heavy costs for many besides these men) than by some targeted bonus or pay initiatives (for example, for college graduates who enlist). It is most difficult of all to argue that a draft in these circumstances would render the military substantially more racially and socioeconomically representative than it is now. As noted above, even with a draft, the racial and economic composition of the military will be dominated by the propensity of those from poorer backgrounds to volunteer and (no less significant) to reenlist.

Third, there are special political, judicial, and personnel management problems associated with military conscription. Politically, resistance to the reestablishment of a military draft is likely to be severe. Judicially, the last years of the draft saw a widening of the deferment for conscientious objection to military service.[13] Claims under this and other headings would be sure to provoke much litigation and contention. Finally, many military personnel officers do not want a truly random sample of able-bodied men (or men and women). The volunteer force gives them those who are there by choice. Pro draft personnel officers would like to reach beyond that, but they seek to enlist those who would not volunteer but will willingly serve once inducted, or (at least) those who are not "true volunteers" but will volunteer if they think that a draft is likely to induct them on less favorable terms. This portion of the youth population (probably a majority) makes good soldiers even if reluctant recruits. Personnel officers would like to avoid a further fraction of the population which rebels against military service even after induction. Those with deep-rooted aversions to military life often wind up in brigs, desert, or become "trouble makers." The presence of this group in the military is unquestionably a cost of the draft; a cost notably reduced under an all-volunteer system.

The first of these problems might be circumvented by a system of universal military service. Here again, however, the underlying demographics restrict the political alternatives. Even at its lowest ebb, even excluding women, the youth cohort between now and the end of the century substantially exceeds any probable military demand. No one, the military least of all, would think it sensible to almost triple our armed forces simply for the purpose of absorbing two million young men each and every year for two-year terms.

Against this backdrop, ideas of compulsory national service, that is systems of service that would allocate some fraction of the youth cohort to civilian service and some fraction to military service, have a substantial appeal to advocates of the draft. At least in the abstract they offer possibilities of dealing with each of the three types of problems mentioned.

First by broadening service opportunities they make universal service plausible. Thus a "rite of passage" is established for each generation, the inequities of having some but not all serve are avoided,[14] and a sense of service as a fact of life is engrained.

Second, once it is established that all will serve in some capacity, the "market" available to the military may change markedly. Middle and upper-class youth will no longer see their choice as between pursuing entirely private ends and enlisting in the military, but rather as between which form of public service, civilian or military, to pursue. Some who have reflected on the matter believe that in this circumstance a substantial number will choose the military. Moreover, it has not escaped those concerned primarily with furthering military ends within a system of national service that the system can be loaded to offer greater rewards (typically pay or educational benefits) for military than for civilian service.[15] Some have suggested yet further enhancing the military mix by imposing high ability or achievement requirements for military service, while setting no such requirements for civilian service.[16] Screens of this sort seem to their proponents to be much more tolerable in the context of universal national service than of selective military service. In the universal system those who pass through the military screen know that those who do not still must serve in a civilian capacity.

Third, a civilian alternative to military service is undoubtedly attractive to some who seek military conscription because it offers the possibility of defusing objections to conscription from many who might tolerate civilian but not military service.[17] Moreover, if those who object to military service can freely opt for civilian service, most (though not all) conscientious objector issues will be circumvented. Finally, a choice between categories of service could be expected to cause those who have a pronounced distaste for military life to screen themselves out of the military branch of the program. This would ease problems of military morale, training, and discipline.

At the other end of the spectrum other visions of national service are viewed by some as potentially helpful to an all-volunteer force. The notion here is that if a system were established where young people expected to devote themselves to a period of service between high school and a job or college, then military recruitment would profit from this expectation.[18] By this view, an expectation of national service as an interlude would make the military more likely than it now is to draw the college-bound and the upwardly mobile. Of course, if a voluntary national service plan drew off those who now volunteer for the military without adding at least equivalent numbers to those who serve, it would undermine the AVF. But if one could move from the present system to a system where almost all young people expected to serve, that expectation would benefit the AVF.[19] It has been suggested that such a transformation of American society might be possible, for example by conditioning federal student aid at the college level to a period of service,[20] or by giving priority for federal employment to those who have served.[21]

ALTERNATIVE FORMS OF NATIONAL SERVICE AND THEIR IMPLICATIONS FOR THE MILITARY

Can national service in one form or another realistically be looked to either to rationalize a draft or to strengthen the All-Volunteer Force? To answer this question one must be more explicit about the specifics of such plans, in particular about when they might be implemented and what forms they might take.

A number of different methods of characterizing national service alternatives have been suggested.[22] Let us consider four variations. A first system might require a very limited commitment from some or all young people so as to expose them to the opportunities and rewards of public service. Senators Nunn and Bradley, among others, have suggested that such programs are attractive enough to warrant experimentation and analysis. In an extended study of national service alternatives for the Ford Foundation, I and my coauthor, Peter Szanton, have designed such a program around a requirement of 240 hours of public service as a prerequisite to receiving a high school diploma. Service would be either on a full-time basis for up to three months, or on a part-time basis during school hours over one school year.

A second type of national service program would aim to encourage volunteering, either by providing priority for government benefits (notably college tuition loans and grants), by outright payments to volunteers, or by subsidizing the charitable organizations that solicit and supervise volunteers.

A third type of program might reenact the military draft but provide draftees facing two years in the military with a civilian service alternative. This alternative service would be similar to that required in past conscientious objector programs save that those who opt for it need not be conscientious objectors. Civilian service would be open freely to any draftee who preferred it. A system of this type now exists in Germany. It seems to me to have a very substantial chance of enactment if a military draft were reinstituted in the United States.

Finally, a fourth form of national service program, the form most often envisioned by the general public, might establish a year of public service at or below the minimum wage (Vista volunteers are now paid two-thirds the minimum wage) as a normal attribute of citizenship. In our Ford Foundation study we have devised an unusual way of enforcing such a requirement. Instead of making nonparticipation subject to prosecution, our version of this plan would impose a recurring 5% surcharge on federal income taxes to be paid each year by every citizen over age 18 who had not yet performed a year of national service.[23] This approach would allow the participant to serve at any time he or she prefers and would thereby hopefully both minimize the intrusion and increase the range of ages (and therefore skills and maturity levels) available for service.

In all these programs, an analysis of the civilian costs and benefits is crucial and this has absorbed the bulk of the effort in our Ford Foundation study. But a sketch of our conclusions about the military implications of these systems should serve the purposes of this chapter.

LIMITED SERVICE AS A PREREQUISITE TO HIGH SCHOOL GRADUATION

Programs of this first type, requiring limited service as a prerequisite to high school graduation, could be tied into the military by, for example, offering a three-month unpaid army basic training course as an alternative to civilian service as a means of fulfilling the national service requirement.[24] What would the practical implications of such a program be for the armed services? The first step in any such assessment must be to estimate the fraction of high school students who would apply for military rather than civilian service. When Gallup polls in 1979 and 1981 asked eighteen and nineteen-year-olds, and in 1982 asked sixteen to eighteen-year-olds, to choose between hypothesized equivalent one-year compulsory military and civilian national service programs, consistently about 45% of the men and 15% of the women chose the military program.[25] If these proportions were to hold in a school-based, part-time program, then the military would face as many as 583,000 applications from physically and mentally qualified men and 195,000 applications from qualified women.[26]

Focusing on the army, which is the service most likely to operate any program like this one, we have calculated the marginal cost of establishing special training battalions for high school, national service participants alongside of regular training units. Such costs would vary between $5,000 per recruit for a small program (around 10,000 trainees) slipped in where the army had extra capacity, to $10,800 per recruit where increments to the training base would be required. This implies that a program that accepted all qualified applicants (i.e., those who chose military over civilian service) would cost over $7.5 billion and would, we estimate, absorb between 10 and 15% of the army's career personnel. Smaller numbers of applicants might result from recognition that the military program would demand more time and dislocation than the civilian program, or from a decision by those with interest in military service to sign up only under the regular, paid, military recruitment program under which service and training would begin after high school.[27] Under any conditions under any such program it is highly likely that the services would be faced with many more applicants than they could reasonably accommodate without disproportionately large allocations of money and manpower to expand the training establishment. The army ought reasonably to respond to this by limiting its program to some 50,000 participants (above and beyond the 233,000 people the army now trains each year).[28] This would entail additional costs of about $540 million per year (8.7% of the army budget authority in fiscal year 1984) plus modest one-time costs of about $40 million to activate training facilities. Such a program would require about 1% of the army's career personnel to provide and manage "national service" training.[29]

For this the army would receive a look at potential recruits with no commitments either by the military or by the recruit. At present, however, the services have the option of discharging unsatisfactory recruits in basic training or later. Thus, a "free look" at potential recruits would be of small value to the military.

Giving potential recruits a free look at the military might be of more value. As a practical matter, recruits can now leave basic training by attrition, and do so approximately 10% of the time. A clearly defined free look, however, might entice participation out of some who are unwilling to make the normally required three-year commitment. Though the evidence is imprecise, interview data suggest that on average those who graduate from basic training do so with about the same regard for the military as they had when they entered training.[30] Thus, the basic training experience is not strikingly likely to enhance the propensity to respond to later military recruiting.[31]

Moreover, by almost any plausible set of numbers, the consequence of any active-force recruitment gains is likely to be almost insignificantly small given a total requirement for some 350,000 active-duty recruits each year. Of somewhat more benefit would be the fact that active-duty recruits who had been through this program would begin their regular enlistments with three months of essentially unpaid training under their belts. This would reduce training costs, extend useful service, and probably reduce attrition rates,[32] yielding an offsetting savings of around $50 million.

Effects on reserve recruitment (where some 60,000 enlistments occur each year) might be of the most benefit to the army. The major stumbling block to reserve recruitment is the initial period of full-time training. This ninety-day period tends to drive away the highest-quality recruits because these recruits tend to have jobs that they are unwilling or unable to leave for so long a time. If basic training had been achieved in high school, the personal sacrifice each recruit would make to enter the reserves would be considerably lowered and reserve recruitment seems likely to be enhanced.[33]

This would be especially true for the individual ready reserve (the IRR). Volunteering might be induced from basic training graduates by offering small annual payments (e.g., $200) for an IRR commitment. The current army shortfall of 240,000 IRR members will be alleviated by a 1983 law committing new recruits to an extended time in the IRR after active duty. Still, if, as is not unlikely, IRR requirements rise, some 34,000 additional men might be on the IRR rolls at any one time as a result of an annual flow of 50,000 participants in the military component of a national service program.

From interviews and my own judgment, however, it would seem likely that the services would regard the defense department dollars spent on a national service program of this type as better spent on other military items, or on other ways of increasing active reserve and IRR enrollments. Equivalent sums seem likely to yield a better return, for example, directed towards extending the IRR enlistments of those who have left the active-duty force and to retaining reservists who are already enlisted. Those whose military experience consists only of ninety days individual training, without unit experience, are only marginally effective soldiers to begin with, and their utility diminishes rapidly as their skills erode with time.

On balance, accordingly, my assessment is that a school-based national service program would be modestly, but only modestly, attractive to the services; that the military would likely participate in such a program without objection if it were part of a larger national policy to do so; but that if the services had to pay the military costs of the program out of their own budgets, they would likely prefer not to participate in such a program. In the latter instance, there would be particularly strong resistance to any proposals that the military accept more than about 50,000 national service participants.

Voluntary National Service

Programs that would use federal funds to enhance the capacity of charitable organizations to elicit volunteers receive some considerable attention in our Ford Foundation study. They are, however, essentially irrelevant to the military, and so will not be discussed here. Programs that would pay volunteers for public service work face a substantial problem because any significant level of payment (even at a fraction of the minimum wage) is likely to elicit heavy enrollments from the unemployed and the underemployed. This both raises costs to probably unacceptable levels and undermines the philosophic premises that this is a service, not a jobs program. Under any conditions, by establishing competing systems of public employment, plans of this character clearly make the military recruitment problem more, not less, difficult.

Accordingly, the only plans of this type that offer possible benefits to the military are those, suggested by Charles C. Moskos, Jr., The Atlantic Council, and others, that would predicate educational (or other benefits) on time in public service.[34] The government is now spending over $5 billion a year in direct support of the 45% of those Americans who attend college, and it is thereby competing with its own military recruitment efforts. If this subsidy were confined to those who served in the military, or at least to those who had performed some public service, military recruitment efforts would benefit. This proposition is logical. The questions, however, are how far this point ought to carry, and how far it is likely to carry, policymakers. In my view the evidence suggests that it is neither desirable nor practical to enhance military recruitment by appropriating the federal portion of the $13.6 billion that now offers tuition support for those attending college.

There is, to begin with, a widespread sense and a well-developed political constituency that regards educational support as an entitlement not to be tampered with. Even if that view could be defeated (and putting aside whether it should be), proponents of this plan have not explained how they would deal with the claims of the vast majority of women and the 500,000 men who would not qualify for military service, or for that matter the claims of another three-quarters of a million or so men who would qualify but would not be accepted because the military will need only some 300,000 male recruits per year.

More seriously still, after several years of discussion a convincing case has yet to be made that the profile of the military force would change significantly for the better under such a plan.[35] A system that offered educational benefits only, or primarily, through the military seems likely to draw proportionately more applicants from lower economic backgrounds and more blacks than does the present system. Moreover, as has often been noted, it would offer strong incentives for the most talented of these recruits to leave the service so as to use their educational benefits as soon as they become available. Finally, with military education benefits presently as high as $20,100 in return for a $2,700 contribution, there is little reason to believe that the present system does not achieve much of what the desired reorientation seeks.

In short, national service programs that reward "voluntary" public service do not appear either very likely to be very attractive to the military or very likely to be passed.

CIVILIAN SERVICE AS AN ADJUNCT TO A MILITARY DRAFT

A national service program that gave military conscripts a choice of civilian in lieu of military service would, I believe, reduce resistance to a draft. Such a program might require an individual's commitment to a civilian alternative as early as the time of draft registration (as in legislation drafted by the National Service Secretariat and introduced into Congress by Pete McClosky)[36] or as late as the time of an induction order (as in the model plan analyzed in our Ford Foundation study). In either circumstance, an outlet for those who were particularly averse to military service might be appealing both to congressmen who had to vote on draft legislation and to young people called upon to accept what had been enacted.

By increasing the fraction of those serving, a civilian alternative would also expand the size of a draft and thereby diminish the sense of ill-fortune and inequity that those conscripted might feel. Excluding the Vietnam War years, the military draft from 1954 to 1971 drew, on average, 11% of the total male cohort.[37] A 100,000-man military draft would conscript less than 5.5% of the cohort in the later 1980s. With a civilian alternative, Gallup poll data suggest that about 125,000 men would choose civilian service before 100,000 conscripted men entered the military.[38] The resulting 225,000-man draft would draw about 12% (or slightly above the historical fraction) of the cohort.

A program that simply afforded a conscript a free and equal choice between military and civilian service would appear likely, however, to offer little benefit to the military. Objections that the conscription process would be rendered complicated and uncertain could be overcome. Projections of civilian-military choices should be fairly simple, and under less than extreme conditions the manpower pool should be more than sufficient to meet military needs. Under a choice at registration plan, abnormal conditions would be coped with by providing for a residual liability for those who choose civilian service: they would not be exempted, but instead would merely fall to the bottom of the draft pool. Under a choice of induction plan, the president could be granted authority to cancel the civilian option if "national security" warranted such action. Of greater concern to the military is the likelihood that conscripts with more privileged backgrounds and higher test scores would opt for civilian service more often than lower-quality conscripts. The national service aspects of the plan therefore would impede improvements in "quality" or representativeness that some draft proponents seek.[39]

This impediment could be diminished by weighting salary and benefits in favor of military service, but it seems likely that at most such steps would moderate the impact of the national service component of the program. National service in this context is therefore a concession that draft proponents might want to make, and that draft opponents might want to secure, on the eve of conscription. But it is not an innovation that would help military manpower problems.[40]

To make a program of this character really attractive to the armed forces, a high threshold (e.g., a strict requirement of high school graduation) would have to be set for military service to keep out the less qualified who would choose that option. Thus the military would, in effect, be drafting only the best while pushing the less desirable portion of the cohort into civilian national service. Some will regard this as a plausible scenario. Others may think it desirable. I think a program so heavily weighted as this would be neither desirable nor politically palatable. So heavily loaded a plan would, I believe, impede a return to the draft and prompt more, not less, active resistance among college students and other elite groups.

In sum, a national service plan of this type would depend on an independent case for resurrecting the military draft. It might facilitate acceptance of that case, but only at the cost of making the resulting draft less attractive to the military.

UNIVERSAL COMPULSORY SERVICE

Only one type of national service program materially aids military recruitment. This is the set of plans under which the entire cohort now reaching age eighteen, or at least the entire male portion of such a cohort, would have an obligation to undertake a substantial period of public service. If, for example, a one-year national service requirement were established, the costs of military service would be reduced because a three-year military hitch would represent a less daunting diversion to potential recruits. In such a situation, the military should be able to improve both the quality and, should it so desire, the quantity of personnel recruited. Gains could also probably be translated into lower pay, or in some cases longer terms if desired.

It should be apparent, however, that the military tail will (and should) be too small to wag the dog of universal conscripted national service. Considerations of effects on the national service participants themselves, or of the costs and benefits of the civilian work associated with such a plan, might arguably warrant such a system. Whether they do is the subject of extensive discussion in our Ford Foundation study. For present purposes it is sufficient to note that the small gains in quality or terms of service of the some 150,000 military recruits that might be affected at the margin could hardly be substantial enough to warrant a system that compelled service from one-and-one-half to two-million men (and perhaps as many women) in each year group, at a cost authoritatively estimated five years ago at about $25 billion dollars per year.[41] If national service comes to affect military manpower policy in this expansive form, it is fairly safe to anticipate that military manpower issues will be in the category of effects much more than in the category of causes.

This view is buttressed by considerations of timing. We are now a substantial way into the twelve-year demographic downturn that poses the most serious challenge to military recruitment prospects. National service did not bulk large among 1984 presidential election issues, particularly given military recruitment achievements that will make fiscal year 1984, like 1981, 1982, and 1983, a successful recruitment year. If 1985 is a poor recruitment year, one can imagine a military impetus for initiating national service programs and serious debate about such topics in the latter part of the year and 1986. But it seems very likely that before embarking on a program of the magnitude just described, this society would move cautiously in testing any national service alternatives for at least two years after the debate had crystallized. Even the most rapid scenario, accordingly, ought to anticipate broad-gauged national service—the only national service plan truly relevant to military manpower problems—as an issue in the 1988 presidential elections.

Universal compulsory national service is thus at most a program that might come in 1989. And this, though it would be a time of the severest demographic depression and therefore least manpower supply relative to demand, would also be close to the time in which the demographic trends would begin to improve. In this circumstance, one may doubt the national willingness to take so bold a step as universal compulsory national service for military reasons. If military needs were the only substantial pressure in this direction I would speculate that the national preference would be to bolster the volunteer system with inflated bonuses or pay rates that were viewed as temporary, or with a draft that might be viewed similarly as an interim measure, but one more easily reversible than a national service system would be.

SUMMARY

National service is an interesting, and for some, seductive concept. But it is not a program that is likely substantially to resolve military manpower problems in the years ahead. It offers a third position in the AVF-draft debate, but that position prompts no near-term options that are more useful for the military than do the alternatives it is supposed to replace. This is not to say that national service is not an interesting and important national issue. It is to argue instead that it is an issue that needs to be evaluated primarily on the basis of effects various national service plans would have on civilian more than on military life. It is also to contend that persistent arguments about modes of recruiting are less important than what I regard as the real problems of the military manpower system: training, retention, promotion, and force-mix. The topic of recruitment lends itself to moving ideological soliloquies, and national service may ultimately be a deus ex machina for military manpower scenarios; but it will come (if it comes) only slowly, late, and in response to a script catalyzed by much more than military requirements. Meanwhile, for military manpower professionals the real action is elsewhere on stage.

NOTES

1. The United States instituted conscription in 1863 (Civil War), 1917 (World War I), 1940 (on the eve of World War II), and again (after a brief AVF interlude) in 1948. On the history of conscription in the United States see Cooper, Richard V.L., *Military Manpower and the All-Volunteer Force* (Santa Monica, CA: Rand Corporation, 1977), pp. 46 ff; John Rafuse, "United States Experiece with Volunteer and Conscript Forces" in *Studies Prepared for the President's Commission on an All-Volunteer Armed Force*, vol. 2 (Washington, D.C.: Government Printing Office, 1970); and Walter Millis, *Arms and Men* (New York: Putnam, 1956).

2. See e.g., *The Los Angeles Times* editorial, "Army of the Poor" 6 April 1981, Part II: "The essential mixture of classes that once characterized the services—which means a mixture of values, attitudes and services—has largely disappeared. The services are less effective for it. The country is less strong than it should be militarily and, we think, morally. The haves are freed from the obligation of military service, the have-nots are sucked in to fill the vacuum. This is a disturbing state of affairs. More to the point, it is a shameful one."

3. Moskos, Charles C., "Social Considerations of the All-Volunteer Force" in Brent Scowcroft, ed, *Military Service in the United States* (Englewood Cliffs, NJ: Prentice-Hall 1982), pp. 137 ff.

4. A letter from Senator Clairborne Pell to Secretary of Defense Caspar Weinberger, dated 9 July 1981, puts this proposition: "In my view the volunteer Army . . . has truly become a mercenary force. . . . In my view, national service can be a powerful force in meeting the military and non-military needs of our nation, as well as strengthing the 'sense of service' which historically has been so important to success as a society." See also the *Wall Street Journal's* editorial advocacy of a study of national service, "A National Service Debate" (May 29, 1981, p.24), to the same effect.

5. The issue of ethnic representation is discussed at length in Binkin and Eitelberg et al., *Blacks and the Military* (Washington, DC: The Brookings Institution, 1982).

6. Cooper, *Military Manpower.*

7. This information was drawn from North Atlantic Assembly, *Manpower Issues for NATO*, Brussels, Belgium (1983), by Gary R. Nelson, Robert F. Hale and Joel Slackman in their supporting work for our Ford Foundation study. The North Atlantic Assembly publications is not precise about the meaning of "eligibles." It appears that the percentages refer to make recruits entering active duty as a percentage of all physically and mentally qualified youth who, for those countries with conscription, do not receive status as conscientious objectors. Cooper's 1977 study (p.61) presents a chart showing the relationship between GNP, total population, force size, and conscription choice in selected countries all over the world. In commenting on his less refined data, Cooper stresses budgetary considerations: ". . . with the exception of the United States . . ., countries [that maintain an all-volunteer force] are either poor (e.g., Jordan), or have small forces (e.g., Canada), or both (e.g., India). Thus, the poorer the nation and the smaller the force, the easier it is to attract a sufficient number of volunteers." (p.60). Cooper does not comment on how Britian's volunteer force meshes with this observation.

8. France requires almost 100% of its young males to serve in a national service program.

9. U.S. figures show total number of male enlisted recruits without prior military service who entered military forces in FY1981 as a percentage of the eligible population of U.S. males The lower percent shows recruits to active duty only; the larger one includes those in the reserves. Eligibles were estimated as the total population of males less 10% for those not mentally fit (category V) and another 10% for those not physically qualified.

10. These restrictions first appeared in the Department of Defense Authorization Act, 1981, Conference Report, Title III, Sec. 302.

11. In the president's budget for FY1984, the navy projected increases of 46,500 (8%) and the air force of 91,000 (15%) people to come onto active duty between 1983 and 1988. The army and marines projected smaller percentage increases, 34,400 (4%) and 8.700 (4%) respectively. Of the 35,000 personnel requested for FY1984, however, Congress authorized an increment of only 8,500. Congressional scrutiny will be similarly vigorous in the future and even service requests will probably diminish in the outyears as fiscal constraints impinge.

12. These numbers are merely illustrative. In a somewhat more detailed discussion, the former director of the selective service system calculated that if the army drew 50% of its manpower requirements from volunteers and 50% from conscription, the net effect would be to raise the percentage of accessions in the highest test score group from 24.3% to 31.6% and to lower the percentage in the lowest acceptable test group from 27.1% to 25.2%. The author concludes that "the draft would do little to change the profile of today's military accessions." Bernard Rostker, "How Can the Draft Be Fair," *Washington Post*, 5 August 1981, p. A23. Binkin and Eitelberg et al., undertake a similar analysis and suggest somewhat more positive results. Their chart (p. 146) estimates that the fraction of high school graduates among army accessions might have increased from 78% to 83%, and lowest mental category entrants might have declined from 30% to 18% if an expansion of 100,000 army men had caused a draft of 51,000 men in FY1981. Of course the impact on the total force profile would be substantially smaller than on the profile of accessions.

13. In a communication with the author, James Lacy, who has researched this matter, has estimated that of ten million males ordered for induction in World War II, only 17,000 refused to enter the service on the grounds of conscientious objection and that the number of CO claims were consistently below 20,000 per year until the Vietnam build up. In 1967 he reports 24,000 claims; in 1968, 29,000 claims; and in 1969, 35,000 claims. By 1970, 42,000 claims were filed, and in 1971, the last year of a substantial draft, 65,000 claims were filed. Between 1965 and 1975, I estimate that there were over 500 conscientious objector cases in the federal appeals courts. In a renewed draft these numbers would probably be greatly affected by *Welsh v. United States*, 398 U.S. 333 (1970), holding that moral or ethical opposition to war, even if not based on religious views, warranted conscientious objector status. For a useful overview of law in this area, see Donald Meikelijohn, "Conscientious Objection in the Supreme Court," 8 *Cumberland Law Review*, 1 (1977).

14. Thus, for example, James Fallows: "The problem of capriciousness in a military draft could also be avoided by a generalized system of national service, which is my own preference. . ." James Fallows, *National Defense* (New York: Vintage Books, 1981) p. 138.

15. "Obviously, we sweeten the deal for those who take the option to go into the military services and once they put in their time will be eligible for the GI bill, which seems to be a major driving force." Testimony by Congressman Marilyn Lloyd in hearings on national service legislation before the Military Personnel Subcommittee of the House Armed Services Committee, March 4, 1980, p. 96.

16. For an example of this point of view circulating among military officers, see "How to Sharpen Uncle Sam's Defense Sword, Increase Home-Front Human Services, Shrink the Government, Cut Taxes, Reduce the Budget and Get America off Its Apathy," *Armed Forces Journal* (November 1980) p. 99. The "Services to America" proposal advanced there under the non de plume "Silver Flash II." entails one year of conscripted civilian or military service, but in the military branch: "No high school dropouts allowed."

17. However, see for example, "National Service—A National Disservice" in the July, 1981 *Washington Newsletter* of the Friends Committee on National Legislation, pp. 2, 4: "Is national service, as it is now being proposed in Congress, just a sugar-coated draft?" And see the comment of Congressman Samuel S. Stratton (an advocate of the draft) to Congressman Marilyn Lloyd (an advocate of national service) in hearings on national service legislation before the Military Personnel Subcommittee of the House Armed Services Committee, March 4, 1980, p. 100: "Isn't this really just an attempt, as you said yourself, to sweeten the deal, that you don't want to upset anybody by suggesting that military service would be mandatory. So you put up a facade by trying to appear that there is some choice in the hope that maybe you are going to get enough people to fill the military needs. Isn't it like burning down the house in order to get the pig roasted?"

18. "As the idea of voluntary service becomes more widely accepted among the young, the numbers who will choose to serve through the military should increase. Thus the move toward universal national service should make military recruiting easier, and help restore the tradition of citizen-soldier now giving way to a mercenary system." *Youth and the Needs of the Nation: Report of the Committee for the Study of National Service* (Washington DC: The Potomac Institute, 1979) p. 100. This 143-page document drafted by a committee of fourteen headed by Jacqueline Wexler and Harris Wofford, provides the most articulate current argument for a voluntary national service system. A minority of the committee apparently would have gone further and endorsed a compulsory plan.

19. Moskos, Charles C. "Making the All-Volunteer Force Work: A National Service Approach." *Foreign Affairs* 60 (Fall 1981), p. 34. "A growing expectation of voluntary service among youths generally will improve the climate of military recruitment. . . . The grand design is that the ideal of citizenship obligation ought to become part of growing up in America." In a similar vein two leading proponents of voluntary national service have written: "If the government expressed its trust in young people by

inviting them to serve for a period in voluntary service, before long many young people would come to appreciate the government's trust by enlisting in the military in sufficient numbers to obviate the need for a draft." Michael W. Sherraden and Donald J. Eberty, eds., *National Service: Social, Economical, and Military Impacts* (Elmsford, NY: Pergamon Press, 1982) p. 109.

20. Ibid., p. 34. "The program should be introduced step by step over, say, the next five years. In the interim, those who enlist in military reserve units or perform a term of civilian service would have priority for federal aid to college students; in time, participation in some form of national service would become a prerequisite for eligibility for federal post-secondary school assistance." Moskos would give especially substantial benefits to those who serve on active duty. His plan is also set out in his essay, "Social Considerations of the All-Volunteer Force" in Brent Scowcroft, ed., *Military Service*, p. 129. In a letter dated 8 July 1981, Congressman Leon Panetta, writting to Lawrence J. Korb, the assistant secretary of defense for manpower, reserve affairs and logistics, advances similar propositions in favor of a voluntary national service plan. Congressman Panetta notes that present tuition aid programs compete with military recruitment and he suggests that if these were conditioned on service, recruitment mught prosper. See also an editorial in the *Washington Star*, "GI Bill Without GI's," 28 January, 1981, urging the elaboration of plans which "make the crucial connection between obligations of citizenship and government assistance."

21. Sherraden and Eberly *National Service* p. 28.

22. The most frequently cited typology was offered in a Congressional Budget Office study, *National Service Programs and Their Effects on Military Manpower* (1978), which distinguished between a "small targeted," "broad-based voluntary" and "broad-based mandatory" national service program.

23. We also considered an alternative means of inducing participation without threat of criminal prosecution. This would be to predicate full social security retirement benefits on four quarters of public service in addition to forty quarters of regularly paid work now required for participation.

24. One can also envision a plan that required all aspiring high school graduates (or perhaps all male graduates) to participate in compulsory military training. The effects of such a "universal military training" (UMT) program and its costs can be inferred from my description of the smaller, and I believe, more plausible, program.

25. Gallup first asked, "Would you favor or oppose requiring all young men to give one year of service to the nation—either in the military forces or in non-military work here or abroad, such as VISTA or the Peace Corps?" They then asked, "Suppose all young men were required to give one year of service, which would you prefer, military or non-military?" Similar questions were asked substituting "women" for "men."

26. Nelson, Hale, and Slackman calculated these yields from the available high school population.

27. It is also possible that those in high school would have different preferences from those in the general population surveyed by Gallup. Those who prefer military service might be disproportionately often not qualified to do it. The numbers in the text should accordingly be treated as a top estimate.

28. The details of this analysis are from the supporting work of Nelson, Hale, and Slackman.

29. Nelson, Hale and Slackman, Table III-2 and page 1 of Chapter III. It may be possible to reduce modestly the $550 million in costs by using reserve personnel. Some reserves serve in units that would conduct wartime training. When they perform their annual two-weeks of full-time military duty, they are often assigned to help in military training. Some might be directed to help in training Program One students. But many of these reserves are already helping meet summertime peak loads for active-duty trainees. Thus savings are likely to be modest. Seasonal concentraton of national service participants would also pose other capacity and cost problems.

30. Kristiansen, Donald, "Attitudes Toward the Army Among Basic Trainees: 1970 versus 1974" (U.S. Army Research Institute for the Behavioral and Social Sciences, 1978) p. 11.

31. Recruiting competition among the services might cause some Department of Defense ambivalence. Army training might be regarded as a recruiting difficulty by the navy, air force and marines.

32. Attrition rates could be expected to decline because recruits and the army would both be unusually well informed about each other after participation in this program.

33. It is difficult to quantify this enhancement. Not only is propensity to enlist in the reserves after a program of this character unknown, there is also no basis for estimating the diversion of potential reserve recruits into the active force and for estimating any mismatch between remaining reserve prospects and unit locations and skill needs.

34. The Atlantic Council, *Report of the Atlantic Council's Working Group on Military Service* (Washington DC: The Atlantic Council of the United States, June 1982). p. 37.

35. The issue is canvassed in two studies by the Congressional Budget Office, "Improving Military

Educational Benefits: Effects on Costs, Receiving, and Retention" (1982) and "Education Benefits: Proposals to Improve Manning in the Military" (1981). Binkin and Eitelberg, *Blacks and the Military*, conclude "At any rate, there is insufficient empirical evidence to support the contention that the adoption of a GI bill will alter the socieconomic or racial profile of the armed forces" (p. 144).

36.   H. R. 2206 (1979).

37.   This calculation, performed for the Ford Foundation study by Nelson, Hale, and Slackman, draws on Department of Defense, *Selected Manpower Statistics* and on historical population studies by the Bureau of the Census.

38.   See footnote 26 and related text.

39.   A 1980 Department of Education survey, described in National Center for Education Statistics Bulletin 81-245B (April 10, 1981) found that whites reported a preference for civilian service in a compulsory program by a ratio of 1.4 to 1, while blacks preferred military service by a ratio of 1.3 to 1. Using Gallup Poll data from 1979, 1981, and 1982 for our Ford Foundation study, Nelson, Hale, and Slackman conclude that "the results raise concern" that military recruits under this program "might not match AVF and draft results" in educational achievement.

40.   An argument could be made that if a reserve membership secured a draft deferment, that a 12% draft (as a result of a civilian alternative) would better promote reserve enlistment thn a 5½% draft. I weigh this argument lightly because: first, I do not anticipate that reserve membership would be ground for deferment in a future draft; second, because even if it were, I doubt that the difference between 12 and 5½% drafts would materially affect reserve recruitment; and third, because under any conditions, I see reserve problems as more the result of difficulties in training and retention than of shortfalls in recruitment.

41.   We have not yet established cost estimates in our Ford study. In 1978, the Congressional Budget Office estimated costs for a program like this at 24 billion then current dollars. Congressional Budget Office, *National Service Programs and Their Effects on Military Manpower and Civilian Youth Problems* (1978). See also Harold Hovey, *Universal Service: An Economical Overview* (Fund for the City of New York: Draft Report, June 1982).

COMMENTARY

DISCUSSANTS

Stanley Resor

I have just one comment on General Thurman's presentation. I think it is another example of one of the wonderful jobs the United States Army has done with a tremendously difficult task. I'm sure that with that kind of sophisticated approach and with help from Congress, it is possible to make the All-Volunteer Force work to the extent of getting the numbers and of recruiting the mix of soldiers which he has described. However, my concerns are based on the tests John Kester has suggested. Specifically, I think that the All-Volunteer Force has to be judged by the kind of fighting capability it creates to carry out our foreign policy and sustain and support our national security interests.

Some of the concerns that Kester has outlined trouble me deeply. Specifically, I think that the All-Volunteer Force has a tendency to make the army smaller than it would be with selected service. Secondly, as it now stands, I think the army does not have an adequate mobilization capability.

As to smallness, I think it's well illustrated by what the Atlantic Council's Working Group on Military Service observed when it studied the situation in 1982. The army active-duty forces are smaller than in June 1964, the last pre-Vietnam draft year. This reduction in size has forced the army to transfer from the active forces to the selected reserves 100,000 positions in units which, in the event of a conflict in Europe, would be required to deploy in the first thirty days.

Past experience with the call-up of the army selected reserves confirms, without exception, that it is wholly unrealistic to expect selected reserve force units to reach a level of readiness which would meet that kind of a schedule. In 1968 some units from the selected reserves were deployed, after the Tet offensive, to Vietnam. It was an ideal situation for deploying reserves. We could see the call-up coming. We got everything ready, including having their beds made before the units arrived on post. It still required nintey days to deploy the first combat unit, which was an artillery battalion, and it was deployed as soon as it was judged deployable. In the Korean War the time to ready units was much longer. For adequate mobilization capability, it is clear that the United States Army has to have an operating selective service to provide additional trained strength in some reasonable time. Such a capability would, of course, be extremely important in an international crisis if one wished to escalate force readiness to increase deterrence in order to prevent a conflict. How can one possibly do this without an operating selective service system? And of course, when the conflict starts, there will be a greater need for additional trained strength; otherwise it will be necessary to raid reserve units for trained manpower at the very time it is necessary to bring them up to strength for deployment.

John Kester has also mentioned the serious problem with the Military Selective Service Act's provision which authorizes exemption for conscientious objectors. Interpretation of that provision by the Supreme Court has created a very subjective test of what a CO is. A study should be done to see if by creating a statutory definition of conscientious objector, the test could be made more objective and the scope more narrow than it has been in practice. If that doesn't appear feasible, then at least if a selective service system were in operation, one would learn the scope of the exemption by seeing how many people successfully exercise it.

Richard Danzig's presentation raises a question: Is conscription workable in the face of the manpower tools projected for the end of the 1980s and the 1990s? Is it feasible or would such a small number come through the draft that it would be politically unacceptable? Kester, in his discussion, recognized that problem and believes it can be dealt with. I also think there are ways to structure a draft so that you would be taking a reasonable proportion of the eligible pool. In fact, James L. Lacey has designed a model which is described in the Atlantic Council study. It's the intermediate or balanced model which would call for about 165,000 inductees each year, or about 35% of accessions. Under that same model, about one-third of the eligible manpower pool would be required to serve. I think this would be an acceptable form of conscription.

Should conscription legislation provide an alternative to civilian national service? If a feasible alternative could be designed, it would make conscription more palatable in Congress and with youth. However, as Danzig goes on to point out, we haven't seen a feasible program as yet. Such a program must deal with two major problems. One, the so called "quality drain-off" runs the risk that the more qualified conscripts would elect civilian service. However, it should be possible to deal with this problem by making the alternative, civilian service, less attractive in terms of pay or term of service. The other problem is the heavy cost of a civilian service program. That is a problem for which I've not yet seen a satisfactory solution. It is in an area that deserves more work. I do not see it as an insoluble problem but rather as one which has not received adequate study as yet.

Finally, just a word about the significant change which has occurred in the strategic context since the All-Volunteer Force decision was made and the possible impact that it could have on public perception of a return to the draft. The All-Volunteer Force, as Kester has pointed out, was essentially a political decision taken in the 1960s as the United States was starting to phase out of an unpopular war. In the fourteen years since then, the strategic context has significantly changed. The Soviet Union has achieved essential equivalence with the United States in strategic nuclear weapons and the United States has codified that new relationship in two treaties. The Soviets have also deployed the SS-20 in Europe, which has affected the relationship in the medium-range nuclear forces.

In this context, General Rogers has pointed out that it is essential that NATO increase its conventional force capabilities in order to reduce its reliance on nuclear weapons. A return to conscription would make a significant and necessary contribution to the capability of our conventional forces. It would also, I believe, reassure our NATO allies as to our seriousness and lend much greater credibility to our conventional force posture, vis-à-vis the Soviets. And as has been trenchantly pointed out here, reassuring our allies today is an essential adjunct to our policy of nuclear deterrence. Conscription in peacetime would, of course, be selective. However, any perceived inequity would, I believe, be justified by conscription's contribution to the enhancement of our conventional force capability. I assume that any method of conscription which was adopted would impose a near-universal liability to selection, and secondly, that it would be based on a random, unbiased means of selection. A lottery draft would meet both these conditions. I believe that is something that we should work to move to as soon as we can so that the serious limitations imposed by the All-Volunteer Force on the fighting capability of our armed forces can be eliminated.

Philip Odeen

In my view, the All-Volunteer Force is a bit like democracy; it is a lousy system with many shortcomings but significantly better than the alternatives. This really is the case if you look in some detail at the various ways the selective service system could be structured. Each has problems and they outweigh the shortcomings of the AVF.

Stanley Resor (see commentary above) made three points. First, he said the All-Volunteer Force causes us to have smaller military forces. I'm not sure that that is true. There are two questions to be addressed. The first is an analytic question. Are our forces today really smaller than they were in 1964 which, as the last pre-Vietnam year, is a good benchmark. Obviously, our forces are smaller in total numbers of military personnel. But there have been substantial overhead manpower savings as a result of the AVF, because of a smaller training and rotation base and other efficiencies that flow from not having two-year draftees, let alone, fifteen or eighteen-month conscripts. If these factors are considered, I suspect that much of that difference in numbers disappears. Secondly, there have been a variety of civilianization actions that replaced military people with civil servants or contractors. This also can be analyzed. Given these considerations, whether our forces are truly smaller in real terms is at least an open question. The real constraint on force size is not the All-Volunteer Force but cost. General Thurman displayed charts showing planned increases in new accessions during the late 1980s—according to the army's latest five-year defense program. I'd be willing to make a substantial bet that this build up will never take place. The reason will not be difficulty in recruiting but cost. We all know of the problem of the deficit and the resulting squeeze on the defense budget. These financial considerations are the real constraint on the near-term size of our forces, not our ability to recruit.

The second issue Stanley Resor raised was the mobilization question, another very complicated and tough question. The kind of forces we have, the way we structure them, and our requirement for the reserves in the first thirty days, is to a large degree a policy issue. We have decided to structure the forces that way, I assume, for good and sufficient reasons. An army the size of ours could be structured a lot of different ways. There are alternatives needing reservists for the early days of a crisis. But that's not the decision that was made. I also doubt very much that the portrait we had of a selective service system not capable of responding is an accurate one. Selective service has done quite a good job of getting a new system in place that could respond quickly and fairly effectively. Most of the mobilization concerns relate to a "strike out of the blue" scenario, a situation where we have a very large, unexpected attack.

In response, we mobilize and deploy forces to Europe after a brief (say twenty-one-day) period of warning. But this is the least likely case. We are far more likely to have a long period of increasing tensions. In such a situation, we have a very different set of factors to deal with, a very different mobilization problem, and a number of ways to respond.

Finally, let me comment on the strategic context that Stanley Resor mentioned. I can see some advantage in terms of the attitude of our allies if we were to return to conscription. On the other hand, we would have to be sure that as a result of conscription our forces were really better. In the longer term, you deter more effectively with strong and effective forces. Would we have a better armed forces today if we had a draft? At least this is an open question, and one I would want to examine carefully before I went back to conscription for essentially political reasons. Moreover, at least in the present environment, we would have a political outcry of great proportions if we should propose to resume the draft. We must make sure that we think through the implications of such a major political battle on the attitude of our allies before we took that step. One could make a case that the net impact on our allies would be negative.

In summary, we ought to look closely at these issues and questions before we push hard to return to the conscript system. There clearly are some advantages, but the problems and risks could well outweigh them. So let's think before we leap.

Irv Greenberg

I've been trying to decide whether I am an ideologue or a pragmatist on the conscription issue. I've decided that I'm a pragmatist. I'm for the AVF if that system can provide the manpower we need for national defense. I'm for peacetime conscription if it is demonstrably necessary.

There are many ideologues at this conference who have taken strong stands for and against conscription. Some are opposed to peacetime conscription because it required involuntary servitude or slave labor. Those who are opposed to the All-Volunteer Force feel that it results in enlisting mercenaries who are driven to enlist by poverty or greed. The positions of the ideologues have not changed from the Gates Commission period to the present. Data on the experience with the AVF are either ignored or interpreted to support their case.

The task of the pragmatists is more demanding. We have to watch the data very carefully and develop solutions to manpower problems that are affordable and politically feasible.

Although the secretary of defense has announced that the volunteer force is a success, I believe the debate will continue, as it should. I would like to suggest a few "rules of engagement" to make future discussions more useful. We should avoid denigrating people who enlist in the armed forces. One form of denigration is to label volunteers as mercenaries. A young man who examines civilian and military job opportunities and pay and bonuses and decides to volunteer is called a mercenary. On the other hand, the extra pay officers receive for submarine duty or for flight duty and reenlistment bonuses for career enlisted personnel enhances their patriotism. I don't understand why the use of money is a good method for retaining career people but a bad method for attracting recruits.

Another way used to criticize the AVF is to label volunteers as poor or disadvantaged. It is difficult to come to grips with this charge because those who make it never define poor, middle class, and upper middle class in terms of income levels. The data I have looked at show that those who volunteer represent a rough cross-section of American youth, especially if we include those who enter as officers.

Those who are concerned about the social and economic composition of the armed forces focus on new enlisted accessions instead of the entire active-duty population. The enlisted career force and the officer corps constitute about 50% of the total active-duty strength. The officer corps and the enlisted career force are certainly not poor. When we consider the force as a whole, I believe we can say that the people in the armed forces are fairly representative of the nation.

I have another suggestion for those who are ideologically opposed to the AVF or to conscription. Don't reject good news just because it blunts your arguments.

Karen Keesling

Some of the things I would have said have already been said. So I'll just try and touch on a few that may be different. One of the things I certainly agree with General Thurman about, although I may disagree with where we start, is that we certainly do need to work with the schools. Not only are we in the military going to be recruiting those high-quality young people who have technical skills, but so is everyone else in the country. I think that we need to start, not in the high schools, but in the junior highs, because if the young people don't have the math and science and the technology, it's almost too late by the time they get to college. I know the navy has a program where they're working with the junior high schools. Those of us in the other services are trying to do what we can to start early. Secretary Orr and the president have spoken out on scientific and technological illiteracy in this country. We need to continue in helping to set the focus for education in this country to make sure we get the kind of people we'll need in the future.

One of the things that we've been trying to do, and the Defense Science Board and various people have brought it to our attention, is in the area of training technology. I think Irv Greenberg mentioned training and I certainly agree we need to do a lot more in the training area.

Fortunately, training is one thing at which we've been fairly good. We need to do more however, as we buy our weapons systems to make sure we get the training equipment at the same time we get the weapons systems. In regard to the training, one of the things I see is that we're trying to develop weapons that are making the jobs easier, not more difficult. At one of our bases that I recently visited, one of the proposals in the construction area would save about 300 manpower slots because of better technology that would make the jobs easier and allow things to be done smarter.

A final comment: although we tend to talk mostly about the army when it comes to recruiting, those of us in the other services need to make sure we continue to talk about the role of all services. In reference to General Thurman's remarks, as I see it, part of the problem is that we tend to deal only with the male cohort and don't address the entire recruiting population, including the female cohort. This is one of the things the air force is trying to do; reach the entire recruit population.

AUDIENCE

Question for John G. Kester (from Gen. Paul Phillips): You mentioned a mixed draft volunteer system and that would pay the draftees less than the volunteers. I'd like to suggest something outrageous to you: you pay the draftees more than you pay volunteers. Unlike the previous draft, it would tend to spread the quality across the services so that the less popular services would get a fair share because there would be less tendency for people to run to the air force and to a lesser extent the navy, in order to avoid being drafted. In addition, since there would probably be few volunteers if you made it less easy to volunteer, or a little more onerous to volunteer, you would have to draft more, and as a result of that, you would be taking in a very much higher proportion, I suspect, of the eligible population.

Kester: I confess I'm flabbergasted at the model you put to me. I've never thought about it. Let me give you just one reaction to it: I don't think that pay is probably the major determinant of the attitude of draftees toward being drafted. I think that for the teenager the idea of spending that time being taken away from whatever else he was doing is the predominantly unpleasant aspect of conscription. If he gets low pay, that's an added insult, perhaps. I think that you might just be throwing money away on the scheme that you suggest. Maybe you have some data that would prove otherwise, I don't know.

Danzig: Let me offer two additional observations. It would be easy to guess your service background from the character of the proposal because I take it that translates into a world where only draftees go to the army. It seems to me that raises some obvious problems in political resistance. If you're willing to encounter those problems, it seems to me more economical and efficient and rational simply to encounter the problem right at the outset. Distribute recruits among the services and deal with balancing, qua balancing, rather than by this indirect method. My second observation is, as with the proposal that would eliminate all volunteers and simply require draftees, that I find it paradoxical and in the end irrational because what is being said in essence is, you can't volunteer at this higher wage rate and we will draft somebody who is unwilling to serve in lieu of you who are willing to serve at this higher wage rate! In fact, we will do that even if you and the other person are otherwise identical. That seems to me to be a misallocation both from the standpoint of individuals and civilian society and even from the standpoint of the military because it substitutes the less willing soldier for the more willing.

Index

About the Editors and Contributors

THE EDITORS

William R. Bowman is Associate Professor of Economics at the U.S. Naval Academy. Since joining the faculty of the Naval Academy in 1980, he has been the course coordinator for the Economics of National Defense and has written widely in the area of enlisted and officer retention.

Roger D. Little is Professor of Economics at the U.S. Naval Academy and was department chairman at the time of the conference. A former U.S. Marine Corps officer, he has served as Adjunct Professor at the Naval Postgraduate School and presently is a Guest Scholar at the Brookings Institution. Professor Little's research has been primarily devoted to empirical studies of military manpower.

G. Thomas Sicilia holds a Ph.D. in Operations Research from the University of Florida. He recently became the Director of the Defense Training Data and Analysis Center (TDAC) in Orlando, Florida after spending 15 years in Washington, D.C. working in the manpower, personnel and training area. Before assuming his current position, Dr. Sicilia was Director, Accession Policy, Office of the Assistant Secretary of Defense.

THE CONTRIBUTORS

Martin Anderson, senior fellow at the Hoover Institution, Stanford University, was a member of both the Defense Manpower Commission and the Military Manpower Task Force. He previously served as Assistant to President Reagan for Policy Development and currently serves on the President's Foreign Intelligence Advisory Board and the President's Economic Policy Advisory Board. Dr. Anderson is author of *The Military Draft* and *Conscription* and edited a volume on *Registration and the Draft*.

Martin Binkin is senior fellow in the Brookings Foreign Policy Studies program. In 1973 he was coauthor of the initial assessment of the all-volunteer armed force for the Senate Armed Services Committee. He is author or coauthor of eleven volumes in the Brookings Studies in Defense Policy series, the latest of which is *America's Volunteer Military: Progress and Prospects.*

William K. Brehm is chairman of the board of Systems Research and Applications Corporation. He has served as an assistant secretary of defense, an assistant secretary of the army, and has held executive positions in the aerospace and consumer products industries. He is a member of the Board of Visitors for the National Defense University.

John R. Brinkerhoff is vice president of Data Memory Systems in Fairfax, Virginia. He served in the Office of the Secretary of Defense as director of manpower programs and as deputy assistant secretary for reserve affairs. Mr. Brinkerhoff has been involved in manpower planning and programming aspects of defense policy and resources analysis for over 20 years.

Lt. Gen. Edgar A. Chavarrie, USAF, is the deputy assistant secretary of defense (Military Personnel and Force Management). A bombardier-navigator in both World War II and the Korean War, he has served on various staffs, including the Supreme Headquarters Allied Powers Europe, the Deputy Chief of Staff for Plans and Operations, the Joint Chiefs of Staff, and the Headquarters United States European Command. General Chavarrie holds a bachelors degree in international relations from the University of Southern California and a master's degree in economics from George Washington University.

David S.C. Chu is director of program analysis and evaluation, Office of the Secretary of Defense. After receiving B.A., M.A. and M.Phil. degrees from Yale University, he served in the army before returning to Yale where he earned a Ph.D. in economics in 1972. Dr. Chu has taught at UCLA and held senior positions at The Rand Corporation and the Congressional Budget Office.

Richard V.L. Cooper is partner-in-charge of economic studies and international trade at Coopers and Lybrand. Prior to assuming his present position, he was director of defense manpower studies at The Rand Corporation. Dr. Cooper has published extensively on the subject of military manpower, and is the author of *Military Manpower and the All-Volunteer Force.*

Richard J. Danzig is a partner in the law firm of Latham, Watkins and Hills in Washington, D.C. He has served as the principal deputy assistant secretary of defense (Manpower, Reserve Affairs and Logistics) and deputy assistant secretary (Program Development). Mr. Danzig has taught law at both Stanford and Harvard Universities and is coauthor of a book on national service written under a grant from the Ford Foundation.

General William E. DePuy retired from the army in 1977 and now works as a consultant to the defense industry. He served as a battalion commander in World War II, and subsequently in various infantry commands in NATO and Vietnam. Before his last tour as commander, Training and Doctrine Command, he was special assistant to the chairman, Joint Chiefs of Staff and assistant vice chief of staff of the army.

Mark J. Eitelberg is adjunct research professor in the Department of Administrative Sciences at the Naval Postgraduate School. Dr. Eitelberg was previously a senior scientist with the Human Resources Research Organization and is the author or coauthor of over thirty-five publications, including a number of works on the subject of population representation in the military and participation in the armed forces.

Richard L. Fernandez joined the economics department of The Rand Corporation in 1978 following graduate study at the University of California, Berkeley. Working in Rand's Defense Manpower Studies Center, he has authored studies of enlistment supply, the effects of postservice educational benefits, and enlistment standards. He recently served as adjunct teaching professor in the Department of Administrative Sciences at the Naval Postgraduate School.

Irv Greenburg was a deputy assistant secretary of defense, capping a government career in military manpower management. After leaving government, he was staff director for the Report to the President on the *Status and Prospects of the All-Volunteer Force*, published in 1982. As a member of the Logistics Management Institute, he continues to provide consulting services to the Department of Defense.

David W. Grissmer is deputy director of the Defense Manpower Research Center at The Rand Corporation. At Rand he has been involved in design and research work on military compensation and benefits, the military sample of the National Longitudinal Survey, surveys of active and reserve personnel, and evaluation of the viability of the All-Volunteer Force. He has studied extensively the attrition and retention of reserve personnel and has applied manpower planning techniques in the fields of social work and education.

Robert F. Hale is the assistant director for the national security division at the Congressional Budget Office where he earlier worked as the principal analyst responsible for defense manpower issues. Before joining the Congressional Budget Office, Mr. Hale was with the Center for Naval Analyses where he researched navy manpower and procurement issues.

Stephen E. Herbits is vice president for corporate development of Joseph E. Seagram & Sons, Inc. During his eleven years in Washington, he worked on Capitol Hill, at The Pentagon and at The White House, devoting substantial time to military manpower affairs. He served on the President's Commission for an All-Volunteer Armed Force, provided research and editorial assistance for *How to End the Draft*, and held the position of special assistant to the assistant secretary of defense (Manpower, Reserve Affairs and Logistics) for AVF matters.

James R. Hosek is director of Rand's Defense Manpower Research Center. His research currently focuses on enlistment and retention behavior and policy simulation. In addition, he has written widely in the areas of labor supply, income tax policy, and welfare participation. He received his doctrate in economics from the University of Chicago in 1975.

John D. Johnston is president of Syllogistics, Inc. which provides consulting services to top-level administrators of large scale activities in both the public and private sectors. He has served on the faculty of the U.S. Air Force Academy and in numerous policy-making and research positions in Washington. He was a Federal Executive Research Fellow at the Brookings Institution where he coauthored a monograph addressing the progress, problems and prospects of the All-Volunteer Armed Forces in a competitive compensation and skills market.

Karen R. Kessling is principal deputy assistant secretary of the air force (Manpower, Reserve Affairs and Installations). Previously she was deputy assistant secretary for manpower resources and military personnel. She is a member of the Virginia State Bar and the Florida State Bar.

Roger T. Kelly is president of Human Resources Management, Inc. and is a senior fellow at Bradley University. Mr. Kelly was vice president for personnel and public affairs at Caterpillar Tractor Company and from 1969-1973 was assistant secretary of defense (Manpower, Reserve Affairs and Logistics).

John G. Kester is an attorney practicing in Washington, D.C. and frequent writer on defense, government organization, law, public policy, and politics. From 1969 to 1972, he served as deputy assistant secretary of the army (Manpower and Reserve Affairs) and from 1977 to 1980 as the special assistant to the secretary and the deputy secretary of defense. He has been a member of the Board of Visitors of the U.S. Air Force Academy and of the Academic Advisory Board of the U.S. Naval Academy. He is a founding member of Democrats for Defense and a contributing editor of the *Washingtonian* and *Military Logistics Forum*.

Admiral Isaac C. Kidd, Jr., USN (Ret.), served on active duty for over forty years before retiring as NATO's Supreme Allied Commander in 1978. He commanded three United States Fleets and was chief of naval material. Admiral Kidd has served on academic advisory boards and boards of visitors at the U.S. Naval Academy, Naval Postgraduate School, National Defense University and currently the National Defense Intelligence College.

Lawrence J. Korb is assistant secretary of defense (Manpower, Installations and Logistics). Before joining the administration, he was resident director of defense policy studies at the American Enterprise Institute for Public Policy Research. Dr. Korb has held academic positions at the University of Dayton, the U.S. Coast Guard Academy and the U.S. Naval War College. He has published over ninety works on national security issues.

Walter B. LaBerge is executive assistant to the president of Lockheed Missiles and Space Company, Inc. A graduate of the University of Notre Dame with a Ph.D. in physics, he has held numerous positions in the federal government including technical director of the Naval Weapons Center, China Lake, principal deputy to the under secretary of defense (Research and Engineering) and under secretary of the army.

Gus C. Lee is vice president of the Human Resources Research Organization. Previously he was in the Office of the Secretary of Defense, serving as special assistant for the All-Volunteer Force and director of manpower requirements and utilization. He is the author of *Ending the Draft: The Story of the All-Volunteer Force*.

William H. Meckling is dean emeritus and James E. Gleason Distinguished Research Scholar in Management and Government Policy in the Graduate School of Management of the University of Rochester. He has been affiliated with the University of Denver, Butler University, U.C.L.A., The Rand Corporation, and was president of the Center for Naval Analyses prior to joining the University of Rochester. He served as director of the President's Commission on an All-Volunteer Armed Force. His research interests have ranged widely, including state and local government finances, the business firm and the theory of organization, radio and space technology, military manpower, and financial markets.

Charles C. Moskos, a former draftee, is professor of sociology at Northwestern University. He has been a fellow at the Woodrow Wilson International Center for Scholars, and a Rockefeller Humanities Fellow. Professor Moskos serves as president of the Research Committee on Armed Forces and Conflict Resolution of the International Sociological Association. He is currently completing a study on national youth service for the Twentieth Century Fund.

Brigadier General Carl E. Mundy, Jr., USMC, is commanding general of the Landing Force Training Command, Atlantic and the 4th Marine Amphibious Brigade. His previous assignment was director, personnel procurement division at Headquarters Marine Corps. An infantry officer, General Mundy served in Vietnam with the 3rd Marine Division.

Robert J. Murray is a lecturer in public policy and director of the national security programs at the John F. Kennedy School of Government in Cambridge, Massachusetts. He has been dean of the Naval War College and the director of Naval Warfare Studies in Newport, Rhode Island. He has served in a variety of governmental posts concerned with the formation, education and training of naval personnel.

Gary R. Nelson is currently a principal of the Systems Research and Applications Corporation, Arlington, Virginia. An economist with over 15 years experience in the analysis and management of the All-Volunteer Force, Dr. Nelson is a former deputy assistant secretary of defense, former associate director for compensation at the U.S. Office of Personnel Management and has worked for the Congressional Budget Office, The Rand Corporation, and the Institute for Defense Analyses. He holds a Ph.D. in economics from Rice University.

Philip Odeen is the managing partner of Coopers and Lybrand's Mid-Atlantic consulting practice. He has served in various senior positions in the Office of the Secretary of Defense and the National Security Council. In addition he was a member of President Carter's "Blue Ribbon" panel on military compensation and has written extensively on national security management and organization issues.

Jesse Orlansky is a member of the staff of the Institute for Defense Analyses in Alexandria, Virginia. He has conducted numerous studies on the effectiveness and cost of various types of military training.

Charles R. Roll, Jr. has served as principal deputy director of program analysis and evaluation in the Office of the Secretary of Defense since December 1983. He received his B.A. degree from the University of California, Berkeley and M.A. and Ph.D. degrees in economics from Harvard University. Dr. Roll has served as a senior scientist at Science Applications, Inc. and earlier was at The Rand Corporation where he directed air force and Office of the Secretary of Defense manpower studies programs and performed research in capital-labor substitution, electronics maintenance and manpower requirements, and NATO manpower. He served on active duty with the U.S. Air Force from 1961 to 1965.

Stanley R. Resor is a member of the law firm of Debevoise and Plimpton in New York City. He has served as secretary of the army, as head of the U.S. Delegation to the Mutual Balanced Force Reduction Negotiations in Vienna, and as under secretary of defense for policy.

General John W. Roberts, USAF (Ret.), has served as deputy chief of staff for personnel and commander of the Air Training Command. He was a member of the 1980 DoD Transition Team and is a member of the Committee on the Performance of Military Personnel of the National Academy of Science.

Bernard Rostker is director of the Capabilities and Force Development Program, Arrogo Center at The Rand Corporation. He has held research and administrative positions at Systems Research and Applications Corporation, Center for Naval Analyses, the Department of Defense and the Department of the Navy. From 1979 to 1981 he was director of selective service. The author of numerous professional reports and articles, he received a Ph.D. in economics from Syracuse University in 1970.

Curtis W. Tarr is dean of the Johnson Graduate School of Management at Cornell University. Dr. Tarr was president of Lawrence University before entering government service, first as assistant secretary of the air force (Manpower and Reserve Affairs) then as director of selective service from 1970 to 1972, and finally as under secretary of state for security assistance. Before assuming his present position at Cornell, he was vice president of Deere and Company. His organizational responsibilities have been in logistics, manufacturing, and human resource managment; his scholarly work has concentrated on leadership.

General Maxwell R. Thurman, USA, is vice chief of staff of the army. He previously served as deputy chief of staff for personnel and commander, U.S. Army Recruiting Command.

Lieutenant General R. Dean Tice, USA (Ret.), served as the deputy assistant secretary of defense for military personnel and force management, Office of the Secretary of Defense from 1979-1983. His 38 year career included command at every level from rifle company to mechanized infantry division. He was the deputy director of army personnel management policies during the transition from the draft to the All-Volunteer Force.

John T. Warner is associate professor of economics at Clemson University. Previously he was with the Center for Naval Analyses and earlier taught at North Carolina State University and the University of North Carolina. Professor Warner is the author of numerous articles on the economics of military manpower.

John P. White is currently the chairman of the board and chief executive office of INTERACTIVE Systems Corporation. Earlier he served in the Carter administration, first as assistant secretary of defense (Manpower, Reserve Affairs and Logistics) and then as deputy director of the Office of Management and Budget. He joined the administration from The Rand Corporation where he was the senior vice president as well as a member of the Rand Board of Trustees. He holds a Ph.D. in economics and in his early career served as a lieutenant in the United States Marine Corps.

Caspar W. Weinberger is secretary of defense and previously served as secretary of health, education and welfare. A graduate of Harvard Law School, he was vice president, director, and general counsel of Bechtel Group of Companies before being nominated by President-elect Ronald Reagan to his present position.